W9-ANA-598

# CHANGING THE STORY

# CHANGING THE STORY

Feminist Fiction and the Tradition

GAYLE GREENE

INDIANA UNIVERSITY PRESS

*Bloomington and Indianapolis*

The paper used in this publication meets the minimum requirements of American
National Standard for Information Sciences—Permanence of Paper for Printed
Library Materials, ANSI Z39.48-1984.

Manufactured in the United States of America

**Library of Congress Cataloging-in-Publication Data**

Greene, Gayle, date.
    Changing the story : feminist fiction and the tradition / Gayle
Greene.
        p.    cm.
    Includes bibliographical references and index.
    ISBN 0-253-32606-0 (alk. paper). — ISBN 0-253-20672-3 (pbk. :
alk. paper)
    1. English fiction—Women authors—History and criticism.
2. Feminism and literature—History—20th century.   3. American
fiction—Women authors—History and criticism.   4. Canadian fiction—
Women authors—History and criticism.   5. Canadian fiction—20th
century—History and criticism.   6. American fiction—20th century—
History and criticism.   7. English fiction—20th century—History
and criticism.   8. Women and literature—History—20th century.
9. Influence (Literary, artistic, etc.)   I. Title.
PR888.F45G7   1991
820.9'9287—dc20                                              91-6849

1 2 3 4 5   95 94 93 92 91

*For Agnes, Paddy, and Jack,*
*who gave me a place to stand*

# CONTENTS

## Part III: Postfeminist Fiction

# ACKNOWLEDGMENTS

This is a book about change. It concerns books about change and books that have changed me.

In the past few decades, a body of fiction has come into existence that names areas of women's experience formerly unnamed and unimagined, and a revolution in literary and critical studies has occurred that has altered the ways we read and think about literature. I was drawn to contemporary women's fiction, after years in the Renaissance, by a search for new stories, for stories that spoke more directly to my experience. I had not quite anticipated what a mid-career change of this sort would involve—how different the questions posed by contemporary women's writings from those presented by Renaissance texts. The attempt to understand these differences, to explore the relation between feminist fiction and "the tradition," is part of the impetus of this book—as, it so happens, the relation of past to present is of vital concern to the writers I was drawn to.

My view of feminist fiction as an open-ended form capable of rendering and facilitating change is derived from my sense of the part it played in my life. As one who has made her way in the world through reading and writing, I'm interested in writers who explore narrative as liberation. I hope that these novels have been similarly empowering for my students; and I'll take this opportunity to thank especially those students—too numerous to name—who worked with me in contemporary women's fiction seminars and applied themselves unstintingly, in papers and discussions, to tracking some idea or unraveling some pattern in ways that helped me immeasurably.

My thanks to colleagues and friends in and around Claremont—Cathie Beitler, Toni Clark and Larry Thornton, Robert Dawidoff, Lynn Dumenil and Norman Cohen, Richard and Margaret Fadem, James Fuller, Sue Houchins, Steve Koblik, Cris Miller, Michael Roth, Ralph Ross, Helena Wall, Nick Warner and Sally Pratt. And to faithful supporters through the years—Arthur Danto, Carolyn Heilbrun, Edward Said. This book took shape in a context of support and encouragement from friends throughout the country, and my warmest gratitude and appreciation goes to an extended network of terrific women, many of whom also happen to be feminist critics, for their friendship and examples as human beings and scholars: Elizabeth Abel, Janet Adelman, Betsy Ermarth, Roberta Johnson, Coppélia Kahn, Wendy Martin, Elizabeth Minnich, Tania Modleski, Carol Neely, Carolyn Porter, Ellen Cronan Rose, Roberta Rubenstein, Madelon Sprengnether—and special thanks to Rena Fraden, Molly Hite, Anne Howells, Ann Rosalind Jones, Lillian Robinson, Christine Stansell, and Jean Wyatt for their readings of parts or all of this manuscript.

Many of us have been suffering through long projects over the past years and it's been enormously helpful to have company along the way.

Thanks also to several organizations—the Shakespeare Association of America, the Doris Lessing Society, the women writers conference in Dubrovnik, Yugoslavia, the Modern Language Association—for providing forums that brought feminist scholars together. Thanks to Scripps College for sabbatical and research support, and especially to Mary Wig Johnson, who always seemed to be behind some generous award or other; thanks to friends in the Renaissance, which I never quite left—Catherine Belsey, Norman Rabkin, Peter Stallybrass, Carolyn Ruth Swift, Frank Whigham. And to special friends Vicki and Larry, Mike and Kathy, my love and appreciation.

Thanks to Cornell University Press for permission to reprint parts of "Women and Men in *The Golden Notebook*," in *The (M)other Tongue: Essays in Feminist Psychoanalytic Interpretation,* edited by Shirley Nelson Garner, Madelon S. Gohlke, and Claire Kahane, copyright © 1985 by Cornell University. Thanks to the University of Illinois Press for permission to reprint "Gail Godwin's *The Odd Woman:* An Old Story," in *Old Maids and Excellent Women,* ed. Laura Doan, and "Margaret Laurence's *The Diviners* and Shakespeare's *The Tempest:* The Uses of the Past," in *Women's Re-Visions of Shakespeare,* ed. Marianne Novy, 1990, pp. 165–82. A version of "Margaret Laurence's *The Diviners:* The Uses of the Past" was also published in *Critical Approaches to The Fiction of Margaret Laurence,* ed. Colin Nicholson; permission is granted from Macmillan and from the University of British Columbia Press. "Margaret Drabble's *The Waterfall:* New System, New Morality" appeared in *Novel: A Forum on Fiction,* vol. 22, no. 1 (Fall 1988). Copyright NOVEL Corp. © 1989. Reprinted with permission. "Margaret Atwood's *Cat's Eye:* A Novel of Our Time," appeared in *Women's Studies,* 1990, permission to reprint, Gordon and Breach Science Publishers. Parts of the essay "The Diaries of Jane Somers: Doris Lessing, Feminism, and the Mother" are reprinted from *Narrating Mothers,* ed. Brenda O'Daly and Maureen T. Reddy. Copyright © 1991 by The University of Tennessee Press. Used by permission. Parts of the essay "Rebelling Against the System: Margaret Atwood's *The Edible Woman*" appeared in *Margaret Atwood: Reflection and Reality,* ed. Beatrice Mendez-Egle, Living Authors Series 9, Pan American University, 1987. Used by permission.

Excerpts from *Cat's Eye* by Margaret Atwood, copyright © 1988 by O. W. Toad, Ltd., used by permission of Doubleday, a division of Bantam Doubleday Dell Publishing Group, Inc., and by permission of Margaret Atwood. Passages from *The Edible Woman,* reprinted by permission of Margaret Atwood © 1969, available in a Warner Books edition. Excerpts from *The Handmaid's Tale* by Margaret Atwood. Copyright © 1985 by O. W. Toad, Ltd. Reprinted by permission of Houghton Mifflin Co., world rights, excluding British Commonwealth. British Commonwealth rights by permission of Jonathan Cape Ltd.

Passages from *Lady Oracle* are used by permission of Simon & Schuster, Inc., Andre Deutsch, McClelland & Stewart Inc., and Margaret Atwood. Thanks to Sheila Ballantyne for permission to quote from *Norma Jean the Termite Queen*. British Commonwealth rights to passages from Margaret Drabble's *The Waterfall* and *The Radiant Way* appear by permission of George Weidenfeld & Nicolson Limited. U.S. rights to *The Waterfall* and *The Radiant Way* from Random House, Inc. and Alfred A. Knopf. Permission to quote from Betty Friedan's *The Feminine Mystique* by W. W. Norton & Company, Inc. Permission to quote from Gail Godwin's *The Odd Woman* by Random House, Inc., Alfred A. Knopf, Inc. Permission to quote from Sue Kaufman's *The Diary of a Mad Housewife* by Random House, Inc., Alfred A. Knopf, Inc. Special thanks to Jocelyn and David Laurence (The Estate of Margaret Laurence) for permission to quote from *The Fire-Dwellers* and *The Diviners*—they were particularly generous. Passages from Doris Lessing's *The Golden Notebook* are used by permission of Simon & Schuster, Inc., and by Michael Joseph Ltd. Excerpts from *The Bell Jar* by Sylvia Plath. Copyright © 1971 by Harper & Row, Publishers, Inc. Reprinted by permission of Harper Collins Publishers. Excerpts from Anne Richardson Roiphe's *Up the Sandbox* by Brandt and Brandt, nonexclusive rights. Permission to quote from Alix Kates Shulman's *Memoirs of an Ex-Prom Queen*, Random House, Inc., Alfred A. Knopf, Inc., and by permission of author. From *Fat Woman's Joke* by Fay Weldon, published by Academy Chicago Publishers and reprinted by permission. Copyright © 1967 by Fay Weldon. All rights reserved. And by permission of Sterling Lord Literistic, Inc.

# CHANGING THE STORY

Many people read novels in order to find patterns or images for a possible future. . . . We do not want to resemble the women of the past, but where is our future? This is precisely the question that many novels written by women are trying to answer. . . . We live in an unchartered world. . . . Our subject matter is enormous, there are whole new patterns to create. . . . Never before . . . have women had so much to say, and so great a hope of speaking to some effect.

Margaret Drabble, "A Woman Writer"

. . . every so often, perhaps once in a century, there's a sort of—act of faith. A well of faith fills up, and there's an enormous heave forward in one country or another, and that's a forward movement for the whole world. Because it's an act of imagination—of what is possible for the whole world. In our century it was 1917 in Russia. And in China. Then the well runs dry. . . . Then the well slowly fills again. And then there's another painful lurch forward. . . .

Yes—because . . . if people can imagine something, there'll come a time when they'll achieve it.

Doris Lessing, *The Golden Notebook*

# *I*

# INTRODUCTION
## FEMINIST METAFICTION AS RE-VISION

> It is part of the business of the critic to
> preserve tradition—where a good tradition
> exists. It is part of his business to see literature
> steadily and to see it whole; and this is
> eminently to see it *not* as consecrated by time,
> but to see it beyond time; to see the best work
> of our time and the best work of twenty-five
> hundred years ago with the same eyes.
>
> T. S. Eliot, *The Sacred Wood*[1]

> We need to know the writing of the past, and
> know it differently than we have ever known
> it; not to pass on a tradition but to break its
> hold over us.
>
> Re-vision—the act of looking back, of seeing
> with fresh eyes, of entering an old text from a
> new critical direction—is for women more
> than a chapter in cultural history: it is an act
> of survival.
>
> Adrienne Rich, "Writing as Re-Vision"[2]

This book addresses a movement in contemporary British, Canadian, and American women's fiction, focusing specifically on a form of feminist fiction— feminist metafiction—that concerns women writers' relation to "the tradition." I am particularly interested in self-conscious fiction by Doris Lessing, Margaret Drabble, Margaret Atwood, and Margaret Laurence that explores women's efforts at liberation in relation to problems of narrative form, fiction that destabilizes the conventions of realism in a project of psychic and social transformation. Though metafiction—fiction that includes within itself commentary on its own narrative conventions—is more often associated with postmodern (i.e., male) writers than with feminist fiction, it is a powerful tool

1

of feminist critique, for to draw attention to the structures of fiction is also to draw attention to the conventionality of the codes that govern human behavior, to reveal how such codes have been constructed and how they can therefore be changed.[3] Whether these novelists make their protagonists readers who speculate about how literature has shaped them or writers who seek new forms in their fiction, they use metafiction to challenge the cultural and literary tradition they inherit.

## Feminist Fiction

The past few decades have seen an unprecedented productivity by women writers. The mid-seventies were particularly rich, not only in fiction, but in poetry, criticism, and theory. Feminist fiction is not the same as "women's fiction" or fiction by women: not all women writers are "women's writers," and not all women's writers are feminist writers, since to write about "women's issues" is not necessarily to address them from a feminist perspective. Nor are feminist writers necessarily so all the time—Lessing is feminist in *The Golden Notebook* and is not in *The Diaries of Jane Somers*—nor do they always identify themselves as feminists. Yet whatever a writer's relation to the women's movement, we may term a novel "feminist" for its analysis of gender as socially constructed and its sense that what has been constructed may be reconstructed—for its understanding that change is possible and that narrative can play a part in it. Feminist fiction is the most revolutionary movement in contemporary fiction—revolutionary both in that it is formally innovative and in that it helped make a social revolution, playing a major role in the resurgence of feminism in the sixties and seventies, the so-called second wave. It is a movement as significant as Modernism, producing texts that combine the excitement and experimentation of Modernism with the social critique of the great age of realism, though literary critics and historians have scarcely recognized it as a movement—perhaps because it's recent, perhaps because it comes from women.

My concern with feminist metafiction determines my focus on white middle-class writers, and my focus on feminist *Kunstlerromane* determines my interest in four writers specifically: Lessing, Drabble, Atwood, and Laurence. Of these four, only Margaret Laurence unequivocally identifies with feminism.[4] Lessing, who is our most extraordinary (and in ways most infuriating) feminist novelist, has refused to identify with the women's movement, "not because" (as she says) "there is anything wrong with [it], but because . . . the cataclysms we are living through" make "the aims of Women's Liberation . . . look very small and quaint."[5] Drabble and Atwood distance themselves from it for reasons that women writers have tended to—resistance to being categorized or dictated to.[6] Drabble objects to "a prescriptive way of looking at books":[7]

> If I end with a marriage, it's going to be seen as a mistake; if I end with a woman alone, it's going to be regarded as a triumph. All you can do is write about how it

seems to you to happen at the time. . . . The truth is more important than ideology.[8]

Atwood resists "that kind of determinism that says because you are *it*, thou shalt be *so*—you know, because you have a womb, your style has to have a hole in the middle of it"[9] and criticizes "a one-dimensional Feminist Criticism" that "award[s] points according to conformity or non-conformity to an ideological position": "novelists and poets are not propagandists or . . . preachers or politicians."[10]

But though both Atwood and Drabble protest the constraints of what Atwood calls "someone else's ideology" ("Paradoxes," p. 186), and though both insist that "imaginative" literature is distinct from ideology, both imply the ideological complicity of narrative forms in metafictions that interrogate the limits of realism. Moreover, both express agreement with a basic assumption of feminism: that art is political. Atwood describes herself as becoming more "political,"[11] and Drabble says "none of my books is about feminism, because my belief in the necessity for justice for women (which they don't get at the moment) is so basic that I never think of using it as a subject. It is part of a whole"[12]—a remark which suggests that if none of her books is "about feminism," in a sense, all are. And though Lessing has disavowed not only feminism, but all forms of organized political activity, she has—or at least has until recently—used her fiction as "an instrument of change," arguing that the writer is "an architect of the soul" who has a "commitment" to the "human beings he influences" and a responsibility to "dramatize the political conflicts of his time."[13]

## "The Tradition"

By "tradition" I mean the canon of "great books" that dominates the study of English literature—what Atwood terms "the Western European literary tradition and its Canadian and American mutations."[14] The writers I'm interested in have a complex relation to this tradition, writing against it but also writing within it, finding it both constraining and enabling. All have strongly humanist values—though they enlarge "human" to include "female"—and all rely on realism in a way that prohibits drastic ruptures of sequence or sentence, though they also interrogate the meanings of the conventions they enlist. Drabble states her belief that novels should be "available to a fairly large reading public"[15] rather than aimed at "a very small elite": "one is obviously going to write to an educated audience—nobody else reads novels. . . . But I do feel . . . an obligation to those who haven't had it very easy, and who could communicate—who could be communicated with."[16] Lessing describes the novel as "the only popular art-form left where the artist speaks directly, in clear words, to his audience . . . as an individual to individuals, in a small personal voice" (SPV, p. 21). Accessibility is a sine qua non for any writing concerned with social change, which is why realism is the mode of feminist writers—as it has been the mode of women writers in the past.[17]

Drabble is the most steeped in "the tradition," having studied literature at Cambridge while Leavis was there (she earned a double first in 1960) and edited *The Oxford Companion to English Literature* (1985). Drabble says "what I've read is as much a part of what I think as the people that I meet and the problems that I encounter" (Cooper-Clark, p. 71). Atwood, always a "voracious and eclectic reader,"[18] earned a B.A. from the University of Toronto's Victoria College (1961), where she took courses from Northrop Frye, and an M.A. from Radcliffe College, Harvard University. Laurence, who describes herself as "an insatiable reader" with "the immense good fortune to be born into a family of readers," graduated with honors in English from United College, Winnipeg (1947).[19] Lessing, though self-educated, claims that she was the better for it because her reading was only "the best—the classics of European and American literature. One of the advantages of not being educated was that I didn't have to waste time on the second-best."[20]

Three of these writers came of age while Leavis's influence was at its height, and his "great tradition," with its view of literature as a civilizing, humanizing force, with its two (out of four) women novelists, was in many ways enabling to them. Alix of Drabble's *The Radiant Way* chose Cambridge "because of Dr. Leavis," and he was a strong presence at Cambridge during Drabble's years there.[21] Yet insofar as "traditions" ossify into a rigid authoritarianism, as Leavisitism did—which began as a revolution against an effete postwar critical establishment but soon turned doctrinaire—they become reactionary and representative of what new writers must overthrow.[22] Drabble has said, "I admire Leavis enormously . . . and the Great Tradition is what I believe in as a novelist" (Creighton, 1985, p. 25; Rozencwajg, p. 341), but she also describes his exclusiveness as "destructive": "it was just good luck that he didn't stop me completely" (Creighton, 1985, p. 26).

All four of these novelists acknowledge their indebtedness to the nineteenth-century novel, agreeing (implicitly or explicitly) with George Lukács's analysis of realism as progressive. Lessing (like Lukács) sees the nineteenth-century novel as "the highest point of literature" and describes her goal of portraying "the individual conscience in its relations with the collective" (SPV, pp. 4, 14). In fact, it is in the nineteenth-century novel that we find the fullest rendering of individual in relation to collective, of the social dimensions of personality. Lukács describes it as representing "man" as "a social animal" whose " 'ontological being' . . . cannot be distinguished from . . . social and historical environment," whose "individuality cannot be separated from "context": for the realists "every action, thought, and emotion of human beings is inseparably bound up with the life and struggles of the community, i.e., with politics."[23] Lukács contrasts Modernism—which views man as "solitary, asocial, unable to enter into relationships with other human beings" and therefore presents "social and historical phenomena as static"—to realism, with its understanding of individuals as related to society, and suggests that it is this understanding that makes realism progressive, for it is "the complex tissue of man's interaction with the environment" that allows people to change, to "form" and be "formed by" the world, whereas "the denial of history" is the denial "of development" ("Ideology of Modernism," pp. 35, 34, 28, 31, 20).[24] According to Lukács— and Lessing's remarks in "The Small Personal Voice" indicate her agreement— "major realist art" (by Shakespeare, Scott, Balzac, Tolstoy) is "dramatically engaged with the . . . 'typical' conflicts and dynamics" of its society, with "the vital 'world-historical' forces . . . which make for change and growth" (Preface to *Studies in European Realism,* p. 18).

Drabble allies herself with realism against Modernism when she remarks, "I'd rather be at the end of a dying tradition which I admire than at the beginning of a tradition I deplore" (to a BBC interviewer, 1967); and she speaks of her "affinities" with nineteenth-century novelists, "the people I must have been influenced by, people I read when I was younger and indeed do still read and reread."[25] She refers to Eliot as "my ideal novelist" (Rozencwajg, p. 336), noting that what she especially values is her breadth and social conscience, and that the writers she "most admire[s] are the people who strive to retain their links with the community" (Cooper-Clark, p. 73).[26] Atwood describes herself as "trained as a Victorianist," refers to her "favorite" "old nineteenth-century chestnuts" such as Dickens, and calls *Middlemarch* "the greatest single novel of the nineteenth century" ("Writing the Male Character," SW, pp. 412–30; p. 422). (Such remarks corroborate Showalter's assessment of *Middlemarch* as the novel "that has most obsessed feminists";[27] in fact, in the interest and controversy it sparked in its time, it occupied a position comparable to that of *The Golden Notebook* in our time.)

The nineteenth-century novel is a strong influence on these writers and they pay it the highest compliment, of imitation, achieving at their best its breadth, seriousness, comprehensiveness, and its understanding of individuals as related to social milieu, class, and generation—as "weeds upon the tide of history," in a term from Drabble's *The Ice Age.*[28] At the beginning and end of the sixties, Lessing published epic novels *The Golden Notebook* and *The Four-Gated City,* which, together, look back to the late forties and forward to the end of the century and not only render the "ideological 'feel' of our mid century" (as she describes her intent in *The Golden Notebook,* introduction, p. xi), but also dramatize the historical dynamics of these decades, fulfilling Lukács's ideal of "realist literature." Drabble has praised Lessing as "one of the very few novelists who have refused to believe that the contemporary world is too complicated to understand,"[29] and the same may be said of her: her recent works *The Ice Age, The Middle Ground,* and *The Radiant Way* are "condition-of-England" novels that investigate "what is happening now," as she says, examining the causes and cures of England's current crises and the complex fabric of English society,— "social attitudes, the way people behave, the way they dress or think."[30] Laurence speaks of the novelist as a "sociopolitical being" and the novel as "political" and "social commentary" (NASB, pp. 15–16) and describes her attempt to render a "strong sense of place and of our own culture . . . to give Canadians a . . . sense of who they are, where they came from, and where they may be going . . . by forging our myths and giving voice to our history, to our legends, to our cultural being."[31] Her Manawaka series (so termed because it is set in the fictional town of Manawaka, a version of Laurence's native Neepawa) portrays characters in relation to community, as Eliot does in *Middlemarch*. And Atwood says, "I believe with the Victorian novelists . . . that the novel isn't just a vehicle for private expression but that it also exists for social examination."[32]

But if realism is enabling, it is also constraining, and these writers express a mingled sense of identification with the tradition and alienation from it, of indebtedness and opposition—the sense described by Woolf of being both "inheritors" and "critics" of culture.[33] Oscillating between "ambiguously hegemonic and ambiguously non-hegemonic positions,"[34] the woman writer (or the white, middle-class woman writer) occupies what Wendy Mulford describes as "a differently gendered place" in a tradition which "is never ours in the same way":

> For me there is always a barrier, a sense of "otherness" about this tradition. . . . I can't *assume* [it]. . . . I have, as it were, only a colonial relationship, . . . inhabiting a language and a culture which I'm not quite at ease in, which doesn't quite fit.[35]

Three of these writers are "colonials" in more than a metaphorical sense: Lessing is southern Rhodesian, Atwood and Laurence are Canadians. As Laurence says, "Anyone who writes in the English language is in some way an inheritor of Shakespeare and Milton, of Fielding and Jane Austen, of Dickens and Thackeray. Our task is not to reject the past but to assimilate it"; yet she also refers to Canadians as "Third World writers" who, "like African writers, have had to find our own voices and write out of what is truly ours, in the face of an overwhelming cultural imperialism" (in W. H. New, 1978, pp. 19, 17). These writers express their ambivalences by creating protagonists who themselves negotiate complex relations with the dominant culture and by critiquing realism in terms more like Roland Barthes's than Lukács's.[36]

I am also concerned with defining these writers' relationship to other women writers. Since our culture continues to exert prohibitions against female literary expression that make female authorship a transgression of social taboos,[37] women writers continue to derive empowerment—and to need this empowerment—from their awareness of predecessors.

Drabble expresses affinities with women novelists: "I was conscious from a very early age that writing novels was a thing that women did do and had always managed to do best;"[38] "I entirely agree with Virginia Woolf . . . when she says that there are links and we owe debts"; and besides Eliot, she cites Woolf, Lessing, and Mary McCarthy as influences.[39] Atwood says, "It is very important to me that other women write successfully":

I went to high school in Canada in the '50's when what was on the curriculum was mostly British literature, some of which was by women. This is different from the experience many American women have when they studied American writing—what they got was mostly by men. I was aware of Jane Austen and the Brontës and George Eliot from the time I was aware of novelists in general. So I never got the idea you had to be male in order to write.[40]

She cites Drabble and Fay Weldon among her favorite contemporaries (Van-Spankeren, p. 233). Laurence found "not many" "women writers who spoke to my childhood" (p. 240), though she does mention Nellie McClung and L. M. Montgomery, whose characters gave her "the sense that a woman could be—and it was *all right* for her to be—an intelligent, independent-minded person who was determined to pursue her own vocation as well as being a wife and mother" (Verduyn, p. 241); and the protagonist of *The Diviners* quotes, "A woman, if she is to write, Virginia Woolf once said (or words to that effect), must have a room of her own."[41] Lessing says little about women writers, but suggests certain affinities by naming the protagonist of *The Golden Notebook* "Wulf" and locating the action of *The Four-Gated City* in Bloomsbury.

One could argue that the writers considered in this study comprise "a tradition of their own"; traditions have been based on less. But if we view them as a "tradition," we should view "tradition" *not* in the Leavisite sense of a timeless, universal entity, but as "tradition making" and unmaking, as a process wherein fiction performs complex negotiations with the works of the past, negotiations which are both appropriations and subversions.[42] In the late sixties and early seventies, feminist fiction accomplished counterhegemonic interventions that were socially effective: it made things happen.

### Feminist Fiction, Feminist Criticism

The publication between 1972 and 1974 of Margaret Drabble's *The Realms of Gold*, Margaret Atwood's *Surfacing*, Margaret Laurence's *The Diviners*, Erica Jong's *Fear of Flying*, and Gail Godwin's *The Odd Woman* indicates that by the early seventies a new genre, feminist metafiction, had come into existence: the protagonist looks to the literary tradition for answers about the present, speculates about the relation of "the forms" to her life and her writing, seeks "an ending of her own" which differs from the marriage or death to which she is traditionally consigned, and seeks "freedom" from the plots of the past. Behind these are the major works of Doris Lessing, *The Golden Notebook* (1962) and *The Children of Violence* (1952–69), prototypical *Kunstlerroman* and *Bildungsroman* of contemporary women's fiction, in which questing protagonists seek "something new": and "something new," a term which recurs in Lessing's works, means more than individual freedom or fulfillment—it means something radically oppositional to "the nightmare repetition" of the past.[43]

Metafiction is a form of literary criticism, a fictional expression of critical positions and assessments, and feminist metafiction is a form of feminist literary criticism. As feminist critics undertake what Annette Kolodny calls a *"re-visionary rereading"* of the literary inheritance,[44] feminist writers also embark on "re-visions," though critics reenter old plots to reevaluate them and novelists reenter them to rewrite them or to "write beyond" earlier endings, in Rachel Blau DuPlessis's suggestive term for the project of twentieth-century women writers. In 1975 Showalter described a "vital interaction" between feminist criticism and fiction;[45] and in 1989, Cora Kaplan, looking back on the seventies, recalled links between the development of feminist criticism and "the new renaissance of women's writing" and "feminism as a social movement," describing "a unified and dialectical cultural practice that spoke into and out of the imaginative project," the sense feminist critics had of "creating a space not solely for a critical project, but for the imaginative project itself."[46]

Like early feminist critics—Mary Ellmann in *Thinking About Women,* Kate Millett in *Sexual Politics,* Carolyn Heilbrun in *Toward a Definition of Androgyny,* Annette Kolodny in *The Lay of the Land,* Judith Fetterley in *The Resisting Reader*—the protagonists of feminist fiction critique "images of women" and the plots of the past. " 'Did you believe that stuff when you were little?' " asks a character in Atwood's *Surfacing;* " 'I did, I thought I was really a princess and I'd end up living in a castle. They shouldn't let kids have stuff like that.' "[47] Jane Clifford of Godwin's *Odd Woman* "ransacks novels for answers to life" only to find that survival depends on eluding "already-written stories."[48] Jane Gray of Drabble's *Waterfall* seeks understanding of her affair with her cousin's husband in "old-fashioned" novels *(The Mill on the Floss, Jude the Obscure, Jane Eyre, Thérèse Racquin, Nana),* only to realize that their punitive morality would have killed her for less.[49] Martha Quest reads "like a famished person," "starved," only to discover "a gap between her self and the past" (MQ, pp. 200, 27, 10): "Is it really conceivable that [women] should have turned into something quite different in the space of about fifty years? Or do you suppose they didn't tell the truth, the novelists?" (PM, p. 205). Mira of French's *The Women's Room* seeks "books she could find herself and her problems in. There were none . . . nothing helped. Like the person who gets fat because they eat unnourishing foods and so is always hungry and so is always eating, she drowned in words that could not teach her to swim."[50] Atwood in *Lady Oracle* and Fay Weldon in *The Fat Woman's Joke* similarly associate unsustaining fiction with unnourishing food, and in Piercy's *Braided Lives* the protagonist's mother reads with "a vast hunger for something. That same hunger that terrifies her in me."[51] Feminists write to fill the "gap" between past and present, and to satisfy women's "hungers" with more nourishing words.

Feminist writers, like feminist critics, engage in "re-visions" of the tradition. "Re-vision", as Adrienne Rich says, is "more than a chapter in cultural history: it is an act of survival" (LSS, p. 35). But re-vision is *also* a chapter in cultural history and a chapter in social history as well, specifically, in the history of the women's movement. Feminist fiction was produced by feminism—though it also produced feminism—and feminist metafiction, which focuses on women as readers and writers, points to the key role of reading and writing in the women's movement. As Rich and others suggest, feminism is a renaming of the world: "in order to change what is, we need to give speech to what *has been,* to imagine together what *might* be."[52] As women who knew the power of reading began writing fiction, they wrote about reading and writing—hence the emergence of feminist metafiction, the most developed form of which was the feminist *Kunstlerroman.* Versions of the feminist *Kunstlerroman* existed earlier in the century,[53] but the genre reached its fullest expression during the second wave of feminism.

That reading and writing emerged as key issues, and often as problematic issues, had to do with the paradoxical situation of women in the postwar period, as they found themselves caught in the crossfire of conflicting signals—in the clash between increased socioeconomic opportunities, on the one hand, and a restrictive domestic ideology, on the other hand.[54] "In the 1950s, one of the surest ways forward for an intellectual young woman from the provinces, for a socially disadvantaged young woman from the provinces, was through Oxford, through Cambridge," says the narrator of Drabble's *The Radiant Way* (p. 86); and Drabble's protagonists here, as in *A Summer Bird Cage, Jerusalem the Golden,* and *The Waterfall,* seek "escape through university" (RW, p. 141). In the United States, an expanding postwar economy allowed women to regain some of the ground they had lost since the second decade of the century, whereas in England new opportunities were created by social legislation: "at eighteen the world opened for them and displayed its riches, the brave new world of Welfare State and County Scholarships, of equality for women, they were the elite, the chosen, the garlanded of the great social dream" (RW, p. 88). Sheila Rowbatham describes "a lot of feminists . . . from working-class families, who had gone to university for the first time, or . . . from a lower-middle-class uneducated background . . . a lot of us were in this process of class transition"; Sally Alexander describes herself as "a child of the welfare state . . . born into the right to education, subsistence, housing and health—that birthright gave my generation the confidence to expect more."[55] Angela Carter refers to the 1944 Education Act, which provided all children the right to education (first to age fourteen, then to fifteen, then to sixteen), as "the most single important cultural event in recent British history": it "granted the ambiguous benefits of a grammar-school education to certain children of the upper working and lower middle class such as myself who might otherwise have driven trains and delivered milk."[56]

But "ambiguous benefits" is right, for though education raised women's expectations, it also made many of them unhappy, creating ambitions that were frustrated by the rigid domestic ideology that urged them back into the home, the ideology described by Friedan as "the feminine mystique."[57] When women's aspirations clashed with this ideology, the result was the malaise—"the problem that has no name"—that produced the ferment that made the women's movement. The protagonists of Drabble's *A Summer Bird Cage,* Atwood's *Edible Woman,* Sylvia Plath's *Bell Jar,* Sue Kaufman's *Diary of a Mad*

*Housewife,* Shulman's *Memoirs of an Ex-Prom Queen,* Sheila Ballantyne's *Norma Jean the Termite Queen,* Godwin's *Odd Woman,* Lois Gould's *The Final Analysis*—all have college degrees that are useless to them. The second wave of feminism in the late sixties and early seventies, in America, Britain, and Canada, was created by middle-class, college-educated women who had learned to want more—who, like the protagonists of this fiction, had expectations their worlds were not meeting: "from books I learned there is something else and I want it bad," says the protagonist of Piercy's *Braided Lives* (p. 9); "books had betrayed her, leading her to want what she could not approach," says the protagonist of Piercy's *Small Changes.*[58]

These protagonists turn to reading for validation of themselves and escape from their circumstances. Martha Quest reads seeking answers, and Lessing suggests that her search is typical and that, contrary to the ivory-tower aestheticism prevalent in the fifties, writers have a responsibility to it:

> For she was of that generation who, having found nothing in religion, had formed themselves by literature. . . . And so she knelt in front of a bookcase, in driving need of the right arrangement of words. . . . Which suggests that it is of no use for artists to insist, with such nervous disinclination for responsibility, that their productions are only . . . "a reflection from the creative fires of irony," etc., etc., while the Marthas of this world read and search with the craving thought, What does this say about my life? (PM, pp. 61–62)

Tina of Kaufman's *Diary of a Mad Housewife,* a "mad housewife" with a B.A. from Smith, keeps copies of Chekhov, Mann, Flaubert, Austen, Marvell, and E. M. Forster on her bedside table, using them as "a way of calming myself without pills or booze"; she finds the means of terminating an unfortunate affair in an Elizabeth Bowen novel—"God bless you, Elizabeth Bowen."[59] For Norma Jean, who has a B.A. from Berkeley, reading is a source both of discontent and strength; as her husband complains, "she reads everything. They're stacked to the ceiling next to the bed: women's lib, ancient Egypt, sociology, the newspaper"; they "take her places where I have no access."[60] Sasha of *Memoirs of an Ex-Prom Queen* finds in her father's library escape from her "baffling life" ("they made me forget I was a piece of meat, albeit a prime piece according to specifications of my mounting pile of *Seventeen* magazines") and finds in philosophy temporary relief from an imprisoning self-consciousness (pp. 51–52, 146).

Often, however, what the protagonist finds in the texts of the culture is reinforcement of the very stereotypes that are the source of her problem, for if "the tradition" inspired woman's aspirations, it also frustrated her dreams by marginalizing and denigrating her. "I have been suspecting for a while now that everything I ever read was lies," says the narrator of *The Women's Room* (p. 210). Jong's Isadora takes "refuge behind books" as though they were "a bullet-proof shield, an asbestos wall, a cloak of invisibility," while also lamenting that she has been taught to see "through the eyes of male writers":

Of course, I didn't think of them as *male* writers. I thought of them as *writers,* as authorities, as gods who knew and were to be trusted completely.
Naturally I trusted everything they said, even when it implied my own inferiority. I learned what an orgasm was from D. H. Lawrence. . . . I learned from Shaw that women never can be artists; I learned from Dostoyevsky that they have no religious feeling; I learned from Swift and Pope that they have too *much* religious feeling. . . . I learned from Faulkner that they are earth mothers. . . . I learned from Freud that they . . . are ever "incomplete" because they lack the one thing in the world worth having: a penis.
But what did all this have to do with me?[61]

Atwood catalogues "stereotypes of women . . . from the Western European literary tradition"—the "old Crones, Delphic Oracles, . . . Three Fates, Evil Witches, White Witches, White Goddesses, Bitch Goddesses, Medusas . . . Mermaids . . . Snow Queens . . . Medea . . . Lady Macbeth . . . Eve, . . . and Mother," "the Whore of Babylon, the Whore with the heart of gold . . . the Scarlet Woman, the Red Shoes, Madame Bovary . . . Molly Bloom and her chamber pot and her eternal yes, Cleopatra and her friend the asp"—concluding, "what do I have to do with thee?" (SW, pp. 219–21). Piercy's Jill tries to adjust novels and biographies "to invent roles for myself," but "a female Hamlet or a female Count of Monte Cristo taxes my inventiveness. Hamlet gets to hog the whole play" (BL, p. 21). Morag of Laurence's *The Diviners* wonders what the lady in a poem by John Donne "might have said of *him*" (p. 191); a character in Edna O'Brien's *Girls in Their Married Bliss* wonders if Shakespeare isn't part of her friend's tragic end: "oh, Shakespeare deepest and powerfulest of friends, father of us all. Father—the crux of her dilemma."[62] It is remarkable how similar such critiques are to those being voiced by feminist critics during these same years.

Feminist writers and critics especially critique the love story, "the old story"—though, as Godwin's Jane Clifford admits, "that is the story we still love most. . . . Even 'emancipated women' . . . love to hear the old, old story"; Baba of *Girls in their Married Bliss* also calls it "the old, old story" (pp. 387, 459). These protagonists may "love" it, but they nevertheless realize that it is likely to leave them dead (in the old versions) or confine them to living deaths (in contemporary versions). Martha Quest, who "sees herself . . . through literature" (MQ, p. 7), expects to find her "end" and deliverance in a man, only to discover that marriage consigns her to ancient and inexorable patterns of repetition, biological and social. Sasha of Shulman's *Memoirs of an Ex-Prom Queen* "wallowed in fable, searching for guidance" and "read every romance as a parable for the future," only to find herself "at thirty . . . without income or skill, dependent on a man and a fading skin"—it was "there in all the texts I'd ever studied," "the fulfillment of a curse!"[63] Mira of French's *Women's Room* also feels cursed: "It had all happened anyhow. Oedipus couldn't escape his fate, and neither could she. The scenario had been written before she was ever born" (p. 99); so too does Miriam of Piercy's *Small Changes* (p. 397). In *How to Save Your Own Life,* Jong's Isadora protests,

all of the greatest fiction of the modern age showed women falling for vile
seducers and dying as a result. They died under breaking waves, under the wheels
of trains, in childbirth. *Someone* had to break the curse, *someone* had to wake
Sleeping Beauty. . . . *Someone* had to shout once and for all: Fly and live to tell
the tale![64]

## Other Ends

The critique of romance is a critique of the ending, for the love story allows
woman one end: her "end," both in the sense of "goal" and "conclusion," is a
man. Feminist critics have analyzed marriage as the one plot available to
woman, her sole means of success or survival, the quest and vocation that
absorbs all possible *Bildung* and defines her transition to adulthood: marriage
symbolizes her integration into society and death symbolizes her failure to
negotiate that entrance and symbolizes, as well, the culture's failure to imagine
her existence apart from marriage—to allow her "something else to be," in Toni
Morrison's term.[65] Feminists are by no means the first to critique endings:
Modernists also associated endings with the constraints of nineteenth-century
realism,[66] and contemporary theorists similarly relate closure to the conservative tendencies of realism, describing it as "aimed at containment,"[67] as an
"imperative to disclosure" which tends toward the revelation of a single, univocal truth—a tendency that neutralizes potentials for change.[68] Feminist writers are especially concerned with endings as bearers of gender ideology, as
"tropes for the sex-gender system," in DuPlessis's term (WBE, p. ix), but they
also critique them for their "containments" and conservatism.

Jane Clifford rejects what she calls the "Emma Bovary syndrome"—"literature's graveyard positively choked with women who . . . 'get in trouble' (commit adultery, have sex without marriage; *think* of committing adultery, or having
sex without marriage) and thus, according to the literary convention of the
time, must die" (OW, p. 302). The nightmarish power of this plot is suggested by
a passage in Alice Walker's *Meridian* which is reiterated three times, as though
in a spell: "She dreamed she was a character in a novel and that her existence
presented an insoluble problem, one that would be solved only by her death at
the end." The reiteration suggests the compulsive and obsessive nature of this
"dream," and "even when she gave up reading novels that encouraged such a
solution—and nearly all of them did—the dream did not cease."[69]

Some of these writers contrast the neat shapes of fiction to the muddles of
"real life." Reading has taught Martha Quest to assume that her life will be
shaped by the dramatic denouements of fiction, but her expectations are
thwarted by the slow, shapeless series form of *The Children of Violence*. Mira of
French's *The Women's Room* protests:

> In the great literature of the past you either get married and live happily ever after,
> or you die. But the fact is, neither is what actually happens. Oh, you do die, but

never at the right time . . . and you don't live happily ever after, but you do live. (p. 211)

Even Woolf got it wrong, French claims, in envisioning a "violent" and "apocalyptic end" for Shakespeare's sister:

> I know that isn't what happened. You see, it isn't necessary . . . there are so much easier ways to destroy a woman. You don't have to rape or kill her; you don't even have to beat her. You can just marry her. You don't even have to do that. You can just let her work in your office for thirty-five dollars a week. (pp. 64–65)

Ella Price laments, "We don't get chopped down like redwoods, we wither. . . . And we don't jump in front of trains. We just keep going. Not dead but alive. And nobody ever knows. That's what's so awful, that no one knows."[70]

Though French complains "you could never go beyond the end" (p. 24), contemporary women writers do write beyond the end, beyond the telos of romance and its "regimen of resolutions," in DuPlessis's term (WBE, p. 21). Though Ella Price's friend calls Nora's ending " 'absurd. You can't do that. Just walk out, without a job, without any knowledge of the world, leaving the children. It just can't be done' " (p. 91), Ella and other contemporary protagonists do it. In *Bodily Harm* Atwood redefines "terminal" (a word much on the mind of her protagonist, who has just had a mastectomy) to mean not "the end of the line, where you get off" but "where you can get on to go somewhere else" (p. 264).

But "somewhere else" is not so easy to imagine, since few narratives exist that take their protagonists past such revelations and dramatize their new freedoms from old plots.[71] The protagonist of Barbara Raskin's *Loose Ends* would like "to write a novel about an American woman who, after a lifetime of psychological dependency upon men . . . moves out front alone, on her own," but does "not know yet what form such an experience takes . . . because it hasn't happened yet."[72] Thus *Loose Ends* ends, like *Ella Price's Journal*, Atwood's *Bodily Harm*, *Surfacing*, and *Edible Woman*, with the protagonist poised on the brink of an unimaginable future.

Open ends are, of course, nothing new in twentieth-century fiction. In 1966 Alan Friedman described the open end as true to the contemporary sense of life, to altered "assumptions about character, society, self, world, sequence, consequence."[73] But by the mid-seventies, "a form of conclusion that would once have been shocking and new has become thoroughly expected and conventional," as Marianna Torgovnick says of *Fear of Flying;*[74] and in Drabble's 1974 *Realms of Gold*, it is the happy ending that requires comment: "So there you are. Invent a more suitable ending if you can."[75] Shulman's 1969 *Memoirs of an Ex-Prom Queen* concludes with Sasha poised on the threshold—" 'I'm leaving,' I said from the doorway"—overcome by ennui: "It all sounded vaguely familiar, like snatches of an old play" (p. 225–26). It had struck Martha Quest as "an old play" years before this, in Lessing's 1952 *A Proper Marriage:* "there's something so *vieux jeu* . . . in leaving like Nora to live differently! . . . One is bound to fall in love with the junior partner, and things will begin all over again" (p. 274).

Martha was right; things do "begin over again." Martha, Sasha, and Isadora leave one husband for another; and, reading beyond the endings of Jong's *Fear of Flying*, French's *The Women's Room*, and Raskin's *Loose Ends* to the follow-ups of these successful first novels—*How to Save Your Own Life, The Bleeding Heart*, and *Hot Flashes*—we find the most amazing recuperation of romantic fantasy: "how to save your own life" turns out to be—find a new man.

Clearly, leaving home is not enough. Change requires more than moving out, resolution, or will: it requires a process of re-envisioning which allows an evolution and alteration of desire and consciousness, both protagonist's and reader's—a "working through" like that which occurs in psychoanalysis.[76] The most convincing of this fiction—*The Children of Violence, The Golden Notebook, The Diviners, Lady Oracle*—places the end of the affair or the marriage in the middle and writes beyond it. The novels I discuss in Part II—*The Golden Notebook, The Waterfall, The Diviners*, and *Lady Oracle*—depict change as a process and devise narrative modes that enact working through.

### Vicious Circles, Liberating Circles, Self-Begetting Novels

In the fiction I focus on, working through is rendered by the structure of circular return, a pattern wherein episodes set in the past alternate with episodes set in the present and are completed when past becomes present, a structure enabling a circling back over material which allows repetition with revision. This pattern is so frequent in contemporary women's fiction as to be practically a distinguishing feature, occurring not only in Drabble's *The Waterfall*, Laurence's *The Diviners*, Godwin's *The Odd Woman*, Jong's *Fear of Flying*, Atwood's *Lady Oracle, The Handmaid's Tale, Cat's Eye*, and Anne Richardson Roiphe's *Up the Sandbox*, but also in novels as various as Octavia Butler's *Kindred*, Marge Piercy's *Woman on the Edge of Time*, Fay Weldon's *Praxis*, Lisa Alther's *Kinflicks*, Ursula K. LeGuin's *Dispossessed*, Anne Tyler's *Earthly Possessions*, Alison Lurie's *The War Between the Tates*, and Marilyn French's *The Women's Room.*

In some sense women's quests have always been circular. In traditional fiction by and about women, women moved from the homes of fathers to husbands, exchanging "one domestic space for another," as Elizabeth Abel says; Mary Anne Ferguson describes "the pattern for the female novel of development" as "largely circular" because women are initiated into "rituals of human relationships, so that they may replicate the lives of their mothers."[77] Cixous's sense of this process is grimmer: "they have wandered around in circles, confined to the narrow room in which they've been given a deadly brainwashing."[78]

While cyclic and linear notions of time ("time's circle" and "time's arrow") have associations not only with female and male, but with east and west, archaic and modern, myth and history, nonrational and rational modes of apprehension,[79] nevertheless, circles and cycles remain resonant symbols for things female, for women's physiology, their sexual and psychosocial experience, and their experience of time. Women's lives are defined by cycles, both natural and social—menstruation, pregnancy, birth, the repetition involved in childbearing, childrearing, and domesticity. "Women's time," as Kristeva describes it, is characterized by "cycles, gestation, the eternal recurrence of a biological rhythm," cycles which have nothing to do with "time as project, teleology, linear and prospective unfolding—in other words, the time of history."[80] Circles and rings have been used to signify the vulva ring and birth canal, associations suggested by the punning of Shakespeare and Donne; related to this is the egg, a symbol which figures prominently in contemporary women's fiction (e.g. *The Stone Angel, The Handmaid's Tale, Memoirs of a Survivor, The Good Terrorist*).

In fact, if there is a "female form" in Western literary representations, it is the circle—though I am by no means suggesting a biologistic analogy between physiology and textuality (women are round and so are their narratives). But the linear sequence of traditional quests and *Bildungsroman* plots have struck many feminist critics and writers as formally inappropriate to female experience.[81] Pearson and Pope describe the "assumption that life occurs in a logical, linear order" and is "determined by linear, causal relationships" as fundamentally patriarchal (pp. 216–17). Patricia Tobin links time as a line, an irreversible arrow whose trajectory is determined by original intention, the causality of past event controlling future, to "the genealogical imperative":[82] when events "come to be perceived as begetting other events within a line of causality similar to the line of generations, with the prior event earning a special prestige as it is seen to originate, control," when "ontological priority is conferred upon mere temporal anteriority," time becomes "a linear manifestation of the genealogical destiny of events" (p. 7); "the prestige of cause over effect . . . is analogous to the prestige of the father over the son" (p. 12). This concept of time is "as intimate and peculiar" to Western thought as "patriarchalism" and reflects patriarchal ideas of authority (p. 12). It is so familiar that we forget that it is unique to the West, that it reflects culture, not "nature"; and it is the notion of time that "pervades the structure of realistic narrative" (p. 7).

But if language, narrative, and reading are linear—as Kristeva notes, "this linear time is that of language considered as the enunciation of sentences (noun + verb; topic–comment; beginning–ending)" (1981, p. 17)—how can a writer disrupt linearity and still remain comprehensible? Attempts on the part of writers to disrupt sentences and sequences often disrupt sense as well and become, like avant-garde experimental texts, inaccessible and esoteric. The pattern of circular return is a brilliant response to this problem since it leaves intact the linear sequence of language and narrative, retaining its coherence and comprehensibility while also critiquing its limitations and suggesting alternatives.

Besides, the circle is a dual symbol, for while it signifies absence, nothingness, blankness, powerlessness, it also signifies totality, perfection, power[83]—a duality exploited in contemporary women's writings, where it is used to symbolize action and passivity, stasis and movement, quiescence and revolution. Whereas in Pauline Reages's *The Story of O* (1954), "O" signifies the openness and blankness of the sexually available woman, and in Friedan's *The Feminine Mystique,* the "vicious circle" (pp. 146, 281), a "tortuously tight circle" (p. 127), signifies the closed circuit of female conditioning, in *Les Guérillères* Wittig shifts the "O" away from a symbol of female sexuality to an emblem of women's revolution against men—"the zero, the O, the perfect circle that you invent to imprison them and to overthrow them."[84] Cixous describes *l'écriture féminine* as "breaking out of the circles" (LM, p. 263), but she also describes it as inscribing another kind of circle—as "always endless, without ending: there's no closure, it doesn't stop."[85] Irigaray describes a "feminine syntax" as having "no beginning or end," as "confound[ing] the linearity of an outline, the teleology of discourse."[86]

I would suggest that "gynesis," "putting the feminine into discourse"— besides making what is muted dominant, what is marginal central, and fore-grounding gaps, discontinuities, blank spaces, and silences (as DuPlessis, Abel, Jardine, and others have described it)[87]—also involves structural or imagistic play on circularity. Since, as Ellen Moers notes, there is not even a female equivalent for a "phallic symbol,"[88] one function of circular structures and images is to provide an alternative sexual vocabulary, as they do in Drabble's *The Waterfall,* where they are associated with the limitless energies of female libido and the revolutionary powers of *jouissance.* Most important, the transfor-mation of closed, "vicious" circles to liberatory cycles is a transformation of the fixed structures of the past to open, processive forms that accommodate change. Whereas the "vicious" circles of Lessing's matrophobic texts *(The Grass Is Singing, A Proper Marriage, The Summer Before the Dark)* circumscribe protagonists in nightmarish repetition and signify the triumph of the past, circles become, in Lessing's later fiction—and in Drabble's *The Waterfall* and *The Middle Ground* and *Kunstlerromane* by Atwood and Laurence—open structures associated with change. The return to the past signifies not the triumph of the past but becomes, rather, the means to a transformed present and new possibilities for the future, allowing repetition in order for there to be escape from repetition, in order for there to be progress or change.

The pattern of circular return allows repetition with re-vision, a return to the past that enables a new future. The *Kunstlerromane* which are the subject of Part II—*The Golden Notebook, The Diviners, Lady Oracle*—enlist circular struc-tures of a particular sort: they are "self-begetting novels" that end with the protagonist ready to begin writing the novel we have just finished reading.[89] Like the reader protagonist who contemplates her relation to earlier pro-tagonists and plots, the writer protagonist also contemplates her relation to the forms of the past, but since she herself is a writer, she has the power to devise new plots. A woman who assumes "the power of the pen" in a culture that defines literary authority in patriarchal terms assumes a power that is customarily male;[90] since woman (as Irigaray says) has been denied "access to language, except through recourse to 'masculine' systems of representation which disappropriate her from her relation to her self and to other women," when she becomes a "speaking subject," she "destroy[s] . . . the discursive mechanism" ("Power of Discourse," pp. 85, 76). To make a protagonist an "author" is to give her control over conventions that have traditionally controlled her. It is also to grant her the powers of imagination, intelligence, inventiveness that women writers have traditionally withheld from their protagonists.[91]

It is not surprising, then, that issues of power in contemporary women's fiction center on questions of language. In the simplest metafictions, protagonists keep journals. Tina of Kaufman's *Mad Housewife* keeps "accounts" in order to write her way back to sanity, hoping "to spot some trend, some key that will help explain why I've gotten in this state" (p. 7); as, two decades later, Ellery of Marianne Wiggins's *Separate Checks,* institutionalized and recovering from a breakdown, keeps a journal to write her way back to health, and Anastasia of French's *Her Mother's Daughter* consults her journals to understand "how I got the way I am, how I got sick."[92] Ella Price's journal (in *Ella Price's Journal*) records how the reading and writing assigned in an English class transform her life; Jong's Isadora uses journals and poetry as means of self-knowledge and "survival" (FF, p. 114); Mira of *The Women's Room* says, "I will write it all down, go back as far as I have to, and try to make some sense out of it" (p. 18).

But in the complex metafictions I discuss in Part II—Lessing's *The Golden Notebook,* Laurence's *The Diviners,* and Atwood's *Lady Oracle*—the protagonists are professional, self-supporting, self-conscious writers whose writing empowers them to live on their own. Their interrogation of narrative convention is the correlative of their efforts to live unconventionally—as their authors themselves do[93]—and their writing is a means of "chang[ing] the rules of the old game," in Cixous's term for *"l'écriture féminine"* (LM, p. 250). Writing is for them a form of activism, as it was for many in the early years of the women's movement.[94]

## Marginals and Metafictions

To be a woman is to be an outsider, to be "from another culture," as the protagonist of Atwood's *Surfacing* calls herself (p. 83); as Dale Spender says, women are *"taught* the official version of experience, the world of men, and they *live* the unofficial version, the world of women"; this enables them "to get outside the male frame of reference, to be 'anthropological observers' . . . of a culture whose values they know but do not share."[95] Three of the writers I focus on are "doubly dispossessed"[96] in being female and "colonial." Lessing is doubly dispossessed in the additional sense of being twice exiled, an experience she describes in *The Marriages Between Zones Three, Four, and Five* and *The Sirian Experiments.* She spent her youth in Africa feeling exiled from England, and then, after moving to England in 1949, she felt exiled from Africa—and she actually *was* exiled in that she was declared a "prohibited immigrant" on account of her Communist Party affiliations and criticisms of racism. She has remained what Mona Knapp terms "an outsider on principle, in voluntary exile from all collectives and movements" (p. 21). At times, as in the Canopus series, she assumes the perspective of a visitor from outer space; more often, as in *Children of Violence* and *Memoirs of a Survivor,* she makes protagonists ethnologists like herself, students of their own, alien cultures.[97]

Laurence spent formative years in Africa, in Somaliland (1950–52) and the Gold Coast (1952–57), which she left the year it became Ghana. Her first novel, *This Side Jordan* (1960), concerns characters who are caught between two worlds—Africans torn between past and future and colonials alienated both from Africa and from England—and the "dispossessed" remain a central focus of her fiction. She attributes her interest in colonialism to her sense of being from "a land that had been a colony, a land which was in some ways still colonial" (NASB, p. 22):

> My sense of social awareness, my feelings of anti-imperialism, anti-colonialism, anti-authoritarianism . . . developed considerably through my African experience. It was not very difficult to relate this experience to my own land, which had been under the colonial sway of Britain once and was now under the colonial sway of America. (NASB, p. 24).

She adds that "our situation . . . like that of all peoples with colonial mentalities, was not unlike that of women in our society" (NASB, p. 23). Atwood describes herself as "citizen of a country which was until recently dominated by one imperial power and is now dominated by another" (SW, p. 358). Drabble is the closest to what might be considered "mainstream," but even she is from the north of England and identifies with her mother's working-class origins and what she terms her "difficult transition into the middle class" (Creighton, 1985, p. 17). She has recently described herself as "a foreigner in London": "I don't feel I can get inside. . . . I'm not from London, I'm from Yorkshire."[98] The three women in *The Radiant Way*—Alix, Elizabeth, and Esther—share "a sense of being on the margins of English life, perhaps, a sense of being outsiders, looking in from a cold street through a lighted window into a warm lit room that later might prove to be their own. Removed from the mainstream" (p. 90); so too do the protagonists of *Jerusalem the Golden, The Waterfall,* and *The Middle Ground.*

In *A Room of One's Own* Woolf described the advantages of being "locked out": "I thought how unpleasant it is to be locked out, and I thought how it is much worse perhaps to be locked in" (p. 24). To be an outsider is to be the opposite of "provincial"—in the sense that Lessing defines "provincial," being "bounded" by one's culture (SPV, p. 15). Nor does this principle apply only to women; as Morris Dickstein notes, "a staggering number of contemporary writers were strangers in a strange land: Americans in Europe, Poles writing in English, Anglo-American Irishmen . . . self-exiled questers. . . . Such deracination could be a source of strength," permitting them "a perspective on modern society unavailable to the insider"[99]—allowing what Teresa de Lauretis calls "a view from 'elsewhere.' "[100] Their sense of being outsiders explains why women writers often make their protagonists archaeologists, anthropologists, or ethnologists. Frances Wingate of Drabble's *The Realms of Gold* is an archaeologist; Kate of Drabble's *The Middle Ground* speculates about Lévi-Strauss and Mary Douglas in contemplating the primitive, xenophobic customs of contemporary England; the protagonist of Raskin's *Hot Flashes* is a professor of anthropology; Zora Neale Hurston was herself an anthropologist. Anthropology figures prominently in feminist science fiction, especially in that of Octavia Butler and Ursula K. LeGuin (the "K" stands for Kroeber), whose novels *The Dispossessed* and *Always Coming Home* explore the workings of social systems.

In a sense all innovative novelists occupy an uneasy relation to the tradition they inherit, which is why they develop new forms. For if the novel is a form that resists change, it is also a form that is always changing. As Wallace Martin suggests, it is by unmasking older conventions, by calling attention to their artificiality, that "the writer clears a space in which departures from convention will be taken as signs of authenticity";[101] thus old forms are modified and new forms evolve. Metafictional devices are intrinsic to the novel from the beginning, even in works that are not obviously experimental,[102] though they become especially prominent in Modernist and contemporary fiction: in fact they are what keeps the novel novel.

In the most minimal form of metafiction, fictionality is explored as a theme, forms and endings are problematized, but fictionality is finally recontextualized in the "real." More extreme metafictions posit the world as a fabrication of competing semiotic systems and resist such recontextualization (Waugh, pp. 53, 115–49). The writers I'm interested in occur at the near end of this spectrum. They thematize fictionality and make their protagonists artists and artist figures who critique the ending and contemplate their relation to the plots of the past. Weaving literary allusions into their narratives structurally and thematically, they problematize "intertextuality"[103] and enlist it to suggest that experience is structured by the stories we inherit. But except for *The Golden Notebook*—and even it seems tame by comparison with the dazzling pyrotechnics of Barth, Nabokov, and Pynchon—they reaffirm a knowable reality.[104]

However, feminist metafiction may have more radical implications than male post-modernist texts, in having more urgency and edge, more relevance to lived experience: for when women write of being trapped in an alien tradition, they write from a sense of living in a culture not their own. As Molly Hite argues, women's narrative innovations "are *more* radical in their implications than the dominant modes of fictional experiment, and more radical precisely inasmuch as the context for innovation is a critique of a culture and a literary tradition apprehended as profoundly masculinist."[105] Women writers enlist metafictional devices not as gamesmanship or self-display, or to make "the confession of futility a chief end of . . . writing"—for which Gerald Graff criticizes post-modernist fiction; language is, rather, critiqued as "social fact," and such fiction thereby reestablishes the connection Graff urges, "with recognizably central patterns of individual and social experience."[106]

### Feminist Metafiction and the Franco-Anglo-American Debate

Allowing the woman writer a way of articulating her ambivalent relation to the tradition, a way of working both within and against the dominant discourse, feminist metafiction resolves a problem at the heart of feminist debate: can we "adapt traditionally male-dominated modes of writing and analyses to the articulation of female oppression and desire," or should we "rather reject tools that may simply re-inscribe our marginality and . . . forge others of our own?" (in Mary Jacobus's terms).[107] In "Is There Such a Thing as Women's Writing," Xavière Gauthier describes the "contradiction" in which women are "caught": throughout history women "have been mute . . . outside the historical process. But, if they begin to speak and write *as men do,* they will enter history subdued and alienated." To speak and write "as men do" makes us part of a process we should oppose, but to remain mute, to abandon language because it inscribes patriarchal ideology, is to abandon the possibility of challenging that ideology. Another kind of speaking and writing is required, but as Gauthier asks, "how can women speak 'otherwise'?" (Marks and Courtivron, pp. 162–63); as Jacobus asks, "when we speak . . . of the need for a special language for women, what then do we mean? Not, surely, a refusal of language itself; nor a return to the specifically feminine linguistic domaine which in fact marks the place of women's oppression and confinement" (1979, p. 12).

Thus Hélène Cixous and Luce Irigaray propose an alternative discourse deriving from the female body, from the rhythms and sensations of female sexuality. Cixous defines *"l'écriture féminine,"* "writing the female body," as the basis of a *"new insurgent* writing" that subverts cultural structures and "wreck[s] partitions, classes, and rhetorics, regulations and codes," thereby "chang[ing] the rules of the old game" (in "The Laugh of the Medusa," the manifesto of *l'écriture féminine* [pp. 250, 256]).[108] Irigaray describes women's language as figured by the female genitals, and therefore as multiple, diffuse, fluid, and open ("When Our Lips Speak Together"). Gauthier suggests that women's writing *"make audible* that which . . . suffers silently in the *holes of discourse,* in the unsaid, or in the non-sense," citing Wittig's use of "O" in *Les Gúerillères* as exemplary (p. 163): "O" is "whatever they have not laid hands on . . . [what] your masters have not been able to fill with their words of proprieters and possessors, this can be found in the gaps, in all that is not a continuation of their discourse, in the zero, the O" (p. 114). (As these descriptions suggest, *"l'écriture féminine"* is a somewhat fluid notion that can connote both writing the female sexual body—with the essentialist implications of that position— and the creative textuality of self-conscious play.)[109]

Disagreement about language is the crux of the debate between Anglo-American and French feminism, and it is a disagreement not only about "women's writing"—what it is and ought to be—but about criticism as well;[110] it also reiterates earlier debates about realism and modernism, as Felski notes (p. 3). Whereas Anglo-American feminist criticism ("gynocriticism," in Showalter's term, "the study of women *as writers,* . . . the history, styles, themes, genres, and structures of writing by women")[111] rests on the assumption that women's writing can "reflect" women's experiences and that language is a transparent medium on a preexistent reality, French feminist theory, which derives from post-Saussurean linguistics, structuralism, and Derridean deconstruction, assumes that language is a set of signifying practices which is constitutive of reality. Feminist critics who accept French feminist assumptions—Toril Moi, Alice Jardine, Mary Jacobus, Jane Gallop—argue that the view of texts as unproblematically transmitting "truth" is precisely the view on which the canon has been predicated and that it conceals assumptions about language and literature that are empiricist, humanist, and bourgeois—assumptions that reaffirm the traditional paradigm of knowledge and the system we should be challenging.[112]

To return to the question posed by Jacobus: should women adopt traditional modes or forge others of their own? Jacobus suggests that "the options polarize along familiar lines: appropriation or separatism" (1979, p. 14). Appropriation implies that we accept language as a neutral tool and separatism implies that we repudiate it as tainted. But in practice, all writers must appropriate language since there is (as Jacobus admits) "no 'outside' of discourse."[113] Thus it is misleading to view the alternatives as separatism *or* appropriation, a choice between forging an alternative discourse or appropriating the language; we should, rather, view the *process* of appropriation as itself constituting an alternative: that is, it is the woman writer's engagement with the tradition that is distinctive about women's writing. Jacobus herself suggests something like this when she describes women's writing as "a process that is played out within language, across boundaries," "that exposes those very boundaries for what they are—the product of phallocentric discourse and of women's relation to patriarchal culture": "though necessarily working within 'male' discourse, women writers . . . would work ceaselessly to deconstruct it: to write what cannot be written" (1979, pp. 12, 17).

The novelists who are the subject of this study write within a realist, empiricist tradition which generally assumes the reliability of language. But by making their protagonists readers and writers who question the old forms and devise new ones, they expose the limits of linguistic and narrative forms from within those forms. In their negotiations with realism, they fall somewhere between the two types of fiction Rita Felski describes—the popular, widely read realist narratives of confession and self-discovery that are "not interested in the issue of the fictionality of literary representation as such" (p. 151) and "an aesthetically self-conscious experimental writing which challenges stylistic conventions and calls into question established modes of representation" (p. 16)—the kind of writing many feminist critics are currently touting as revolutionary, against which realism is measured and found wanting. Like Felski I am uneasy about this polarity and doubtful that "aesthetic radicalism" is necessarily the same as "political radicalism" (p. 61), and like her, I feel that "one of the strengths of feminism has been precisely [its] partial reintegration of literature into the everyday communicative practices of large numbers of women" (p. 162). Though realistic fiction may be anachronistic from certain theoretical stand-points, it remains a major literary form for oppressed groups, a means of defining problems of self and cultural identity (Felski, p. 78). The fiction I focus on bridges this gap between naive realism and esoteric experimentalism, enlist-ing realism while also deploying self-conscious devices that interrogate the assumptions of realism,[114] challenging the ideological complicity of the sig-nification process while also basing itself in that signification process (to use Annette Kuhn's terms).[115] Feminist metafiction is a kind of nontransparent realism that enlists strategies of the "writerly" text and—in Barthes's terms for this text—is open to "play," to process, and change.[116]

"Women's writing" has often been described in terms of disruption and transgression, but most analyses tend to be ungrounded in discussion of women's texts.[117] What Jacobus, Moi, and Jardine describe theoretically, I demonstrate in the actual textual practices of contemporary women writers. My analysis of a process-oriented, open-ended mode has affinities with descriptions of women's writing by DuPlessis and Jane Marcus,[118] though I do not attribute these qualities to female "boundary fluidity."[119] I am less concerned with "women's writing" than with feminist fiction, and more specifically with femi-nist metafiction, a highly self-conscious mode that I associate with female identity only when the writer herself does—as Drabble, Lessing, and Atwood in fact do. I am more interested in the writer's exposure of boundaries as a means of exploring systems than as expression of female "boundary confusion." I am also less interested in the woman writer as a figure of "female creativity," as Susan Gubar (1981) and Lee Edwards have discussed her,[120] than as con-sciously and deliberately concerned with reformulating tradition. I am not making claims for a "women's writing" so much as describing a literary movement which is allied with a specific historical moment.

Like Joanne Frye, I am interested in narratives that are capable of effecting change, and like her, I describe a narrative practice that can both *represent* women's experience and . . . *redefine* the premises of representation."[121] Frye argues that the first-person pronoun allows the protagonist "agency" and means to change (p. 79) and attributes subversive powers to first-person nar-rative like those which I attribute to metafiction. Her argument, however, does not take account of those first-person narrators who fail to achieve agency (Tina of Kaufman's *Diary of a Mad Housewife*) and those third-person protagonists who *do* attain it—Morag in *The Diviners* and Jane in *The Odd Woman*. My qualification of her approach applies to my own as well: neither first-person narratives nor metafictions nor circular structures are inherently radical or reactionary or inherently *anything;* all are forms that assume particular mean-ing only in combination with particular content.

## British, Canadian, American, African-American

I suspect that the belief in individualism which is entrenched in American thought makes it difficult for American writers to grasp the nexus of individual and collective, to render the connections between consciousness and history that I find most interesting in feminist fiction. The belief in the autonomy of the self that goes back to Emersonian individualism—what Nina Baym describes as the American myth "that individuals come before society, that they exist in some meaningful sense prior to, and apart from, societies in which they happen to find themselves"—makes it difficult for even the avowedly feminist writer to conceive of character as enmeshed within and formed by social relations.[122]

It has often been said that the relation between individual and society in English fiction tends to be one of support rather than conflict, whereas in American fiction the isolated hero asserts self in face of an alien or hostile environment; in the English novel the individual gains life from the community, whereas the American novel characteristically pits individual against community.[123] This failure to conceive of identity as grounded in collective produces what Charles Molesworth terms an "impoverished political vocabulary" and a psychological vocabulary which "has tended to drive out all others."[124] When asked about her view of art as political, Atwood responded that only in the United States, where "somehow it's been decided generally that the Freudian subconscious is OK for art, but one's conscious political decisions are not," would it occur to anybody to question that art is political (in VanSpanckeren, pp. 233–34).[125]

Protagonists of "mad housewife" fiction resolve their problems by asserting the autonomy of the self: Plath's Esther proclaims, "I am, I am, I am"; Margaret of Anne Richardson Roiphe's *Up the Sandbox* claims, "that I am what I am is by my own choosing"; Camilla of Johanna Davis's *Life Signs* asserts that "she was whoever she chose, she would belong to herself."[126] French, Piercy, and Jong may show their characters participating in political causes and their lives as affected by public events—as when Isadora's first husband is drafted into the Vietnam War—but this is not the same as rendering consciousness as structured by society, as enmeshed within ideology and produced by history, which the most interesting novels of Drabble and Lessing do. The feminism of Jong, Shulman, Godwin, and Raskin represents what Rich calls " 'life-style liberation,' personal solutions, to the few—and those few, overwhelmingly white" ("Disloyal to Civilization," LSS, p. 309)—which leaves untouched the vast majority of women and the social structures that oppress them.[127] Of American writers, only African-American women writers—coming out of a tradition which is preoccupied with the survival of a people, where the formation of self is resolved not in individualistic terms but by identification with black culture—convincingly portray the interdependence of individual life with community.[128]

It was with reluctance that I omitted Toni Morrison, Alice Walker, and Paule Marshall from this study, but American women of color do not write metafiction of the sort I focus on here. Not that they do not write metafiction: in Morrison's *The Bluest Eye,* Pecola's mother, Pauline—who is, like Sula, an "artist with no art form" (p. 121) and therefore dangerous—learns at the movies the standard of beauty that destroys her daughter; in *Brown Girl, Brownstones,* Marshall evokes Greek and Shakespearean tragedy to suggest the fatalistic forces her protagonist, Selina, contends with and has her create a new form in dance;[129] Gloria Naylor invokes Dante in *Linden Hills* and Shakespeare in *Moma Day;* and Walker shows the protagonist of *Meridian* living beyond the traditional endings, not only of marriage and romance, but of martyrdom. But I have found no feminist metafiction by black women writers that relates the rewriting of old plots specifically to women's search for freedom as Drabble, Laurence, and Atwood do. I suspect that this is because the white male "tradition" is a matter of less urgency to them than it is to white women. As Angela Carter puts it,

> There are black Africans, Afro-Caribbeans, Indians, Pakistanis, Cypriots, Chinese and numerous others in and outside Britain who use the English language as a means of imaginative communication and to whom the Great Tradition and, indeed, the whole history of the novel in England since Defoe, means precisely piss-all since they have other fish to fry in it.[130]

Canadian literature is often said to be more concerned with community and what David Jeffrey terms the quest for "cultural identity" than American literature is: "in Canadian fiction the old identity questions . . . are usually translated not so much in terms of personal identity as by expressions of a search for an identity which is collective and cultural."[131] This seems odd in a country so sparsely populated as Canada, but the "Canadian tradition" is to some extent a British legacy, as is clear from Atwood's description of the British literature she studied, and to some extent a fabrication in response to the *absence* of past or community. Atwood describes what it was like to want to be a writer at a time when "Canadian writer" was "an oxymoron" ("Canadian-American Relations," SW, p. 381), when "the only writers I had encountered in high school had been dead and English" (VanSpanckeren, p. xiii). Her response to this situation was to define a Canadian literary tradition: "One of the reasons I wrote [*Survival*] was that nobody else had" (SW, p. 385); and *Survival* struck a chord, becoming "the most widely read work of literary criticism in Canada" (VanSpanckeren, p. 3). Atwood also describes certain advantages to having "no longstanding tradition": "there are no huge giants hovering over you, you're very free . . . you can do anything."[132]

## Canon Re-Formation

My focus on feminist metafiction accounts for my omission of African-American women writers. It also accounts for my omission of feminist fiction which is not metafictional—by Piercy, French, Alther, Lurie—and of major women writers—Iris Murdoch, Muriel Spark, Beryl Bainbridge, Joyce Carol Oates—who are not feminist.[133] Murdoch and Spark employ metafictional devices—artist figures, speculations on fictionality or the function and morality of art—but not in a way that is related to gender. In Spark's hilarious first novel, *The Comforters* (1957), which she describes as "a novel about writing a novel about writing a novel,"[134] a woman who is writing a book on "form in the modern novel" gets stuck in the chapter on realism, convinced by the night-marish sound of typing that an authorial presence is trying to take over her life; but Spark makes no connection between her protagonist's situation and her gender. Similarly, in *The Driver's Seat,* a woman sets out in search of her executioner, only she assumes control over the plot, systematically organizing every detail of her death, making her own decisions the driving force of the story in a way that challenges authorial control (as Stevenson suggests; p. 181). But like *The Comforters,* this grim little fable is uninformed by feminist con-sciousness.

My study is gynocritical in that it reads women writers in relation to one another and in relation to history. I am concerned to show these writers as "thinking back" not only through "mothers" (as Woolf says women writers do, p. 101), but through elder sisters as well, reworking the feminist quest articu-lated by Lessing in *The Golden Notebook* and *The Children of Violence.* My selection of texts is based on content, focusing on fictions that focus on women, and I do close readings; my approach is thus empirical and unashamedly Anglo-American. But far from assuming an unproblematic relationship be-tween language and reality, I am interested in the way texts signify and in these *writers' awareness* of the way texts signify, in their critiques of conventions as bearers of ideology, for these are sophisticated writers whose concerns have been shaped by an age when criticism and theory are powerful.

Of the numerous studies of twentieth-century women writers which have appeared since 1975,[135] so few have focused on contemporary fiction (Christ, Rigney, Rubenstein, Felski, Mickelson, Frye, Hite, Waugh, Alexander, Kenyon) that one senses a reluctance on the part of feminist criticism like that which characterizes mainstream criticism to engage with recent fiction. (Perhaps it is still true that, as Atwood quipped, to be a "great author" you have to be dead and male.) My project takes the feminist effort of canon re-formation into the area of contemporary women's fiction, and it is motivated by a pragmatic concern—to draw attention to major women writers so that they have a better chance of surviving. For they are an endangered species: Lessing, who should long ago have received the Nobel Prize, lost many readers when she turned to space fiction and mysticism, and critics who dismiss her feel justified in writing off her feminism as well, discounting it as another form of "spacing out"; Drabble is often out of print in this country; Laurence is practically unknown in the United States; only Atwood regularly makes best-seller lists. Most of my male colleagues, most men I know, even those who keep up with contemporary fiction, do not feel the responsibility to read these writers; and (as I show in the next chapter) contemporary women writers have barely begun to penetrate the consciousness of those who write literary history.

I use the term "tradition" knowing that it raises vexed questions concerning the canon and the relation of women's writing to it: do feminists really want a canon, even a countercanon of women writers? My own feeling is that though canons are ideologically suspect, they are inevitable, and they are based on distinctions, which are also suspect and also inevitable. This study suggests distinctions—between the fiction of Gail Godwin and Erica Jong, whose forms recuperate the ideology they purport to critique, and that of Laurence, Atwood, Lessing, and Drabble, who offer complex interrogations of form in a radically deconstructive feminist practice. I am also aware that one of my criteria in evaluating this fiction is the old new critical standard of complexity, though I value complexity not because it illuminates "the human condition" but because it exposes the world as constructed and therefore as capable of change. I am also aware that some of the least complex novels formally and stylistically—*The Diary of a Mad Housewife, Fear of Flying, The Women's Room*—have had the most effect on the most women and that one reader's "revolutionary text" may be another's dud.

Chapter 2, "Women Writing in the Twentieth Century: The Novel and Social Change," historicizes feminist fiction of the sixties and seventies. I posit a relationship between the backlash against feminism that occurred after the first wave of feminism, after women won the vote, and the "decline of the novel" subsequent to Modernism, and a further relationship between the gains women made in education and the professions in the sixties and seventies and the renaissance in women's fiction during those decades. Chapter 3, "Mad House-wives and Closed Circles," discusses a group of sixties and seventies novels that name what Friedan termed "the problem that has no name," but fail, for the most part, to name it politically or to challenge the ideology that is its source. In these works the protagonist suffers alone and imagines that her misery is unrelated to anything outside; lacking the literary and critical powers of writer protagonists and with no way of connecting personal to political, she ends up reaffirming the domestic ideology that has been driving her "mad." Chapter 4 focuses on two metafictions—Erica Jong's *Fear of Flying* and Gail Godwin's *The Odd Woman*—whose protagonists have more literary and critical acumen, but who resist one set of conventions to succumb to another.

Part II concerns feminist *Kunstlerromane* which challenge the forms, both narrative and social, and whose narrative modes depict processes of break-through. This section begins with Lessing's *The Golden Notebook*, the most influential novel written by a woman in this century, as the numerous testi-monies to its transformative power suggest. In *The Waterfall*, a novel directly indebted to *The Golden Notebook*, Drabble's Jane Gray, failing to find guid-ance in "the old novels," uses her writing to make a "new system" and "new morality" that allows her to continue her adulterous, incestuous affair and to forge a "feminine ending" that accommodates transgression (pp. 211, 248).

Atwood's protagonist in *Lady Oracle*, like Anna Wulf and Jane Gray, similarly writes beyond earlier conventions—in this case, the Gothic formula that has sustained but also "contained" her and the "family romance" on which that formula depends—to evolve a "feminine form" bursting with subversive energy. In *The Diviners*, Laurence draws on Joyce's *Portrait of the Artist* and Shakespeare's *Tempest* for her "portrait of the artist" as contemporary, Canadian, and female, allowing her protagonist to develop powers of "the artist" which Laurence has considerably redefined. I analyze Laurence's intertextual play with *Bildungsroman, Kunstlerroman,* romance, and epic as she appropriates works at the heart of a male-defined, male-centered canon; I read Lessing's critiques of the ideology of form in relation to Marxist aesthetics and deconstructive textual practices. Drabble's novel is discussed in terms of French feminist theories of *"l'écriture féminine,"* while Atwood's is analyzed in relation to feminist critiques of Gothic romance by Tania Modleski, Claire Kahane, and others. Each of these chapters draws on different critical methods—Marxist and deconstructive for Lessing, French feminist celebration of rule-breaking and role-breaking for Drabble, gender difference in intertextuality for Laurence, psychoanalytic for Atwood.

Framing the book with historicizing chapters on the fifties and eighties, I conclude with a chapter on postfeminist fiction which explores the way women's fiction in the eighties participates in the retrenchment of the decade, focusing on metafictions which no longer envision writing as re-vision and on novels by Lessing, Atwood, and Drabble in which personal is severed from political and from the wider vision of social change that animated seventies fiction. To trace the evolution of three major novelists through three decades is to see how writers change with their times: to watch them move into new decades and new literary forms is to learn something about the relation of historical moments and movements to individual talents. Feminist metafiction was produced by a few writers who were attuned to the exhilarating possibilities of a new age and sufficiently gifted to forge "something new." It was ambitious and innovative while also being widely read—and it was revolutionary in that it *changed people's lives.*

# Part I

# Feminist Fiction
# The Beginnings

# II

## WOMEN WRITING IN THE TWENTIETH CENTURY
### THE NOVEL AND SOCIAL CHANGE

> Women are writing, and the air is heavy with
> expectation: What will they write that is new?
>
> Julia Kristeva, "Women's Time," 1981[1]

> To recall the great figures of the early years of
> the century is to decide that something has
> been generally wanting in the later years . . .
> while the need has been felt for fundamentally
> new starts—a new use of language, a new
> sense of values and of the literary work, a
> response to . . . new conditions . . .—that has
> come along with an inability wholly to adapt
> or to solve the problems and difficulties, as if
> these have been just too great for those who
> confronted them.
>
> John Holloway, "The Literary Scene," 1983[2]

In 1963, in an article in *Harper's,* Ellen Moers described contemporary
women's fiction as "timid, narrow in scope," "conservative," "complacent and
pedantic":

> Talented women appear content today to write in small letters about the small
> scene—which is exactly what they have always been told they *should* write. [Their
> work] offers no grand intellectual preoccupations . . . it does not venture beyond
> the home or the hometown . . . or further than childhood and marriage.

Moers contrasted women writers "today" with those "angry young women of
the nineteenth century" who wrote "epic novels" that "were big and passionate,
bold in subject, experimental in style."[3] A decade and a half later, however, in
her preface to *Literary Women* (1977), she "marvels at the change."[4]

31

Indeed, a change had occurred between 1963 and 1977, a revolution in women's writing sufficient to earn Showalter's term "renaissance."[5] In the years between the early sixties and the early seventies, women writers found their voices, and their voices were "big and passionate," "angry," and "bold." The early years of the decade were particularly rich:[6] 1972 to 1975 saw the publication of Margaret Atwood's *Surfacing*, Marge Piercy's *Small Changes* (1972), Toni Morrison's *Sula*, Erica Jong's *Fear of Flying* (1973), Margaret Laurence's *The Diviners*, Gail Godwin's *The Odd Woman*, Fay Weldon's *Female Friends*, Ursula K. Le Guin's *The Dispossessed* (1974), Margaret Drabble's *Realms of Gold*, Maxine Hong Kingston's *The Woman Warrior*, Sheila Ballantyne's *Norma Jean the Termite Queen*, Joanna Russ's *The Female Man* (1975), and Doris Lessing's *The Summer Before the Dark* and *The Memoirs of a Survivor* (1973–74)—to name only a few. Of these and the numerous other novels published by women in the course of the seventies,[7] many were very good, some were major, and the variety dazzles: they include feminist quest, feminist metafiction, autobiography, social satire, science fiction, fantasy, and works like *The Woman Warrior* and *Memoirs of a Survivor*, which defy generic classification.

### "Something New"

Moers's assessment on the eve of this extraordinary outburst shows how difficult it is to be a historian of the present when changes are always occurring that can only be seen later. Surveying the state of fiction in 1963, one would be looking back on the fifties, when the Cold War blighted more than politics and both women and men wrote small. As Lessing said in 1957, "We are not living in an exciting period but in a dull one. We are not producing masterpieces, but large numbers of small, quite lively intelligent novels. Above all, current British literature is provincial";[8] and the "conventional short novel" *Free Women* she uses to frame her long, unconventional *Golden Notebook* expresses this critique. At the end of the decade, "protest" was being voiced by the "Angry Young Men" in England and the "Beats" in America, but on the basis of these male voices it would have been impossible to predict the dramatic changes that were about to occur in women's fiction. Incentives *not* to be identified as a "women's writer" were suggested by Mary McCarthy's association of "this 'WW' business" with "drapery" and "decor"—"George Eliot *certainly* wasn't [a WW] and George Eliot is the kind of woman writer I admire"[9]—and by Norman Mailer's indictment: "The sniffs I get from the ink of the women are always fey, old-hat, Quaintsy Goysy, tiny, too dykily psychotic, crippled, creepish, fashionable, frigid, outer-Baroque, *maquillé* in mannequin's whimsey, or else bright and still-born." As Showalter remarks, "If these were the terms of membership, what writer coming of age in the 50's would have wanted to . . . get involved in the 'WW' business?"[10]

Yet there were indications of the upheavals that were about to transform the terrain of women's fiction in the publication, in 1962–63, of Betty Friedan's *The Feminine Mystique* and of three novels, by an American, a British, and an expatriate Southern Rhodesian in London: Sylvia Plath's *The Bell Jar,* Penelope Mortimer's *The Pumpkin Eater,* and Doris Lessing's *The Golden Notebook.* All three novels dramatize what Anna Wulf calls "the disease of women in our time"; all corroborate Anna's assessment that these countries are "full of women going mad all by themselves," each thinking, "There must be something wrong with me."[11] All name what Friedan names "the problem that has no name," though there is a world of difference in the ways they name it—between Mortimer's resignation, Plath's retreat, and Lessing's breakthrough. Also in 1963, a *Report of the Commission on the Status of Women* was published which corroborated that there was indeed "something wrong," that women in America were at a lower point in education and the professions than they had been at any time since the twenties. As Nancy Cott observes,

> After the late 1920s all the numerical indices of women's progress in academia leveled or dropped off, including the proportion of college students who were female, the proportion of Ph.D.s, and the proportion of faculty members . . . plummeting abruptly in the early 1950s to a proportion close to that of 1900 (about 9 percent).[12]

Though a survey by the editors of *Harper's* in 1962 observed that few women showed "any interest in feminism,"[13] when "the problem" was "named"—by Friedan, Lessing, and others—the message "spread like a nuclear chain reaction," as Friedan herself describes the effect of *The Feminine Mystique.*[14]

Where did this remarkable outburst of women's fiction come from? The short, easy answer is that it came from the women's movement. Feminist fiction of the late sixties and early seventies, like the feminism of which it was a part, crossed national boundaries to assume the character of an international movement; for though conditions varied in the United States, Canada, and England, the women's movement materialized in these countries at approximately the same time and with similar energies.[15] But the short, easy answer does not account for the major role feminist writing played in making feminism: Lessing's *The Children of Violence* and *The Golden Notebook* antedated the resurgence of feminism, and nonfictional works by Friedan, Simone de Beauvoir, Germaine Greer, Shulamith Firestone, Juliet Mitchell, and others were also enormously influential. Interactions between the social and literary movements were complex, for this was a revolution in which reading and writing played unprecedented roles. So close was this fiction to the pulse of the times that it is possible to use it as documentary of and commentary on the social and political scene, as I do in this chapter, combining historians' accounts with the voices of women writers and their characters.

Many women writers acknowledge their indebtedness to Lessing. Drabble refers to her as a "touchstone," and her influence on specific works is demonstrable;[16] even where it is not, the quest she articulated entered the culture with the force of a new myth. In *The Golden Notebook,* prototypical *Kunstlerroman* of the new movement, Anna's quest for "something new" is portrayed in specifically metafictional terms; in the five-volume *Children of Violence* (1952–69), prototypical *Bildungsroman,* Martha Quest's quest is depicted in more general terms, though these novels also have metafictional elements. Martha vows that she would *"not* be like her mother" or like any of the older women she knows, but this leaves her wondering "who was she going to be like?"[17]—so she turns to books, to find herself "named" as "British," "adolescent," "twentieth-century," "female," and "doomed." Overwhelmed by the sense that *"it had all been done and said already"* (PM, p. 34), she wonders, "If this has all been said, why do I have to go through with it? . . . it was time to move in to something new" (MQ, pp. 8–9). But "go through it" she must, as in the course of the series, she lives through each of the roles conventionally allotted to woman—"woman in love," wife, mother—enduring each process thoroughly, exhaustively, before she can "move in to something new."

### Modernism, Feminism, and Metafiction

In her study of "the artist as heroine," Grace Stewart notes that women's *Kunstlerromane* "are clustered in groups—at the turn of the century, in the thirteen years from 1915 to 1928, and . . . [from] 1962–1976"; she asks, "Why is there a void in the 1940's? the 1950's?"[18] Though there is no way of saying for certain why some ages are "void" of and others flourish with certain literary forms—why some ages produce major fiction and poetry and others do not—it seems obviously to have to do with some combination of "individual talent" and historical moment. There were major women writers in the first part of the century, in the decades associated with Modernism: Virginia Woolf, Dorothy Richardson, Katherine Mansfield, Gertrude Stein, Djuna Barnes, Rebecca West, Edith Wharton, Ellen Glasgow, Anzia Yezierska, Willa Cather. While they are not feminist in the sense that sixties and seventies writers are—their concerns are not so closely related to a women's movement—they do critique patriarchal ideology and institutions and some even register these critiques at the level of narrative.[19] Nor are they traditionally associated with Modernism (except perhaps for Woolf and Stein), nor is Modernism associated with them; in fact, the star figures in Modernism—Eliot, Pound, and Joyce—are male writers whose works typically exclude the "feminine." But what is significant is that the same period that saw this flourishing of fiction and poetry was also that of the first wave of feminism: women won the vote in 1918 in England and in 1920 in America. That the high point of English literature in this century corresponds (approximately) to a time of gains for women[20] suggests that the same social and cultural ferment that produced one also produced the other.

While Modernism is by no means monolithic, what is nearly always attributed to it—both by those who lived through it and by those who evaluate it from a later perspective—is the sense that times were changing. Even before the outbreak of World War I, technological revolutions in the 1880s and 1890s, social and political upheavals in the first decade of the twentieth century—agricultural depression, coal workers' strikes, protest against the Boer War, unrest in Ireland, acts of terrorism—reveal a society in the grip of change.[21] With the advent of the war, writers and artists experienced their time as an age when the systems of the past—social, ethical, religious—lost explanatory force. They described their age as different from all others, as—in Stephen Spender's term—"unprecedented, and outside all the conventions of past literature and art": D. H. Lawrence says that in 1913 the old world ended; Gertrude Stein writes that on August 1, 1914, the twentieth century was born; according to Virginia Woolf, "on or about December, 1910, human character changed."[22]

This sense of difference from the past produced an intense interest in the past and the nostalgia for "the tradition" that we find in T. S. Eliot.[23] Still, there was something exhilarating about the toppling of old orders, even for those who lamented the world that was lost. Eliot, Woolf, Lawrence, Conrad, and Pound used their writing to reinvest the world with meaning, to provide what the culture could not, to make new forms and new languages, new meanings and myths.[24] This sense of art as a means of remaking, reviving—"re-vising"—the world gave it enormous vitality and endowed it with a quasireligious mission. I would suggest that this sense of change is a condition—a necessary, though not a sufficient, condition—of major fiction and poetry: what is essential is a sense of movement sufficient to disturb categories that are fixed in more stable times (including gender definitions), but not so cataclysmic as to render the aesthetic response irrelevant, so that art can be envisioned as the means of "making it new." It was this that produced the extraordinary creative energy of Modernism—what Bradbury and McFarlane term "an explosiveness that destroyed the tidy categories of thought, toppled linguistic systems . . . disrupted formal grammar and the traditional links between words and things," enabling "new juxtapositions, new wholes," and a new "coalescence" and "fusion."[25] It was a similar sense of change that produced feminist fiction of the sixties and seventies.

When fiction is viewed as the means of remaking the world, it becomes a subject in its own right. Whereas nineteenth-century novelists did not write novels about writing novels, art now becomes, in Lawrence Durrell's term, "the great subject of modern artists,"[26] and metafictional elements become prominent; in fact, Modernism has been described as "less a style than a search for a style" (Bradbury and McFarlane, p. 29). Woolf's *To the Lighthouse,* Joyce's *Portrait of the Artist,* Gide's *The Counterfeiters* interrogate the relation of art to life, the value of art, the meaning of narrative and linguistic forms; and the early decades of the century saw a flourishing of "artist fiction."[27] As Lessing observes in the introduction to her *Kunstlerroman, The Golden Notebook,* "heroes a hundred years ago weren't often artists," but "the artist-as-exemplar" is the "theme of our time" (p. xii).

Feminist writers of the sixties and seventies, like early-twentieth-century artists and writers, experienced their time as an age of change. "The times they are a-changin' "—and the Bob Dylan refrain captured the spirit of the age, a

decade of turmoil that produced the antiwar movement, the civil-rights movement—and the women's movement. It is difficult to communicate the excitement, energy, and hope of those years, the extraordinary optimism women
experienced, the heady sense that they might change their lives and be part of
the making of history.[28] As Michelene Wandor recalls, "We felt that we were
pioneers, visionaries who would make a world . . . in which inequalities . . .
social injustice, would all come to an end."[29]

Feminist writers view change as exciting, often as excruciating, but always as
a central fact of existence. As Anna says, " 'there are whole areas of me made by
the kind of experience women haven't had before' " (GN, p. 471); according to
a character in Fay Weldon's *Down Among The Women,* "We are in the throes of
an evolutionary struggle which we must all endure, while we turn, willy-nilly,
into something strange and marvelous. We gasp and struggle for breath, with
painful lungs, like the creatures who first crawled out of the sea and lived on
land."[30] Like Modernist writers, feminist writers see their situations as "unchartered" and use fiction to create "blueprints for the future" (GN, p. 495): as
Drabble says, "One of the reasons that women's novels are particularly interesting at the moment is that women are charting this ground where the rules have
changed"; "in writing novels we create not only a book but a future, we draw up
. . . 'our beautiful, impossible blueprints.' "[31]

Growing out of a sense of the unprecedentedness of contemporary experience, feminist fiction seeks new forms to express change, which is why it is
often—like Modernist fiction—self-reflexive. As with Modernism, the sense of
discontinuity with the past produces an interest in the past, an interrogation of
the literary and critical tradition. But by this time Modernist texts have themselves
become part of the tradition that is being critiqued: in *The Diviners* Laurence
evokes *The Waste Land* and *A Portrait of the Artist as a Young Man;* in *The
Middle Ground,* Drabble evokes *Mrs. Dalloway.* Lessing is haunted especially
by Eliot; in *Landlocked,* the fourth novel of *The Children of Violence,* she
draws on *The Waste Land* as Eliot draws on the Grail story to ask whether
cataclysmic destruction—for Lessing, the Second World War; for Eliot, the
First—will lead to new creation; Drabble also, in *The Radiant Way,* evokes the
ruined city of Eliot's *Waste Land* to suggest questions about renewal. In their
engagement with the works of the past, however, these writers do not tend to
nostalgia.[32] They view the return to the past as a means to a new future,
differentiating memory from nostalgia and depicting it as an agent of change.[33]


## Critical Omissions

For those of us who have imagined that feminist criticism has made a
difference in redefining standards of aesthetic judgment, literary periods, and
the shape of the canon, it is sobering to turn to studies of the twentieth-century
novel and see how untouched descriptions of Modernism,[34] the thirties, the
postwar period, and postmodernism have been by the study of women writers.

Modernism is generally acknowledged as the high point of English literature in this century and "one of the most fruitful periods in the whole history of English literature,"[35] and literary historians concur that the novel declined in decades subsequent to it. Bernard Bergonzi voices the general lament when he describes British fiction between 1930 and 1970 as traditional, backward-looking, nostalgic, and "used up," as a form in which "nearly everything possible to be achieved has already been done" (p. 19). He acknowledges a certain amount of "inventiveness" in these years, but "not the sense of development and spectacular advance that was apparent between 1890 and 1930" (p. 20), and predicts that novelists in the near future are "likely to continue making variations on familiar themes or carrying out intricate stylistic maneuvers within a basic *impasse*" (p. 213). But this account is based almost entirely on fiction by men. While one can perhaps understand Bergonzi's omission of women writers in 1970, in 1983 John Holloway's description of "something . . . wanting in the late years" (quoted at the beginning of this chapter) and Gilbert Phelps's judgment that "English fiction since the war does not measure up to that of the earlier part of the century" ("The Post-War English Novel," both in the 1983 Boris Ford *Pelican Guide to English Literature: The Present,* p. 449), are inexcusable: both merely echo the old lament, oblivious of the many novels by women which had appeared between 1970 and 1983.

Literary history continues to be the history of literature by men, and generalizations—the thirties are political, postwar fiction is nostalgic, American fiction is postmodern, contemporary fiction is "bleak"—continue to exclude women writers. At their best, male critics pay women writers a kind of superficial tribute (Phelps), but more typically, they ignore them (Holloway, Stevick, Bradbury, Swinden) or dismiss them (Karl, Grindin, Burgess; see my Chapter 5 on men reading *The Golden Notebook*). Gilbert Phelps suggests that "one of the most striking features of contemporary English fiction has been the large number of talented women novelists" (p. 440), but his grouping of Muriel Spark, Jean Rhys, Barbara Pym, Penelope Mortimer, Brigid Brophy, Edna O'Brien, A. S. Byatt, and Beryl Bainbridge as "writers of more or less 'feminist' persuasion" who tend to "detachment," "tiredness and defeatism" (pp. 418, 441) is wildly inaccurate. And while admitting that Margaret Drabble is neither narrow nor "aloof"—she does write "a 'condition of England' novel"—his characterization of her as "probably still best known for her early novels about 'the condition of women'" (p. 439) slots her safely back into the category "women's writer." Holloway claims that he has "reluctantly left . . . aside" "the writing . . . which has come out of the recent Women's Movement" because "his own limitations and the space available would have foredoomed his comments to a seemingly 'patronizing' brevity" (p. 123); thus, rather than being "patronizingly brief" on the subject, Holloway is silent. In 1973 Philip Stevick proposes "an aesthetic" based on "new fictions," none of which is by a woman.[36] In 1979 Malcolm Bradbury refers to the "international debate" about "the business of the novel" which is being carried on by "a broad community" of contemporary novelists (pp. 12–14)—a "community" consisting of thirty-one men and four women!—and in 1983 Bradbury's listing of 113 major American authors since 1890 includes sixteen women.[37] Even Morris Dickstein's excellent study of the sixties (*The Gates of Eden,* 1977) hardly mentions a woman writer; from his discussion of fiction of the fifties and sixties, one would scarcely suspect that women *could* write. As recently as 1984, a work titled *The English Novel of History and Society, 1940–1980* makes not one reference to Lessing or Drabble,[38] and in 1985 *The Political Novel Since 1945* dismisses *The Golden Notebook* (in passing) as a "novel of sensibility" and includes one woman writer, Nadine Gordimer, as a "political novelist."[39]

Of the fifty-six reviewers and novelists surveyed in the 1978 *New Review* on the subject of fiction in the past ten years, most do not even mention feminist fiction,[40] though it was by far the most significant movement that occurred in the decade they were asked to evaluate, from the mid-sixties to the mid-seventies. According to David Lodge, "The most striking feature of fiction-writing in Britain for the last decade, and longer, has been . . . the absence of any significant school or movement" (*New Review,* p. 40). Those surveyed concur that "times have never been worse," that "the English novel in the Seventies . . . has shared the fortunes of this country in the Seventies, becoming poorer, more cost-conscious, and less outgoing."[41] This disregard of so con-spicuous a movement is striking.

Clearly, the numerous studies of twentieth-century women writers which have appeared since 1975 (cited in chapter 1, n. 134) have not redirected the "mainstream" of literary history. "What we have today," as Robert Stepto says of American literary history, "is a proliferation of histories—black, chicano, women's, mainstream"—but "the prevailing history has been left largely in-tact."[42] Besides, though the twentieth century is nearly at an end—and this is the century that has produced more major fiction by women than all ages preceding—no literary history of twentieth-century women writers has yet been written. This is particularly striking in relation to the novel, the genre in which women writers and readers have figured most prominently.

It seems possible that a fuller understanding of women novelists in these decades might qualify the sense that the novel declined so precipitously in the years subsequent to Modernism. (It is no coincidence that the literary historian who finds the most interest in the fiction of these decades, Randall Stevenson, also happens to be the one who finds the most interest in women writers.) But more work needs to be done on individual women writers before we can even begin to know about how knowing more would transform our understanding of fiction of the thirties, forties, and fifties; and such work needs to be assimi-lated by literary historians. I'm not suggesting that this will make these decades into the great age of the novel; probably they were not. But if they were not, this can hardly be unrelated to the silencing of women that occurred between the mid-twenties and mid-sixties: these were decades when women were not em-boldened to voice their experiences, let alone challenge the world.

### Between the Waves: Post-Feminism and the Decline of the Novel

What follows is a hypothesis offered to anyone undertaking a literary history which includes women writers in this century—an account of the "decline of the novel" in relation to the backlash against feminism and the polarization of male and female experience that occurred in the decades subsequent to Modernism.

In the thirties, the pressure of public events produced a reaction against Modernism for being "personal," "aesthetic," and apolitical. Looking back from 1940 Virginia Woolf wrote, "in 1930 it was impossible . . . not to be interested in politics; not to find public causes of much more interest than philosophy," and impossible to "go on discussing aesthetic emotions and personal relations."[43] The Depression, the rise of Fascist and totalitarian dictatorships, the sense of being trapped *entre deux guerres*—all created a sense of impending doom and a valorization of the political as what was "real" and important. Since men were without jobs, women were discouraged from competing and confined to work that was part-time and marginal; traditional roles were reasserted and in the United States the proportion of women in the professions and the number of women on faculties declined, and the percentage of women receiving doctorates declined in relation to men (Chafe, pp. 91–92). In Canada, also, women were urged into areas of employment where they would not threaten men.[44] The political consciousness of the decade, far from expressing itself in feminism, fostered a reaction against change for women: leftist groups saw women's issues not only as less important than the struggle of the proletariat, but also as potentially divisive.[45]

The valorization of the public and "male" was part of what Showalter calls "the feminist crash of the 1920s—the unexpected disintegration of the women's movement after the passage of the Nineteenth Amendment" (CLH, p. 823). As Friedan observes, feminism "ended as a vital movement . . . with the winning of . . . the vote": by the mid-twenties "no one was much concerned with rights for women: they had all been won."[46] Just as today, when the threat of nuclear war and the destruction of the planet make "the aims of Women's Liberation . . . look very small and quaint" (GN, p. ix), women deferred to more "important" issues. Parallels between that backlash and the backlash of the eighties are chilling:[47] in fact, the term "postfeminist," which sprang so brilliantly to the pages of *The New York Times* in October 1982 and spoke directly to a new generation of young women who imagined themselves "past all that," was actually first used in 1919, when (as Cott tells us) "a group of female literary radicals in Greenwich Village" founded a new journal announcing its interest "in people . . . not in men and women," declaring their stance "post-feminist."[48] "Feminism" became—then as now—a dirty word, a "term of opprobrium," as Dorothy Dunbar Bromley said in 1927.[49] Lillian Hellman described "the emancipation of women" as "stale stuff";[50] Rebecca West described "anti-feminism" as "strikingly the correct fashion . . . among . . . intellectuals" (in Gilbert and Gubar, 1985, p. 1237).

As these examples suggest, it is possible to generalize about women in England, the United States, and Canada, since the big events of the century—the Depression, the wars, backlash after both wars, the baby boom—affected women in these countries similarly. There were also, of course, significant differences: England and Canada did not experience the social turmoil that swept the United States in the sixties, and the major impetus for the second wave came from America. The women's movement in Britain did not take off until slightly later, influenced by the events of 1968, by the revolutionary student movements in Europe, and by feminist theory from the United States imported through American women in London and the networks of radical journals.[51] But as Juliet Mitchell observes, "Feminism in England and North America has interacted extensively, reflecting in this, the general political and economic involvement of the two countries";[52] and as Banks says,

> What was most striking . . . were not the differences but the similarities between the two countries. Time and time again developments occurred at the same time in the two countries, in spite of very large differences in the social and political context as well as in the styles of leadership. (p. 262)

For the Canadian movement also, impetus came from the United States, and it too was shaped by that country's involvement, cultural and political, with the States.[53]

The thirties was a "masculine decade" in which "the literature of the Right often looked rather like the literature of the Left" and both were "produced by and for men" (Benstock, pp. 400, 410). Even those women writers who were involved in radical political activity and shared the goals of male revolution-aries—Meridel Le Sueur, Tess Slesinger, Josephine Herbst, Grace Lumpkin, Ruth McKenney, Agnes Smedley, Tillie Olsen—had difficulty getting published, finding readers, staying in print. Showalter describes women on the Left as lost even to the lost generation, "lost to literary history and to each other," "iso-lated" and without "support either from women's groups or Communist Party networks" (CLH, pp. 822, 832). This was a "period of conflict, repression, and decline" for American women writers, of "hostility toward female authorship and feminine values in academia and the literary establishment," of "frustra-tion, fragmentation and silencing" of women poets and novelists, when "left-wing aesthetics and expectations made "taboo" "the subjects . . . the styles and subjectivities of women writers" (CLH, pp. 822, 824, 835, 832).[54]

This polarization of male and female made impossible the kind of "coales-cence" and "fusion" that energized Modernist art. While male writers—George Orwell, Evelyn Waugh, Christopher Isherwood, Graham Greene, Anthony Burgess, John Steinbeck—addressed the public and political, women writers—Ivy Compton-Burnett, Rosamond Lehmann, Elizabeth Bowen, Elizabeth Tay-lor—turned inward to write about the personal and private. Modernism was hardly a movement dominated by women's voices, but it was more congenial to women and to the "feminine" than was the mood of ensuing decades. Produced by the same social and intellectual ferment that produced the first wave of feminism, its energies were more inclusive, encompassing some "fusion" of public and private, of "male" and "female" as they are traditionally defined—the "collaboration" "of opposites" that Woolf recommends.[55]

In the forties and fifties, as women continued to lose ground in education, employment, and the professions, female and male spheres remained polarized. For a brief time during the war women were needed in the work force and encouraged to enter "male" fields, but when the GIs returned, women were urged back into the home with a powerful propaganda program waged by the media, educators, popular psychologists, and sociologists. Women were fired, demoted, and had difficulty entering colleges crowded with ex-GIs whose educations were funded by government money. Men and women were marrying younger, and more of them were marrying, and on both sides of the Atlantic the baby boom reinforced the ideology that woman's destiny was essentially domestic.[56] "The feminine mystique" asserted a division between male and female experience more extreme than in any preceding decade of the century, persuading woman that her "world was confined to her own body and beauty, the charming of man, the bearing of babies, and the physical care and serving of husband, children, and home" and that her "fulfillment" was in "sexual passivity, male domination, and nurturing maternal love" (Friedan, pp. 36, 43).[57] As an editor at *McCall's* told Friedan, " 'Our readers are housewives, full time. They're not interested in the broad public issues of the day. They are not interested in national or international affairs. They are only interested in the family and the home' " (p. 37)—though this was a myth that, as Friedan explains, such magazines had themselves helped to create.

By 1960 the assumption that woman was destined to be a mother and homemaker was so widely held that it was as if there had never been a women's movement": "Really, anyone would think that the emancipation of women had never happened," observes the protagonist of Mortimer's *Pumpkin Eater*.[58] "There were two cultures—the world, which had men in it, and [women's world] . . . which had only women and children," as Mira of French's *The Women's Room* says; "there were things going on in the world while Mira was caring for her children. Eisenhower had been elected. Joseph McCarthy was having some trouble with the United States Army."[59] Plath's Esther is instructed by a *Reader's Digest* article that "a man's world is different from a woman's world and a man's emotions are different from a woman's emotions."[60] It was this separation of spheres that Simone de Beauvoir addressed in *The Second Sex,* only far from celebrating woman's confinement in "immanence" and man's freedom to seek "transcendence," she critiqued these as cultural constructions in need of change, as did other early feminist analyses, by Alice S. Rossi, Greer, Firestone, Heilbrun.[61]

But the postwar glorification of happy families and traditional values was a reaction *against* change, nostalgia for a simpler era when men and women knew their places, for many women did not go home again; many remained in the workplace, where their presence disrupted the traditional polarity between male and female spheres (Chafe, pp. 208, 224). Underlying the vision of the happy family—and in large part accounting for it—was anxiety: about the arms race, the bomb, the Cold War, the Red scare. As Sinfield suggests, it was because women's working outside the home threatened male control that women were urged back into the home; it was this that produced "the heavy ideological work around domesticity" (p. 206).[62]

Writers and intellectuals responded by withdrawing, by abandoning politics,[63] and protest was further silenced by Red-baiting and by an unprecedented affluence created in large part by military expenditure. As Friedan says, "It was easier, safer, to think about love and sex than about communism, McCarthy, and the uncontrolled bomb":

> What happened to women is part of what happened to all of us in the years after the war. . . . The American spirit fell into a strange sleep. . . . The whole nation stopped growing. All of us went back into the warm brightness of home. . . . Women went home again . . . just as thinkers avoided the complex larger problems of the postwar world. (pp. 187–88)

It was this climate that produced the new criticism, and one can see its depoliticization and degendering of literary studies, its isolation of text from social and historical context, as part of the general retreat.[64]

As in other periods when political realities are too horrifying to confront, the family is made the source of stability and fulfillment, and woman, the center of the family, is made the bulwark of social order. In 1970 Philip Slater described this tendency: since "in their jobs the husbands must accept change—even welcome and foster it—however threatening and disruptive it may seem," they "use their wives as opiates to soften the impact," as "island[s] of stability in a sea of change."[65] But to assign women this role is also to make them scapegoats for whatever goes wrong, which is what happened:

> Mom got herself out of the nursery and the kitchen. She then got out of the house . . . she also got herself the vote and, although politics never interested her (unless she was exceptionally naive, a hairy foghorn, or a size forty scorpion) the damage she forthwith did to society was so enormous and so rapid that even the best men lost track of things . . . a new all-time low in political scurviness, hoodlumism, gangsterism, labor strife, monopolistic thuggery, moral degeneration, civic corruption, smuggling, bribery, theft, murder, homosexuality, drunkenness, financial depression, chaos and war.[66]

Thus spoke Philip Wylie in *A Generation of Vipers,* a work which focused the discontent of the period in what Friedan terms the "unremitting attack on women" that became "an American preoccupation" (p. 203): "blame the woman" was the message of fiction, film, and media. In *Modern Woman: The Lost Sex* (1947), Ferdinand Lundberg and Marynia Farnham attribute the ills not only of modern woman, but of all society, to woman's abandoning the home for male spheres of activity; as Friedan remarks, this book "was paraphrased ad nauseam in the magazines and in marriage courses, until most of its statements became a part of the conventional, accepted truth of our time" (p. 119). Even as women were urged to devote their lives to family and marriage, "everything was all mom's fault—she was trying to run her husband and was ruining her children."[67] As Stacey of Laurence's *The Fire-Dwellers* complains, "some wise guy is always telling you how you're sapping the national strength";[68] as Sasha of Shulman's *Ex-Prom Queen* observes, "they made us do it, then blamed us for it. . . . They found nothing more hateful than a clinging wife—except a dominating mom."[69]

Postwar fiction is saturated with nostalgia. As Rosamond Lehmann wrote in 1946, writers "turn back to the time when, the place where they knew where they were"—and in Britain this meant to some time of lost innocence before the war.[70] Still, even amidst the general retreat, British fiction continued to divide along gender lines. The eleven volumes of C. P. Snow's *Strangers and Brothers* (1940–70) and the twelve volumes of Anthony Powell's *A Dance to the Music of Time* (1951–75) chronicled the life of the times, though these sagas tended toward complacency and nostalgia in their depiction of English society.[71] But women novelists such as Elizabeth Taylor, Ivy Compton-Burnett, Isobel English, Elizabeth Jane Howard, Rachel Trickett, Monica Sterling, Barbara Pym, Rosa Macaulay, and A. L. Barker wrote novels of sensibility remarkable for what Rebecca O'Rourke terms their " 'fine' use of language," "exploration of personal relationships," and narrowness of "range, in both subject and characterization"[72]—"narrow, timid, complacent," in Moers's terms. In the United States, some male writers—Norman Mailer and Herman Wouk—took on public issues, while women writers focused almost exclusively on the personal, and though one finds the occasional strong woman or critique of marriage in Mary McCarthy (*The Company She Keeps* [1942], *The Groves of Academe* [1952], *A Charmed Life* [1954]), Eudora Welty (*Delta Wedding* [1946]), and Carson McCullers (*The Heart is a Lonely Hunter* [1940], *The Member of the Wedding* [1946]), their novels are almost entirely without feminist consciousness.

When the Cold War thawed and protest began in the late fifties, it was men who voiced it—men and Doris Lessing. "We are all of us, directly or indirectly, caught up in a great whirlwind of change," Lessing wrote in 1957 (SPV, p. 20). Nineteen fifty-six, the year of the Suez crisis and the Hungarian uprising, was, as Lessing said, "a climactic year, a watershed, a turning point, a crossroads," a time "of change, breaking up, clearing away, movement," a "year of protest and activity and lively disagreement" when "a great many people, in one way or another, said: No, enough, no more of that" (FGC, pp. 277–78); and her *Four-Gated City* is unsurpassed for its depiction of those years, the nastiness of the fifties and the exuberance of change in the sixties. The appearance of Britain's "Angry Young Men" (John Wain, John Braine, Kingsley Amis, John Osborne, and Alan Sillitoe) signaled the emergence of a generation of writers who differed from the older generation of postwar writers in that they welcomed change rather than regretting it (Stevenson, p. 123)—though the Angry Young Men seemed angry at the system primarily for excluding them[73] and expressed protest in fiction that was formally conservative and strikingly misogynist. In

America, Jack Kerouac's *On the Road* (1957) and Allen Ginsberg's *Howl* (1956) sounded the note of dissent that became louder throughout the following decade, but their protest was for the most part without ideological content; as Gerald Graff suggests, the "rebel without a cause," epitomized by Jimmy Dean, Elvis Presley, and Holden Caulfield, lent "a certain heroism to aimless youth in the fifties," but it was "without cause"—"a-historical, a-political, and nonideological."[74] Alienation was a style, as Zane, protagonist of Alix Kates Shulman's *Burning Questions,* discovers when she comes to New York in the late fifties in search of the revolution, which she finds hanging out in Greenwich Village coffee shops, decked out in black stockings and turtlenecks.

### Doris Lessing and the Fifties

Given the conservatism of the fifties and the nonpolitical nature even of the protest that emerged at the end of the decade, Doris Lessing's appearance on the literary scene in 1950 was remarkable indeed. (Two other major women writers, Murdoch and Spark—born within a year of Lessing and of one another, in 1918 and 1919—also began publishing in the fifties: Spark might at times be termed a "women's writer," but Murdoch, with her male protagonists and abstract, philosophical concerns, could never be so categorized.) Lessing was immediately hailed, upon the publication of her first novel, *The Grass Is Singing* (1950), as a bright new talent, and was grouped with the Angry Young Men— an association she did her best to deny, since she saw their work as characterized by the "pettiness and narrowness" it protested and as "extremely provincial," not in the sense that "they come from or write about the provinces" but that "their horizons are bounded by their immediate experience of British life and standards" (SPV, p. 15). She published the first three *Children of Violence* novels in fairly close sequence: *Martha Quest* in 1952, *A Proper Marriage* in 1954, and *A Ripple from the Storm* in 1958; she then interrupted the series with *The Golden Notebook* (1962) and returned to it in the late sixties, completing it with *Landlocked* (1965) and *The Four-Gated City* (1969). In the context of postwar retrenchment, the *Children of Violence* novels were "something new" indeed: there was nothing like Lessing's radical critique of Anglo culture, nor was there anything like her satire of nostalgia in a postwar fiction that was saturated with nostalgia. With *The Children of Violence,* Lessing invaded a male preserve: in chronicling the life of her times, she did what male series writers did, and in protesting the life of the times, she did what male protest writers did, and in protesting the life of the times, she did what male protest writers did—except that her protest had ideological edge and her portrayal of colonial and English society, far from being complacent or genial, was savage.

Where did Lessing come from? How does one account for her? She cannot be explained by the women's movement, which she antedated (though *The Second Sex* was published in 1949, a year before *The Grass Is Singing*); nor by the remarkable Olive Schreiner, the only radical feminist writer to precede her from southern Africa, and a writer of whom she was well aware. It seems astonishing that she came from Southern Rhodesia, but perhaps it is not so surprising when one realizes that colonial societies make glaringly apparent the structures of oppression that are more masked elsewhere and so encourage a "view from elsewhere."[75] African writers Chinua Achebe, Amos Tutuola, and Ama Ata Aidoo, and African-born white Nadine Gordimer, were also addressing colonial oppression. The impetus for Laurence's early writings came from Africa;[76] as she says, "It was . . . Africa which taught [her] to look at [her]self" and to know Canada.[77] Other anomalous radicals in the fifties were also writing about dispossessed peoples: Harriette Arnow's *The Dollmaker* (1954) concerns southern immigrants to the industrialized north; Paule Marshall's *Brown Girl, Brownstones* (1959), which concerns Barbadians in Brooklyn, seems fifteen years ahead of its time (as in 1969, Marshall's *The Chosen Place, The Timeless People* will also seem).

From the start, Lessing's feminism was linked to an understanding of racism gained from her years in Africa and to an understanding of class related to Marxism. Even the small-scale and conventionally well-made *Grass Is Singing* renders the relation of individual to collective and of sexism to racism. Historically, the struggle against women's oppression has often been allied with the struggle against racial oppression; it was linked with early abolitionist efforts, and in the 1960s it grew out of the civil-rights movement. But Lessing was ahead of her time in relating sexism to racism and analyzing both in a Marxist framework. Of her contemporaries, only de Beauvoir was making comparable connections, and she was not making them in her fiction; her major political novel, *The Mandarins,* relegates women to the private sphere while it allows men agency in the political arena. Only much later, in the late sixties, as women who participated in the New Left turned to socialist theory for a radical theoretical framework that could explain the oppression of women in relation to that of other groups, would feminists begin to appreciate the connections Lessing made in the early fifties.

Lessing invaded male territory but went beyond what male writers were doing, in combining her depictions of English society with protest and combining protest with ideology. Yet her fiction also documents a distinctively "feminine" world, for the early *Children of Violence* novels read like case studies for *The Second Sex* and *The Feminine Mystique.* Lessing brings together male and female spheres—public and private, personal and political—to express a "new kind of knowledge" in new narrative forms: though *The Children of Violence* has been dismissed as old-fashioned realism, in this epic that takes Martha from her childhood in southern Africa through apocalypse, Lessing moves beyond realism, ending with a move "off into fantasy," as she says, for "I could no longer say what I wanted to say inside the old form."[78] Lessing's is a lone and remarkable voice in the fifties, unique, anomalous, the first feminist novelist of the mid-twentieth century.

### Education: "The Key to the Trap"

Besides combining areas and energies that had been polarized into "male" and "female," Lessing focuses on education in a way that points the direction that would be taken by the new feminist fiction. It is somewhat startling to come to the end of *The Four-Gated City,* final novel of the *Children of Violence,* and find the statement: "This book is what the Germans call a *Bildungsroman.* . . . This kind of novel has been out of fashion for some time. This does not mean that there is anything wrong with this kind of novel" (p. 615). It is surprising because neither *The Four-Gated City* nor *The Children of Violence* resembles the *Bildungsroman* as we know it,[79] and the ambiguous referent (this "book"?) makes it unclear whether Lessing is referring to the final novel or to the series as a whole. But if we take *"Bildungsroman"* to mean a work that is concerned with education, the term is right: and this concern is central not only to *The Four-Gated City* and to the series, but to the whole of Lessing's oeuvre and to feminist fiction generally. All Lessing's work is concerned with change—what enables it, what prevents it, why it is necessary. Though she dissociated herself at an early age from formal systems of education, she has always written about education—learning, remembering, connecting one thing with another to make "something new."

Friedan describes "the problem with no name" as a problem of education— "Our culture does not permit women to . . . grow and fulfill their potentialities as human beings" (pp. 76–77)—and attributes women's "lack of identity" (p. 181), their "bored, diffuse feeling of purposelessness, non-existence, non-involvement with the world," to "vicarious living" (p. 291). So, too, do many women writers of the sixties and seventies: " 'How is it possible to say how you feel, after so many years of others, others?' " says Norma Jean of Ballantyne's 1975 *Norma Jean the Termite Queen;*[80] "What's left of me? Where have I gone?" says Stacey of Laurence's 1969 *The Fire-Dwellers;* "I don't know who I am, I don't know what I'm like," says Mrs. Armitage of Penelope Mortimer's 1962 *Pumpkin Eater* (p. 191); "How could she want something if she couldn't even give it a name?" asks Beth of Marge Piercy's *Small Changes.*[81] These writers depict women as cut off from other women, from a sense of community and history, each blaming herself: "I know I'm a Very Lucky Girl and really must be crazy to get into this state," as Tina of Kaufman's *Mad Housewife* says; "How dare you complain? . . . I've had everything I always wanted," as Stacey says (p. 67).[82] Piercy describes the world of the fifties as allowing her no way to grow "but through the cracks," as lacking "a sense of possibilities": "I could not make connections"; "just as there was no community to mediate for me between individual and mass, there was nobody to write for, nobody to communicate with about matters of being female, alive, thinking, trying to make sense of one's life and times."[83] As long as each woman is isolated, each thinking there is "something wrong" with her and that her anguish is so private that it cannot even be named, there is no possibility of change.

"Consciousness raising" was a corrective to this isolation and confusion, offering women a way of naming the problem and connecting with other women, of understanding that experience which seemed private and idiosyncratic was (in Rich's term) "shared, unnecessary, and political."[84] Consciousness raising was both a teaching and a learning, and feminism itself has been called "a *teaching* movement," a "learning experience," a "perspective transformation";[85] though it was also in important ways an unlearning—an unlearning of old roles and a learning of new roles and relationships to the world.

Formal education was important in this process. Reformers ranging from Christine de Pisan, Bathsua Makin, Mary Wollstonecraft, and John Stuart Mill to Betty Friedan and Adrienne Rich have known that if women want to be equal to men, they need equal access to education and the same kind of education. Though it is not easy to say which is cause and which effect, education and feminism are causally linked. The first wave of feminism in this century, like the second, was accompanied by gains in education. The first decades of the century saw a 1,000 percent increase of female enrollment in public colleges and a 482 percent increase in private schools in America (Chafe, p. 89); "the high point in women's share of professional employment (and attainment of advanced degrees) overall occurred by the late 1920s" (though, as Cott notes, this was a time when academic salaries were particularly depressed, whereas in the fifties, when salaries were booming, the proportion of women on college faculties dropped to a nadir [pp. 222–23]). But these gains were "followed by stasis and/or decline not reversed to any extent until the 1960s and 1970s" (Cott, p. 220).[86]

In 1963 the Commission on the Status of Women, established by John F. Kennedy and headed by Eleanor Roosevelt, issued a report that revealed widespread discrimination—that fewer women were being educated and that they were receiving a different kind of education from men, and not only in secondary schools but in colleges, both coeducational and single-sex (Friedan, pp. 165–66). In England in the years between 1947 and 1967, the number of boys and girls in higher education increased while the *proportion* of girls to boys remained the same, with far more boys than girls.[87] On both sides of the Atlantic, popular psychologists, social scientists, and women's magazines cooperated with educators to define severely restricted options for women: "there was no middle ground, no way to combine marriage and a career, a job and motherhood. A woman became either a well-adjusted home-maker or a feminist neurotic" (Chafe, p. 210).

Friedan sees this as accounting for the "preoccupation with sex and sexual phantasy" that was pronounced in the period: since women were defined as "sex creatures," their "whole identity [based] on . . . [the] sexual role," sex was made to "fill the vacuum created by the denial of larger goals and purposes" (pp. 261, 265, 262). "Sexuality was expressed in popular culture largely in a repressive manner," "coyly or salaciously"; females were expected to "play a sex game" involving exaggerated mannerisms and elaborate artifice, a game which diverted attention "from the real dangers and controversies of the world" (Miller and Nowak, pp. 159, 168). The styles of the period—the sheath dresses, tight skirts and sweaters, high-heeled shoes and beehive hairdos, padded bras and merry widows—"trained us to await babies and cancer and rape, dumb as a centerpiece of waxed fruit," as Piercy recalls: "the clothes jailed us" (p. 210). Margaret Laurence recalls, "wearing our long hobble skirts . . . with . . . miserably pinched-in waists and crippling spike-heeled, pointy-toed shoes, we weren't going to be doing much competing with men in the labour market."[88]

Friedan describes education as "the key to the trap" and concludes *The Feminine Mystique* with an impassioned plea to "educators and parents" to reshape "the cultural image of woman" in a way that will allow woman a "maturity, identity, completeness of self, without conflict with sexual fulfillment" (pp. 364–68). In the sixties and seventies, some of the changes she called for occurred, as more women went to school and in areas that had formerly been reserved for men:

> From its nadir of 24 percent in 1950, women's percentage of bachelor's and first professional degrees rose to 43.5 percent in 1968. Most of this increase occurred between 1960 and 1965, when the number of degrees earned by women went up to 57 percent compared to only a 25 percent increase for men. (Freeman, p. 29)[89]

In the seventies the number of women pursuing the doctorate grew each year of the decade, as the number of men pursuing it fell—"while in 1970 males outnumbered females six to one in the receipt of doctorates, a decade later the ratio stood at 2.5 to one, an impressive narrowing of the gap" (Daniel, p. 360)—though again, this occurred as the doctorate plummetted in value. Friedan claims,

> If today American women are finally breaking out of the housewife trap in search of new identity, it is quite simply because so many women have had a taste of higher education—unfinished, unfocused, but still powerful enough to force them on. (pp. 368–69)

Whether education was "the key to the trap," whether it was more and better schooling that caused the resurgence of feminism or the resurgence of feminism that made for educational reform[90]—or (as is more likely) both were *effects* of deeper causes, of an expanding postwar economy, a climate of protest and reform, the sexual revolution and general loosening of restrictions—education was crucial in the women's movement in several ways. Feminist leaders have always been educated women: in the first wave of feminism, "the strong presence of women who had been to college and even graduate or professional school . . . was remarkable in an era in which only a tiny proportion of women or men had higher education" (Cott, p. 40); in the second wave, the organizers of NOW were middle-class, college-educated women, and later in the decade, the younger group of feminists from the antiwar and civil-rights movements, recruits from SDS and FSM, were even more directly from college campuses. In the United States the women's movement tended not to be a grass-roots movement: it was middle-class women who "had the education and the political skills necessary for rebellion, and indeed, the leisure time that made it possible for rebellious ideas to be translated into political action" (Banks, p. 5); though in England, feminism did have more connection with working-class activity—the Hull campaign for better safety standards on fishing trawlers; the Ford women's strike, which produced the National Joint Action Committee for Women's Equal Rights; the Equal Pay campaign.[91]

Education demystified the feminine mystique and made women more receptive to feminism. College narrowed the division between male and female spheres and promoted an "androgynous personality" (one study on "The Effects of Going to College" demonstrated "a perceptible narrowing of traditional differences between the sexes in interests, attitudes, and behavior patterns").[92] Women's experiences in college—in an atmosphere of relative equality, free exchange, and the company of other women—raised their expectations and made them discontented with careers as housewives, as a 1960 *New York Times* article cited by Friedan (p. 22) and a 1979 Gallup poll cited by Chafe suggest (p. 240). In college women encountered the works of de Beauvoir, Mitchell, Millett—not in curricula, as they would ten years later, but as underground reading passed from student to student.

But it was education in conjunction with discrimination in the workplace that caused many women to experience the "relative deprivation" that produced feminist consciousness, for between 1940 and 1964, as their participation in higher education increased, their participation in the professions declined (Banks, p. 210); while "the educational preparation of women for middle-class jobs approximates that of men more closely each year," their "share of both quantitative and qualitative occupational rewards decreases each year" (Freeman, p. 31). Besides, though more women were working, the jobs they held were at the bottom of the hierarchy, and they were paid less for them; very few—fewer than 6 percent—held any kind of executive position in the sixties; a third had clerical jobs, and many did work out of their homes, such as selling Avon or Tupperware (Miller and Nowak, p. 163). Thus "relative deprivation" gave women an experience of marginality, and since marginality permits "criticism of existing arrangements," the sense that the world is "neither legitimate nor inevitable," it is "the psychological precondition" . . . for the ability to conceive of and organize for change.[93]

Woman's situation in the early 1960s was characterized by dizzying discrepancies between ideology and actuality. The reality was that more women worked, more women were educated, yet the ideology instructed them to find fulfillment as housewives—and the ideology was used to deprive them of good jobs and equal pay. "Torn between myth and reality . . . American women were plagued by a deepening sense of bewilderment" (Freeman, p. 25); as Piercy recalls, "Seldom has the role of women been more painful, the contradictions more intense" (1974, p. 208). Part of what drives Plath's Esther "mad" is the mixed signals she gets from her culture: "Look what can happen in this country, they'd say. A girl . . . gets a scholarship to college and wins a prize here and a prize there and ends up steering New York like her own private car." But the girl who is told she can have everything and who wants "to be everything" learns how restricted her options really are: marriage requires that she give up her brains and career requires that she give up marriage, family, love, sexuality (pp. 2, 83). Hence, the "madness" of the mad housewife was adjustment to a screwy situation, madness in the sense described by R. D. Laing (whose *Politics of Experience* was published in 1967). The feminine mystique dictated that woman choose "between femaleness and humanness" (Friedan, p. 304): she could fulfill her "feminine role and be loved, or she could fulfill her human identity and forfeit love.

## Reading, Writing, and Consciousness Raising

If feminism was a "teaching movement," it was also a "reading movement" and a "writing movement," for it was feminist writing—fiction, poetry, and nonfiction—that transformed confusion to consciousness, enabling women to understand the changes they were living through and to interpret their "relative deprivation" as a collective phenomenon rooted in inegalitarian social, economic, and political structures.

Feminism, like Modernism, generated numerous journals, periodicals, and publications that issued manifestoes defining, explaining, and extending the new movement,[94] but with this difference: feminist publications were part of a wide social movement. They were a means of education and community building, a vehicle by which information spread from the United States to England, "a communications network" that enabled the movement to "develop past the point of occasional, spontaneous uprising" (Freeman, p. 67). Between March 1968 and August 1973, more than 560 newspapers and magazines came into existence; the 1983 *Directory of Women's Media* lists 379 women's periodicals ranging "from general purpose political newspapers to academic, literary and spiritual journals, as well as specialised publications written by and for lesbians, women of colour, and older women" (Gatlin, p. 157). In Canada, also, "literary and political journals and newspapers multiplied," often "shortlived but crucial for communication within the women's movement" (Prentice et al., pp. 360–61). In the United States, academic journals such as *Signs, Women's Studies,* and *Feminist Studies* defined feminist scholarship as interdisciplinary and extended its range, exploring the relation of Anglo-American feminism to French feminism and to structuralism, poststructuralism, and postmodernism.

Individuals' descriptions of their consciousness raising, like general accounts of the development of the women's movement, usually begin with mention of the same several books: *The Second Sex, The Feminine Mystique,* Juliet Mitchell's *Women's Estate,* Mary Ellmann's *Thinking about Women* (1968), Kate Millett's *Sexual Politics* (1969), Shulamith Firestone's *The Dialectic of Sex,* and Germaine Greer's *The Female Eunuch* (1970). *The Feminine Mystique* was an immediate best-seller.[95] So, too, were other works of feminist theory: for the first time in history, a Columbia Ph.D. dissertation, Kate Millett's *Sexual Politics,* reached a mass audience; the second to do so was Nancy Milford's *Zelda.* One historian hypothesizes that feminism reached more people through the works of Germaine Greer and Shulamith Firestone than through the various women's groups and organizations in cities and on campuses throughout the country (Daniel, p. 302; see also Gilbert and Gubar, 1985, p. 1675). Dale Spender begins *For the Record* with this observation: "Over the last decades I have learnt as much if not more about feminism from books as from any other source. And I suspect that many of the same books that have influenced me have also made a dramatic difference to other women and to the way they live their lives" (p. 1). Susan Bolotin says, "I came to feminism the way so many others did in the 1960s—through books," and she mentions Woolf, Austen, Plath, de Beauvoir, and Friedan ("Post-Feminist Generation," p. 29).

Fiction played an important part in this process. As Janet Batsleer et al. suggest,

> Groups of women . . . exchanged titles and authors, swapped books and discussed fictional situations and characters in terms of what they had to say about our relation to each other, to men, to the world. . . . Fictional situations provided one set of indicators against which to think about actual experience, as well as a source of knowledge about the lives of women in situations different from but recognizably like our own, reinforcing that anger and solidarity about women's position from which feminism developed.[96]

"This was my life she was writing about," says Lynn Wenzel of Alix Kates Shulman, and "I wasn't alone anymore."[97] Nora Johnson describes her response to "mad housewife novels" as "primal and only half-critical; I listened for cries that matched mine, novelty and hope (however illusory) in the dark night"[98]—and other women expressed a similar sense of recognition. "We discussed fictional women in the same way we discussed our friends," says Diana of Raskin's *Hot Flashes;* "we . . . gossiped about writers as often as about friends. We . . . spent a good portion of our lives reading."[99] Cora Kaplan refers to the mid-seventies as a time when those involved in the women's movement "read poetry and novels as they came out much more than we read them now. We read them because these texts were part of the ongoing debate of the social movement of which we were part."[100] Alison Light describes herself as "made by books"; "books were the way out of my home, and . . . out of my class" ("Feminist Criticism in the 1990s," in Carr, p. 29). Anthea Zeman describes "the woman's novel as perform[ing] a function especially necessary to women; that of telling them accurately where they stood at a given moment," of "monitoring reports on new freedoms, lost ground, new dangers, new possibilities."[101]

Drabble describes the importance of de Beauvoir to her in college and speaks of Lessing as "a mother and seer."[102] Many other women also single out de Beauvoir and Lessing for particular mention: as Elizabeth Wilson writes, "in the strange cultural landscape of 1960 [Lessing and de Beauvoir] loomed up, Cassandras of women's experience";[103] according to Jenny Taylor, "for women who found reading and discussing novels an important reference-point, often a crucial form of self-perception and analysis, Doris Lessing loomed up—wherever one looked, she seemed to be waiting," and *The Children of Violence* was not simply "promoted as the epic, archetypal story of our time, but was read, often compulsively, as prototypical."[104] Martha Quest is "a character whom readers mentally lift from the page and incorporate into their own lives as a reference point."[105] Jean McCrindle describes reading *The Golden Notebook* "as a way of finding out about the world and who I was and where we stood in the world and what love and emotions were all about" ("Reading *The Golden Notebook* in 1962," in Taylor, p. 50). Wilson says she first read *The Golden Notebook* "as a manual of womanly experience" (in Taylor, p. 71); Annette Kolodny says she used it as a way of interviewing prospective lovers (in conversation, October 1989); Joanne Frye describes "the response of those many women who read the novel, share it with friends, find in it the basis for offering to each other the initial feminist response: 'me too.' "[106] Laurie Stone writes, "I first read Doris Lessing in my early twenties . . . her truculent, anxious, hungry heroines . . . this band I knew. It was the early 1970s and meeting myself in literature felt like a confirmation of reality."[107] Annis Pratt calls *The Golden Notebook* "one of those novels that seemed to speak directly to a whole generation's experience."[108] Susan Lydon describes *The Golden Notebook* as "almost . . . a Little Red Book" of "women's liberationists," "probably the most widely read and deeply appreciated book on the woman's liberation reading list, Simone de Beauvoir's *The Second Sex* and Betty Friedan's *The Feminine Mystique* notwithstanding."[109] Jong's Isadora Wing includes Anna Wulf on a list of actual women (along with de Beauvoir, Plath, and Woolf) who have failed her as role models: "And Doris Lessing's Anna Wulf can't come unless she's in love, which is seldom."[110] Ella of Dorothy Bryant's *Ella Price's Journal* identifies with Anna, despite their differences:

> I don't know anything about women like this—free, independent women who earn their own living, raise their own children, sleep with whoever they want, make their own rules. But in some strange way their lives don't seem to be much different from mine. (p. 88)

Margaret Drabble describes Lessing as "the kind of writer who changes people's lives" and *The Golden Notebook* as "a transforming work. There is nothing at all like it" (*Ramparts,* pp. 50, 52). There are many testimonies to the transformative power of the novel: Jane Marcus says, "I never would have gone [to graduate school] if it hadn't been for Elaine Shinbrot, who gave me Doris Lessing's *The Golden Notebook*."[111] John Leonard says, "*The Golden Notebook* changed my life."[112] According to Nancy Porter, Lessing "has changed the way many women understand their lives."[113] Lisa Alther says, "Any number of my friends speak of the crisis of self-examination that accompanied their first reading of *The Golden Notebook* and the *Children of Violence* series, unabashedly admitting these books 'changed their lives.' And almost every woman writer I know acknowledges a debt to Doris Lessing"[114]—a debt that is apparent in her own novel *Other Women*. According to Dee Seligman, "Lessing readers have often been changed by what they have read . . . are moved to see their lives in a different perspective"; Rose and Kaplan describe Lessing as having "changed the direction of the professional lives of a significant number of academics."[115] Rachel Blau DuPlessis expresses a sense shared by many readers of being haunted by *The Golden Notebook* and needing to return to it again and again:

> A self-questioning, the writer built into the center of the work, the questions at the center of the writer, the discourses doubling, retelling the same, differently. . . .
> Of course I am describing *The Golden Notebook* again. Again.[116]

McCrindle calls the book "prophetic": it "does prefigure all sorts of things that were actually to happen in the next ten years—to me personally, and in the external world. I think I even felt that I wouldn't fully understand it until I had actually lived another ten years of my life. I can still pick it up now and say, 'God, *now* I know what she is saying about that' " (in Taylor, pp. 55–56). The novel has occasioned even more extravagant praise: Susan Lardner calls it "the sacred text for most of her admirers," "a feminist gospel, a representative of Modern Woman."[117] Drabble calls it "the Bible of the young";[118] John Leonard refers to it as "one of the sacred texts of our time"[119]—though he is one of the few men I know of to praise it so lavishly, for as my discussion of male critics of *The Golden Notebook* in Chapter 5 demonstrates, men usually found ways of dismissing it.

### Feminist Fiction in the Sixties

But, apart from *The Golden Notebook,* there was not—in the mid-sixties—much feminist fiction to choose from, though there would be more by the end of the decade. Dickstein demonstrates, by his very omissions, how male-dominated the "serious" fiction of this period was and describes the way it backed itself into narrower corners: from the exuberant, expansive black humor and apocalyptic modes of the early sixties to the smaller, solipsistic, and self-conscious modes which became, in the last years of the decade—the years when the women's movement was taking off—detached, "impersonal and abstract" (p. 215), as in the experimental short fiction of Donald Bartheleme, John Barth, William H. Gass, and Robert Coover, metafiction which makes "its own devices . . . its only subject" (p. 234). Dickstein describes the decline of the commercial market which made publishers "stop buying novels" and "retreat to old middlebrow staples like history, biography, and reportage, which provide the narrative element many of the novelists have abandoned" (pp. 91–92, 232). Moreover, fiction of this period is marked by a misogyny verging on the pathological. Mary Allen describes the reactionary trend in novels by Barth, Pynchon, Purdy, Kesey, Roth, Updike, and Oates, a fiction conservative in its views of women's work, birth control, and abortion, yet "adamant as to the abuses of motherhood."[120] She notes that women characters in fiction by men are "ineffectual, "unenlightened," without "skills or talents," "miserable, verging on madness" (p. 185): "the housewife in fiction is a trapped being who wanders around her house trying to figure out what trivia to attend to next" (p. 183). Allen concludes "this is a terrible myth. An old one. May the future prove it a lie" (p. 185).

The future proved that "mad housewives" were no "myth," but as the object spoke and made herself subject, she discovered that she was not alone. What Dickstein and Allen fail to note is the women's fiction that comes to the fore at the end of this decade, offering the narrative element lacking in experimentalist fiction and providing much else besides for the many women who turned to fiction seeking understanding of the changes they were living through. In the late sixties, as male fiction was losing its audience and energy, the "mad housewife" novel—Sue Kaufman's *Diary of a Mad Housewife,* Fay Weldon's *The Fat Woman's Joke* (1967), Laurence's *The Fire-Dwellers,* Drabble's *The Waterfall* (1969)—reclaimed the commercial market and claimed new subjects for fiction, subjects like female sexuality and physiology, female socialization and objectification, women's relations with mothers, daughters, and with other women. In 1964 Margaret Laurence published *The Stone Angel,* the first of the five-volume Manawaka series, which included *A Jest of God* (1966), *The Fire-Dwellers* (1969), *A Bird in the House* (1972), and *The Diviners* (1974). Drabble published her first novel, *A Summer Bird Cage,* in 1963, after which she published four more in short sequence—*The Garrick Year* (1964), *The Millstone* (1965), *Jerusalem the Golden* (1967), and *The Waterfall* (1969)—all of which met with spectacular success: "I found I had unwittingly tuned into a mood that was spreading through the country. Far from being isolated, I was part of a movement. . . . The times were changing. The captive housewife spoke."[121] Atwood, who was born the same year as Drabble (1939), published her first novel, *The Edible Woman,* in 1969. Other feminist writers also began publishing in this decade: Edna O'Brien (*The Country Girls,* [1960], *Lonely Girl* [1962], *Girls in Their Married Bliss* [1964], *Casualties of Peace* [1966]); May Sarton (*Mrs. Stevens Hears the Mermaids Singing* [1965]); Jane Rule (*Desert of the Heart,* [1964]).

Nineteen sixty-nine saw the publication of important works: Laurence's *The Fire-Dwellers,* Atwood's *The Edible Woman,* Drabble's *The Waterfall,* and Shulman's *Memoirs of an Ex-Prom Queen,* as well as Sheila Rowbotham's *Women's Liberation and the New Politics* and Kate Millett's *Sexual Politics;* 1970 saw the publication of Germaine Greer's *Female Eunuch* and Eva Figes's *Patriarchal Attitudes.* What is astonishing is how many of these 1969 novels implement the same device at the same time, using divided pronouns to express the sense of dividedness and contradiction described by Piercy and Plath. Atwood and Drabble split their narratives into "I" and "she"; so, too, does

Laurence, but she splits the narrative further, into a veritable polyphony (or cacaphony) of voices. Lessing had experimented with divided voices and pronouns as early as 1962, and though by 1969 she was "off into fantasy" (p. 45, above), this split—about which I have more to say about in Chapter 3—remains prominent in women's fiction throughout the sixties and seventies.

Nineteen sixty-nine was a breakthrough year for feminist fiction because an audience and market had come into being: in 1968 the women's-liberation movement emerged as a movement with an ideology, membership, and structure, coming to the fore just as the New Left was fading. It attained national visibility with the picketing of the Miss America pageant in September 1968, the first feminist event to get front-page coverage, and by 1969 the movement was getting considerable, if usually negative, publicity; "mentions of the women's movement in national press increased tenfold between May 1969 and March 1970."[122] (Many date the beginning of the women's movement in England from 1970, with the Ruskin College conference in Oxford.[123]) As feminism attained national visibility on both sides of the Atlantic, publishers targeted it as a new market: the success of Friedan, Greer, Millett "encouraged major publishing houses to create or expand their 'women's issue list' "; anthologies appeared that made articles from alternative presses available to mass markets—Robin Morgan's *Sisterhood Is Powerful* (1970), Altbach's *From Feminism to Liberation,* and Vivian Gornick and Barbara K. Moran's *Women in Sexist Society* (1971)—so that "what had been esoteric knowledge in 1969 was broadly available in 1972 and commonly recognized by 1974" (Ferree, p. 74).

Feminist writers had wide appeal, as their sales testify. More than 900,000 hardcover copies of *The Golden Notebook* have sold in the United States since Simon and Schuster brought it out in 1962; since it was first issued in paperback by that company in 1973, it has remained on Bantam's active backlist, continuing to sustain substantial reorders from booksellers; almost half a million of these paperbacks are in print.[124] (Lessing describes how "ten years after I wrote it," "I can get, in one week, three letters about it, from three intelligent, well-informed, concerned people, who have taken the trouble to sit down and write to me" [p. xxi]). Drabble was immediately hailed as one of England's important young writers; according to an editor at Weidenfeld and Nicolson, her British publisher, "sales of her books are among the highest for living British novelists."[125] Drabble attributes her popularity to her representativeness—"Well, millions of others were in exactly the same position, but I didn't think about that at the time";[126] "There must be a lot of people like me;"[127] and her work has been referred to as "an English *Passages* for a particular generation of middle-class women."[128] She has described herself as " 'a woman's page writer' " who "belongs to the 'nose in the washing-machine' school of fiction,"[129] and her lack of pretension has appealed to a wide readership, though it has also occasionally caused her to be dismissed as a "serious" writer. Like Lessing, she is a writer who changes people's lives: Joyce Carol Oates compares her with Lessing for "tak[ing] upon herself the task, largely ignored today, of attempting the active, vital, energetic, mysterious recreation of a set of values by which human beings can live" and "chang[ing] us for the better."[130]

An early review of Laurence's *The Diviners* claims that "Laurence is unforgettable because she is us";[131] another early review of *The Fire-Dwellers* states, "Mrs. Laurence realizes that there are millions of other Staceys, sorting dirty laundry and wiping dripping noses;"[132] and another:

> The Housewife as Heroine . . . appears to have been considered a subject of too paltry significance to warrant treatment beyond stories in ladies' magazines. . . . Miss Laurence decided to risk the perils of inconsequentiality in deference to that neglected, unappreciated household drudge conventionally known as Mom, who might just have something to say after all.[133]

Laurence says, "I didn't realize how widespread some of these feelings are."[134]

Jong, too, expresses surprise at learning that "my thoughts, nightmares, and daydreams were the same as my readers": "when I wrote about a fantasy I thought was wholly private, bizarre, kinky . . . thousands of other people had experienced the same private, bizarre, and kinky fantasy."[135] *Fear of Flying* sold ten million copies,[136] and in the highly autobiographical sequel *How to Save Your Own Life,* Isadora, a writer who is faced with the problem of surviving her success, expresses astonishment at the popularity of her protagonist, Candida Wong: "When I invented Candida Wong . . . I was convinced that she was either unfit for print or else so precious that no one but a few other wise-ass Jewish girls from the Upper West Side could relate to her. But I was wrong. As Candida felt, so felt the nation"; "astoundingly enough, millions of women all over the world felt exactly as Candida felt!"[137] Jong was inundated by letters from women seeking advice and approval—"people would say, you're the first person who understood me, you make me feel less lonely."[138]

Several of these novels—*The Pumpkin Eater, Up the Sandbox, The Diary of A Mad Housewife, The Bell Jar, A Jest of God (Rachel, Rachel)*—were made into movies. Not surprisingly, their success occasioned jealousy, as in the sadly revealing statement of Auberon Waugh in the 1978 *New Review:*

> Soon, I suspect, novel writing will become the virtual monopoly of housewives and academics. . . . Housewives can and do write admirable novels, but their experience of the world tends to be limited. . . . For my own part, I gave up writing novels six years ago when my fifth and last novel failed to find a publisher in the U. S. and ended by earning a grand total of 600 pounds. (p. 71)

Also in *The New Review* William Trevor wrote, "The big literary selling point of the Sixties continued: a woman and her typewriter in a state of undress" (p. 69). "There must be a quarter of a million Jewish girls of marriageable age living in New York City, and I sometimes have the panic fear that every one of them is going to write the story of her life" (Godfrey Smith, in Zeman, p. 120).

What does it mean when a generation of women readers claim that *The Golden Notebook* changed them? Notwithstanding the power of narrative to resist change,[139] people still do speak of books as changing them. Numerous conversations I've had with friends (Lillian Robinson, Elizabeth Abel, Myra Goldberg, Ann Rosalind Jones, Annette Kolodny, Tania Modleski, Molly Hite, and Dorothy Kaufman) corroborate my sense of *The Golden Notebook* as a transforming experience, a touchstone for my generation. It certainly changed my life; Lessing and de Beauvoir made me a feminist, and *The Golden Notebook* haunted me so that I returned to it year after year and finally reorganized my professional life around it, changing my field from Renaissance to contemporary literature. From this postfeminist era, it seems unwise to make extravagant claims for the effect this has had on the world, but surely it has made some difference that I have been an educator teaching feminism for more than two decades. And teaching *The Golden Notebook*, I see that it still exerts enormous power on young women—though some are more critical of Anna's passivity, of Lessing's homophobia, than women of my generation were.

Feminist writers know that books make a difference and make this a focus of their fiction. When they express coming to consciousness—in fiction that charts the coming of age of a generation—they foreground reading and writing as part of the process, which is why (to return to the question asked at the beginning of this chapter) women's *Kunstlerromane* re-emerge in the sixties and seventies. In order to demonstrate how crucial powers of reading and writing are to the process of change, I'll turn to a group of mad-housewife novels that do not envision such powers for their protagonists and do not break the closed circuit of female conditioning.

# *III*

# MAD HOUSEWIVES AND CLOSED CIRCLES

> How to write a novel about a person to whom nothing happens? A person to whom nothing but a love story is *supposed* to happen? A person inhabiting a world in which the only reality is frustration or endurance—or these plus an unbearably mystifying confusion?
>
> Joanna Russ, "What Can a Heroine Do? or Why Can't Women Write?"[1]

### Naming the Problem with No Name

This chapter focuses on a dozen or so "mad housewife" novels published in as many years—1962 to 1975. There has been remarkably little work on these novels, individually or as a group, though they were widely read and influential. They dramatize woman's socialization as sexualization and evoke the ideological feel of these decades, down to the details of dress—pleated skirts, cashmere sweaters, white dickeys, charm bracelets, bobby sox, mink tail neckerchiefs.[2] They document the "increasingly severe pathology, both physiological and emotional" that afflicted women trapped in the domestic sphere and name what Friedan terms "the problem that has no name."[3]

Indeed, Friedan is so accurate a chronicler of white middle-class women's experience in these years that *The Feminine Mystique* provides historical documentary for what the novels portray fictionally. Friedan writes, "We did not want to be like [our mothers], and yet what other model did we have?" (pp. 74–75); Martha Quest vows, "she would *not* be like" her mother but wonders "then, who was she to be like?"[4] Friedan discovered, interviewing women of her generation, that "many of us could not see ourselves beyond the age of 21. We had no image of our own future" (pp. 69–70);[5] and in *The Bell Jar* Esther's crisis is precipitated by her realization, the summer before her senior year, that she had "absolutely no idea what to do next": "try as I would, I couldn't see . . . beyond [my] nineteenth [year]" (p. 101).[6]

Friedan refers to woman's condition as "a trap" (p. 309), a "slow death of self," like being buried alive (p. 336),[7] and in all these novels—Penelope Mortimer's *The Pumpkin Eater* (1962), Sue Kaufman's *The Diary of a Mad Housewife,* Fay Weldon's *The Fat Woman's Joke* (1967), Margaret Laurence's *The Fire-Dwellers,* Alix Kates Shulman's *Memoirs of an Ex-Prom Queen* (1969), Anne Richardson Roiphe's *Up the Sandbox* (1970), Dorothy Bryant's *Ella Price's Journal,* Johanna Davis's, *Life Signs* (1972), Barbara Raskin's *Loose Ends* (1973), Sheila Ballantyne's *Norma Jean the Termite Queen* (1975)— protagonists are confined in houses, apartments, basement flats, "cells of brick and glass" (PE, p. 212), "boundaries . . . [of] four walls" (FD, p. 64), bell jars or "pumpkin shells," looking back on their lives and wondering how they managed to get stuck in a situation from which there is no exit.[8] Weldon's Esther is "trapped in this body, in this house, in this marriage" (FWJ, p. 99); Ella Price is "buried alive" (EPJ, p. 41); " 'The days wrap around me; I suffocate,' " says Norma Jean; "I have no part of my life that I can call my own" (NJTQ, pp. 14, 39). Mrs. Armitage of Mortimer's *The Pumpkin Eater,* who is so completely defined by marriage that she has no name besides "Mrs. Armitage," is in the throes of a depression brought on by a lifetime of living for others: "I don't know who I am, I don't know what I'm like" (p. 191); and she ends as she began, "kept" in a "pumpkin shell," incarcerated emotionally as well as physically, the circular structure of the narrative—final scene returning to first scene—affirming the triumph of the past.

Friedan describes woman's conditioning as a "vicious circle" (p. 146) which "completes itself, from mother to sons and daughters, generation after generation" (p. 203), and circular images and structures are everywhere in this fiction. In the early *Children of Violence* novels, Lessing used circles to symbolize the "cycle of birth" and "cycle of procreation" that ensnare Martha (PM, pp. 152, 251): the Ferris wheel spinning outside Martha's bedroom window "like a damned wedding ring" (pp. 29–30); the circles of women that entrap her (pp. 36, 249, 255, 272); the nets, webs, cages, bonds, and traps (pp. 28, 81, 91, 95, 99, 137, 201, 202, 250, 266, 337) suggest—as they do in *The Oresteia*—an "appalling fatality" (p. 34). Friedan describes woman's work as "endless, monotonous, unrewarding" (p. 307);[9] "endless" too are the "whirl[s] of . . . community activities" which "led in no direction for her own future" (p. 345). French's Mira fears the "narrow circle" (p. 267), the "endless kaffee-klatches," that trap her friends: " 'It's that they go round and round. They never get anyplace. . . . They go around doing and saying the same things. . . . It feels like hell to me. . . . To go round and round like that forever' " (WR, p. 188). Weldon's "fat woman" complains,

> Dusting and sweeping, cooking and washing up—it is . . . an eternal circle which lasts from the day you get married until the day you die, or are put into an old folk's home because you are too feeble to pick up some man's socks and put them away any more. (p. 73)

In the "necropolis" where Norma Jean lives, "every street [is] a sterile avenue, winding in circles, coming out where it began. . . . All of us sealed in, entombed, dying" (p. 113). Of her neighbor's redecorating tasks, Norma Jean thinks, "No new ground is broken, no boundaries extended; just the same old boundaries endlessly rearranged" (pp. 182–83).

Yet these novels do speak "something new" into existence, naming not only the housewife's malaise but also articulating areas of women's lives that were formerly taboo. They address female sexuality, pregnancy, child rearing, women's relation to their bodies, "body image," eating—starving, fasting, purging, gorging. Sasha of *Memoirs of an Ex-Prom Queen* realizes that there are no words to describe the "nameless" part of herself which she "caresses to a nameless joy," no words to discuss sex ("intercourse . . . Fucking? Relations? Have Sex? Fornicating? Sleeping with?"), and she finds a "conspiracy of silence about motherhood . . . even wider than the one about sex. Philosophers ignored it and poets revered it, but no one dared describe it"; "Why didn't the women speak? Evidently they were too busy" (EPQ, pp. 45, 20, 254, 250). Isadora Wing senses that "despite her [mother's] bohemian talk . . . sex . . . was basically unmentionable" (FF, p. 153): so Jong "mentions" it. "Those things weren't mentioned then [in 1964]," as Norma Jean says; "we all suffered alone" (pp. 37, 7).

But more than "mention" them, these novels make them the main events: central events in these novels derive from the fact that women live in women's bodies—this becomes the focus of fiction for the first time.[10] Crises are precipitated and/or resolved when the protagonist gets a diaphragm and loses her virginity *(Bell Jar);* when she is sterilized *(Pumpkin Eater);* when she gets a period and ends an affair or when she doesn't get a period and has a baby or an abortion *(Mad Housewife, Up the Sandbox, Ella Price's Journal);* when she gains weight or loses weight *(The Fat Woman's Joke, The Edible Woman).* "This is not the stuff of fiction," says Mira of *The Women's Room:* "It has no shape, it hasn't the balances so important in art" (p. 292)—so these writers make new "stuff" and shapes for fiction.

Published during the decade and a half when the women's movement was at its height, this fiction accomplishes—like consciousness raising—what Selma James terms "the charting of personal experience."[11] But though these novels give literary expression to the female sphere in a way that is unprecedented in fiction, they do not portray it as the source of an alternative or oppositional energy. They confront the question addressed by major feminist fiction—the possibility of finding freedom from the constraints of the past, of forging "something new." But they do not, for the most part, make the connections— between individual and social, personal and political, past and present—that might enable them to challenge the situations they depict.

## Divided and Conquered

Locked into the female sphere, women are prisoners not only of domestic spaces, but of a stifling self-consciousness. Shulman's Sasha learns early that "there was only one thing worth bothering about: becoming beautiful" (p. 20), and by the time she is a teenager her concerns have contracted entirely to her appearance: "There was only one way for a girl to control her future: choose her man. There weren't many things a girl could do to command the choice, but . . . methods were spelled out . . . in *Seventeen*" (EPQ, p. 74). Sasha never loses sense of herself as an object on display, "toss[ing] her head back . . . and unleash[ing]" an "outlandishly Hollywood, hold-it glamour smile" (pp. 102–103), using her "eyes with the old bus-stop swagger" (p. 219). Raskin's Coco similarly lives her life

> like the star of a low-budget European movie, playing her existence into an invisible camera which she envisioned suspended six feet in front of her, eternally recording each of her theatrically poignant scenes. (p. 91)

As John Berger says, "to be born a woman has been to be born, within an allotted and confined space, into the keeping of men. The social presence of women has developed as a result of their ingenuity in living under such tutelage within such a limited space."[12] Within this space she develops what Frigga Haug terms "competence in non-competence," "familiarity with the requisite standards, with proportions, with strategies of concealment and emphasis"— strategies that "work to consolidate our social incompetence" by teaching "expertise in operating within existing standards."[13]

Thus Coco embarks on a "reclamation routine" that consists of "filing, cutting, shaving, trimming, clipping, gluing, plucking, polishing, and squeezing" (p. 8). Regimens were "spelled out" in women's magazines, and though Miriam of *Small Changes* realizes that "if she followed . . . even one or two of them, the upkeep of her body would consume her entire free existence" (p. 314), such regimens promise salvation—"by dyeing one's hair blond or by having another baby" women could solve "the problem with no name" (Friedan, p. 61). Tina gets a cut and curl because her husband " 'is tired of the way it is' " (p. 80); Sasha has a second baby and *then* resorts to a new hairstyle, though neither effort succeeds in reviving her husband's waning attentions (p. 294).

Female objectification leads to the self-division Berger describes: "A woman must continually watch herself. She is almost continually accompanied by her own image of herself" (pp. 46–47). This sense of being "split in two" (as Berger puts it, and as Jong's Isadora puts it [p. 157]), of being "separated from herself" (as Laurence's Morag describes herself [p. 263]), is explained by de Beauvoir: man's "vocation as a human being . . . his social and spiritual successes endow him with a virile prestige. He is not divided," "whereas it is required of woman that in order to realize her femininity she must make herself object and prey, which is to say that she must renounce her claims as sovereign subject."[14] Such contradictions were exacerbated by the conflicting signals of the postwar period, intensified as a restrictive ideology that objectified woman diverged from social circumstances that held out new possibilities of agency and autonomy.

One form of this division was the split between femininity and career experi-

enced by many of these protagonists. Isadora learns from her mother that
" 'women cannot possibly do both . . . you've got to choose. Either be an artist
or have children' " (p. 40); Sarah in Drabble's *A Summer Bird Cage* realizes
" 'You can't be a sexy don. It's all right for men, being learned and attractive,
but for a woman it's a mistake";[15] Miriam of *Small Changes* is told that "only
homely women" become brilliant scientists (p. 371). As we shall see, the most
interesting of these novels—Atwood's *Edible Woman*, Drabble's *The Waterfall*,
Laurence's *Fire-Dwellers* and *The Diviners,* and Ballantyne's *Norma Jean*—
explore such divisions at the narrative level, by splitting the narrative into "I"
and "she."[16]

Some of these protagonists are uncomfortable as objects. Esther keeps thinking "how stupid I'd been to buy all those uncomfortable, expensive clothes,
hanging limp as fish in my closet" (p. 1) and is appalled by her image in mirrors
(pp. 83–84, 92, 162–63); Atwood's Marian is similarly dissociated from her
reflection (pp. 66, 155); Tina, deluged by "drifts of beaded, spangled, feathered
dresses in violent purples, greens and reds," feels menaced by "the three-way
reflection" of her "skin sickly glimmering" (pp. 113–14); and Godwin's Jane
Clifford is similarly disoriented by the images that assault her from the mirrors
of Saks Fifth Avenue.[17]

Several come to the realization that they are playing a game they cannot
possibly win; and the game is a frequent image in this fiction, though it tends
not to be used as an emancipatory strategy[18] (except in *The Waterfall*), but
rather, as a symbol of sexual politics—"no game at all, or if it was, it was a
game that required you to be buried alive," a "possibly fatal game," as Alice
Munro's Del realizes.[19] In Laurence's *The Diviners,* Morag's husband, Brooke,
an authoritarian Englishman, puts her through Nora-like games which reenact
on a personal level Canada's subordination to England. Fay Weldon's "fat
woman" knows " 'It isn't a game. It's very serious and very painful' " and " 'if
you're a woman you never win,' " so she stops playing, choosing obesity over
objectification: "There's more dignity, if one is neither young nor beautiful, in
simply giving up. Which is what, being middle-aged, I am finally allowed to
do' " (pp. 89, 58). Sasha figures out the rules of the game early on, though she
does not realize the stakes until too late—"It was all there in all the texts I'd ever
studied" (p. 293), leaving her "at thirty . . . without income or skill, dependent
on a man and a fading skin––it can only be the fulfillment of a curse!" (p. 285).
Sasha dreams of mastering chess—for "in chess the queen is more powerful"
(pp. 206–207)—but in *Memoirs of an Ex-Prom Queen*, all she gets to play is
"prom queen" (though the protagonist of Shulman's next novel, *Burning Questions,* does master chess).

Objectified, sexualized, woman is the prime target of advertising. These
protagonists are promised magical transformations through the power of purchasing: it is shoes "bought in Bloomingdale's" that make Plath's Esther the
"envy" of everyone (p. 2); the "glistening shade of Yardley's honey-beige" gives
Coco a "reassuring" "allure" (p. 18). As an advertising executive told Friedan,
"properly man' )ulated, . . . American housewives can be given the sense of

identity, purpose, creativity, the self-realization, even the sexual joy they lack—
by the buying of things" (p. 208); women, as Friedan and others have noted,
"wield seventy-five percent of the purchasing power in America."[20] The role of
homemaker further implicates women in consumerism, especially in these years
when they were isolated in the suburbs and brainwashed to believe that they
should spend all leisure time and money perfecting the home.[21] Tina of Kaufman's *Mad Housewife* puts herself to sleep on bad nights by imagining herself
"a paragon-housewife, a lady with an apron," moving through the house
"taking . . . inventory" of the soap, towels, glasses, plates, cups, wax, polish,
lightbulbs (pp. 67–71); and this novel precisely itemizes the items and names
the brand names necessary to keep the upwardly mobile young couple upwardly mobile. Laurence's Stacey has a wry sense of herself as caught in a system
she "hate[s] but perpetuate[s]"; and the catalog of "Polyglam" objects (i.e.,
Tupperware)—"plastic vessels gleaming softly . . . picnic plates . . . sandwich
cases. Pie containers. Cookie jars. Breadboxes. Buckets and dish pans. Dogs'
feeding bowls. Infants' cereal bowls. Mixing bowls. . . . Ice-cube trays. Vats."—
gives the sense of an avalanche (FD, pp. 3, 24). Atwood's *Edible Woman* offers a
brilliant analysis of woman as consumable in consumer capitalism: when
Marian turns out in a tarty hairdo and red dress that make her feel like a
"callgirl" and her fiancé responds, "Yum, yum," she gets the point—that in
objectifying herself, she has made herself "edible."[22]

When these protagonists turn to doctors, counselors, psychiatrists, psychologists, as nearly all of them do, they are advised to conform to the feminine role:
"When in doubt, seek examination. Especially if you are female" (NJ, p. 32).
"Postwar America was the era of the expert," as Elaine Tyler May and others
have observed; "when the experts spoke, postwar America listened," and what
the experts advised was conformity to cultural norms.[23] When Tina tells Dr.
Popkin that she wants to be a painter, he replies, " 'That is precisely what you
cannot be. You must be what you are,' " "a bright but quite ordinary young
woman, somewhat passive and shy . . . equipped with powerful Feminine
Drives—which simply means I badly wanted a husband and children and a
Happy Home" (p. 25). Esther's therapist is "young . . . good-looking . . .
conceited" and displays a photograph that makes her "furious": "How could
this Doctor Gordon help me anyway, with a beautiful wife and beautiful
children and a beautiful dog?" In fact, he is useless, barely registering her
existence, though vividly recalling his visit to her college—" 'I remember your
college well. I was up there during the war. . . . My, they were a pretty bunch of
girls' " (pp. 107, 118).

The advice of the doctors is reinforced by stories and articles in women's
magazines. A friend urges Mrs. Armitage to read the women's magazines:

> "It says in one of them you must do this *every* night if you don't want a double
> chin by the time you're twenty. They have terribly serious articles too, you know,
> about cancer and having the curse . . . and what to do if your husband is
> unfaithful and all that". . . . "I'm reading *Jane Eyre*," I said. . . . "But that

doesn't *tell* you anything!" . . . "You really ought to read them, you know. They'd do you much more good than old *Jane Eyre*." (pp. 77–78)

But far from "doing good," the information they offer usually makes the protagonist feel bad, for current pop psychology (as Friedan observes) blames the woman. As Stacey of Laurence's *The Fire Dwellers* reflects, "Some wise guy is always telling you how you're sapping the national strength"; the articles in the magazines at her hairdressers are titled " 'Nine Ways the Modern Mum May Be Ruining Her Daughter' " (p. 11); " 'Are You Emasculating Your Husband?' " (p. 49); " 'Are You Increasing Your Husband's Tension?' " (p. 71); " 'Mummy Is the Root of All Evil?' " (p. 273) Sasha, too, observes, "Of all the experts I'd ever consulted, none . . . was unequivocally on my side. They made us do it, then blamed us for it" (p. 269). Of the crimes of violence Norma Jean reads about in the newspapers, "there always seems to be an aborting, absent, negligent or seducing mother somewhere in the background"; "The message is everywhere, and it says: The problem is all yours" (pp. 127–28). But by 1975 this protagonist knows enough to blame *Ladies' Home Journal* "for selling me this bill of goods" (p. 125).

The main development that occurs in the mad-housewife novel in this decade and a half is the development of feminist consciousness that allows the protagonist to understand that her experience is "shared, unnecessary, and political." In *The Bell Jar, The Pumpkin Eater, The Fire-Dwellers,* and *Ex-Prom Queen,* protagonists imagine that their situations are solitary and self-incurred. With no way of relating their misery to that of other women, they blame themselves (Kaufman's Tina: "I know I'm a Very Lucky Girl, and really *must* be crazy to get into the state I'm in these days, when I have everything A Girl Could Want" [p. 44]; Laurence's Stacey: "This is madness. I'm not trapped. I've got everything I always wanted" [p. 64]. These protagonists may suspect that (as Anna Wulf puts it) "this country's full of women going mad all by themselves,"[24] but they have no terms or vocabulary for connecting their misery to anyone else's; nor is it clear that the authors themselves understand such connections. Mortimer's Mrs. Armitage has a glimpse of someone worse off than she is and imagines "advising" her:

> What should I say to Mrs. Evans? . . . Dear Mrs. Evans, my friend, Dear Mrs. Evans, for God's sake come and teach me how to live. It's not that I've forgotten. It's that I never knew.
>
> .   .   .   .   .   .   .   .   .   .   .   .   .   .   .   .   .   .   .   .   .   .   .   .
>
> You have a vote, Mrs. Evans . . . I have a vote. Really, anyone would think that the emancipation of women had never happened. (pp. 149–50)

One would indeed think, on the basis of this novel, that "the emancipation of women" had never occurred; nor does Mortimer give a clue how it might. At one point Kaufman's Tina comes face to face with another housewife, who answers her door dazedly and "stood tweaking back lank blond hair from a tired face, blinking. . . . I blinked back, just as dazed: It's *ma semblamble, ma soeur,* I thought" (p. 116); but nothing is made of this connection, by Tina or Kaufman. Tina tries to articulate a connection between her "crack-up" and the madness of New York:

> "I'm talking about what goes on in this city, or any big city like it nowadays. It's all a sign of the times, the terrible pressures we live under. The exhibitionists in the park and subways, the rapists in elevators, the muggers . . . they're all a sign of the times. . . ."

> "It means that some people just can't take all the pressures we live under—the Russians, the Chinese, the war in Vietnam, the Negro Revolution, and of course The Bomb—some people just crack." Crack. I listened to the word. (p. 65)

"The point is, everything's cracking up" is Anna's opening line in *The Golden Notebook,* a novel which, published four years *earlier,* delineates the relation between individual "crack-up" and the crises of the twentieth century. But Kaufman explores no such relationships: Tina is left at the end in a "private totalitarian state" (as Esther terms marriage; p. 69); so, too, are Plath's Esther, Weldon's Esther, Mrs. Armitage, Roiphe's Margaret, Davis's Camilla.

Later protagonists who have the benefit of feminist analyses are able to see the connections between themselves and other women and to question the standards that declare them "mad." By 1973 Coco of *Loose Ends* retorts to her analyst, " 'Maybe my problems aren't *peculiar* to me. Maybe all women like me have *exactly* the same problems . . . maybe we've gotten to be this way because of cultural and societal and political reasons. . . . So maybe we're not really *crazy* ' " (p. 49). Jong's Isadora says to one of her analysts, " 'Don't you see that men have *always* defined femininity as a means of keeping women in line? Why should I listen to *you* about what it means to be a woman? . . . Why shouldn't I listen to *myself* for once? And to other women?' " (p. 18). Unfortunately, as the actions of Coco and Isadora declare, feminist rhetoric is no guarantee of change. Isadora expresses her "liberation" by traveling through Europe with a lover and then returning to her husband when the lover ditches her; and Coco, who also takes a lover to escape her marriage, is so sunk in "pre-lib" ploys that she remains in a "confinement" as complete as Mrs. Armitage's more than a decade before, cut off from other women and imprisoned in a house and in herself.

The most frequent means of escape for these protagonists is an affair. Some of these novels enlist contemporary versions of what Jean E. Kennard terms the "two-suitor convention," in which the husband is associated with the repressive patriarchal order and the lover represents a less conventional alternative:[25] in *The Fire-Dwellers* and *Mad Housewife,* the lover is a writer; in *Ella Price's Journal,* he is a professor. Only in Jong's *How to Save Your Own Life,* sequel to *Fear of Flying,* does the protagonist leave the husband for the lover; and only in *The Edible Woman* and *Ella Price's Journal* does the woman face her life alone. Usually the function of the lover is to resign her to her marriage, and these novels end, as Anthea Zeman suggests, on a cheerful note of adaptation" which makes them "rather alarming."[26]

A few of these protagonists fantasize writing as a means of escape. Plath's Esther imagines writing a novel—"that would fix a lot of people" (p. 98). Martha Quest, having failed at "various inconclusive attempts to escape" (p. 209), resolves to "be a writer":

> If others, then why not herself? . . . How was she to suspect that at least a hundred young people in the same small town stuck in the middle of Africa, kept desks full of poems, articles, and stories, were convinced that *if only* . . . they could be writers, they could escape into glorious freedom and untrammelled individuality—and for no better reason than they could not face the prospect of a lifetime [at their jobs]? (MQ, pp. 211–12)

Tina sees her journal as a means of "writ[ing] [her]self back to sanity" (p. 79), but her "accounts" (as she calls them; p. 2) only provide her a way of renaming a dead end as a chosen strategy, and (like Esther and Martha) she fails to write her way free. Two later protagonists of 1973 novels, Jong's Isadora and Raskin's Coco, imagine writing as the route to fame and fortune: Coco sees "coming out in paperback and society" as the "path to personal salvation" (p. 25) and imagines further satisfactions in getting back at her husband (pp. 25, 253–54); but neither Jong nor Raskin dramatizes writing as the means to change because neither imagines what real change might mean.

These novels demonstrate how difficult it is to dramatize or even to conceive of change. Despite their powerful rendering of female entrapment, they engage in various dodges and retreats from insights too painful to be sustained, and from the connections—between personal and political, between past and present—that might make sense of the suffering they portray. Even those writers who do glimpse the connections between their protagonists' individual experience and their social and historical contexts fail to incorporate this understanding into their narratives. Only one of this group—Ballantyne's *Norma Jean the Termite Queen*—understands the connections between personal and political and renders the process of working through, delving the past in a way that transforms the present.

## Closed Circles

*The Bell Jar* is the most disturbing of these novels because its failure to confront the issues it raises resonated tragically beyond the text, to be dramatized by Plath's suicide a month after it was published in January 1963 (she killed herself in February 1963; *The Bell Jar* was not published in America until 1971, when it was immediately hailed by the women's movement). Beginning from an end in which the protagonist is "all right again"—an "all right" defined as "playing with baby" (p. 3)—the narrative moves in a circle and ends with Esther's integration into the domesticity she has tried to kill herself to avoid; and Plath suggests that this is a happy ending. "There ought . . . to be a ritual for being born twice," Esther reflects as she steps before the doctors to be pronounced "cured," to end "patched, retreaded, and approved for the road" (p. 199); but this conclusion emerges not from any working through of her problems, but from Plath's compulsion to have it "all right again." Though Esther is temporarily helped by shock therapy, she has no understanding of the bell jar, where it comes from or why it goes away: "How did I know that someday—at college, in Europe, somewhere, anywhere—the bell jar, with its stifling distortions, wouldn't descend again?" (p. 197).

Though Esther has more freedom of movement than those protagonists who are confined in domesticity, *The Bell Jar* is in some ways the most claustrophobic of these novels. "Supposed to be having the time of [her] life" the summer she spends in New York, recipient of a prestigious women's-magazine prize, Esther is stifled not only by the hot, sticky weather, but also by a bell jar that cuts her off from everything and everyone. Her disconnectedness is confirmed by the structure of the novel—the short, choppy sections on which the novel is structured, wherein, like the landscape Esther observes from the train window returning home from New York, "one fragment bears no relation to another" (p. 92)—and by Plath's failure to connect one thing with another.

Plath interweaves memories of the past (Esther's childhood and near-engagement to the smug medical student Buddy Willard) with episodes set in the present (the month in New York, Esther's return to her mother's, her suicide attempt, hospitalization, treatment and "cure"), but she does not use this structure to bring the past into vitalizing relation with the present, to explore the connections that might allow change. Esther neither understands the events she recalls nor understands their relation with the present; nor is it clear to the reader how this present will lead to the future, the "end" from which she looks back when she is "all right" and "playing with baby." Though Plath told A. Alvarez that she thought of *The Bell Jar* "as an autobiographical work" which she had to write in order to free herself from the past,[27] the novel seems, rather, to have reaffirmed the hold of the past.

Esther arrives in New York armed with her "little successes" from college, but the month in the city, though promising initiation into adulthood, is an experience absolutely discontinuous with anything in her past, for she realizes that "all the little successes I'd totted up so happily at college fizzled to nothing outside the slick marble and plate-glass fronts along Madison Avenue" (pp. 1–2). The most obvious escape from such confusions would be marriage, but this, too, represents absolute discontinuity with who she is and what she has accomplished: cooking and washing up after meals "seemed a dreary and wasted life for a girl with fifteen years of straight A's" (p. 68). Buddy Willard confirms even worse fears,

> saying in a sinister, knowing way that after I had children . . . I wouldn't want to write poems any more. So I began to think maybe it was true that when you were married and had children it was like being brainwashed, and afterward you went about numb as a slave in some private, totalitarian state. (p. 69)

Esther runs dead end against the choices allowed by her society, marriage or career: as she tells Buddy, " 'If neurotic is wanting two mutually exclusive things at one and the same time, then I'm neurotic as hell' " (p. 76).

But Esther *is* "neurotic as hell." There is something frozen about her that persists unrecognized throughout: the bell jar, "blank and stopped as a dead baby" (p. 193), represents her own stillborn emotions. She is as estranged from others as she is from herself: the telephone "could have connected me up with things, but there it sat, dumb as a death's head" (p. 16). People are barely real to her, registering themselves as disembodied parts: her friend Joan is a face "float[ing] . . . bodiless and smiling, like the face of the Cheshire cat" (p. 192); her mother is a face "anxious and sallow as a slab of lemon" (p. 107), "a pale, reproachful moon" (p. 193); a "Negro's face" is "a molasses-colored moon" (p. 150). People are mannequins (p. 81), "shop dummies, painted to resemble people and propped up in attitudes counterfeiting life" (p. 116), and in proportion as they go dead, the inanimate world assumes menacing life: "goggle-eyed headlines" announcing the Rosenberg execution "stare up . . . on every street corner and at the fusty, peanut-smelling mouth of every subway" (p. 1); "fashion blurbs, silver and full of nothing, sent up . . . fishy bubbles in my brain . . . surfaced with a hollow pop" (p. 81); "letters . . . get cocky and wiggle about" (p. 112); "words . . . twisted all awry, like faces in a funhouse mirror" (p. 102).

Esther never does get "connected up." She is chilling as she engineers the loss of her virginity, choosing a man, maneuvering him into place, billing him when she hemorrhages and cutting him off when he expresses concern—"I was perfectly free" (p. 198).[28] Even more disturbing is her response to the suicide of her friend Joan, a lesbian whose advances she has repelled: though Esther has in some sense triggered this suicide, showing up at Joan's house bleeding, she responds to it with a combination of self-centeredness—"I wondered what I thought I was burying" (p. 198)—and exhilaration: "I am, I am, I am" (p. 199). The "perfect freedom" (p. 198) she achieves is a freedom from connections, and though her ruthlessness may be exonerated as desperation, it does raise the question of how she accomplishes a future in which she is "playing with baby," a condition implying that some connections have been made. Just as Esther can see no relation between her past as a straight-A student and her future as a sex object or wife, neither can the reader (or this reader) understand the relation between the present we see her living through and that future of blissful domesticity.

Only once, when she is skiing down a mountain, plunging toward a broken leg, does Esther have an intimation that the key to her "freedom" might be in her past:

> People and trees receded on either hand like the dark sides of a tunnel as I hurtled on to the still, bright point at the end of it, the pebble at the bottom of the well, the white sweet baby cradled in its mother's belly. (p. 79)

But this is the merest glimpse, and besides, it is regressive, a fantasy of return to the womb to escape the years "of doubleness and smiles and compromise"

(p. 79) rather than a return to the past which works through that duplicity and compromise. There is a momentous event in Esther's childhood, the death of her father, which requires understanding, because Esther comments that after it, "I had never been really happy again" (pp. 60–61): but this is barely mentioned. Far from delving into the past as a means of understanding the present, this novel leaves past and present absolutely discontinuous, which is why the change Esther asserts at the end is unconvincing.[29]

Only once is there a suggestion that Esther's pain may be connected to larger historical processes—when she says, "I knew something was wrong with me that summer, because all I could think about was the Rosenbergs"; "It had nothing to do with me, but I couldn't help wondering what it would be like, being burned alive all along your nerves" (p. 1). What it has "to do with" her becomes clear when Esther herself is subjected to electric shock therapy: but is there not a deeper connection between the repressive ideology that is crushing her and the Cold War ideology that kills the Rosenbergs? The anticommunism of the period and women's brainwashing are hardly unrelated phenomena, yet the weirdly dissociated sensibility of the novel makes it difficult to know what Plath knows.[30] She seems to approve of her protagonist's consigning herself to "the experts," and the circle closes, unbroken—the circular structure of the novel corroborating the closed circuit of female conditioning—though it will subsequently be shattered by her furious, vengeful poetry and her suicide.

So, too, does the circle close on Tina of Sue Kaufman's *Diary of a Mad Housewife*, who has similarly been "shrunk, thoroughly, and presumably with success" and now claims to be happily adjusted to "the Feminine Role," "playing Passive Female to Jonathan's Dominant Male," spending her days "between the . . . playground, the A&P, and the laundromat" (pp. 30, 40). She and Jonathan join "The New People," "couples, mostly youngish, like us, but about twenty times richer than we are, whose only aim in life seems to be to climb out of the set they're in and make it into the one above" (p. 43). Though Tina is "paralyzed . . . paranoid . . . so depressed I can't talk . . . afraid of most anything you could name" (pp. 4–5), she is sure that her condition has nothing to do with the Feminine Passive Role but with Jonathan's insistence that she grow out of it, that she "leave the seclusion of the lair and re-enter The Great World" (p. 73).

Tina seeks escape in an affair with George Praeger, a cold, narcissistic playwright to whom she is driven by the domestic role that she claims suits her so well: a Thanksgiving with Jonathan home sick and the children home sick, so horrendous that Tina takes the initiative and phones George to arrange a meeting. As she contemplates this man's power over her—"George is the classic Heel, the Sadistic Rake . . . and I . . . the perfect Willing Victim"—she comes to realize that their relationship is not so different from her marriage:

> Why not face the truth? It's an enormous relief to have that sort of thing out in the open and act it out, instead of having to deal with it in a disguised form, all veiled and gussied up with domestic overlay as it is with Jonathan and me. The only

> thing I can't help wondering is how in hell I got to *be* such a goddamn masochist and Willing Victim? Is it the outcome of overdoing the Feminine Passive Role, of overplaying Limp Lady to Jonathan's Forceful Male? If so, I have . . . really been had. (pp. 190–91)

But the reward for this recognition is a "bolt of pain" in the head so acute that she never goes near it again. This novel is fascinating for the way it offers and retracts such insights.

Crisis is precipitated when Tina thinks she has become pregnant by George. Terrified, without money of her own even to pay for an abortion, she realizes that "the very idea of my divorcing Jonathan or of Jonathan divorcing me fills me with terror, puts me on the brink of the abyss. *Why?* . . . Why, when life with Jonathan has been such hell?" Because, she concludes,

> I've finally begun to perceive that the life I've been living is right for me, that I'm in the right niche. That if I divorce Jonathan or Jonathan divorces me, I'll never find the right niche again. (p. 269)

Tina was more honest earlier, when she admitted "that unless I wanted to divorce Jonathan, or have Jonathan divorce me, I had to jump when he said Jump," and since "I went into a tailspin at just the very thought of trying in my current condition, to go it alone . . . I knew I would jump" (p. 110)—but again, this is not an insight she sustains.

When she discovers she is not pregnant and is "free to pick up the pieces and start again. . . . Free to pick up the pieces and start *what* again?" she reinvokes the fantasy of the "lady with the apron":

> I know at last what I'm going to settle for and who I'm going to be. Who? Who is that? Why, . . . The lady with the apron. And check-lists. And keys. It's me. Oh, it's *very* me, and I can't for the life of me see why I didn't realize that before. (pp. 281–82)

"Why" is supposedly because Jonathan has not allowed her to, and Jonathan conveniently cooperates by admitting how awful he's been and confessing to an affair. Tina is about to confess to having an affair as well, but she draws up short: "It was a giant step for me. . . . I decided I would never tell him about George . . . for the first time in my life I was being completely realistic, without any gratuitous masochism thrown in. . . . I knew what I meant to have and be, and I was going to go after it" (pp. 290–91). Though one can perhaps understand Tina's need to lie, there is something screwy about making a virtue of this necessity. But then there has been something screwy all along: Tina *claims* that her problem is the conflict between what Jonathan wants of her and what she wants of herself, while actually admitting that she is so terrified of facing life on her own that she does not know what she wants, and she seems to see no contradiction between these positions.

The novel ends with Tina liberating a cockroach from the kitchen clock after watching it go "round and round":

> I lifted the clock off its hook and shook it and the roach began to run. Obviously not even badly wounded from its bout with the second-hand, it ran crazily round and round the numbers, too frenetic to get out the same way it had got in. . . . Then, with a little jump, it climbed out onto the glass . . . ran down the clock's side and across the counter to the wall, where it vanished down a hole in the plaster between the tiles—damaged but undaunted—home to wifey and the kids. (pp. 292–93)

The insect bolting dazedly for home, is presumably, an image of herself. Thus Tina liberates Tina to be Tina—though one suspects that her retreat, unlike the roach's, will not put an end to her "crazy round."

Margaret Reynolds, protagonist of Anne Richardson Roiphe's *Up the Sandbox,* also suffers the claustrophobia of raising two children in a New York apartment, with a "brick wall behind the kitchen window [which] lets in no light" (p. 9). In her fantasies, however, she refuses to be "shut up in any single life-box with bolted doors" (p. 29). The contradictory impulses which burst out erratically in *Mad Housewife* are expressed here in formal alternations between fantasy and reality, though this novel takes its protagonist to the same end, a dead end similarly reimagined as a creative solution.

In "real life" (in chapters titled "In Week One," "In Week Two," etc.), Margaret has a keen sense of herself as "no romantic heroine or creature of historical importance. I'm just Margaret Reynolds, wife and mother, not yet thirty . . . too old for an identity crisis and yet not past the age of uncertainty" (p. 14). But in her fantasies ("Out of Week One," etc.), she does play "romantic" and "historically important" roles, blowing up bridges, interviewing Castro, voyaging down the Amazon, traveling to Vietnam, having "an extramarital fling" (p. 29):

> I have as much right to be a private, or a cowboy, or a fortune hunter as anybody else. My sex is not as limiting as people . . . thought. . . . I am no man's object. . . . I am able to dabble in life, to taste, experiment and expand myself, test my mettle. (p. 29)

Her fantasies enlist not only feminist rhetoric ("I want the same separateness [as my husband] . . . I want to learn something myself" [p. 57]), but sixties protest rhetoric as she pits herself against "a system I despise" (p. 27). But Margaret does not really "despise" the system: all she wants is a bit of excitement, the excitement of "belonging" (p. 34). Though Roiphe implies that Margaret's fantasies express "another identity, a counter-personality" (p. 27), her "pirates and cowboys" actually reiterate rather than challenge the clichés of the culture.

Margaret analyzes the separation between male and female spheres in terms like de Beauvoir's, though unlike de Beauvoir, she does not contest this division. While Margaret's husband Paul "sits in the library, in his classroom, and . . . tries to find some . . . design that will . . . in adding to our knowledge, add to our redemption," "I repeat each day the sameness of everything" (pp. 45–46). But though she is pained by the "terrible inequality of love"—that he is ab-

sorbed in his work whereas "I would put anything down to go for a short walk
with him. . . . I am so reduced" (p. 12)—she is grateful that he consents to
remain married to her: "I am so ordinary a person, and since the children have
arrived I am even more ordinary. Where once I read poems of Baudelaire . . .
now all I do is read Benjamin Spock" (p. 82). She is comforted that "the children
make for [her] a universe with a design and a rhythm and a function" (p. 12):

> My life is not my own any more, it belongs in part to [my daughter]. . . . She
> must be the better part of me. She must be the more beautiful, the more graceful,
> the more loving part of me. I am in and of myself no longer complete. I need her.
> (p. 51)

She is consoled by repetition and continuity—"eat, eliminate, prepare food,
clean up, shop, throw out the garbage"; "my life hardly differs from that of an
Indian squaw settled in a tepee on the same Manhattan land centuries ago . . .
she was my sister" (p. 18). Margaret loves "the oval playground . . . its simple
way of giving me somewhere to go, something to do. . . . I am doing what every
peasant woman has always done. I am nurturing" (p. 45). She does not even
mind "the biological tie" that has "destined" her to become her mother: though
she once hoped "to be as unlike her as possible . . . I find that I am feeding and
caring, just like her" (p. 84).

But this novel does something slightly more interesting, in opposing what
Sara Ruddick terms "maternal thinking"[31] to the sterility of male theorizing
and affirming the superiority of "woman's knowledge." Margaret's husband
may go off each day to the library in search of new knowledge, but what he
comes home with is an appalling theory of psychohistory that posits a repetition bleaker than anything in Margaret's experience, a theory of generational
conflict in which "fathers are trying to kill their sons . . . and that's why we have
war each generation" (p. 82). Against this, Margaret pits her faith:

> I'm certain that, despite his historical evidence, revolutions must take place and
> one day one of them will be led by a real hero who will neither sell out his cause
> nor find himself knifed in the back. Some day there will be a revolution with
> genuine heroes and the way of life for that country will change. (p. 104)

But though the female sphere in this novel provides an oppositional space, it
is finally conceived of in conventional terms, since motherhood is the only
action Margaret can imagine, "the only arena to really test [her] mettle . . . to
give [her] a self" (p. 152):

> After all, I can't build a bridge across a jungle and plant a city. I can't make
> statues . . . or paintings. . . . I can't start a factory or discover a new element. . . .
> I can't equate the universe in a new mathematical relationship. . . . But I can
> make another human being. (p. 135)

Though she qualifies this, asking, "What else can I do? . . . I must believe
evolution is not complete" (pp. 153–54), Roiphe's conception of woman's

knowledge is entirely conventional. Margaret insists that she has chosen her situation: "In America, of course, any mobility is theoretically possible. . . . I could have been anyone, a Playboy bunny, an industrialist's diamond-studded wife. . . . The fact that I am what I am is by my own choosing, and remains so for the rest of my life, since radical options continue to be open. What a dreadful responsibility" (p. 99). But what dreadful "options," so banal that one questions the "choice" involved.

The last chapter, in which Margaret tells her husband she is pregnant again, though titled "Out of Week Six," takes place in "reality" rather than in fantasy like the other "out of" the week chapters, which suggests that fantasy is no longer necessary as she embarks on the great adventure of motherhood. Paul is "very proud of his extraordinary fertility. We are, he says, a social unit, the two of us, our children. We are part of history. . . . We are doing what the Neanderthals, the Indians, the Babylonians and the Assyrians, etc., have all done" (p. 155)—though considering his view of history, this is hardly reassuring. Roiphe implies that pregnancy resolves the tension between Margaret's aspirations to significant action and her confinement in domesticity, but since she has not actually demonstrated that such tension exists, the narrative device falls flat. In *Up the Sandbox,* feminist rhetoric is enlisted to reinforce the old boundaries: feminist aspirations are childish stuff, and to "grow up" is to step back within bounds.

Stacey of Margaret Laurence's *The Fire-Dwellers* also ends resigned to her situation, though her resignation is more convincing—she is not rationalizing her way to another child, but accepting, at age forty, the three children she has, as well as the aged father-in-law who moves in at the end. Readers of *A Jest of God,* the preceding novel in the Manawaka series, or those who have seen its film version *Rachel, Rachel,* have encountered Stacey Cameron, protagonist of *The Fire-Dwellers,* as a fantasy in her sister Rachel's consciousness—as the one who got away, who escaped their mother and Manawaka to make a new life in the big city, Vancouver. What a disappointment to meet Stacey here as a dumpy, unhappy housewife who is as trapped as her sister Rachel, but in a misery more perplexing because it seems to be of her own making: "Whose fault? Okay mine" (p. 64). A dream she has of herself stumbling through a wilderness— *"She has to continue, bringing what she is carrying with her. . . . The head she has been carrying is of course none but hers"* (p. 109)—expresses her sense of her truncated, encumbered life.

Stacey is so cut off from the world that she knows nothing about her city or the people in it: "nearly twenty years here, and I don't know the place at all or feel at home" (p. 5); "by the time the day ends, I'm too beat to seek rich cultural experiences, whatever that may mean" (p. 64). One of her failed efforts at "cultural experience" is symbolized by the unread copy of *The Golden Bough* on her night table, left over from an unsatisfactory night course, "Mythology and Modern Man." But though she is alienated from the world, she is bombarded by it—by advertising that promises magical transformations and miraculous rebirths (p. 74), by radio and television messages, alarming and invasive, that intensify her isolation and confusion: "I'm surrounded by voices all the time but none of them seem to be saying anything, including mine" (p. 71). She is the victim of what Rosalind Coward calls "discursive bombard-ment," which teaches women to consume while "limit[ing] communication . . . [and] keep[ing] people apart."[32] The news bulletins transmitted through the EVER OPEN EYE blare messages of murder, arson, suicide, violence, war, doom—"*Doom everywhere*" (p. 52). The screen is lit by Vietnamese villages in flames; "EVER-OPEN EYE   STREETS IN CITIES NOT SO FAR AWAY ARE BURNING   BURNING IN RAGE AND SORROW" (p. 274). Stacey is haunted by visions of her own house in flames and by the ominous "Ladybird, ladybird, / Fly away home; / Your house is on fire, / Your children are gone" (p. 1). These horrific images provide a correlative rather than a contrast to her life, for Stacey knows that violence is everywhere.

Stacey's world is a cacaphony of voices, internal and external. Third-person pronoun alternates with first-person, and the topography of consciousness is indicated typographically: thoughts are introduced by a dash; daydreams and dreams are set in italics; memories are indented; and counterpointed with these are external voices—radio, television, and conversation, reported without quotation marks and often without final punctuation. But for all this noise, Stacey is in an isolation so deep that those who are closest to her are unreach-able: "If I could only talk about it. But who wants to know, and anyway, could I say?" (p. 14) She fantasizes a utopia where people talk to one another ("*out there in unknown houses are people who live without lies, and who touch each other*" [p. 79]) and wonders "what would happen if just for once" she wrote the truth to her mother: "Please write immediately and let me know what was actually in your mind all those years because I haven't a clue" (pp. 132–33). She finds intimacy, briefly, in an affair with a younger man (a science-fiction writer) who has not yet closed off, and imagines running off with him, shedding "baggage" (p. 211), "start[ing] again. . . . No lies. No recriminations. No un-merry-go-round of pointless words" (p. 184). But when he offers to take her away, she realizes "where she belongs" (p. 249).

The novel concludes with Stacey resigned that there will be no magical rebirth for her or for Mac: "Now I see that whatever I am like, I'm pretty well stuck with it for life. Hell of a revelation that turned out to be" (p. 268). But this is not as bleak as it sounds, for she has had a dream that imaginatively transforms her "prison" to an "island": "*This place is a prison but not totally so. It must be an island, surely, some place where people are free to walk around but nobody can get away . . . there is nowhere to go but here*" (p. 232). Stacey achieves "freedom" within boundaries, but this is not the "competence in non-competence" that comes from mastering the rules of a demeaning game or an idiot celebration of her "niche"; it is, rather, an acceptance of responsibility for the life she has made. Besides, though she is resigned to her isolation, she generalizes her situation in a way that enables her to feel connection with the world: "I was wrong to think of the trap as the four walls. It's the world" (p. 272). She learns to respect her family's silences—"all I can do is accept that it is a language, and that it works, at least sometimes" (p. 266)—and as though in reward for this, she hears her two-year-old daughter utter her first sentence (p. 269). When at the end, as at the beginning, we move around the bedroom noting the unread *Golden Bough* on the night table, final pages reiterate first pages in a closing of a circle. But this circular movement provides a measure of change: whereas at the beginning Stacey despised the "trivialities" (p. 83), now "maybe the trivialities aren't so bad after all" (p. 276)—though she (like Roiphe's Margaret) puts her hope in evolution: "Give me another forty years, Lord, and I may mutate into a matriarch" (p. 277).

Fay Weldon's *The Fat Woman's Joke* similarly consigns its protagonist to the domestic situation from which she began, but this resignation is more disturbing since Weldon has so forcefully demonstrated all the reasons Esther should leave. *The Fat Woman's Joke* offers brilliant analysis of sexual politics and especially shrewd commentary on the relation of food to sex. Esther and Alan Wells's marriage comes apart because they go on a diet. Their lives are so involved with food—its planning, buying, cooking, fixing, serving, eating—that dieting unhinges them, catapulting Alan, precariously lightened, into fantasies of becoming a great writer and an affair with his secretary, Susan. Esther takes herself off to a basement flat where she eats, deliberately, defiantly, and excessively. Gaining weight is her means of resistance, for she discovers that, in rejecting marriage, she has challenged "the whole structure of society" (p. 158). When her friend Phyllis comes to her, seeking explanations, Esther does her best to explain, though she cautions that this is not a pleasant tale and "there has never been a tale quite like this before" (p. 16).

And indeed, there never has been a tale quite like this, with its blend of hilarity, bite, and pronouncements of doom—" 'You are right to feel afraid' "; " 'Because you are growing old. Because you have a vision of loneliness . . . the glue factory . . . we are all alone' " (pp. 13–14). Weldon's humor—like that of Iris Murdoch, Muriel Spark, and Beryl Bainbridge—is tinged with the grotesque; but *The Fat Woman's Joke* is unique in its combination of black humor with feminist satire, its analysis of the double standard, of the conditions that drive women to marriage, and of marriage itself. " 'It is a fearful thing to be a woman in a man's world. . . . It would perfectly acceptable being a woman if only men didn't control the world' " (p. 137), Esther tells Phyllis. " 'Nothing changes. Women want to get married and have babies just as they always did,' " which is why " 'they get away with everything, men' " (p. 133): " 'there's one law for husbands and another for wives' " because " 'wives need husbands more than husbands need wives . . . such is the structure of our society' " (p. 97). As Esther tells Alan, "femininity" is defined by men to suit men: " 'Men are always accusing women of being unfeminine, and at the same time making sure that the feminine state is as unendurable as possible' " (pp. 97–98). When he retorts, " 'quite the suffragette,' " she points out, " 'and that is still the worst term of abuse a man can think of to say to his wife' " (p. 98).

Esther reverses the usual view that marriage offers women security and happiness, observing, with appalling clarity, " 'Men don't make women happy.

Men make women unhappy' " (p. 102). Marriage is " 'a con trick' " (p. 77), destructive to both sexes but especially to women: " 'Wives are a miserable lot. I shall never be a wife again' " (p. 101). Esther defines woman's work as "bother" (p. 18) and housekeeping as aggression: " 'To spend my life waging war against Alan, which was what my housewifeliness amounted to, endeavouring to prove a female competence which was the last thing he wanted or needed to know about—what a waste of time!' " (p. 74). Her final pronouncement on their marriage is that it was " 'a battle which we should never have embarked upon' " (p. 174) and which neither can win (p. 188).

Weldon is scathing on the role of romantic fantasy in both male and female self-delusion. Esther is right; in Alan there "lurks" "a rich fantasy life," fantasies Susan feeds in order to flatter her image of herself as capable of transforming him into something other than a middle-aged, sold-out ad man: " 'I want to save you. I want to rescue you' " (p. 154). Susan needs to play a romantic role because, as she says, it makes her feel " 'truly alive' " (pp. 80–81): " 'If I didn't have boyfriends, I don't think I would exist' " (p. 88).

Esther is very persuasive. Her defiance of conventional boundaries is heroic compared with the purging and hacking which her friend Phyllis resorts to. Esther demonstrates that Phyllis's "femininity" is more grotesque than Esther's obesity:

> I suppose you really do believe that your happiness is consequent upon your size? That an inch or two one way or the other would make you truly loved? Equating prettiness with sexuality, and sexuality with happiness? It is a very debased view of femininity. . . . It would be excusable in a sixteen year old. . . . But in a woman of your age it is vulgar. (p. 11)

"Femininity" has deformed Phyllis physically and emotionally: she has surgically altered the shape of her body, she is frigid, and her desire to consume her husband makes Esther's straightforward gluttony seem wholesome: " 'At least I just eat food. You'd eat him, if you could' " (p. 109). Esther argues that obesity leaves her "free" (p. 11): " 'I live by myself. Just me. Self-sufficient. . . . I live with the truth' " (p. 34); " 'I can control everything, and I can eat. I like eating' " (pp. 10–11). All that is required of her is occasional trips to the store for more books and more food: " 'Food. Drink. Sleep. Books. They are all drugs. None are as effective as sex, but they are calmer and safer' " (p. 14). But for all her wit and energy, she is persuaded by her husband to return home in the end, since " 'It doesn't seem to make much difference where one is' " (p. 188).

Weldon's "fat woman" and Atwood's "edible woman" are the only protagonists of these novels who do not seek professional help but administer self-therapy through the body. Though the characters in *The Edible Woman* are younger, still facing the decisions that will determine what they will "turn into," they are discovering that the work available to them grinds them into a system of "production-consumption" that—as Duncan, Marian's "second suitor," says—"makes one kind of garbage into another kind" (p. 147). The company

Marian works for, Seymour Surveys, teaches people to "consume," and is, as she suspects, immoral and exploitative: playing on anxieties, it creates needs which it then offers to fill by "consumption," promising magical transformations in exchange for purchasing. But the real transformation Seymour Surveys accomplishes is to turn people to things, and Atwood depicts this transformation brilliantly, suggesting that Marian's co-workers, the "Office Virgins" (who represent what Marian will "turn into" if she stays at Seymour Surveys), are metamorphosing into metal.[33] Like Plath, but more like Dickens, Atwood renders the thingification of people and animation of things—what Dorothy Van Ghent terms a "principle of reciprocal changes between the human and the nonhuman."[34]

An even less reflective protagonist than Esther, Marian drifts into engagement with Peter, a conventional ad man, and then into involvement with Duncan, an offbeat graduate student. With her engagement, the narrative shifts from "I" to "she"—appropriately, since in making herself "an object destined for another" (in de Beauvoir's term; p. 360), Marian makes herself the object of another's discourse. But as though in protest against this objectification, her body cuts itself off from food, at first rejecting only things "that had once been, or might still be living" (p. 183), but then extending its concept of "living" to carrots, cake, and the mold growing in her sink and refrigerator. As Marian goes dead with the effort of repression, her imagination brings the environment alive: telephone wires are like snakes (p. 138), the city coagulates with traffic (p. 103), the toilet paper crouches sympathetically in the ladies' room, "helpless and white and furry" (p. 71)—a confusion of animate and inanimate that threatens her already tenuous sense of self and intensifies her terror of dissolution. Turning to Peter as escape from Seymour Surveys, she has exchanged one trap for another, for her objectification as Peter's fiancée has the same effects as her objectification in a world of alienated work; both threaten her with annihilation.[35] So, too, does the Toronto summer, which "condenses around her like a plastic bag" (p. 12), the air like soup (p. 16), like "a layer of moist dough" (p. 37)—images that combine a claustrophobia like Esther's with an additional terror of being eaten.

The one counter to these processes is Duncan, who is in every way Peter's antithesis: if Peter is a stereotype, Duncan is a shape-shifter; if Peter confines Marian to a stereotype, Duncan leaves her free, mainly ignoring her. As a graduate student, he is from another world, though it is not really a different world, for Atwood presents the academic world as participating in the same futile process of production-consumption—"publish or perish" (p. 202)—that reduces people to mechanisms: Duncan himself is thingified, his skin turned to "tissue paper or parchment" from slaving "in the paper-mines" (pp. 103, 100). Marian tries to get him to rescue her from Peter while pretending to be rescuing him, and when Duncan assures her that he does not wish to be rescued or to rescue (p. 254), she bolts back to Peter—at which point her body "cuts itself off" from all foods (p. 264). Her response is to bake a cake in the shape of a lady which she offers to Peter as a "substitute" for herself, a sacrifice which can undergo the fate she thereby escapes: "You look delicious. . . . Very appetizing. And that's what will happen to you; that's what you get for being food" (pp. 277–78). When Peter flees, she eats the cake herself.

Atwood's extended though implicit wordplay on "consumption" illuminates the symbolism of the cake lady and expresses a vision of human relations in capitalism. "Consuming" refers both to the ingesting and digesting of food—as in the "body's consumption" (p. 200)—and to the purchase and use of commodities, in which Marian is implicated both by being a young woman on "the market" (p. 244) and by her work as a market researcher: it refers both to physiological and to economic processes. Food metaphors are everywhere, as though the novel were written by a starving person who can think of nothing but food—which is what Marian becomes when her body stops consuming. The two meanings of "consume" are suggested by Duncan's wordplay on "system," when he explains Marian's refusal to eat: " 'You're probably representative of modern youth, rebelling against the system; though it isn't considered orthodox to begin with the digestive system' " (p. 197). Atwood's analogy between the digestive and the socioeconomic "systems"—"machines and mouths" (p. 10)—suggests that a "consumer society" makes us consumers not only of goods but of one another, forcing us into roles of predator or prey. This novel renders the relation of individual to collective lyrically, imagistically, wittily, in an original blend of black humor and Marxist-feminist critique.

As a symbol of Marian's control over processes which have been controlling her, baking and eating the cake lady is enormously effective. It also has therapeutic value, for in the final section, she returns to the first-person pronoun, cleans house, becomes sufficiently interested in herself to be bored by Duncan's self-absorption, and begins eating again. Her cake lady is a way of saying "no" to a system that would commodify her. It is a refusal of her part in the marriage plot and her role as consumable—as "sugar," "sugar and spice," "sugar pie," "honey," "honey-pie," "pumpkin," "sweetie," "sweetheart," "dish," "tomato," or "tart." Though this defiance puts her ahead of most other protagonists of this fiction, it remains metaphorical: it is not clear how it will translate to action, what she will do next, what she will "turn into." Besides, as Duncan points out, the return to "reality" makes her "a consumer" again (pp. 286–87)—his comment fusing the physiological and socioeconomic meanings of the word, making the implicit pun explicit—and in becoming a consumer Marian resumes her place in the system that threatens her life. She has evolved, in the terms of the novel, from prey to predator. Atwood's next novel, *Surfacing*, concludes with the statement "There ought to be other choices," but in neither this novel nor in *Surfacing* are there other choices:[36] or if there are, they are *in potentia* and *in utero*, in the unborn child that the *Surfacing* protagonist may be carrying—in evolution again. The protagonist of *The Edible Woman*—like the protagonists of *Surfacing*, *Lady Oracle*, *Bodily Harm*, and *Life Before Man*—ends poised on the edge of an unimaginable future.

The protagonist of Alix Kates Shulman's *Memoirs of an Ex-Prom Queen* enjoys more freedom of movement than do most women in this fiction, yet she also ends up going in circles. Sasha resolves "to take matters into [her] own hands" (p. 79), to "be somebody" "because, of course, somebody could get a much better husband than nobody" (p. 80). But bouncing from boy to boy, then from man to man, she seeks identity in all the wrong places: "In fact, from the eighth grade on, no matter how I talked up freedom," "I always had "at least one man to count on, and frequently two"; "in high school they called it 'boy crazy'; in college . . . 'oversexed.' To me it was life insurance" (pp. 14–15).

In the course of the novel she marries Frank, leaves Frank for Willy, and then, at the end, is about to leave Willy. The novel begins with Sasha "about to cut free of" Frank, after which, episodes set in the present alternate with episodes set in the past, as we follow her back through childhood, adolescence, and through the marriage she is trying to terminate. But Shulman does not make this structure function as a therapeutic return to the past, for Sasha is as unreflective as Plath's Esther and considerably more dependent. Depending on her husband for his view of her as beautiful ("that was his insidious power over me"), she is, midway through the novel, on a boat returning from Europe, returning to Frank, "like a junkie getting a fix" (p. 15): "the concentric circles were shrinking. My future was doubling back on itself" (p. 209); "with no one on board to save me. . . . End of journey. Unless . . ." (p. 210).

Rescue appears in the form of another man, but even with Willy in the wings Sasha clings to her marriage because she is afraid of growing old, sick, or fat; and "with Frank, whatever happens to me, he'll just have to take care of me" (p. 221). When she finally does leave, she phones her best friend, Roxanne, who has blazed the trail by writing her way out of her marriage, and who advises, " 'all it takes is freedom, determination, and very hard work' " (p. 171). But Sasha chooses, rather, a second marriage:

> Willy expected it, poets encouraged it, it was part of the package. And as a job, motherhood seemed to offer more possibilities of advancement than the Clayton Advertising Agency's research library. (p. 247)

Motherhood, however, is an experience for which nothing has prepared her, requiring self-discipline beyond her farthest imaginings: "not one word" from "the learned professors" about

> what the tiniest baby will do to the woman. Stretching her belly and waist into the ghastliest shapes . . . ruining her breasts . . . and that only the beginning. In time comes the ugly crease in the brow between the eyes . . . the rasp in the voice, the knot in the gut, the regret. (pp. 277–78)

As Sasha becomes more involved with her children, her husband withdraws, and she responds by making a desperate attempt, at the beauty parlor, to resurrect her prom-queen image, for which she is rewarded by the revelation that "the whole process was out of control" (pp. 284–85): "To find myself at thirty locked under a dryer . . . without income or skill, dependent on a man and a fading skin—it can only be the fulfillment of a curse!" (p. 285)[37] When

Willy is enraged at her new haircut, Sasha reaches for the phone to call Roxanne. That this reiterates the action with which she terminated her first marriage suggests that she is about to end this one, too, and this exit looks back to the middle of the novel as the middle looked back to the beginning; but it is not clear what it looks forward to, since Sasha's development has been so inexorable a "shrinking" (p. 209), a closing of the circle.

*Memoirs of an Ex-Prom Queen* offers the same disturbing vacillation between insight and denial encountered elsewhere in this fiction. It is full of wonderfully witty bits, but it also bogs down in vast wastes of sexual escapades unredeemed by irony or analysis: Sasha's first gropings in high school, travels in Spain (pp. 32ff), adventures as a waitress (pp. 88ff), adventures with an Italian lover (pp. 129ff). At one point Sasha falls in love with philosophy (p. 137), which has the advantage of taking her mind off her appearance ("for the only time in my life, I didn't care how I looked" [p. 146]) but the disadvantage of embroiling her in an affair with her married philosophy professor; and for a time during her first marriage she sleeps with men for money (pp. 197ff). But there seems to be no connection between the woman who turns tricks and the woman with a passion for philosophy and the responsible mother who contemplates the culture's failures toward motherhood. Not that such shifts are unimaginable, but they do require some acknowledgment or comment; Shulman's narrative voice seems simply confused.

## Extending the Boundaries

Sheila Ballantyne's *Norma Jean the Termite Queen* (1975) is the best of these works, not only in its protagonist's determination to change and her understanding of what change requires—and this in spite of the fact that she stays in her marriage—but also in Ballantyne's forging of new forms to accommodate change.

At the outset, Norma Jean feels reduced to a "termite queen," "a giant receptacle, an endless repository" for the needs of others (p. 210), and is in the grip of "a rage so inarticulate that even to attempt to describe it is to court accusations of insanity" (p. 39). Her response is to reach "back in time" to retrieve "some original self which lay buried, deep as any pharaoh" (p. 24), as, recalling her "sense of purpose during the years spent in the college library" (p. 18), she turns to her undergraduate interests—in Egypt and ceramics. She is fascinated by Egypt because she thinks it is a matriarchy—"It meant anything was possible, even for me" (p. 25)—and is especially drawn to the God Osiris, "he who giveth birth to men and women a second time" (pp. 39–40), sensing her own need for a second chance. The ceramics she makes puzzle her for their resemblance to Egyptian canopic jars until she realizes that they are "a beginning," "the way the Egyptians regarded death as a beginning" (p. 42).

But when she tries to explain this to her husband, Martin—" 'I always dreamed of doing something in the world; I certainly never dreamed of just keeping house' "—he tries to push her back within boundaries, calling her "abnormal," "unnatural," "unfeminine," "crazy" (pp. 164–68), enforcing the old choice between work and love (p. 191). She tries to make him understand, " 'Your work didn't preclude your having the gratification of a family. Why are you asking *me* to make that choice?' " to which he replies: " 'Why did you have a family if you wanted to be an artist?' "[38] This argument ends with her shouting, " 'people change! Their times change, and their own needs change' " (p. 163); and the novel is about change—changing people, changing times, extending existing boundaries to make "something new" (p. 98).

Norma Jean's main ally in this struggle is her reading. She reads voraciously, seeking connections. As in *The Fire-Dwellers,* quotes from the protagonist's readings are woven into the narrative fabric, and the narrative moves back and forth between first- and third-person pronouns in a polyphony of voices, internal and external. Headlines and stories are quoted from the newspaper, which Norma Jean "mainlines" (p. 28) each morning as she sits at the kitchen window, and besides these there are passages from *The Horizon Book of Lost Worlds, The Lost Pharaohs, The Pyramids of Egypt, Osiris and the Egyptian Resurrection, Religion and Thought in Ancient Egypt,* interspersed with quotes from Alvin Toffler's *Future Shock,* Philip Slater's *The Pursuit of Loneliness,* and Ferdinand Lundberg and Marynia Farnham's *Modern Woman, The Lost Sex.*

The newspaper especially is Norma Jean's " 'window' to the outside world, it not only informs and alerts, it reactivates feelings connected with that world" (p. 5); she pores through it every morning, taking it "seriously" as "a reflection of the time and place in which we live" (pp. 4, 29). What it "reflects" by way of social and natural disasters is more alarming than the media's messages in Laurence's 1969 *Fire-Dwellers*—"the end of civilization" (pp. 147–48); "MAN MAY VANISH SOON"; "PENTAGON PLANS LASER 'DEATH RAY' . . . MORE BOMBS FOR VICTORY" (p. 28). It tells of more violence within families: "MOTHER LOCKS IN KIDS, BURNS HOME . . . . QUIET MOTHER MURDERS HER FAMILY" (pp. 28–29); "YOUTH, 15, ADMITS SLAYING MOTHER" (p. 102), "BATTERED CHILD SYNDROME ON IN-CREASE" (p. 104). Like Stacey, Norma Jean scrutinizes these stories with a sense of their relevance to her life, but she has a clearer perspective on them which she has gleaned from her reading.

Reading Slater, Norma Jean understands her isolation as related to " 'the flight into the home [which] was . . . part of a general post-war retreat from the world' " (pp. 113–14). She "did what most of her friends did: worked a few years, married, and had children," "choices" she finds described as " 'the natural route taken by women in the fifties who wanted to achieve and preserve the identity required of them by their culture' " (p. 19). She knows that she is living through a period of rapid and bewildering change when "the old values are breaking down" (p. 255), that her neighborhood is "a place in time marked by a high rate of social mobility and resistance to definition," and analyzes its customs with the eye of an anthropologist (p. 3). She ponders the loss of community and laments "the quickness with which families dissolve, friends scatter" (pp. 102–103); "there were interconnections between people, whole networks of links and roots, . . . now, what's there to hold you?" (p. 186).

She also has a sense, corroborated by Toffler, that change is accelerating (pp. 228, 268) but that people's needs are "the same or greater in the face of all this change" (p. 235). She understands that change puts pressure on the family and particularly on the woman—which Martin himself demonstrates when he insists, " 'If you're not *there* at mealtimes, it's like the children and I are just . . . floating around. There's no center' " (p. 109). But without the supports of community, neighborhood, or extended family, each nuclear unit has to fend for itself: "It is up to just the two of us to make this family run. We must bring unimagined efforts to bear on the task. It requires everything we have." This fosters unwholesome relationships: "You're all shut in there together. . . . Under such conditions, it's only natural to absorb one another; what else have you got to eat?" (p. 254)

Norma Jean has also "read the feminists," and as her arguments reveal, she has assimilated them as well. She quotes Shulamith Firestone: " 'Women are the slave class that maintains the species in order to free the other half for the business of the world" (p. 107). Trying to explain her frustration to Martin, she draws on de Beauvoir:

> by some invisible arrangement, on reaching adulthood . . . the woman moves abruptly backwards, assumes the management of a home itself, occupies its center as her mother before her, *becomes* that mother . . . revokes whatever goals for achievement and involvement she may have entertained, and whatever freedom she may previously have enjoyed. The man's life, by contrast, continues . . . the outwardly moving pursuit of freedom. (pp. 109–10)

Whereas his profession, teaching, allows Martin to participate in the creation of "something totally new" (p. 193), raising a family dooms Norma Jean to repetition: "Eat eat eat, in and out, in and out. What good does it do anyone? You can't read it, you can't exhibit it, it does not endure" (p. 82).

The easiest way to change is to have an affair or get a divorce, and Norma Jean sees this happening all around and fantasizes doing it herself. But she does not leave, nor does she stay in the marriage as it was, in Martin's idea of it; freeway survival skills have taught her *"You can't go back"* (p. 177). Rather, she stays and makes changes in the marriage. It is her work that gives her inspiration and example to do this, and as her ceramics push "beyond established limits" (p. 176), one larger "Piece" emerges which "is nothing like anything that has ever been before" (p. 105). Norma Jean addresses it: "By declaring new boundaries for yourself, you have extended mine. You . . . have convinced me . . . That people are not fixed; our possibilities are fluid and infinite" (p. 160); and it addresses her, *"Go ahead; you are free"* (p. 202).

But "freedom" is this novel is not in cutting loose from others: it is, rather, in relationships. Ballantyne brilliantly renders the "shifts" and "currents" as Norma Jean and Martin battle each other, jockeying for position and territory, engaging in border skirmishes which escalate to full-scale war over such issues as who will make breakfast or "WHO WILL SEW THE HOLE" in their son's bathing suit (p. 241). Initially these end in stalemate: " 'I want my wife back,' he demands indignantly"; " 'I want my life back,' she . . . whispers" (p. 111). Signs of victory occur when Martin shows evidence of change—a "victory" "shared equally. . . . There are no losers" (p. 243): when Martin begins to assume some responsibility for the children, Norma Jean can begin to enjoy them and see that they, too, are her creations and have changed her "absolutely and forever. . . . My little Pieces, that I should also be your product alters everything. . . . I think I am grateful" (p. 233). From motherhood she learns that change is a reciprocal process involving others, and from ceramics she learns the art of balance and control: "you have to extend the boundaries outward at the same time being careful not to lose your grip on the center. It requires both hands" (p. 125). The novel ends with Norma Jean's decision to apply to graduate school and to have an exhibition of her artwork.

Norma Jean forges connections and understands connections, not only with her family but with the world beyond her four walls, finding "a link between myself and the things I see" (p. 272). She has a vision of unity with the universe, which she imagines communicating to her children: "Listen. There is something you must know. Your lives are connected to [the ocean] in mysterious ways. In your veins are swimming all the fish of the sea; under your luminous bones the green underwater moves, precise, cool, forever in love" (pp. 144–45). She imagines a time when human life was aligned with the tides and seasons, when "a cycle as fundamental as women's" brought man "into harmony," "regulated him" (p. 237). Understanding her life as related to cosmic processes fills her with hope, for "if the universe can expand, so can I" (p. 267).

Though Norma Jean does not mention reading feminist fiction, one bets that Ballantyne has. Published a few years later than the other novels considered in this chapter, *Norma Jean* is filled with intertextual resonances.[39] Like *The Golden Notebook* in a comic vein, this novel relates its protagonist's "crack-up" to a society in the grip of bewildering and accelerating change, dramatizing the relation of individual to social and historical forces. Like *The Bell Jar,* which concludes with "a ritual for being born twice," this novel concludes with Norma Jean's fantasizing a ritual of rebirth for herself, about to receive a benediction from the god Osiris:

> Awaken, O sick one, thou who has slept . . .
> He whose head was restored to him
> After it had been cut off;
> Never again shall thine head be taken from thee
> In the future never again for all eternity
>     shall thine head be taken from thee.
>         Christine Desroches-Noblecourt, op cit, p. 274 (p. 278)

But whereas Esther's "rebirth" consisted of being "patched" and "retreaded" by the experts, Norma Jean does her rebirth originally and effectively—so effectively that she earns even, a restoration of the severed head. Whereas Maria in

Didion's *Play It As It Lays* (1970) drives the freeways in a self-destructive drift, Norma Jean drives to master skills of survival. Whereas Norma Jean Baker killed herself in 1962, that watershed year in feminism, this Norma Jean lives on and assumes new forms. As Norma Jean gives birth to a new "Piece" and new pieces, she fulfills the hope of evolution expressed by Roiphe's Margaret and Laurence's Stacey: rather than adjusting to the available forms, she breaks through to "something unique" (p. 277), reconciling the claims of biological and artistic creation, of family and career, and making her "madness" the source of new vision and strength.

## The Limits of Realism

In an essay written in 1972, "Humanbecoming: Form and Focus in the Neo-Feminist Novel," Ellen Morgan describes woman's story "in this period of transition" as "the story of an education, of a coming to consciousness . . . of rebellion and resolution."[40] As Morgan suggests, at a time when "the future is uncertain and largely unimaginable," women's stories are likely to express the "doubt, uncertainty, and inconclusiveness which are the experience of many women" (p. 185). These novels express that doubt and uncertainty, but they do not dramatize much rebellion or coming to consciousness. Lest I sound too harsh on them, though, I should add that most of them are well worth reading (or rereading); and if their wit is sometimes a dodge, a deflection or a denial of pain, they are nonetheless lively and entertaining. My disappointment is that they do not push hard enough against the forms to accomplish the release that their protagonists so obviously seek.

Several conclude with protagonists resigned to situations from which they can imagine no exit, though there is a world of difference between the despair of *The Pumpkin Eater* and *The Fat Woman's Joke,* the yea-saying of *Mad House-wife* and *Up the Sandbox,* and the seasoned acceptance of *Fire-Dwellers.* Several—*Ex-Prom Queen, Edible Woman, Ella Price's Journal, Loose Ends*—gesture toward unimaginable futures. The most interesting—*The Fire-Dwellers, The Edible Woman, Norma Jean*—use divided voices to express divided selves and, paradoxically, those which most fully understand the divisions are those which most convincingly render the connections, portraying consciousness enmeshed within a collective which is given over to consumption and violence and in the grip of convulsive change. Only in Ballantyne's novel, a kind of "tactile/sculptural *Kunstlerroman,*"[41] are the narrative innovations a part of the protagonist's breakthroughs.

It may be that—contrary to what George Lukács argues—"the novel of social realism and the novel of social change . . . are contradictions in terms" (as Susan Kress suggests);[42] that "it is next to impossible for a realistic novel to be written which defies the sex-role system, for society everywhere upholds this system, and social realities are staples of the realistic novel)" (as Ellen Morgan asserts [pp. 189–90]). Certainly the feminist writers who were turning to science fiction in this period did so from a sense of the constraints of realism.[43] The feminist metafictions that are the subject of Part II endow their protagonists with critical and creative powers that enable them to probe the limits of realism—to break the circle of mimetic representation—and write their ways through to "something new." Before turning to these, however, I'll look at two novels that tailor the formula of feminist metafiction to the popular market: *Fear of Flying* and *The Odd Woman*.

# IV

## "OLD STORIES"
### ERICA JONG'S *FEAR OF FLYING*
### AND
### GAIL GODWIN'S *THE ODD WOMAN*

> A stiff prick, Freud said, assuming that *their* obsession was *our* obsession.
>
> *Fear of Flying*[1]

> Yes, that is the story we still love most. . . . How some woman went to work and got her man. Even "emancipated women". . . love to hear the old, old story one more time.
>
> *The Odd Woman*[2]

*Fear of Flying* (1973) and *The Odd Woman* (1974) express a next stage of women's liberation in that the obstacles confronted by their protagonists are less material and external: rather than being confined by early marriage and children, they face subtler, less tangible pressures—psychological, emotional, sexual. Both Isadora Wing and Jane Clifford have attempted to be "free." Jane describes "her goal . . . to become her own woman" which she followed "to its end" (p. 149), but now she cannot see "what use, what joyful use, she could possibly make of this freedom" (p. 149). Isadora wonders why, if we were "free women,"

> did our lives seem to come down to a long succession of sad songs about men? Why did our lives seem to reduce themselves to manhunts? Where were the women who were *really* free, who didn't spend their lives bouncing from man to man, who felt complete with or without a man? (p. 100)

The term "free women" recurs in *Fear of Flying,* "a phrase which means nothing without quotes" (p. 110) both because it alludes to *The Golden Note-*

*book,* Jong's intertext in *Fear of Flying,* and because it rings as ironically in 1973 as it did in 1962.

Both novels follow the formula of feminist metafiction. In their search for freedom from the past, protagonists turn to the past—to women in fiction and in the family—and try to make new plots and endings of their own. In both novels, the protagonist sets out in search of romance, and in both, the "search for the impossible man" (FF, p. 101), for a love "that exists in a permanent, eternal way" (OW, p. 286), turns into a search for the self. Both try to depict women who change, and their failures are instructive.

## "Round in Circles"

Accustomed as I am to having to defend my interest in *Fear of Flying,* I'll state at the outset why I find it important. Sexual liberation was an essential part of the early women's movement, and *Fear of Flying* has been taken seriously, if not as "literature," as an expression of sexual liberation—most recently, by Susan Suleiman, who describes it as "a significant gesture, both in terms of sexual politics and in terms of . . . sexual poetics," praises its "freshness and vitality" of language, and calls it a "fictional counterpart" to such books as *Our Bodies, Our Selves* (1973) and Shere Hite's *Sexual Honesty, By Women for Women* (1974), which similarly reclaim female bodies and sexuality for females.[3] I confess to having liked the novel when it first appeared, though it does not bear up to rereading and I don't finally share Suleiman's enthusiasm. But as the only instance of feminist metafiction I know of to sell ten million copies, it was important as a vehicle for the dissemination of feminist ideas and for the controversy it sparked,[4] and it deserves attention as a cultural document.

Disappointed by the women of the past—in history, literature, and her family—Isadora is left to chart her own way. Turning "to our uncertain heroines for help," she encounters only "spinsters or suicides":

> Simone de Beauvoir never makes a move without wondering *what would Sartre think?* And Lillian Hellman wants to be as much of a man as Dashiell Hammett. . . . And the rest—the women writers, the women painters—most of them were shy, shrinking, schizoid. Timid in their lives and brave only in their art. Emily Dickinson, the Brontes, Virginia Woolf, Carson McCullers . . . Flannery O'Connor . . . Sylvia Plath sticking her head into an oven of myth. . . . What a group! Severe, suicidal, strange. Where was the female Chaucer? One lusty lady who had juice and joy and love and talent too? Where could we turn for guidance? (pp. 100–101)

"So the search for the impossible man went on" (p. 101), she laments, implying that the failure of her literary foremothers is responsible for her dependence on men. She sees an even more direct connection between the failure of her mother and her dependence on men: "So I learned about women from men" (p. 154).

Like other contemporary women novelists, Jong writes to fill the gap between the fiction of the past and women's experience in the present.

Jong implies that she is telling "the other side of the story":

> A stiff prick, Freud said, assuming that *their* obsession was *our* obsession. Phallocentric, someone once said of Freud. He thought the sun revolved around the penis. And the daughter, too.
>
> And who could protest? Until women started writing books there was only one side of the story. (p. 24)

Recalling the Wife of Bath's claim that if women wrote, the stories would be different, Jong implies that she is "the female Chaucer," the "lusty lady" with "juice and joy and love and talent too."

Like other women protagonists, Isadora seeks escape in an affair, and as in other contemporary versions of the "two-suitor convention," the husband represents the oppressive patriarchy and the lover represents liberation;[5] for Adrian—whom she picks up at a psychiatrists' convention in Vienna, which she is attending with her husband, Bennett Wing—is Laingian, bearded, English, and sexy, and promises "spontaneity, existentialism, living in the present," against the dull security of Bennett. Adrian proposes that they have an "odyssey"—" 'you'll discover yourself' " (p. 132)—and urges Isadora " 'to go down into [herself] and salvage [her] own life' " (p. 249), to "find patterns in [her] past" (p. 183). As they drive through Germany and France, Isadora tells him "everything": "What was this crazy itinerary anyway if not a trip back into my past?" (p. 249); "we . . . picked up the threads of these old patterns of behavior as we made our way through the labyrinth of Old Europe" (p. 178).

But the best Isadora can come up with is that she keeps being attracted to men who are poor risks (p. 183)—which is not very original but at least explains her attraction to this jerk, who is not only married but impotent; and though she senses that she is repeating this pattern with Adrian, she does not examine this too closely. Nor does she examine anything else too closely; her recounting of her past has no bearing on her present; it is merely episodic, merely there. So, too, is the structure of the novel, which, in its alternation of episodes set in the past with episodes set in the present, might provide a vehicle for plumbing the past, but does not; for Isadora's past has as little to do with her present problems—with her boredom in her marriage and fear of leaving it—as the labyrinth of old Europe has to do with the labyrinth of herself: Europe also is merely there, an exotic backdrop.

Adrian promises Isadora that she will discover her strengths and learn to "stand on [her] own two feet" (p. 132); and he becomes, "perversely, an instrument of [her] freedom" (p. 271) when he drops her in Paris, without warning, to return to his wife. He tells Isadora he's " 'not here to rescue [her]' " (p. 122), and she accepts this, drawing the moral that "I wasn't Adrian's child, and it wasn't his business to rescue me. I was nobody's baby now. Liberated. Utterly free. It was the most terrifying sensation I'd ever known in my life. Like teetering on the edge of the Grand Canyon and hoping you'd learn to fly before you hit bottom" (p. 271).

She finds her "wings" by surviving a night alone in a hotel room in Paris. Talking herself through a panic, trying to get hold of her fear, she rehearses, again, the names of women of the past:

> Me: Think of Simone de Beauvoir!
> Me: I love her endurance, but her books are full of Sartre, Sartre, Sartre.
> Me: Think of Doris Lessing!
> Me: Anna Wulf can't come unless she's in love. . . .
> Me: Think of Sylvia Plath!
> Me: Dead. . . .
> Me: Well—think of Colette.
> Me: A good example. But she's one of the very few.
> Me: Well, why not try to be like her?
> Me: I'm trying. . . .
> Me: Then why are you so afraid of being alone?
> Me: We're going around in circles. (p. 278)

But it is her own writing, not theirs, that pulls her out of this tailspin, as she realizes, reading through her journals, how much she has changed (p. 288). That night, she "assigns herself dreams as a sort of cure" (p. 289),[6] and these dreams, which include "a book with her name on the cover" (p. 290), instruct her that she would not "be a romantic heroine" but that she would "survive": "I would go home and write about Adrian instead. I would keep him by giving him up" (p. 300).

The "book with her name on the cover," the book she will write, is the novel we have just read, and *Fear of Flying* ends with the protagonist ready to begin. Isadora has presumably learned "to go down into myself and salvage bits and pieces of the past" (p. 117), to plumb "inner space. . . . My writing is the submarine or spaceship which takes me to the unknown worlds within my head . . . a new vehicle, designed to delve a little deeper (or fly a little higher)" (p. 210). Whereas once she had difficulty admitting that she was "a woman writer"—

> I didn't want to risk being called all the things women writers . . . are called. . . .
> No "lady writer" subjects for me. . . . I languished in utter frustration, thinking
> that the subjects I knew about were "trivial" and "feminine"—while the subjects
> I knew nothing of were "profound" and "masculine" (p. 118)

—presumably now she has the courage to tell "the other side," in authentic female voice, and *Fear of Flying* is the fruit of those lessons.

Isadora shows evidence of change when, at the end of the novel, on her way back to Bennett in London, she has the chance of a "zipless fuck" with a "stranger on a train"; though such a prospect once fueled her sexual fantasies, she now finds the idea "revolting" (p. 302). She realizes that it was wrong to want "to lose [her]self in a man, to cease to be [herself], to be transported to heaven on borrowed wings" (p. 300). By learning to take her writing seriously, she has, supposedly, grown wings of her own. Flight is a recurrent image in women's writing, as we'll see in Laurence and Atwood, and is often a metaphor for women's writing, signifying what Grace Stewart calls the desire to escape "the polarity between woman and artist";[7] and since in French *voler* means not only "to fly," but "to steal," it has further associations with "stealing the language"—a connection stressed by Suleiman, who sees Jong as accomplishing both feats (p. 122).

But Isadora's ending suggests that her "wings" are still Bennett's—Bennett Wing's—since she has followed her husband to London, let herself into his room, and ends up soaking in his bathtub, contemplating her options:

> Perhaps I had only come to take a bath. Perhaps I would leave before Bennett returned. Or perhaps we'd go home together and work things out. Or perhaps we'd go home together and separate. It was not clear how it would end.

At which point, the novel ends:

> But whatever happened, I knew I would survive it. I knew, above all, that I'd go on working. Surviving meant being born over and over. . . .
>
> .   .   .   .   .   .   .   .   .   .   .   .   .   .   .   .   .   .   .   .   .   .   .   .   .   .   .   .
>
> I hummed and rinsed my hair. As I was soaping it again, Bennett walked in. (p. 311)

Notwithstanding Isadora's assertion of open-ended possibilities and her insistence that she is free to leave, strong probabilities are suggested by the force of her past, which the novel does nothing to exorcize, and by her situation in the present—she is naked in her husband's bathtub. Isadora may have outgrown her desire for zipless fucks, but she has not overcome her need of Bennett. Besides, we know from the sequel, *How to Save Your Own Life* (perhaps the most embarrassing novel written in recent decades by a woman with literary pretensions), that she does not leave Bennett until she has another man lined up to take his place.

The blurb on my paperback copy of the book proclaims *Fear of Flying* "a dazzlingly uninhibited novel that exposes a woman's most intimate sexual feelings," and besides the reviewers who praised it for telling it like it is from the female sexual viewpoint,[8] we have Jong's testimony to the numerous women readers who share her fantasy of the zipless fuck (cited in Chapter 2). But women's "most intimate sexual feelings" sound depressingly familiar: cunt, cock, prick, ass, tits, fuck, fuckable, blowing and being blown. These do not break new ground.

There have been various attempts to defend Jong's use of male sexual vocabulary, most notably by Suleiman, who claims that it is a way of "filching" the language from men, "a parody of language of tough-guy narrator/heroes of Miller or Mailer," a "reversal of roles *and* of language, in which the docile . . .

silent, objectified woman suddenly usurps both the pornographer's language and his way of looking at the opposite sex."[9] But even granting this as Jong's purpose, to reverse the terms is not to challenge the terms. The problem with this sexual vocabulary is that it inscribes a power struggle in which women have been "had"; to wield it is not to steal the language or demonstrate "authenticity," but to reveal a more insidious form of alienation. The challenge facing women who write about desire is to articulate new terms for sexuality that will transform the old power struggle and change "the rules of the old game"—as Drabble does in *The Waterfall*.

Jong confuses liberation with sexual liberation and confuses sexual liberation with the freedom to act and talk like a man, but the bold language that so impressed readers masks a conventionality, a failure to imagine otherwise. Isadora is right—she does "talk a good game" (p. 131)—and there are wonderfully quotable bits in *Fear of Flying*, which I've filched throughout chapters 1 and 2, but they are suspiciously excerptable, on the surface, as is the feminism of the novel. The novel does not, finally, challenge "the old story" at the level of plot, language, or meaning. When Isadora is falling for Adrian, she senses the presence of a "hackneyed plot" (p. 173), "the vocabulary of popular love songs, the cliches of the worst Hollywood movies. My heart skipped a beat. I got misty. . . . He was my sunshine" (p. 121); and *Fear of Flying* is itself caught in the hackneyed, for Isadora resists one set of clichés to succumb to another and is left going "in circles" (p. 181), "round in circles" (p. 278), on a "merry-go-round" (p. 121), a "constant round" (p. 275).

Thus the ending of *How to Save Your Own Life* comes as no surprise:

> It was no good. All her feminism, all her independence, all her fame had come to this, this helplessness, this need. She needed him. She needed this man.
> When he entered her, when his hot cock slid into her, she was moaning something about that, about surrender.[10]

"A stiff prick"? On the basis of Jong's fiction, "their obsession" would seem to be "our obsession."

### Godwin's Odd Woman: Formal Complicity

Godwin's *The Odd Woman* addresses more seriously the question of change and the relation of forms to "the times." Though Jane is not a writer, she is someone who believes in words, whose "profession" is words, "the articulation, interpretation, appreciation, and preservation of good words. She believed in their power" (p. 9). Taught by her reading to expect a traditional ending, her expectations are thwarted by her experience: she seeks "eternal love" (p. 175), only to find that "nothing in this world is certain" (p. 120); she seeks "clear answers" (p. 26), only to find that experience is "booby-trapped with uncertainties" (p. 120); she seeks nineteenth-century resolutions, only to encounter twentieth-century irresolutions. With her longing for a happy ending, she must accept being alone, for her lover, "Gabriel," is no redeemer, but a middle-aged man who offers her the occasional weekend and whose life's work, contained in eleven shoeboxes of notecards on types of love in pre-Raphaelite paintings, reminds her uncomfortably of George Eliot's Casaubon's "Key to all Mythologies."

Godwin suggests that Jane's yearnings are nostalgic:

> As the world spun faster, maddeningly, toward the year 2000 . . . wasn't it a cowardly retreat for her to expect clear answers, articulable standards . . . firm shapes? Wasn't the challenge—always in human progress—with the unformed rather than the solidly formed, the set, the congealed? But she was not a reformer. Damage distressed her too much. She liked to work with the materials of excellence, undamaged. (pp. 26–27)

With her longing for certainty, Jane must accept open-endedness; with her longing for product, she must resign herself to process. She faces "the hard task of self-change," in Eliot's term for Gwendolen Harleth,[11] the only heroine Eliot did not kill or marry off, in a work which (as Jane says) "poses some questions I can't even answer yet" (pp. 151, 426).

But Jane is not only a "starry-eyed" "novel-reader" (p. 379); she is also a teacher and critic of literature who understands the relation of "the forms" to "the times." Though she feels the lure of "the old story"—" 'I love a love story; you know me' " (p. 196)—she can also critique it. She knows that the romantic fiction her mother, Kitty, wrote is "the old story" at its most reductive and formulaic, "the same old plot again and again; the plot of a girl . . . . who threw everything out the window to get her man" (p. 192)—terms that suggest repetition without revision, always to the same end. She is aware that even the best nineteenth-century novels—by Charlotte Bronte, Jane Austen, George Eliot—offer variations on this theme (pp. 59, 28). This message is the same as her grandmother Edith's—"you had your choice: a disastrous ending with a Villain; a satisfactory ending with a Good Man" (p. 29)—and it has been reaffirmed by nearly all the women in Jane's family: Edith taught it by exhortation and Edith's sister, Cleva, who met a bad end with a villain, taught it by example; and even Kitty, who rebelled against Edith, enacted it by her romantic elopement, her sacrifice of career to family, and by the romantic fiction she wrote for a living.

Of more relevance to Jane's situation are those nineteenth-century novels which do not end in marriage or death. But there seem to be very few of them, and those few are unsatisfactory:[12] Ellen Glasgow requires her women to live without love (pp. 61, 276); Gissing in *The Odd Women* subjects his women to "horrible ends" (p. 61): "ESCAPE THROUGH DRINK—PARTIAL REHABILITATION TO 'A USEFUL MEMBER OF SOCIETY' "; "STARTING ALL OVER AGAIN IN A CHILD"; "FINDING 'FULFILLMENT THROUGH OTHERS' "; "SUBLIMATION OF PERSONAL DESIRES AND FURIES INTO A 'CAUSE' " (pp. 301–302). Jane's reaction to Gissing's novel is a tangle of contradictions. She finds herself circling the outcry of Rhoda Nunn, "the young spinster career woman with whom she most identified"—" 'Love— love—love— . . . What is more vulgar than the ideal of novelists? They won't represent the actual world. . . . In real life how many men and women *fall in love?* ' "—and wonders "Was Rhoda right? Was 'love-love-love' never to be found outside the ideals of novelists?" But she also chides her for "playing this feminist power game" and finds her renunciation unacceptable: "who the hell" would "want to live without love of any kind?" (p. 119)

Besides, even in *The Odd Women,* lives have shape and significance, loose ends are tied up, for, as Jane's summaries of Gissing's characters suggest, there is something inherently simplifying in literary representation. This is, of course, why Jane loves literature, as her friend Gerda points out: " 'real people are sloppy and unpredictable and often boring. You like to have . . . a guarantee that everything is going to turn out in some coherent, aesthetic way' " (p. 151). Jane's mother, Kitty, tells her, " 'You're such a good little *student.* You've always been one to look up your life in books. . . . You're living in myths' "; but " 'the trouble with myths . . . is that they leave out . . . all the loose ends, all those messy, practical details that make living less than idyllic' " (pp. 176–77). Jane finds Sheldon, her "good student," reassuring because he seems to confirm that "if only she kept on reading the right books, doing research . . . the mystery of her life would come clear" (p. 25). Though she is criticized for these tendencies by her mother, her best friend, herself, hers is the response of "the artist"—the longing of Yeats's Byzantium poet for an artifact that transcends "the fury and mire of human veins," the longing of Drabble's Jane Gray for "a poem as round and hard as a stone."[13] Jane Clifford imagines "Art" as "the great exempter. Like Death, it excused you from the annoyances and limitations of time" (p. 152). But her terms also suggest the problem: that such "exemption" is a kind of death.

Given this longing for eternal forms, it is understandable why Jane is drawn to a view of literature as expression of "universals," "things we all experience, which tug at all of us, however different we are." She enlists Matthew Arnold's description of literature as "the best that has been known and thought," and she tells her student Howard (her "bad student") that

> ". . . literature is the collection of the best expressions of these universal emotions and thoughts. By 'best' we mean the ones which have a special, extra power to tug at us. The ones which have endured because of a richness of language, an amazing distillation of many, many connected things, arranged in such a way that we see connections we hadn't seen before." (p. 23)

Howard is right—" 'I have this feeling you're just repeating things some teacher repeated to you' "—because Jane is parroting new-critical wisdom that she would have learned in graduate schools in the sixties. But the conversation takes an interesting turn, as Howard makes an appeal to direct experience over language, which he believes "gets in the way," assuring her that "we would have felt the same thing" about "this fabulous moon the other night," and Jane replies, " 'I'm not so sure. You would experience, God knows, some sort of Zen moon, and I—what would I see?' " As Jane reaches for Coleridge to explain what she might have seen (p. 24), she undercuts her appeal to universals (though she does not seem to notice), for if something as concrete as the moon is mediated intertextually, appearing different even to people who inhabit the same culture at the same time, how much less "universal" is something as complex as a literary text, especially when interpreted by people of different cultures at different times. Jane thus calls into question the possibility of "universals," though neither she nor Godwin seems to see this.

Besides, if literature expresses "universals," Jane ought to be able to translate herself to a Jane Austen or a George Eliot novel, but she knows that she cannot because these works express their times (p. 28). Godwin is clear about her characters' relations to their times and delineates each woman in Jane's family in relation to her generation: Edith, Jane's grandmother, was "always in style" (p. 62), with her white gloves and impeccable appearance, in harmony with her *Zeitgeist;* Emily, Jane's younger sister, is in harmony with hers, in her pragmatic, unromantic ordering of her life; whereas Jane and her mother, Kitty, have both fallen (as Kitty says, in the conversation they have while sorting through Edith's possessions, when they come upon her white gloves) "in the interstices of the *Zeitgeists.*" Kitty tells Jane that she felt torn between ambition to write and love of her babies, that she was "born too late or too early," with "one foot in one era and the other foot in the next" (p. 178); and Jane, like her mother, is "in transit" and confused about what she wants. But Godwin does not see the contradiction between this view of people and literary forms—that, as Kitty says, "we are products, we are prisoners of our times" (p. 178)—and the ideal (which Godwin seems to share with Jane) that literature expresses "universal thoughts and emotions": a view that Godwin reiterates in her notorious review of the Gilbert and Gubar *Norton Anthology of Literature by Women.*[14]

Jane raises a further problem when she asserts that "the real thing" is knowable after "at least fifty years had elapsed":

> There was the real thing, and there was the approximation, the imitation, and the barefaced hoax. She became increasingly convinced, more so since she had read a collection of nineteenth-century reviews praising as master-pieces novels no one now remembered and explaining why people like Hardy and Emily Brontë were flashes in the pan, that the world could not tell the difference till at least fifty years had elapsed. (p. 153)

But neither she nor Godwin confronts the question why fifty years should provide the final test, or what it means when, a hundred years later, that "master-piece" falls back out of fashion again and the same work that moves one generation to tears moves the next generation to laughter. Thus the 1905 melodrama *The Fatal Wedding* moved Great-aunt Cleva to defy family for a grand passion—actually, to exchange one shackling convention for another. Jane has an uneasy moment when she senses that her own responses may be as time-bound as Cleva's, and she wonders what a great-grandniece of hers "some seventy years in the future" will think of her from a perspective on her like hers on Cleva: Jane imagines her thinking *"What was wrong with her? Couldn't she see that it's all a matter of. . . ."* (p. 337). It follows that those qualities that "have special power to tug at us," those criteria by which we define the "master-piece," will seem as quaint as Edith's white gloves, for in our judgments we are as bound by our *Zeitgeists* as stage-struck Cleva was by hers. If Edith's decisions were "written out of some etiquette book, copyrighted about 1890" (p. 48), surely the question follows, what "book" "writes" us?

Godwin brilliantly renders a sense of reality as process, as subject to the shaping power of imagination and "written" according to the exigencies of the present. Her depiction of Jane's consciousness demonstrates that reality—past and present, our selves and others'—is a creation of the fictionalizing imagination, that meanings take shape from interpretation and reinterpretation. The past, too, is a creation of the stories we tell ourselves and others. Jane has always been intrigued by her family's "mythmaking" (as Gerda calls it; p. 62), especially by Edith's use of Cleva as a cautionary tale, and she realizes that she herself is "mythmaking" when she makes Edith into a "perfect Southern lady" for the benefit of her friend Sonia (p. 62). She is also aware that we reconstruct the more immediate past, realizing that she and Kitty will remake their meeting, "do it over in [their] memories" (p. 89), according to what each needs to believe.

Jane is fascinated by how many of our efforts are taken with self-creation, what she calls the "terrible task of personality" (p. 279). She is "amazed" at Gerda's "continued ability to re-create herself" (p. 42) and impressed by Sonia's willingness to "revise herself" (p. 58). Her sense of the "undefined, unresolved self" is so acute that she wonders if the very concept of self is "a bygone literary convention" (p. 27). She knows that the self is a creation of time and circumstance, tailored to occasion and audience, and is continually checking her image in mirrors, as though seeing herself might help her to know herself. So dependent is she on reflections from others that when she is alone, dissolution threatens (pp. 69, 72).

Jane also understands that we create others by our ideas of them and that those ideas are determined by our needs and desires. This is particularly evident in men's views of women: *"You are the most— woman I have ever met because that's what I want you to be, by God"* (p. 375). And such images are persuasive: Jane realizes that her family's "image of her" exerts a powerful hold, is the "most compelling weave of all" the nets they cast on her (p. 89). Knowing another person is a matter of choosing a version of that person to believe, as Kitty does with Emily (p. 97). A relationship is a kind of reciprocal creation that works as long as one person's image of the other squares with that person's self-image. Thus Jane initially sees Gabriel as her savior, and as long as she needs to be saved, she puts up with anything he asks, but when her needs change, the balance shifts; and her decision to leave him is a repudiation of his image of her as "the most patient woman" he has ever known.

Jane understands that words shape reality. She "creates" Gabriel with words—"I dreamed him and then summoned him with words" (p. 371). She feels also that his words "summon" her, and indeed, his delicate distinction between "irrevocable" and "irredeemable" (he tells her that choices in his life have "hardened into the irrevocable" but not the "irredeemable") is "a bit of etymological foreplay" (pp. 261, 265). She also understands that literary forms shape reality: " 'we are always in some play or other . . . do we create the roles, or do they create us?' " (p. 358). No sooner has Jane written the farewell note to Gabriel than she finds herself "rehearsing" the incident "for a future scene" (p. 371), and as she is leaving, she has to resolve to make the scene "her scene," to "play it as I see fit" (p. 348).

Given Godwin's sense of reality as process—as structured by imagination and language and shifting with the needs of the moment—it is no wonder that Jane has difficulty finding an "eternal constant" (p. 14). Early in the novel, the morning after Edith's death, Jane has an important "insight about stories," or rather, about the limitations of stories:

> You could learn from stories, be warned by stories. But stories, by their very nature, were Procrustean. Even the longest of them had to end somewhere. If a living human being tried to squeeze himself into a particular story, he might find vital parts of himself lopped off. Even worse, he might find himself unable to get out again.

She concludes,

> You remained indestructible by eluding for dear life the hundreds and thousands of already written, already completed stories. . . . You reminded yourself that . . . you had to write yourself as you went along, that your story could not and should not possibly be completed until *you* were: i.e., dead. . . .
> *She* was not dead yet. Nothing was finished, nothing at all . . . she had not written herself into any premature endings . . . there was, she felt, still time, still hope to do, be anything. . . . (pp. 49–50)

This insight gives her the exhilarating sense that, since she is still alive—"THIS IS NOT THE FINAL DRAFT" (p. 241). The problem Godwin faces is like that faced by Lessing—to find a form which is neither a surrender to conventional form nor to formlessness, a form that accommodates the process of change.

What is disappointing is that, having so skillfully raised these questions, Godwin's narrative rigidifies to so fixed a form. Godwin's novel is very much a final draft—finished, "completed." Though Jane is made to accept uncertainty and irresolution, the novel as a whole suggests a narrowing of possibilities in its adherence to the Aristotelean principles Jane defines as "a good plot," a progress "from possibility to probability to necessity" (p. 151)—principles that are ideologically complicit.[15] Godwin is, like Jane, no "reformer." Progress, as she suspects, requires "damage" ("break-down" or "crack-up," in Anna Wulf's terms); and rather than pushing through "the unformed" to new forms, she retreats to the "solidly formed," the "set" and "congealed."

At the beginning of the novel, "possibilities" have narrowed to the "probability" that Gabriel will not leave his wife. Jane is beginning to outgrow Gabriel's image of her, and "necessity" is asserting itself in the form of her own needs. Nevertheless, she keeps trying, the day she spends in New York waiting for him, to tailor herself to his needs, to remake herself in his image—both in attempting to make herself as he likes her (i.e., patient) and to remake herself like him. Gabriel is the silent type, and Jane's attempt to renounce "word-knowledge" and know him "wordlessly" is an extreme effort of self-renunciation. She tries "to empty herself of a lifetime of preconceptions in order to approach what she could not figure out in words about this man": "Never had she so completely doubted every form of reason; never had she doubted herself, all that she had based her life on, so completely" (p. 294). But she cannot relinquish reason, language, or her "conscious," "recording" ego (pp. 297–98). Whether Gabriel cares about any of this is unclear, but Jane does; and the standard evoked (though Godwin does not say so) recalls D. H. Lawrence's view of women as caught within an imprisoning ego and rationality—a compelling cultural stereotype and one to which Jane, as an avid reader who is timid about her sexuality, would be vulnerable. (As Jong's Isadora testifies, Lawrence's pronouncements on female sexuality have made more than one woman feel inadequate; FF, p. 154.)

Neither can Jane remake herself according to the standard represented by Saks Fifth Avenue. Though she tries to "refurbish her image" in the mirrors at Saks (pp. 309, 316), she realizes that it is too late to remake herself as a beautiful object. The scene in the department-store fitting room, when she panics at losing herself among the dresses, is a high point of comedy in the novel and one of those scenes in contemporary women's fiction—like the construction-worker scene in Lessing's *Summer Before the Dark*—that women readers remember as epitomizing some essential experience. The dresses on the racks at Saks do not fit Jane any more than other people's stories do—"she would not look in any more mirrors for awhile" (p. 318); and she hardly cares when she loses the dress she has just bought, leaving it on the seat of the taxi, since it was never really hers in the first place.

Her next destination, the library, shows more awareness of who she is. At the library she decides to track down the truth of Aunt Cleva, enlisting the tools she has developed as scholar and critic and bringing them to bear on her past. What she finds, in researching "the old play"—that "the villain" of Cleva's life was the hero of the play, the incongruously named Edwin Merchant, rather than, as in Edith's moralization, the stage villain played by Von Vorst—is further uncertainty, how difficult it is to get "to the bottom of anything" (p. 420).

Gabriel's postponement of their meeting stretches Jane's patience and makes her departure more "probable," though not yet "necessary." What provides the "necessity" is Gabriel's postponing the meeting yet again, but even in the cab on the way to the airport, she asks "What is this drama? Did you choose it? Or are you letting some facile director . . . force you into this premature denouement?"

To this question "necessity" at last asserts itself: "Oh God, I don't want to be *patient* in somebody's eyes, I want to be *first!*" (pp. 372–73).

Jane Clifford is not redeemed by passion, though she would like to be; she learns, rather, to relinquish illusion, accept herself, and depend on her own efforts. When Jane returns home and hears of Sonia's "interesting bit of news," her heart leaps at the possibility that Sonia has found the perfect man for her—someone who will combine the attractions of a Knightley and a Heathcliff; but Sonia's news concerns, instead, a job opportunity. And when the phone rings and Jane anticipates hearing Gabriel's voice at the other end, it is, instead, a student—someone who requires, rather than offers, rescue. Though Godwin makes gestures toward open-endedness—we don't know if Gabriel will get the Guggenheim or if he will ask Jane to accompany him to England—probabilities are strongly suggested: Jane is left alone with herself, depending on her own efforts, attaining the self-awareness and self-reliance that make it impossible for her to pick up and follow Gabriel to England or anywhere else.

In the final scene of the novel, as in the opening scene, Jane is in bed with insomnia, imagining herself in conversation with the "enema bandit." But the advice she imagines offering him—"turn your oddities inside out like a sock and find your own best life by making them work for you" (p. 429)—indicates a new self-acceptance. The circular return provides a measure of change: having traveled back through her familial past and excavated the true story of Aunt Cleva, having divested herself of illusions concerning not only Gabriel, but Gerda, she returns knowing that she must make her own story—that she must accept her own "oddities" and make them "work for" her.

But occurring at the end of a movement which is a narrowing down of possibilities, the circular structure creates a sense of constriction, a sense which is reinforced by the careful symmetry, the contrasts and parallels, on which the novel is structured.[16] Each woman in Jane's family is shown in relation to her generation; Jane's voice opposes Gerda's, Gabriel's opposes Zimmer's, Sheldon the good student opposes Howard the bad; Sonia, the colleague who has "it all"—success, marriage, children—is contrasted to Marcia, the graduate student Jane meets as she travels to Edith's funeral, who flounders professionally and personally. Coincidence obtrudes when Von Vorst just happens to be interested in the same questions Jane is thinking about—of the relation of literature to life—and when Jane just happens to encounter "a sort of alternate fate" (p. 405) in the story of Nan Frampton, a young woman who has managed to win her lover from his wife. At such points one feels the strong hand of the author.

Godwin is her own best critic on this. In a fascinating essay, "Becoming a Writer," she describes "the most serious danger to [her] writing [as her] predeliction for shapeliness":

> How I love 'that nice circular Greek' shape . . . a nice, neat conclusion with all the edges tucked under. And this sometimes leads me to 'wrap up' things, to

force dramatic revelations at the expense of allowing the truth to reveal itself in slow, shy, and often problematical glimpses.[17]

Even as *The Odd Woman* gestures toward open-endedness, its "nice circular . . . shape" "wraps things up": Godwin's awareness of this danger does not enable her to avoid it.

When as a child, Jane asked Kitty, " 'Why don't you write a story about a woman who teaches school at the college and writes love stories on the weekend and has a little girl like me?' " Kitty answered, " 'It wouldn't sell, that's why' " (pp. 32–33). Godwin extends this discussion in the essay "Becoming a Writer," where she describes the romantic fiction her mother wrote for a living: "GIRL MEETS MAN. MUTUAL ATTRACTION. THINGS DEVELOP. A PROBLEM ARISES. CONFLICT AND DOUBT. RESOLUTION OF CONFLICT. FINAL EMBRACE. The formula was unvarying. All the stories . . . were imprisoned in that plot," on that "romantic treadmill . . . the mutual attraction, the developing passion, the necessary conflict, the happy ending."[18] Godwin wonders whether her mother had "moments when she was tempted to rip out the 'happily-ever-after' lie she was perpetuating . . . and tell her own story": "It would have been much more interesting. But who would have bought it?" "When you write for the market, you lock yourself willingly into the prison of your times" (pp. 234–35).

Godwin speculates about women writers today:

> [Today's] fictional terrains support . . . divorced mothers, unmarried mothers, even well-to-do suburban wives who may or may not "keep" that unplanned-for last child. And I think of the writers of these stories, safely within the ideologies of their *zeitgeist,* and I wonder what parts of their own stories they still feel obliged to suppress, what dark blossomings of their imaginations still lie outside the realm of the current "market"? Yes, even in these "liberated" times.

She adds, "It is the dark blossomings, the suppressed (or veiled) truths that I court. Not always successfully. Like my mother, I, too, am the child of my times" (p. 234).

We may understand some of the "suppressed or veiled truths" that elude her by comparing her to writers who take greater risks. Lessing's Anna Wulf descends into madness; Laurence's Morag Gunn becomes single parent to a dark-skinned child in a racist society; Drabble's Jane Gray finds inspiration for her writing in an adulterous, incestuous affair. But Jane Clifford takes no such chances; they go against Godwin's grain—as Godwin herself suggests in a passage in *A Mother and Two Daughters,* where she mocks the excesses of her contemporaries, targeting especially Atwood's *Surfacing.*[19]

In a revealing passage, Jane describes her education as an education in pleasing men—"She had connived to win her degrees . . . partially through the charms of her sex"—and compares the way she trimmed and tailored her mind to the way other women shape their bodies:

the college term papers, carefully researched, accurately footnoted . . . then shaped and tinted (as other women shaped their figures with foundation garments, tinted their skins with make-up) with a delicate wit, an irresistible . . . turn of phrase. (pp. 148–49)

There is all the difference between this careful styling and Jane Gray's abandon and abandonment to the sticky mysteries of sex and birth. Jane Clifford's fear of letting Gabriel hear the sounds of her bodily functions, so extreme that she returns home constipated after spending a weekend with him, becomes more significant by contrast with other protagonists' acceptance of "shit": in *The Diviners* Morag learns to accept the "muck" represented by her stepfather, the town scavenger, and in *The Middle Ground,* Kate "turns shit to gold."[20] As Gerda says, " 'until you can let him hear you shit, there is going to be *no* free dialogue' " (p. 134); and perhaps this is the meaning of the mysterious "enema bandit" with whom Jane has imaginary late-night conversations—this is Jane's "free dialogue."

Jane's caution and conventionality are related to her fastidiousness about sex. Jane fears "the menacing relationship between blood and impurity" and would like "to have it over with," "to be respectable and old" (pp. 246–47)—an asceticism also apparent in her nostalgia for the winter she spent writing her dissertation (on George Eliot), which she remembers fondly for its "pure" frozen stillness (p. 222). As in *The Waterfall,* fastidiousness is associated with the longing for perfect form: Drabble's Jane Gray wanted to write "a poem as round and hard as a stone," but immersed in the processes of birth and sex as she becomes, she realizes that "a poem so round and smooth would say nothing" (p. 69); and the narrative form Drabble forges is as unconventional as the form her protagonist works out in her life—an open-ended, unfinished tale of unpunished passion that allows for "conflict" and "compromise" (p. 247). But Godwin does not risk the damage that she rightly senses is required to make "something new."

In *The Golden Notebook* Anna descends to "the place . . . where words, patterns, order, dissolve" (p. 634), risking a confrontation with formlessness that leads to a new understanding of form and forging "out of the chaos, a new kind of strength" (p. 467). Lessing, like Drabble, suggests a sense (like Yeats's) that form, the eternal artifact, is inseparable from "the fury and mire" of mortal life—that product is inseparable from process, dancer from dance, that "the artifice of eternity" is attained through immersion in process, in "what is past, or passing, or to come" (Yeats's terms in "Among School Children," "Sailing to Byzantium," and "Byzantium"). But Godwin opts for eternal artifact. The image with which the novel concludes—"the barely audible tinkle of a soul at the piano, trying to organize the loneliness and the weather and the long night into something of abiding shape and beauty"—though haunting and lovely, reasserts this impulse to order.

I can't help feeling that this failure is related to another of the novel's problems: the caricature of Gerda and the dismissal of feminism. Godwin seems initially to allow Gerda a real criticism of Jane's illusions, making her a kind of double who represents some of the anger and vitality Jane herself lacks, though also suggesting that she has suppressed the "inner life" to throw herself into fad after fad, the most recent of which is the women's movement. But this tension is not sustained, for Gerda emerges, finally, as silly and trendy. Rather than giving her a voice which would allow for a genuine tension or complexity, Godwin resolves all into a univocal perspective—Jane's perspective. Gerda's feminism, far from being presented as a viable alternative, is reduced to that deadliest of stereotypes, man-hating, as she and her cronies try to enlist Jane's assistance in compiling a list of "One Hundred and One Ways He Uses You Every Day" (p. 373).

The world of this novel lends itself to analysis in feminist terms. There is Jane, stuck in one-year teaching appointments, marginalized professionally, unable to take herself seriously or challenge her situation; there is Gabriel, secure in a tenured job and a marriage, with a mistress on the side (though, to be fair, the portrayal of Gabriel is good: he has problems of his own). Surely these are related phenomena, but Godwin does not suggest a relationship. When Jane arrives home at the end of the novel, she finds

> Nothing new on national news. A few shots of a war, in a place where snow never fell, a war she had been watching, in its perfunctory snippets and shots of continual coverage, for years. A politician's angry face appeared briefly, denouncing an opponent. Nothing new. (p. 415)

Even Plath, with her weirdly dissociated sensibility, suggests a possible connection between the Rosenbergs' execution and Esther's self-immolation. But Godwin shows no sense that the war may be relevant to Jane, that it may be part of the politics that is at least partly responsible for her unhappiness and part of the power structure that determines the shape of the literary marketplace Godwin herself serves—that Jane's personal problems may have a political dimension and that both personal and political are related to questions of "form." Whereas in *The Golden Notebook* Anna's "writer's block" is related to her problems with men and to the political horrors of the century and to the literary marketplace—personal is political is aesthetic—Godwin suggests no such connections.

There is a powerful moment in the novel, when Jane stumbles, panicked, out of Saks Fifth Avenue, seized by a vision of "the end" that makes all other destinations irrelevant (p. 328), of New York reduced to rubble and her own flesh "returning to dust"—an apocalyptic vision recalling moments in Woolf's *Mrs. Dalloway* and Lessing's *Four-Gated City*. Jane imagines a time centuries later, when "a curious visitor from another planet, with archeological interests" will come across a fragment of Jane (pp. 325–27). And Jane is panicked by time, that "tempus fugit" (the name she gives her alarm clock), ticking away her childbearing years. But her response—and Godwin's—is nostalgic, toward fixed, solid forms, reactionary rather than revolutionary. As good as Godwin is at articulating the relation of literary to social convention and at contrasting nineteenth-century certainties with twentieth-century complexities, her protagonist's longing for order and clarity is, finally, her own. No reformer and no re-former, she accepts the world she inherits and assures her imprisonment in its forms.

# Part II

# "Something New"

Stories are where we need to go, she wrote. . . . It doesn't matter that the stories aren't true, they're our metaphors for our existence—stories about men and women, but especially stories about women, are the metaphors we use for our existence, on which we must rely, on which we must rely as much as we rely on what our mothers taught us.

Marianne Wiggins, *Separate Checks*
(p. 233)

# V

## DORIS LESSING'S
## *THE GOLDEN NOTEBOOK*
### NAMING IN A DIFFERENT WAY

> That they were both "insecure" and
> "unrooted," . . . they both freely
> acknowledged. But Anna had recently been
> learning to use these words in a different way,
> not as something to be apologised for, but as
> flags or banners for an attitude that amounted
> to a different philosophy.

> I had to "name" the frightening things, over
> and over, in a terrible litany, like a sort of
> disinfecting. . . . But now . . . it was not
> making past events harmless, by naming them,
> but *making sure they were still there.* Yet I
> know that having made sure they were still
> there, I would have to "name" them in a
> different way.
>
> 

*The Golden Notebook*[1]

In the introduction to *The Golden Notebook* published nearly a decade after the novel appeared, Lessing expressed disappointment that no one had noticed its complex structure and that critics had reduced it to a "tract about the sex war," a "trumpet for Women's Liberation" (pp. x–xi).[2] Though she had grounds for complaint, in fact the novel received very different kinds of readings from men and women. Male critics condemned it for deviating from party line—not Soviet, but new-critical, party line—reacting exactly as Lessing describes critics reacting: "What they do very well, is to tell the writer how the book or play accords with current patterns of feeling and thinking, the climate of opinion. They are like litmus paper" (p. xvi). But women, untroubled by the novel's violation of new-critical canons or its status as "art," were thrilled to find themselves named: "The shock of recognition of oneself, the sense of 'Yes,

someone is writing about *my* life exactly as it is' is overwhelming";[3] "after years
of our attempts to identify ourselves with Quentin Compson, Augie March,
and the Invisible Man, not to mention Lolita and Franny Glass we were
presented with a novel whose persona was an intellectual, a political activist, an
artist, as well as a lover, a mother—a woman."[4] "And not censored: love,
politics, children, dreams, close talk. The first Tampax in world literature."[5]
Women read asking Martha Quest's question, "What does this say about my
life?"[6] and "what we discovered, when we read *The Golden Notebook* or the
Martha Quest novels, was a writer who, it seemed, knew us better than we
knew ourselves . . . *this,* we felt, was what was lacking in our study and teaching
of literature."[7]

## Men and Women on *The Golden Notebook*

To contrast male and female responses to *The Golden Notebook* is to see,
beyond a doubt, that men and women read differently, and to demonstrate the
needs feminist criticism evolved to address.[8] To be sure, some men recognized
its importance,[9] but the majority of male reviewers and critics—even those who
deplored the general timidity of postwar British fiction—found ways of discounting it. Anthony Burgess laments that novelists today "do not feel sufficiently strongly about anything to be urged into attempting some large-scale
work of individual vision which . . . [will] radically change our view of life,"[10]
but he dismisses *The Golden Notebook* as "a crusader's novel," "unacceptable"
as a "work of art." How does Burgess manage to overlook this so obviously
"large-scale" work which actually did change people's lives? His grounds for
dismissal are embarrassing:

> [Anna] say[s] some hard things about male arrogance, crassness, sexual impo-
> tence and incompetence, and her own sexual frustrations (which are, of course, to
> be blamed on men). . . . She is intelligent, honest, burning with conviction, but
> she ends up as a bit of a bore. So, for that matter, does Mrs. Lessing's own
> experiment. . . . There has been too much diversion of aim, too little digestion of
> deeply held beliefs into something acceptable as a work of art. The crusader's best
> medium is the manifesto, which is not quite the same thing as a novel. (p. 100)

Offended by Anna's attack on "male arrogance" and "impotence," Burgess
counterattacks by calling her "a bore," in a move very like Richard's in a scene
in *The Golden Notebook,* when, in response to Anna's rebuff of a pass, he
counters by insulting her (p. 45). Burgess cannot let it go, either, for he returns
to say in another context:

> We have seen how in Doris Lessing's *Golden Notebook* there is a powerful
> expression of resentment of the male—not purely social (in the old suffragette
> manner) but sexual as well. Woman has a sexual need of man, but she objects to
> having this need; she wants to reject man, but she cannot, and so she seeks to

dominate him . . . and the literary expression of the female dilemma is often harsh, sensational, explosive. (p. 122)

P. W. Frederick McDowell similarly criticizes the novel, suggesting that Anna's "intellectual difficulties . . . arise from her sexual frustrations" and the novel is "disorganized," "subjective," "a cross between a standard novel . . . and a confession."[11] Other critics concede that it has interest for what it reveals about women's lives but deny that it is "art." Walter Allen admits that *The Golden Notebook* is "impressive in its honesty and integrity, and unique . . . as an exposition of the emotional problems that face an intelligent woman who wishes to live in the kind of freedom a man may take for granted," but he concludes that it "fail[s]" "as a work of art": "the structure is clumsy, complicated rather than complex. . . . Its main interest [is] . . . sociological."[12] Patrick Parrinder describes it as "an almost legendary weapon in the armoury of 'consciousness raising' about politics, psychoanalysis, feminism. . . . There is no lack of witnesses to the 'importance' of this novel, but I do find a strange absence of agreement or even serious debate, about its artistic success."[13] Frederick R. Karl calls it "the most considerable single work by an English author in the 1960's," but he too dismisses it on "purely literary" grounds:

> It is a carefully organized but verbose, almost clumsily written novel. . . . The book's strength lies . . . certainly not in the purely literary quality of the writing, but in the wide range of Mrs. Lessing's interest, and, more specifically in her attempt to write honestly about women.[14]

James Gindin criticizes "Miss Lessing's addiction to historical categories" and "the historically conditioned character" as "an aesthetic shortcoming"[15]:

> Doris Lessing's intense feeling of political and social responsibility is carefully worked into specific historical situations. But the positive convictions can become heavy-handed, and the specific situations journalistic, while the strict allegiance to time and place can limit the range of perception about human beings. Miss Lessing . . . produces an enormously lucid sociological journalism, honest and committed, but . . . she lacks a multiple awareness, . . . a perception that parts of human experience cannot be categorized or precisely located, a human and intellectual depth. Intense commitment can cut off a whole dimension of human experience. (p. 86)

This was in 1962, and Gindin's assumptions—that "intense commitment" and the "historically specific" are at odds with "human and intellectual depth"— reflect, "like litmus paper," the new-critical dicta of the day.

One notes how consistently these critics draw attention to Lessing's marital status even when they do not know what it is: whatever else they may know, they do know and insist on the fact that she is a woman, a rhetorical move that corroborates their categorization of *The Golden Notebook* as a "women's novel." In the context of such judgments, one appreciates Bernard Bergonzi's admission that *The Golden Notebook* is "not at all easy to place or evaluate": he calls it a "disturbing achievement" which breaks down "the traditional distinction . . . between literary and sociological ways of looking at the world," "a work of great, if cold brilliance."[16] One suspects that if this novel had been written by a man, more critics might have shown some humility in approaching it; of course, if it had been written by a man, it would not be *The Golden Notebook*.

What one senses in these responses is an irritation, the real grounds of which are unacknowledged. New-critical criteria—"complexity," "multiple awareness," "pure literary quality"—are then enlisted to dismiss the novel as "inartistic," "unaesthetic," "clumsy," "unacceptable as a work of art." Because it violates some new-critical standards, it is faulted for violating all of them—for "lack of multiple awareness"! Lessing knew that "to say, in 1957, that one believes artists should be committed, is to arouse hostility and distrust"[17]—and sure enough, *The Golden Notebook* gets dismissed as "sociological," "journalistic," "manifesto." But even today, when the prevalent critical approach is better suited to appreciating the novel than it was in the fifties, few men are much better at reading *The Golden Notebook;* few (in my experience) *have* actually read it, let alone read it carefully. As recently as 1983, John Holloway and Gilbert Phelps omit *The Golden Notebook* from their surveys of contemporary literature.[18] A 1987 collection of essays on *British Novelists Since 1900* contains nothing on Lessing.[19] A critic I know who claims to be writing about the novel in seventies Britain has not felt it necessary even to read Lessing; her turn to mysticism has given him an excuse for dismissing her as politically incorrect, though this same critic spent years studying Ezra Pound. Of the fifty-six writers, critics, and reviewers surveyed in the 1978 *New Review,* a few mention Lessing as among the major novelists of the day, though only one singles her out as "the outstanding novelist of our time" (p. 47).[20] In his learned and provocative study of the novel, *Resisting Novels* (1987), Lennard Davis says, "There has never been a novel, to my knowledge, that actually seriously addresses" or "reveal[s] the ideology of the novel through the novel"[21]—yet this is precisely what *The Golden Notebook* does.

But *The Golden Notebook* presented problems for some women readers as well. From the beginning, its portrayal of women provoked widely varying responses. On the one hand, Ellen W. Brooks describes Lessing's depiction of women as "the most thorough and accurate of any in literature";[22] Elayne Antler Rapping calls the novel "a nearly pure expression of feminine consciousness . . . honestly reflecting the truths of feminine experience" and places Lessing in the tradition of "feminine sensibility" for her portrayal of women as the center and source of value in the modern world;[23] Margaret Drabble hails it as "a document in the history of liberation."[24] On the other hand, Alice Bradley Markos sees Lessing's women as the most badly mangled victims of the contemporary world, "almost humans manque";[25] Elaine Showalter and Ellen Morgan argue that it is alienated "from the authentic female perspective";[26] Catharine R. Stimpson sees Lessing as apart "from the 'feminine' and from feminism";[27] Jenny Taylor claims that "the novel certainly isn't an explicitly feminist text."[28] One can see in these assessments the concerns of early feminist criticism: the search for strong "role models," "explicit feminism," and for "accuracy" and "authenticity." If one reads the novel according to such prescriptions, it is likely to disappoint. But one approaches it this way at one's risk, for Lessing's parody of the Soviet "literature of health and progress"—"where are the working masses in this book? Where the class conscious fighters?" ask Soviet reviews of Anna's *Frontiers of War* (pp. 443–45)—make it unlikely that she will create characters who are models of heroic behavior.

That Anna is no model of feminist strength and independence, she would be the first to admit. Catapulted out of a long, draining relationship with a man who has denigrated her as a writer and mother and who ditches her for the security of a dead marriage, Anna is "in pieces," a state of "awful moral exhaustion" (p. 44). " 'Free women,' said Anna, wryly" (p. 4)—and the reiteration of "Free Women" in the chapter headings drives home the irony: "Women's emotions are still fitted for a kind of society that no longer exists. My deep emotions, my real ones, are to do with my relationship with a man. One man" (p. 314). But from this unpromising beginning Anna writes beyond "the end of the affair," forges "a new way of looking at life" and "new imaginative comprehension" (p. 61), and makes "something new" (pp. 472–73). *The Golden Notebook* concerns change—breaking "a habit of nerves from the past," "shedding a skin": "what is happening is something new in my life . . . a sense of shape, of unfolding" (p. 479)—and its narrative renders the process of change, taking its protagonist (and many of its readers) through an evolution of consciousness and desire.

Joanne Frye claims that the novel "does not argue a feminist position or even center exclusively in female experiences; instead it examines broadly the crises of twentieth-century society and the problems of characterizing those crises in novelistic form."[29] But Frye's divisions are not Lessing's: the novel *does* center in "female experience," *and* it relates that experience both to novelistic form and to the crises of twentieth-century society. It charts female experience compellingly, unsentimentally, and originally: Anna is delineated in relation to her body ("the first Tampax in world literature"), to her child, to men, women, work, and politics. Its depiction of the centrality of female friendship is unprecedented in fiction: Irving Howe rightly praises the "precise and nuanced dialogue" of the "remarkable conversations between Anna and Molly as some of the strongest writing in the novel" (p. 178). Anna describes herself as "a completely new type of woman" (p. 4) who is " 'living the kind of life women never lived before' " (p. 472), "made by the kind of experience women haven't had before" (p. 471); and her juggling of roles—of single parent, political worker, writer, lover, friend, and woman on her own—epitomizes the "role conflict" many women experience today.

Anna does not separate her personal experience from problems of narrative form or from the crises of the twentieth century; as she says of her "writer's block," " 'if I saw it in terms of an artistic problem, then it'd be easy, wouldn't it? We could have ever such intelligent chats about the modern novel' " (p. 41). The first novel of the sixties to name "the disease of women in our time" (p. 333) as a political "disease," this work is fundamentally concerned with "relationship"—with (in Lessing's words) "the personal [as] general," "look[ing] at things as a whole and in relation to each other" (pp. xiii–xiv). *The Golden Notebook* depicts "form" as a literary *and* a personal *and* a political problem, for it is only when Anna can cast off conventional forms in her life that she can risk "something new" in her fiction; and the freedom she imagines—" 'I want to walk off, by myself, Anna Freeman' " (p. 471)—comprehends, if it does not accomplish, a world in which all can be free. I will argue that *The Golden Notebook* is a feminist novel, both in terms of content and textual strategies—"feminist" not in offering strong female models who infiltrate existing social structures (which Adrienne Rich defines as "tokenism," not feminism), but in envisioning "a profound transformation of world society and of human relationships."[30]

## Men and Women in *The Golden Notebook*

*The Golden Notebook* concerns change on individual, collective, and narrative levels. It is about people who "try to be something else" (p. 466) and try to change the world—"world-changers" (p. 624). Lessing describes writing it as a process which changed her: "Writing *The Golden Notebook* completely changed me. When I started it I was a Marxist and a materialist . . . [but] I suddenly found myself writing easily about things with which I had no personal acquaintance";[31] and as the numerous responses of women cited in Chapter 2 indicate, it was a transformative experience for many readers. In a conversation that takes place in *The Shadow of the Third,* the novel Anna writes in the yellow notebook, Ella's father claims " 'A man is what he is. He can't be anything else. You can't change that' "; to which Ella replies, " 'That's the real difference between us. Because I believe you can change it' " (p. 466). When Ella imagines "writ[ing] about that—people who deliberately try to be something else, try to break their own form as it were' " (p. 466), she realizes that "something else" cannot be expressed within the familiar "patterns of defeat, death, irony" or "patterns of happiness or simple life." What she envisions—"a man and a woman—yes. Both at the end of their tether. Both cracking up because of a deliberate attempt to transcend their own limits. And out of the chaos, a new kind of strength" (p. 467)—prefigures what happens later, when, in the blue notebook, Anna and Saul break down into each other.

On the collective level, the novel concerns humanity's slow, painful progress toward (in Anna's phrase) " 'the end of being animals' " (p. 276). This is not an easy time to believe in progress—" 'not an easy time to be a socialist' " (p. 21)—as leftists, "determined to be honest, yet fighting every inch of the way even now not to have to admit the truth about the Soviet Union" (p. 481), "are reeling off from the C. P. in dozens, broken-hearted" (p. 448). But to Tommy's " 'what do you live by now?' " Anna replies,

> "Every so often, perhaps once in a century, there's a sort of—act of faith. A well of faith fills up, and there's an enormous heave forward in one country or another, and that's a forward movement for the whole world. Because it's an act of imagination—of what is possible for the whole world. In our century it was 1917 in Russia. And in China. Then the well runs dry, because . . . the cruelty and the ugliness are too strong. Then the well slowly fills again. And then there's another painful lurch forward." (pp. 275–76)

Meanwhile it is our "acts of imagination" that "keep the dream alive": " 'Yes—because every time the dream gets stronger. If people can imagine something, there'll come a time when they'll achieve it' " (pp. 275–76). A version of this hope is stated by Anna's fictional character Paul in "The Shadow of the Third": " 'All our lives . . . we'll put all our energies, all our talents, into pushing a great boulder up a mountain. The boulder is the truth that the great men know by instinct, and the mountain is the stupidity of mankind.' " Though Anna has him conclude " 'we are the failures' " (p. 210), she later, in the golden notebook, dreams a character, a composite of Paul and Michael, who reverses this judgment:

> "But my dear Anna, we are not the failures we think we are. We spend our lives fighting to get people very slightly less stupid than we are to accept truths that the great men have always known. . . . It is our job to tell them. Because the great men can't be bothered. Their imaginations are already occupied with . . . visions of a society full of free and noble human beings . . . [but] they know we are here, the boulder-pushers. . . . And they rely on us and they are right; and that is why we are not useless after all." (p. 618)

In this crucial instance of "naming in a different way," "boulder-pushers" are renamed as "not failures," "not useless," and the second version goes on to envision "a society full of free and noble human beings."

Lessing refers to *The Golden Notebook* as expressing her "dissatisfaction" with "the conventional novel" (introduction, p. xiv), and she expresses this dissatisfaction by making her protagonist a novelist who is similarly dissatisfied: as Anna says, " 'I keep trying to write the truth and realizing it's not true' " (p. 274). Though Lessing describes "the artist" as the "theme of our time"— "every major writer has used it, and most minor ones" (introduction, pp. xi–xii)—*The Golden Notebook* is one of only two novels where Lessing "uses" it (*The Diaries of Jane Somers* is the other) and the only one where she endows the novelist/protagonist with her own considerable talents. It is actually surprising that Lessing addresses this "theme" at all, in view of her contempt for "the cult of the artist" and her sense of why most people wish to write—their desire to attain fame and to escape the tedium of their lives (MQ, pp. 211–12). But, as she explains in the introduction, she is not interested in "that isolated, creative

sensitive figure" which is the usual subject of the *Kunstlerroman*; she finds
"intolerable" "this monstrously isolated, monstrously narcissistic, pedestalled
paragon":

> I decided [the theme] would have to be developed by giving the creature a block
> and discussing the reasons for the block. This would have to be linked with the
> disparity between the overwhelming problems of war, famine, poverty, and the
> tiny individual who was trying to mirror them. (p. xii)

"The reasons for the block" are political as well as personal, for, as Anna says,
the " 'moment I sit down to write, someone comes into the room, looks over my
shoulders, and stops me. . . . It could be a Chinese peasant. Or one of Castro's
guerilla fighters. Or an Algerian fighting in the F.L.N. . . . They stand here in
the room and they say, why aren't you doing something about us, instead of
wasting your time scribbling?' " (p. 639)

In order to write "the only kind of novel which interests" her, a work
"powered with an intellectual or moral passion strong enough to create order,
to create a new way of looking at life" (p. 360), Anna must "enter those areas of
life [her] way of living, education, sex, politics, class bar [her] from" (p. 61). In
order to do this, she must remain vulnerable to "the overwhelming problems"
of others: rather than closing and dividing herself off, as the male characters do,
she must keep herself "open for something"; this becomes the means to new
creation, the "gap" through which "the future . . . pour[s] in a different shape"
(p. 473). In the final episodes, when Anna and Saul " 'break down' into each
other, into other people, break through the false patterns they have made of
their pasts" (as Lessing describes them; pp. vii–viii), Anna "break[s] . . .
[her]own form"; and, "changed by the experience of being other people" (p.
602), she "expand[s] [her] limits beyond what has been possible" (p. 619). It is
her ability to risk the dissolution of the self that enables her to expand the
boundaries of the self.

It is precisely those qualities of female identity analyzed by Chodorow—
boundary confusion, empathy, relatedness—that enable Anna to change.[32]
Whereas the female "experiences herself . . . as a continuation or extension of
. . . her mother in particular, and later of the world in general," the male "has
engaged, and been required to engage, in a more emphatic individuation and a
more defensive firming of experienced ego boundaries."[33] Lessing articulates
differences between men and women—" 'because we aren't the same. That is
the point' " (p. 44)—to women's advantage, portraying women as "tougher . . .
kinder" (p. 663), and establishing this contrast in the first scene, in the conflict
between Richard and Molly/Anna for the loyalty of Tommy, Molly's and
Richard's son. Whereas Richard prides himself on "preserv[ing] the forms,"
Anna and Molly pride themselves on not "giving in" (" 'to what?' " Richard
asks; " 'if you don't know we can't tell you,' " they reply [pp. 25–26]); and
Tommy understands that "the forms" by which Richard defines himself (money,
status, power) fix him and freeze him, whereas the "formlessness" of the
women's lives would allow them to " 'change and be something different' "

(p. 36). Yet Tommy, in Anna's "Free Women" version, is so terrified of formlessness that he kills off a part of himself rather than risk it; and this measure, though extreme, symbolizes what most of the men do, who "stay sane" "by block[ing] off at this stage or that . . . by limiting themselves" (p. 469), by a "locking of feeling . . . [a] refusal to fit conflicting things together . . . [which] means one can neither change nor destroy" (p. 65). The men Anna becomes involved with after the end of the affair with Michael (Paul in the yellow notebook), "sexual cripples" (p. 484) who are afflicted with "mother trouble" (p. 581) and frozen in postures of "cool, cool, cool" (p. 545), illustrate what has been described as "the limits of masculinity" and "the confines of masculinity."[34] Even Saul, the one man in the novel who risks "freedom" in the most basic sense (of being unmarried) and risks breakdown and survives able to write—even he remains locked into an "I" which rattles through his speech like a machine gun (p. 556), and he leaves at the end, unable to love, "not mature yet" (p. 642).

## Working It Through: Textual Feminism

Lessing demonstrates that both male and female behaviors represent crippling adjustments to a destructive society, but that men are more crippled because they lock themselves into postures that prohibit change. In "the sex war" (p. 572) Saul and Anna engage in as they break down into one another, they assume typical, stereotypical, male–female roles, which they play out in extreme form. Enacting the various potentials of woman as Saul enacts those of man, "play[ing] against each other every man-woman role imaginable" (p. 604), he becomes "the position of man," "a classic . . . story of our time" (p. 560), as she is " 'the position of women in our time' " (p. 579). Anna begins "stuck fast in an emotion common to women of our time" (p. 480), "self-pitying," "Anna betrayed" (p. 596), to which Saul responds with "his need to betray" (p. 597). He admits that he resents her success as a writer and that he " 'enjoys a society where women are second-class citizens' " (pp. 604–605), that he's " 'competitive about everything' " " 'because I'm an American. It's a competitive country' " (p. 578). They enter into a "cycle of bullying and tenderness" (p. 581), he railing against "women the jailers, the consciences, the voice of society," she responding with "the weak soft sodden emotion, the woman betrayed" (p. 630), "the white female bosom shot full of cruel male arrows" (p. 636). He is "repeating a pattern over and over again: courting a woman with his intelligence and sympathy, claiming her emotionally; then, when she began to claim in return, running away. And the better a woman was, the sooner he would . . . run" (pp. 587–88). But out of these unpromising materials, they forge a new kind of relationship, noncompetitive and supportive—" 'You're going to write that book, you're going to write it, you're going to finish it . . . because if you can do it, then I can,' " he tells her (p. 639); and they part as a "team"—" 'we're a team, we're the ones who haven't given in, who'll go on fighting' " (p. 642); "I felt towards him as if he were my brother, as if, like a brother, it wouldn't matter how we strayed from each other, how far apart we were, we would always be flesh of one flesh, and think each other's thoughts" (p. 641).

In this relationship, as in the novel as a whole, "something . . . [is] played out . . . some pattern . . . worked through" (p. 583). As in *The Children of Violence*, "working through" requires repetition; as in *The Four-Gated City*, where Martha's circular returns allow her to learn on deeper and deeper levels, so here, the organization of material into several notebooks allows Anna to rework the material of her life until she can get it right. In the course of her breakdown, she circles closer in on cathected material, and, as her self dissolves, so, too, do the basic categories of experience: she loses all "sense of time" (pp. 593–94) and "words . . . become . . . not the form into which experience is shaped, but a series of meaningless sounds," "the secretions of a caterpillar" (p. 476). This is why she would like to communicate through nonverbal shapes, a circle or square (p. 633)—and in a sense the "wordless statement" made by the form does just this, for (as Rubenstein notes) "the major divisions of the novel into four groups of four are abstractions of the square" (p. 107), as opposed to which are "the cyclic repetitions, layerings, and recombinations of the same essential emotional events from a variety of perspectives" (p. 75): *The Golden Notebook* "moves forward in time and in the narrative unfolding of the novel, while turning back on itself both in the repetition of images and themes in the circularity of the organization" (p. 90).[35] Reworking the material in four notebooks and two novels, Anna can relive "the end of the affair" in imagination and actuality, in fictional and "real-life" versions, repeating the loss of Michael in the loss of Paul, and repeating the loss of Michael/Paul in the loss of Saul/Milt in a way that puts an end to repetition. The form of *The Golden Notebook* allows repetition which is a release from repetition and allows Anna to revise, reevaluate, redescribe—to know "on deeper and deeper levels" (p. 239) and " 'name' . . . in a different way" (p. 616). And as in *The Four-Gated City*, where four parts of four yield to a fifth, to the new dimension of the "Appendix," so, too, in *The Golden Notebook* do four sections of four notebooks yield to a fifth, the golden notebook, which similarly portrays break-through to a fifth dimension.

In the introduction, Lessing stressed the importance of the form: "My major aim was to shape a book which would make its own comment, a wordless statement: to talk through the way it was shaped . . . this was not noticed" (p. xiv). It was "not noticed" because *The Golden Notebook* was ahead of its time, and, like other innovative works, it had to teach us how to read it. After Lessing published the introduction, the next decade of criticism focused on form, but most readings emphasized Anna's attempts to find wholeness, efforts that lead her to Jungian psychology and Marxism—which, as Lessing says, "looks at things as a whole and in relation to each other—or tries to" (p. xiv).[36] A more recent stage of criticism has been less concerned with the text's unities than with its disunities, its uses of splitting and fragmentation, and less concerned to resolve Anna into a homogeneous, unified self than to celebrate her complex, heterogeneous identity.[37] This shift illustrates (like litmus paper) the shift from the new-critical focus on unity to contemporary theory's interest in discontinuity, and illustrates as well feminists' reassessments of subjectivity, their shift from the search for unity and authenticity to a celebration of heterogeneity.[38]

But the political implications of Lessing critique of "the forms" have still not been much noticed, which is why the novel's feminism continues to be misunderstood. Lessing drew on Marxist critiques that were coming out of the Left in the fifties and sixties for her analysis of the ideological complicity of the forms, conventions, and institutions of literary production. The novel combines Marxist exposure of the ways ideology is inscribed within literary forms with deconstructive critiques of an epistemology based on hierarchical oppositions, with a feminist analysis of personal as political and of female identity as processive, in a radically feminist text which is also a "writerly" text (in Barthes's term), a "polyphonic" text (in Kristeva's term), an "interrogative" text (in Belsey's term).[39]

## Ideology and Form

Like Adrienne Rich and Mary Daly, Lessing sees "naming" as crucial to remaking the world: "It would be a help at least to describe things properly, to call things by their right names" (p. xvi). But how "to call things by their right names" when "names" are themselves "contaminated, full of traditional associations," as Lessing terms them?[40] Anna seeks truth in words, only to find "untruths" everywhere—encoded in slogans, jargon, "parrot-phrases" (pp. 21, 401, 590–91): "how many of the things we say are just echoes" (p. 52).

Lessing was drawn to Marxist aesthetics because it was concerned with questions that concerned her—about the ideological complicity of language and convention, the relationship of politics to art, the possibility of revolutionary form. Though she left the Communist Party in 1956, her break precipitated, like that of many other British leftists, by Stalin and the invasion of Hungary, she was on the first board of the *New Left Review* in 1960, on the editorial board of the *New Reasoner,* and took an active part in the emerging New Left, which focused on analyses of literature, media, communications, and the possibility of "cultural intervention."[41] She knew Brecht's drama and probably also knew Walter Benjamin's work on Brecht;[42] she had read Lukács and was aware of his analysis of the novel as counteracting the alienation and fragmentation of capitalism and recreating the totality or relatedness of life;[43] Antonio Gramsci's *Prison Notebooks,* written between 1927 and 1935, was translated into English in the fifties (or at least portions were, in *The New Prince*) and was being discussed in leftist circles.[44] Louis Althusser's refinements of the "vulgar Marxist" definition of ideology in "Marxism and Humanism," in *For Marx* (1965) and "Ideology and Ideological State Apparatuses" (in *Lenin and Philosophy*)[45] were published a few years after *The Golden Notebook,* but his ideas were in the air.

Anna uses the word "myth" as Gramsci and Althusser use "ideology," to mean that system of beliefs and assumptions—unconscious, unexamined, invisible—by which we imagine and represent the world. "It all comes out of the myth" (p. 349), Anna says, referring to the "flat, tame, optimistic . . . curiously jolly" (p. 349) Soviet fiction she and her friend Jack read, "the literature of health and progress" (p. 445):

> The writing is bad, the story lifeless, but what is frightening . . . is that it is totally inside the current myth. . . . This novel touches reality at no point at all. . . . It is, however, a very accurate recreation of the self-deceptive myths of the Communist Party at this particular time; and I have read it in about fifty different shapes or guises during the last year. (p. 346)

Though, as Althusser says, "the accusation of being in ideology only applies to others, never to oneself" ("Ideology," p. 175), the numerous parallels Lessing suggests between communist and "capitalist publishing racket[s]" (p. 346) make the point that Western literary and critical practices are every bit as enmeshed in ideology as Soviet propaganda is. As Lessing says, everyone is "a prisoner of the assumptions and dogmas of his time, which he does not question, because he has never been told they exist" (p. xvi); as Anna says, " 'Well, surely the thought follows—what stereotype am I?' " (p. 49).

Though originating in particular social and political conditions, ideology authorizes those conditions as "natural" or "universal."[46] Gramsci analyzes ideology as working through "1. language itself, which is a totality of determined notions and concepts . . . 2. 'common sense' . . . 3. the entire system of beliefs, superstitions, opinions, ways of seeing things and of acting, which are collectively bundled together under the name of 'folklore.' "[47] Althusser describes two types of "State Apparatuses" which "ensure *subjection to the ruling ideology*" ("Ideology," p. 133): the Repressive State Apparatuses such as the army and police and the Ideological State Apparatuses, mainly "the educational" but also including "the communications apparatus" (press, radio, and television) and "the cultural" (literature, the arts)" (pp. 143, 145, 154). His analysis of "the School" as "the dominant Ideological State Apparatus" (pp. 153, 156–7) resembles Lessing's critique of formal education as inculcating "received opinion" and a respect for authority; and his analysis of coercion as both psychological and materialistic (like Gramsci's) represents a "union of Marx and Freud"[48]—"Grandfathers Freud and Marx," as Anna calls them (p. 643). Ideology masks contradictions, offers partial truths and a false coherence, thereby obscuring actual conditions and prohibiting change; as Coward and Ellis say, "It defines the limits for, and works to fix the individual within, a certain mental horizon" and masks the very "contradictions, ambiguities, and inconsistencies" which might function as "a source of possible change" (pp. 74, 67–8; see also Althusser, "Ideology," p. 162, and *For Marx*, p. 233).

Literature transmits ideology not merely or most significantly in content; rather, as Eagleton suggests (drawing on Lukács), "the true bearers of ideology

... are the very forms" (p. 24): "in selecting a form ... the writer finds his choice already ideologically circumscribed"; "The languages and devices a writer finds to hand are already saturated with certain ideological modes of perception, certain codified ways of interpreting reality" (pp. 26–27). Jameson says "formal processes" "carry ideological messages of their own, distinct from the ostensible or manifest content of the works";[49] Barthes says that "every Form is also a Value": "It is under the pressure of History and Tradition that the possible modes of writing for a given writer are established ... writing ... remains full of the recollection of previous usage, for language is never innocent."[50] Raymond Williams describes conventions as "involving ... social assumptions of causation and consequence";[51] DuPlessis applies this specifically to romance, which she analyzes as a "trope for the sex gender system."[52] Forms, conventions, and language are bearers of ideology; and so, too, are genres, which emerge in response to specific historical situations, as the novel did to meet the needs of the bourgeoisie in the eighteenth century. In fact, Jameson extends *the ideology of form*" to apply to "the aesthetic act" itself: "the production of aesthetic or narrative form is ... an ideological act in its own right, with the function of inventing imaginary or formal 'solutions' to unresolvable social contradictions" (p. 79).

### Representation and Its Discontents: The Four Notebooks

The central question of *The Golden Notebook*—how to oppose a system by means of linguistic and literary conventions that have been forged by that system—is a central question facing feminist theory today: can we use the master's tools to dismantle the master's house?[53] Anna's four notebooks contain commentary, explicit and implicit, on the ideological complicity of literary and critical forms—novels, short stories, journalism, parody, "propaganda," literary criticism, reviews. Their discussion—and demonstration—of the complicity of forms with the systems, capitalist and communist, that produce them, offers a kind of "worst possible case," exploring the possibility that all discourse is inextricably and inevitably bound to "reproduction," bound to a circular process of reproducing the ideology which produces it, determined and determining.

In the yellow notebook, Anna explores the conventions of the "women's novel" by writing "The Shadow of the Third," which "comes out of" the myth of romantic love—"the property of the women's magazines" (p. 204), as Ella calls it. The red notebook, a record of Anna's political activities, consists of Soviet short stories and speculations about Soviet art. The black notebook is a record of transactions relating to Anna's first novel, *The Frontiers of War,* including attempts of the capitalist literary marketplace to commodify it and Soviet reviews which condemn it for deviating from party line. The blue notebook, a journal, contains "facts," attempts at parodies and discussions of parody, and notes on film, "High Art," and pastiche, including Anna's last-ditch effort to "cage the truth" by means of the newspaper clippings she pastes around her walls.

The form that is easiest to critique as ideological—because it expresses someone else's ideology—is the Soviet fiction Anna reads for the communist publishing house she works for. Though the cheerful, bland Soviet writing is superficially the antithesis of the "unhealthy," "immoral" fiction she repudiates in *Frontiers of War,* Anna realizes that this "dead stuff," "this bad, dead, banal writing is the other side of my coin . . . of the psychological impulse that created *Frontiers of War*": "And so this is the paradox: I, Anna, reject my own 'unhealthy' art: but reject 'healthy' art when I see it" (p. 349). The parallels between these forms imply similarities between the societies that produce them. The lonely-hearts letters Ella answers for the women's magazine she works for, *Women at Home,* have their counterparts in the comrades' letters Anna answers for the communist publishing house—and when this publisher advertises its interest in fiction, it is inundated by manuscripts. As Molly exclaims,

> "Everyone was going to be a great writer, but everyone! . . . every one of the old party war horses . . . everyone has that old manuscript or wad of poems tucked away. . . . Isn't it terrifying? Isn't it pathetic? Every one of them, failed artists. I'm sure it's significant of something, if only one knew *what.*" (p. 16)

"What" it signifies is stated in *Martha Quest*—no one can "face the prospect of a lifetime behind a desk" (pp. 211–12). Such manuscripts "come out of" different "myths," but they express the same despair (pp. 38–39, 167–68, 175, 236, 284, 353, 653).

Overt forms of coercion in the Soviet Union are paralleled by blacklisting in the United States. As Nelson, a blacklisted American writer, says, " *'They've beaten me* . . . they don't need prison and firing squads to beat people' " (p. 490). On both sides, the political situation makes it impossible to know the truth: "the communist language" and "the language of democracy" are both "safe unreal jargon," "a means of disguising the truth" (pp. 294–95). "This is a time when it is impossible to know the truth about anything" (p. 302); " 'anything might be true anywhere. . . . Anything is possible' " (p. 163).

But that "anything is possible" makes parody impossible, since truth is so fantastic that it outdoes attempts at caricature, as Anna keeps discovering— "something had happened which made parody impossible" (p. 440). The "journals" of a young American traveler and a "lady author" "afflicted with sensibility," which Anna and her friend write as parody, are accepted as authentic and published (pp. 434–40). Anna's *"Blood on the Banana Leaves"* expresses the melodrama and sensation latent in her first novel, *Frontiers of War,* as "the Romantic Tough School of Writing" (pp. 539–41) expresses a potential of Saul's writing. When Anna assumes the voice of June Boothby, a lovesick adolescent girl, she realizes how close this style is to her own: "I wrote in the style of the most insipid coy woman's magazine; but what was frightening was that the insipidity was due to a very slight alteration of my own style, a word here and there only" (p. 620). Conversely, Anna finds parody where there is none: Comrade Ted's story of his meeting with a Stalin eager to follow his advice is so fantastic that Anna "thought it was an exercise in irony. Then a very skilful parody of a certain attitude. Then I realised it was serious. . . . But what seemed to me important was that it could be read as parody, irony, or seriously"; and this gives her a sense of "the thinning of language against the density of our experience" (p. 302).

The Western literary world co-opts by the power of money, on the one hand, and by the power of "culture," on the other hand, the former reducing art to a commodity, the latter enshrining it as "high Art"; "the literary world is so prissy . . . so classbound; or if it's the commercial side, so blatant, that any contact with it sets [Anna] thinking of joining the Party" (p. 154). Anna's encounters with Reggie Tarbrucke of Amalgamated Vision and Mrs. Edwina Wright of Bluebird Screenplays illustrate "the commercial side." Reggie tries to convince Anna that her novel is "really a simple moving love story" (p. 285), and in an effort to outrage him, Anna suggests making a comedy of it, but again, this attempt at parody is defeated when Edwina, representative of American television, assures her that "it would make a marvellous musical" (p. 292).

The belief in "Art" and "the artist" is represented by Anna's Jungian therapist, Mrs. Marks. "A pillar of reaction" (p. 237) who insists that the artist is "sacred" (p. 235), "a European soaked in art," her room is "like a shrine to art" (p. 253)—" 'all that damned art all over the place' " (p. 5); "the walls are covered with reproductions of masterpieces and there are statues. It is almost like an art gallery" (p. 236). Anna can see that this view of "the artist" is part of the same "myth" that sanctions the term "real woman" and that this myth is "reactionary"—Mrs. Marks "uses this word, a woman, a real woman, exactly as she does artist, a true artist. An absolute" (p. 237); " 'I no longer believe in art,' " Anna tells her (p. 232). The name Anna and Molly give her, "Mother Sugar," refers to "a whole way of looking at life—traditional, rooted, conservative" (p. 5). Besides, Anna can see that Mother Sugar's "complacent smile" "when the word Art cropped up" is another expression of the attitude of the marketplace, of "the money changers, the little jackals of the press, the enemy": "When a film mogul wants to buy an artist—and the real reason he seeks out the original talent and the spark of creativity is because he wants to destroy it, unconsciously that's what he wants, to justify himself by destroying the real thing—he calls the victim an artist" (pp. 62–63). Anna rejects both preciousness and popularization, "culture" and commerce, and realizes that they are opposite sides of the same coin.

Criticism, like literature, "comes out of the myth" and, while purporting to offer new perspectives, only recycles received ideas. Reviews of *Frontiers of War* demonstrate the way criticism monitors what can be thought and said. Soviet journals condemn the novel: "a true artistic work must have a revolutionary life . . . this author must learn from our literature, the literature of health and progress, that no one is benefited by despair. This is a negative novel . . . unhealthy, even ambiguous" (p. 445). In the West, academic taste shifts with political winds, so that an article on China which is refused publication one month becomes lucrative the next month (pp. 157–58); critics and reviewers "adapt themselves to authority figures, to 'received opinion,' " and are incapable of "imaginative and original judgment" (this commentary occurs extratextually, in Lessing's remarks on the critical reception of *The Golden Notebook;* introduction, p. xvi). Anna imagines herself writing a review of *Frontiers of War* which asks "the only question worth asking":

> The most interesting question raised by this new report from the racial frontiers is: why, when the oppressions and tensions of white-settled Africa have existed more or less in their present form for decades, it is only in the late forties and fifties that they exploded into artistic form. If we knew the answer we would understand more of the relations between society and the talent it creates, between art and the tensions that feed it. (p. 60)

In both novels Anna is writing, *Free Women* and "The Shadow of the Third," Anna shapes the rough, raw material of the blue notebook into more conventional, marketable form. In *Free Women,* there are clearer crises and denouements, scenes that are more dramatic and definitive, than anything in the blue notebook: Tommy attempts suicide and blinds himself; Anna offers advice which improves the situation between Tommy and Molly and earns Richard's thanks (pp. 521–22); and the novel ends with Anna " 'integrated with British life' " (p. 666), taking a job as a marriage counselor and giving up writing. In "The Shadow of the Third" Ella has a more conventional job than Anna does, at the women's magazine *Women at Home,* and she and her friend Julia "considered themselves very normal, not to say conventional women" (p. 171); though Ella has qualms about how her magazine "pushes taste on" its readers (pp. 179, 220), she is generally untroubled by questions of the truth or morality of art—she publishes a novel about suicide and has "no politics" (p. 178). Anna names the "coy little-womanish, snobbish" atmosphere (p. 178) of Ella's magazine and adjusts her language to it ("it was Patricia Brent, editress, who suggested Ella should spend a week in Paris" [p. 306]). Romantic love is associated with conventional form: " 'Broken hearts belong to old-fashioned novels. . . . They don't go with the time we live in' " (p. 103), as Paul Blackenhurst says[54]—though this novel concludes more interestingly than *Free Women* does, breaking off into fragments that lead to new beginnings.

Though Anna is critical of the forms, she also makes various nostalgic attempts to fit her life to them. *The Golden Notebook* registers the loss of the systems—social, moral, philosophical, political—that once gave life meaning: " 'My God, what we've lost, what we've lost, what we've lost, how can we ever get back to it, how can we get back to it again?' " Saul exclaims (p. 629). Anna does try "to get back to it," but she is prevented by her own honesty, on the one hand, and by history, on the other hand, which destroy the possibility of romantic or political innocence. The "form" she clings to longest is that provided by romantic love—" 'my strongest need—being with one man, love, all that' " (p. 625). Though she can criticize the system of beliefs that sanctions

Mrs. Marks's terms "true artist" and "real woman," she has more difficulty with the term "real man," which she uses without irony (pp. 391–93, 404, 455, 484, 561): though she strives for liberation from the romantic myth, she is also enmeshed in it, and the emotional thralldom she is exploring in "The Shadow of the Third" is her own.

The "end of the affair" coincides with the end of therapy with Mrs. Marks and the end of her involvement with the Communist Party: "Michael is leaving me, that's finished"; "And I'm leaving the Party. It's a stage of my life finished. And what next? I'm going out, willing it, into something new. . . . I'm shedding a skin, or being born again" (p. 353). Endings occur in the middle, with the second half of the novel "writing beyond" them: the "skin" Anna "sheds" is no less than her conditioning, "a habit of . . . nerves from the past" (p. 365), and her change puts her on a "kind of frontier" (p. 482). Against Mrs. Marks's efforts to fit her experience into an "old pattern," to get her to "put the pain away where it can't hurt, turn it into a story or into history" (p. 471), Anna insists on remaining true to what is "new" in her, to " 'areas of me made by the kind of experience women haven't had before' " (p. 471)—to what is "raw" and "unfinished" in her life (pp. 236–37). Anna's interrogation of literary-critical forms is inseparable from her efforts to move beyond conventional forms in her life. To be true to what is "new" in her requires that she resist "turning it into a story"—or rather, that she invent a new kind of story.

## New Moves

To remain stuck in the role of victim is to validate the "helpless lists of opposing words" (p. 71) Anna named at the beginning—"Men. Women. Bound. Free. Good. Bad. Yes. No. Capitalism. Socialism. Sex. Love" (p. 44)—and so to reaffirm the dualisms which are the basis of Western thought, confirming not only male power but the whole epistemological and linguistic structure that sanctions it. But in the course of the novel, nearly every important event, issue, question, quality, attitude, action comes up for renaming: in the visionary and "re-visionary" final episodes, words, phrases, events recur, the same but different, as the value of "boulder pushing," of "taking a stand," of "the forms," of "making patterns," of irony, and of naming itself—all are renamed as Anna wrests strength from chaos. Most crucial is the principle of destruction represented by her dream of the dwarf, which she names "joy in malice, joy in a destructive impulse" (p. 477); Anna first dreams it negatively, and then, realizing "it was up to me to force this thing to be good as well as bad" (p. 478), dreams it positively, releasing a "third friendly" creature—male and female, "the third" or "the shadow of the third," the figure onto whom she had projected those powers she relinquished in her relationship with Michael/ Paul.

But the way to this power is by giving up power, just as the way to new form is through formlessness. This is why Anna's route in the latter half of the novel seems so bizarre. Rather than finding redemption through the love of a good man, Anna becomes involved with men who are worse and worse, even more divided and destructive than Michael/Paul—Nelson, de Silva, Saul Green—and submerges herself in their destructiveness. They take her through an "emotional no-man's land" (p. 457) to a realm where "it didn't matter" (the phrase that recurs in de Silva's speech), but they also jolt her out of the passive, unthinking stance she assumed with Michael into more active, creative roles which do not fall within the rubric of romantic love or, indeed, within any rubric. Those critics who have blamed Lessing for depicting woman's sexuality as "contained" or "created" by man's (pp. 445, 215)[55] have confused the author with the protagonist, for Lessing shows Anna as needing to outgrow this idea: the cost of being Michael's "creation" has been her own creative self.

Anna's sense of other possibilities begins as she learns, with Cy Maitland, that she can "do the directing" (p. 323); with the Canadian scriptwriter she also "gives pleasure," though she resents this new role, criticizing him on the grounds that "the man's desire creates a woman's desire, or should, so I'm right to be critical" (p. 546). Blaming de Silva on similar grounds—"Of course it's him, not me. For men create these things, they create us"—she has a new insight: "remembering how I clung, how I always cling on to this, I felt foolish. Because why should it be true?" (p. 501). Anna does not easily relinquish the claims of the passive self, but against her clinging to old patterns there struggles a new sense of her powers of creation—as suggested by the short-story sketches concerning the creation of selves in response to relationships (pp. 460–61) and by the insight that a man with an "ambiguous uncreated quality" (p. 532) is more attractive than one who is "formed." By immersing herself in the destructiveness of these men, she comes to acknowledge the destructive principle within her—a process symbolized by the dream of the dwarf, which evolves through various male incarnations before coming to rest finally in her; it is this which enables her to relinquish her role as victim.

As she comes to see herself as participant rather than victim and as her role in relationships becomes more "creative," she can relinquish the illusion that "the truth" is outside, in some external form, and accept that meaning is in the patterning, structuring power of the mind. In her search for "the truth" Anna has assumed that there is a reality independent of the mind, but all her attempts to record "simply, the truth," "the straight, simple formless account" (p. 63), throw her back on her "own ordering, commenting memory" (p. 585). On the day she attempts to record "everything," September 17, 1954, "the idea that I will have to write it down is changing the balance, destroying the truth" (p. 341): "No, it didn't come off. A failure as usual" (p. 368). She realizes that knowing the end has altered the shape: "As soon as one has lived through something, it falls into a pattern. And the pattern of an affair . . . is seen in terms of what ends it"; "literature is analysis after the event"(pp. 227–28). She realizes that memory distorts: "How do I know that what I 'remember' was what was important? What I remember was chosen by Anna, of twenty years ago. I don't know what this Anna of now would choose" (p. 137). She imagines that visual images might provide greater certainty—"the absolute assurance of a smile, a look, a gesture, in a painting or a film" (p. 110): "probably better as a film. Yes, the physical quality of life . . . not the analysis afterwards" (p. 228). But in the dream she has of herself filming her life, she realizes that visual images are also shaped by memory: " 'What makes you think that the emphasis you have put on it is the correct emphasis?' " (p. 619), asks the "projectionist." All attempts to "cage the truth" (p. 660) by means of visual images or "facts" are as dependent as fiction is upon the ordering, selecting faculty of the mind.

When Anna can accept that there is no reality apart from the mind that perceives it and the words that shape it, she can accept that none of her versions is true—or all are true, or truth itself is a fiction, invented rather than discovered. It is this which gives her the power of renaming. New possibilities incur ontological instability, and as Anna's role becomes more "creative," we cannot always tell what is "real" and what is created. Toward the end of the novel Anna's notebook divisions break down: the political meeting where Anna meets Nelson is recorded in the blue notebook rather than the red notebook, and observations occur in the yellow notebook which prompt her to say, "This sort of comment belongs to the blue notebook. I must keep them separate" (p. 537). Both red and black notebooks break off into newspaper clippings; the yellow notebook breaks off into Ella's short-story sketches (pp. 531–34), sketches which prefigure Anna's breakdown with Saul and raise questions—if Ella is "writing" Anna, is she "authoring" her author; if Ella writes Saul, is he "real"—a "real man"? The blue notebook becomes a record of breakdown, which becomes, in the golden notebook, a record of breakthrough; and in both, dreams figure prominently, prefiguring "actual" incidents (or recalling them? it is not always possible to tell). Impugning the blue notebook as "the truth" on which the other notebooks draw, Lessing blurs the boundaries between "truth" and fiction and calls into question not only "the true story" but the "real man."[56] It may be that Anna "invents" Saul, fabricates him from all the men she has known, a kind of composite male who expresses her own "masculine" potential (in Jungian terms, her animus) and guides her through breakdown: she does dream of him as her "projectionist," "a person concerned to prevent the disintegration of Anna" (p. 614).

Though Lessing enlists Marxist critiques of linguistic form as determined and determining, she also critiques this critique and, allowing Anna the power of "naming in a different way," she gives her means of tapping into the subversive and liberatory potentials of language. Coward and Ellis critique Marxist thought about language as being "capable [only] of negative formulations about language, reducing it "to ideology" or "to a passive medium of communication with no effective determinacy of its own"; but language is not "reducible to ideology," for "language and thought . . . engender [each] other: language makes thought possible, thought makes language possible" (pp. 78–

79).[57] *The Golden Notebook* qualifies its Marxist critiques with a poststructuralist sense of the truth of interpretations, that (in Molly Hite's term) "there is no truth apart from the telling, no real story, no authorized version" (p. 90).[58] Not that there is no reality, as in extreme poststructuralist positions, but that—as Raymond Williams suggests—"all human experience is an interpretation": "we create our human world as we have thought of art being created." This view of interpretation as agency, as creative and culture building, is different from relativistic deconstructive positions: it makes the imagination integral to "everything we see and do, the whole structure of our relationships and institutions," and it provides the way through Anna's writer's block by justifying art, making it crucial to culture building, and linking it with life: "to see art as a particular process in the general human process of creative discovery and communication is at once a redefinition of the status of art and the finding of means to link it with our ordinary social life." This is the answer both to "High Art" and commodification, as Williams explains, for it eliminates "the distinction of art from ordinary living, and the dismissal of art as unpractical or secondary (a 'leisure-time activity')," which "are alternative formulations of the same error."[59] When Anna can accept her own fictions, she can allow her various versions to "come together" into the novel we have just read, a form that admits to its own uncertainties and contradictions, to its own processes of production, and that celebrates the "crude, unfinished, raw, tentative" in her life as "precisely what was valuable in it" (pp. 236–37).

## Naming in a Different Way

Before she can know—with a knowledge that is "part of how [she sees] the world" (p. 589)—that "truth" is in the patterning, structuring power of the mind, Anna must first experience the dissolution of language, know that "words mean nothing" (pp. 476–77). This possibility is suggested in several places in the novel and is finally worked through in the golden notebook:

> I think, bitterly, that a row of asterisks, like an old-fashioned novel, might be better. Or a symbol of some kind, a circle perhaps, or a square. Anything at all, but not words. The people who have been there, in the place in themselves where words, patterns, order, dissolve, will know what I mean and the others won't. (pp. 633–34)

This realization prompts Anna's encounter with the "terrible irony," a nihilism that represents the defeat of all human effort, but this low point is also the turning point, for

> Once having been there, there's a terrible irony, a terrible shrug of the shoulders, and it's not a question of fighting it, or disowning it, or of right or wrong, but simply knowing it is there, always. It's a question of bowing to it, so to speak, with a kind of courtesy, as to an ancient enemy: All right, I know you are there, but we have to preserve the forms, don't we? And perhaps the condition of your existing at all is precisely that we preserve the forms, create the patterns. (p. 634)

That the "terrible irony" calls forth "a kind of courtesy" recalls the association of irony with "courtesy" in relation to Tom Mathlong, "a courteous,
ironical figure" "who performed actions, played roles, that he believed to be
necessary for the good of others, even while he preserved an ironic doubt about
the results of his actions"—a quality Anna defines as "something we needed very
badly in this time" (p. 597). "We have to preserve the forms," the phrase
Richard used to justify his idiot complacency, is renamed positively as "creating
the patterns" and transformed from a self-limiting self-justification to a saving
grace; and though Tommy has dismissed "just making patterns" as cowardice—
" 'I don't think there's a pattern anywhere—you are just making patterns, out of
cowardice' " (p. 275)—Anna reenvisions "making patterns" as an act of creative
imagination. Similarly, "it doesn't matter," the phrase that expressed the nihilism of de Silva and the "total sterility" of Anna's dream of her life as a film—
" 'it doesn't matter what we film, provided we film something' " (p. 525)—is
associated now with commitment: "it doesn't matter" which stand we take as
long as we take a stand; " 'We've got to make stands all the time . . . . the point
is to make a stand at all' " (p. 552). "Naming" itself is transformed from a
defensive "fixing," "a 'naming' to save . . . from pain" (p. 489), to the imaginative recreation Anna practices in "the Game" and in the novel as a whole.
"Naming" is reenvisioned as "rescue-work . . . rescuing the formless into form"
(p. 470); and "something new and terrible" (p. 481) becomes something "terrible . . . or marvellous" (p. 473). "Everything has two faces," as Anna tells Mrs.
Marks (p. 251), which is also what Martha discovers in her breakdown: *every
attitude, emotion, thought, has its opposite held in balance out of sight but
there all the time. Push any one of these to an extreme, and boomps-a-daisy,
over you go into its opposite*" (FGC, p. 521).[60] This involvement of each quality
with its opposite, this dialectical interchange of each with other, dissolves the
binding force of binaries.

This release of new potentials enables Anna to dream, again, of her life as a
film; but unlike the "glossy," "conventionally, well-made films" of the first
golden-notebook dream sequence, "all false," "all false" (pp. 614–21), this film
has a "realistic," "rough, crude, rather jerky quality" (p. 634), and it not only
transcends her experience but brings "together" images previously separate:

> The film was now beyond my experience, beyond Ella's, beyond the notebooks,
> because there was a fusion; and instead of seeing separate scenes, people, faces,
> movements, glances, they were all together . . . it became a series of moments
> where a peasant's hand bent to drop seed into earth . . . or a man stood on a dry
> hillside in the moonlight . . . his rifle ready on his arm. (p. 635)

The golden-notebook dream sequences show Anna transcending her own form
and attaining a "new imaginative comprehension" of the Algerian soldier and
Chinese peasant—figures which recur to symbolize the collective life she feared
her art was debarred from (pp. 596, 600, 635, 639). Having confronted the
worst possibility, the "terrible irony"—"All right, I know you are there" (p.
634)—Anna can get on with her life.

After the four notebooks merge in the golden notebook and after Anna's selves merge with Saul's, Anna steps back into the forms and frames the experience with the short, conventional novel *Free Women,* which—unlike the notebooks, which fly off into fragments to become new beginnings—is a closed form which contains or "buttons up" (p. 625). Having dissolved the forms, she can remake them on her own terms and "preserve the forms" that enable her to endure, forging a new relation to the forms which is not a capitulation, but which enables her to take stands, in full recognition of the arbitrariness of these stands, in a spirit of "courteous" irony.

Lessing makes terms with the forms similar to those which she makes with language, terms that acknowledge what Fuoroli calls "the paradoxical nature of referential language—that it is always inadequate and always necessary."[61] *The Golden Notebook* has been criticized for discussing the inadequacy of language in adequate language, for "talk[ing] about disorder in a very orderly way—in an accessible style, and a determinedly everyday vocabulary, one usually non-allusive, even pedestrian" (Sprague and Tiger, introduction, p. 10). Nicole Ward Jouve points to the contradiction between Lessing's radical critiques of convention and her conservatism regarding language;[62] Elshtain objects that though Lessing's articulate characters discuss the limits of language, Lessing herself does not seek "new and innovative forms of expression."[63] It is true that Lessing assumes the efficacy of language for practical purposes; as the protagonist of *Briefing for a Descent into Hell* says, quoting T. S. Eliot, *"I gotta use words when I talk to you"*—besides, as he goes on to say, "that sequence of words . . . is a definition of all literature, seen from a different perspective."[64]

The "wordless statement" made by the form of *The Golden Notebook* affirms the value of forms while also acknowledging their partiality and incompleteness. But these forms are different from those by which Richard defined himself, because form is accepted within full ironic recognition of its limits. It is irony, with its acknowledgement of other perspectives and the incompleteness of each, that makes the difference between adequate and inadequate form—irony, not "terrible," but "courteous."[65] By juxtaposing the forms, Lessing creates a whole which includes and goes beyond them, a whole which is complex, heterogeneous, and processive.

## Breaking the Circle

Though Anna began with the passivity of earlier Lessing protagonists—Mary Turner of *The Grass Is Singing* or Martha Quest of the first four *Children of Violence* novels—drifting into destructive relationships and staying in them too long, she becomes, by the end, "intelligent enough to let [men] go": " 'You could do worse,' " Milt quips; " 'you could keep them' " (p. 568).[66] Anna does not get it "all," and her failure is in some sense a failure to resolve the traditional female conflict between love and writing. But her breakdown into Saul has transformed male–female relationships from a power struggle to a cooperative venture, and her response to the end of the Saul/Milt affair is measure of how far she has come since the end of the affair with Michael/Paul: the "skin" she "sheds" is no less than her sexual and emotional conditioning, the female dependence which is the legacy of the past.

Though *The Golden Notebook* unmasks and demystifies the conventions of realism, it is also a quintessential expression of realism (as described by Lukács): and this tension between the form and its deconstruction is part of the novel's fascination. It fulfills Anna's ideal of "a book powered with an intellectual or moral passion strong enough to create order, to create a new way of looking at life" (p. 61), while also impugning the basic assumption of realist representation, that literary and linguistic forms "reflect" reality. It focuses on an exceptional individual whose subjectivity is felt to matter and whose world is richly specified in relation to society and history. It accomplishes what the great realist novels do, creating a protagonist whose singularity is representative, for Anna is as representative of her age as Julien Sorel is of his. It gives us "a little novel about the emotions"—several of them—while also demonstrating those "emotions to be "a function and a product of a society" (p. 42). It is true that Anna's resolution is an individual resolution—only in the fantasy structures of the science fiction do Lessing's characters get to save the world. But the affirmations of this novel—culture building, boulder pushing, keeping the dream alive—are more than personal.

The main affirmation of the novel is the novel itself. I am assuming that Anna writes *The Golden Notebook*, though I realize that there is some ambiguity about this. The most persuasive argument that she does not is made by Molly Hite, who claims that since Lessing disallows "a hierarchy of ontological levels," it is impossible to decide whether the blue notebook or *Free Women* (in which Anna says she will no longer write) provides the "real" ending (p. 98). Hite argues that if we see Anna as the author of *The Golden Notebook*, we need to posit "a controlling consciousness to preside over *The Golden Notebook*," "an 'invisible Anna' " who is "the 'editor' of the entire work." But where is this Anna, author of *The Golden Notebook*? "If the authorial 'Anna' is not in the story, she is completely unknowable. There is no basis for calling her 'Anna' or for supposing that the experiences she recounts are in any sense her own" (p. 98).

Perhaps it is just that I cannot tolerate this much ontological insecurity,[67] but it seems obvious that Anna writes *The Golden Notebook* because she has been writing it all along: these are *her* notebooks. (As a student of mine commented, "She wasn't suffering from writer's block—she was writing the whole time; she was suffering from a bad attitude.") It is true that Anna nowhere says she intends to bring the notebooks together into a single novel, but she does say that she intends to put all of herself into one notebook, a "golden notebook."

If *Free Women* is all Anna writes as a result of her breakthroughs, it hardly seems worth the effort. In *Free Women*, Anna tells Molly that she will no longer write but intends to be a marriage counselor and work for the Labour Party, and Molly tells Anna that she is getting married; both women are resigned to "the

forms," " 'integrated with British life at its roots' " (p. 666). A tone of what Hite
calls "debilitating irony" (p. 99) informs the ironically titled *Free Women,* a
"tone" which has been defined by Anna as "a locking of feeling, an inability or
a refusal to fit conflicting things together to make a whole . . . [a] refusal
[which] means one can neither change nor destroy" (p. 65)—an irony not
"courteous." But as Lessing explains in the introduction, to use *Free Women* as
a frame for the notebooks was to make a "comment about the conventional
novel," to show " 'how little I have managed to say of the truth, how little I have
caught of all that complexity: how can this small neat thing be true when what I
experienced was so rough and apparently formless and unshaped' " (pp. xiii–
xiv). What is missing from *Free Women* is what is most essential about *The
Golden Notebook:* the wresting of strength from chaos, the transformation of
"terror" to "courtesy," the process of working through, of renaming and
reclaiming.

This situation of an Anna who writes a novel about an Anna who gives up
writing is a closed, self-cancelling circle: like the novel Anna writes about an
Ella who writes a novel about suicide or the "sadistic–masochistic cycle" (p.
606) in which Saul and Anna are caught, "a cycle [in which they]go around and
around" (p. 621), or Anna's dream of the firing squad, a nightmare in which
two men cynically exchange glances as they change places before a firing squad
before being shot—a dream that shows history as "simply a process, a wheel
turning" and that "cancels all creative emotion" (p. 345). But Anna and Saul
break their "cycle," and the novel Saul writes, to which Anna gives him the first
line, reverses the nightmare of the firing squad, for in Saul's novel the two men
talk to each other, though they are shot for it. So, too, does the novel Anna
writes, to which Saul gives her the first line—"the two women were alone in the
London flat"(p. 639)—transform the closed circle to an open, liberatory form,
for the opening line sends us back to the beginning not only of *Free Women* but
of *The Golden Notebook:* end circles back in a "self-begetting novel" that
concludes with the protagonist ready to begin—or, in this case, realizing that
she has already completed a task she had thought impossible. Though the
linearity of narrative means that there is no escaping what John Fowles calls "the
tyranny of the last chapter,"[68] and *Free Women* is the last chapter, it is not the
last word.

That each ending sends us back through the other, searching for a resting
place that cannot finally be found (Hite likens this effect to that of a Mobius
strip; p. 99), enlists the reader's imagination in an exercise of perceiving relationships and thereby strengthens the faculty of sympathetic imagination defined as a saving grace in the novel. For there is another "consciousness" in *The
Golden Notebook:* besides Anna's, besides Lessing's, there is the reader's
imagination—that essential component of any literary enterprise—that brings
the notebooks together and completes them. It is the reader who "imaginatively
fuses" *The Golden Notebook,* who provides the creative moral response, the
"act of imagination" which Anna likens to an "act of faith" (p. 275) and defines
as necessary to the realization of better selves and better worlds: "I was thinking

that quite possibly these marvellous, generous things we walk side by side with in our imaginations could come in existence, simply because we need them, because we imagine them" (p. 637).

As dismayed as Lessing was by readers' failure to understand the novel, she has also admitted to being instructed by her readers: "This novel continues to be, for its author, a most instructive experience." She describes how "ten years after I wrote it, I can get, in one week, three letters about it," one "entirely about the sex war," "the second . . . about politics," the third, about "mental illness": "but it is the same book." What she has learned from such letters is (what one suspects she already knew) about the role of the reader in the production of meaning. She concludes, characteristically, that

> the book is alive and potent and fructifying and able to promote thought and discussion *only* when its plan and shape and intention are not understood, because that moment of seeing the shape and plan and intention is also the moment when there isn't anything more to be got out of it. And when a book's pattern and the shape of its inner life is as plain to the reader as it is to the author—then perhaps it is time to throw the book aside, as having had its day, and start again on *something new*. (p. xxii, emphasis mine)

Naturally, I would like to believe that Lessing's "plan and intention" are plain to me. Nevertheless, *The Golden Notebook* remains "alive and potent and fructifying" because each time one reads it, it yields something new. It provides "a new way of looking at life" (p. 61) and "expand[s] one's limits beyond what has been possible" (p. 619), and its structural innovations affirm the possibility of psychic and political transformation by enacting change formally. Lessing writes not only beyond romantic endings, but also beyond the idea of the ending, with its inevitable nostalgia, and beyond those fictions by women who refuse their protagonists powers equivalent to their own. "A woman if she is to write must have a room of her own," said Virginia Woolf, and Lessing gives Anna "Wulf" not only a room of her own but the literary and critical gifts neither Woolf nor Austen, nor the Brontës, nor Eliot ever lavished on their protagonists, and then demonstrates that this is not enough, for the room in which Anna and Saul break down becomes a place where new possibilities are forged, terrible and marvelous: "the floor . . . bulging and heaving. The walls seemed to bulge inwards, then float out and away into space. . . . I stood in space, the walls gone" (p. 599). *The Golden Notebook* represents more than an "act of imagination" that "keeps the dream alive." It has been for many of us a "lurch forward" (p. 275) into new possibilities; it is what Margaret Drabble calls "territory gained forever."[69]

# VI

## MARGARET DRABBLE'S
## *THE WATERFALL*
### NEW SYSTEM, NEW MORALITY

> I tried for so long to . . . find a style that
> would express it, to find a system that would
> excuse me, to construct a new medium . . . so
> what can I make that will admit me and
> encompass me?

> I must make an effort to comprehend it. I will
> take it all to pieces, I will resolve it to its
> parts, and then I will put it together again. I
> will reconstitute it in a form that I can accept,
> a fictitious form. If I need a morality, I will
> create one. . . .
>
> *The Waterfall*[1]

Subdued by marriage, isolated and agoraphobic, Jane Gray seems to be suffering a terminal case of mad-housewife syndrome: she has relinquished all interests and connections with the world and sunk into near-catatonic stupor. Abandoned by her husband as she is on the verge of delivering a baby, she withdraws to her bed, "empty, solitary, neglected, cold" (p. 8), frozen into an "ice age of inactivity" (p. 7). But what is born in the opening pages is not only a child but a passion—for James, her cousin Lucy's husband—as, "delivering" a child, she is herself "delivered" (pp. 10, 159), and "submit[ting] . . . helplessly to the current" (p. 39), she is saved by love, Sleeping Beauty awakened. Thus Lynn Veach Sadler says "how any feminist could appreciate *The Waterfall* will remain a mystery."[2] Drabble herself calls it "a very neurotic book,"[3] a "wicked book"—"I've been attacked really very seriously and I can only respect the attack by people who say that you should not put into people's heads the idea that one can be saved from fairly pathological conditions by loving a man."[4]

Why include this "old story" in a study of feminist fiction, rather than, say,

*The Realms of Gold* or *The Middle Ground,* with their mature, resourceful, professionally successful protagonists? Because this account of events leaves out what is most important in *The Waterfall*—the reworking of tradition. For Jane is not only a woman abandoned by one man and saved by another: she is also a woman writer—a poet and novelist—who uses "the power of the pen" to repudiate "the old novels" in which "the price of love was death" (p. 256) and to define a new relation to the myth of romantic salvation. As a first-person narrator who is writing a novel about Jane in the third person, she not only enlists romantic precedence to justify her behavior but also interrogates her stylized, romantic fictionalization by means of an analytical first-person critique; and from this processive revision of "I" by "she" and "she" by "I," she forges a new "system" and "morality" (pp. 47, 53). Those who read *The Waterfall* in the way critics often approach Drabble's fiction, as social realism significant for what it reveals "about life,"[5] will be disappointed: but *The Waterfall* is Drabble's most self-consciously intertextual work, a metafiction that draws attention to problems of finding a style and making an ending, a writerly text that invites the reader to participate in the production of meaning and challenges the ideological complicity of realism. Its dialogic structure opposes generic modes, perspectives, and views of language in what Julia Kristeva terms a "polyphonic" text that transgresses "linguistic, logical, and social codes."[6]

Drabble has referred to Lessing as "mother and seer,"[7] and nowhere is her indebtedness more apparent than in *The Waterfall*. As in *The Golden Notebook,* the protagonist's dissolution of self and breakdown into a lover enable her to forge an identity that is both connected and separate, relational and autonomous. In the same way that Anna uses "The Shadow of the Third" to sort out her feelings for Michael/Paul, Jane writes to "comprehend" her experience with James;[8] and just as the conventional novel Anna writes demonstrates Lessing's sense of the constraints of conventional form, the novel Jane writes probes the limits of certain kinds of narrative convention. But Drabble's interrogation of convention goes farther than Lessing's, extending beyond narrative to an investigation of language itself. Whereas the various notebooks and novels with which Anna tries to "cage the *truth*"[9] differ in genre and form, they do not differ in style, for though she may question language, Anna assumes it as a means of representation: but Jane's first- and third-person narratives test modes of representation which rest on different assumptions about the relationship of language to reality and explore various potentials of language. Moreover, Jane creates her new "system" from a verbal medium reconstituted by recombinations of words according to principles that subvert conventional relations between subject and object, by means of which she shakes words free from their usual meanings and liberates them from their customary positions in a discourse inscribing hierarchy and possession. Taking her metaphors where Jane finds her salvation, Drabble makes her protagonist's newly discovered sexuality the source of an alternative discourse with the revolutionary implications of "*l'écriture féminine,*" "writing the female body." *The Waterfall* is—in Cixous's terms from "The Laugh of the Medusa"—"a new insurgent writing" that "wrecks partitions, classes, rhetorics, regulations and codes" and "change[s] the rules of the old game."[10]

## Old-fashioned, Unforgiving Stories

When Jane turns to literary tradition for understanding of her passion—"love is nothing new" (p. 161)—she is appalled at the effect literature has had on her life, its power to "move" her disastrously (p. 92). So keen is her sense of its influence that she "blames the poets" for her marriage to Malcolm: "Love at first sight: I have heard of it, and like a doomed romantic I looked for it" (p. 91). When Jane "falls" for her cousin Lucy's husband, she finds precedent in the heroines of nineteenth-century novels, especially Maggie Tulliver, who was also in love with her cousin Lucy's "man"—"Perhaps I'll go mad with guilt, like Sue Bridehead, or drown myself in an effort to reclaim lost renunciations, like Maggie Tulliver. Those fictitious heroines, how they haunt me." But Maggie "drifted off down the river, abandoning herself to the water . . . and then, like a woman of another age, she refrained" (pp. 161–62), and *The Mill on the Floss* does not help Jane understand her situation any more than the other "old novels" she considers—*Jane Eyre, Jude the Obscure, Thérèse Racquin, Nana*. Like Anna Wulf, Martha Quest, Jane Clifford, Isadora Wing, Atwood's Lady Oracle and Laurence's Morag Gunn, Jane finds the fictions of the past irrelevant to her experience in the present: "In this age [since Freud], what is to be done? We drown in the first chapter" (p. 162).

Drabble evokes *The Mill on the Floss* as representative of the tradition Jane must define herself against. Maggie's ending, her renunciation of her cousin Lucy's man and her return to an unforgiving family ("all that superego gathered together in a last effort to prove that she loved the brother more than the man" [p. 162]), is, as Tony Tanner describes it, a "return to the past and its binding patterns," a "reinsert[ion] [of] herself into a social discourse that will deny her any social identity . . . [and] that effectively prescribes her own annihilation." Maggie is (in Tanner's terms) "cramped up in the room of an old language," unable to reformulate the patterns of the past or to generate new meanings, for there is "no conceivable possibility of her renaming [her brother] and the whole male-dominated society he represents." Her drowning represents a surrender to psychological and social forces more powerful than she is; Tanner describes it as "thalassic" and "regressive," noting that this type of water imagery is frequent in the novel of adultery.[11] And this punitive ending was typical, for nineteenth-century novelists—English, French, Russian, American—were relentless in enforcing obedience to the rules governing female purity. Thus, as unconventional as Eliot was in her life, she condemned Maggie to the "current" she herself escaped; and Jane also cites Zola, who, notwithstanding the strict sexual morality of his fiction, could be seen enjoying the company of his mistress and babes in the Tuileries, "more charitable to the flesh in his life than in his art" (p. 138). Besides Thérèse Racquin and Maggie Tulliver, one might mention—as Godwin's Jane does—Emma Bovary, Anna Karenina, Hetty Sorel, Lily Bart: "literature's graveyard positively choked with women who . . . commit adultery, have sex without marriage . . . and thus, according to the literary convention of the time, must die."[12]

But Jane's passion for her cousin Lucy's husband, far from incurring the punishment that it did in "old-fashioned," "unforgiving" (p. 138) novels, "releases [her] from enclosure" (p. 169), liberates her from isolation, "delivers" her to new life. Unlike "a woman of another age," Jane plunges in, "drowns in a willing sea"(p. 29), "drowns in the first chapter" (p. 162), to discover in passion "salvation" rather than damnation. The birth of passion is vividly recounted in the opening section, along with the birth of a child. Born in a bed still wet with blood and other aftermath of birth, this passion is also "like death"("like death, like birth," p. 158); and though the old pun on "die" is nearly literalized when James almost dies in the car accident, it is finally like "rebirth" (p. 159), as James recovers, their love continues, and Jane finds new energy in all areas of her life. Jane's discovery of sexuality is linked to maternity in an experience of what Kristeva calls *"la mère qui jouit,"* the mother who has *"jouissance,"*[13] with the connection between the two emphasized by the pun on "deliverance" (pp. 10, 16, 159).

In fact, it is Jane's marriage to Malcolm which, though conventionally respectable, confines her to death, for it locks her into silence and a repetition of the past. Her marriage perpetuates the hold of her parents—genteel and middle-class but dishonest and hypocritical (p. 57), "obsessed by notions of class and rank" (p. 61)—by implicating her in their secrecy: "I practiced concealment and married a man who would help me share this conspiracy" (p. 52); and the penalty is "solitude, or a repetition of pain" (p. 50). James, who represents all that her family "was not" (p. 55), is "an exorcism" (p. 55): déclassé, sexual, subversive, illicit, transgressive of boundaries of family and class, destructive of her sexual and emotional containments, he leaves her "no way of returning to the old confines" (p. 248).

Jane's task, then, is to create "a system that would excuse [her]" (p. 47) and "a morality that condones [her]" (pp. 53–54). Though the "convention" she is "reconstituting"—adulterous yet redemptive passion—is "conventional" to the point of cliché, it also raises bewildering moral and philosophical problems. For one thing, it brings social and ethical systems into conflict with emotional and sexual imperatives—conflicts which, as Jane suggests, are not easily resolved:

> I have often thought . . . that the ways of regarding an event, so different, don't add up to a whole; they are mutually exclusive: the social view, the sexual view, the circumstantial view, the moral view, these visions contradict one another, they destroy one another. They cannot co-exist. (p. 47)

For another thing, it wreaks havoc with language and epistemology, for whereas the old Jane modeled her life on the virtues of "abnegation," "denial," "renunciation," the new Jane names these virtues vices (p. 53). Thus, though "delivering" her, this passion also calls into question "the true end of life," and with that, "the qualities" on which the end "depends" (p. 52)—and with those, language itself:

> The names of the qualities are interchangeable—vice, virtue; redemption, corruption; courage, weakness—and hence the confusion of abstraction, the proliferation of aphorism and paradox. In the human world, perhaps there are merely likenesses. (p. 52)

In fact, Drabble shows "transgression" as having effects like those which it had in "the old novels," the dissolution of categories and meanings. As Tanner explains, adultery, like "adulteration," introduces an "irresolvable category-confusion," an "unassimilable conflation of what society insists should be separate categories and functions."[14]

But Drabble sees such dissolution as cause for celebration rather than mourning, as allowing a breaking of boundaries, of containments and confines, and a dissolution of oppositions that releases new possibilities; for her, as for Lessing, breakthrough requires breakdown. "Drowning," in the numerous "seas," "currents," "floods," and "waterfalls" of this novel, is regenerative rather than regressive—or rather, it is regenerative *because* it is regressive, signifying a therapeutic journey back to beginnings, to an experience of sexuality and maternity that becomes the basis of a new discourse. Still, since language is Jane's means of reconstituting experience, her sense of the "interchangeability" of names and the "confusion of abstraction" cannot help but trouble her.

Jane longs for clarity—"I see no virtue in confusion, I see true virtue in clarity, in consistency, in communication, in honesty"—but despairs of achieving it: "so here I am, resorting to that old broken medium" (p. 47), to language and form. She imagines some lost state of innocence where words corresponded to things, and expresses this nostalgia in her response to that song of Malcolm's that so disastrously seduced her—"I wanted to find the source of that sound. . . . I wanted to believe that what I heard was true" (pp. 95–96)—and in her desire for a"name" amid the disturbing sounds and smells of the racetrack to which James takes her,

> She could smell the curious dangerous sulfurous burning smell from the track, and wondered what it was, what name it had: she thought she would ask James, and find if the name corresponded to the hot cinders and petrol and rubber. Perhaps it would be a word she would never again be able to dispense with, an important word. (p. 81)

She will need to relinquish this longing for a Word and resign herself to a struggle with words, to a medium that is "merely a likeness" (p. 52), "broken and fragmented" (p. 47).

## Dialogic Process: Working It Through

Jane's division of her narrative into "I" and "she" enables her to express complex responses to her experience, to voice both surrender to and skepticism of the passion that grips her. But it is also a means of exploring two discourses, two ways of "comprehending" her experience, the "she" testing an "artistic" mode and the "I," an analytic mode. This dialogizing enables her to explore the potentials as well as the limits of each discourse, for, as in *The Golden Notebook,* each version qualifies and is qualified by the other; the analytical "I" sections implicitly and explicitly comment on the limitations of the literary "she" and the "she" sections do the same for the analytical mode.[15]

The third-person sections are stylized and conventional, "structured and orchestrated" (p. 249), and enlist poetic figures—metaphor, analogy, simile—and allusions to literature, legend, myth. By conventional means, these sections express conventional attitudes toward a conventional subject—romantic abandon to an irresistible and (as Jane imagines) doomed passion. In the first section, a striking rendering in the third person of the birth of Jane's child and her love for James, Jane draws on an array of literary associations to tell an archetypal tale of bereavement and deliverance. She evokes a stylized and ritualized image of a woman weeping, waiting—"like a victim she waited: meek like a sacrifice." The conventions of this mode require passivity of the woman, submission and surrender, and prescribe the complementary role of rescuer or savior for the man—a role James cheerfully accepts:

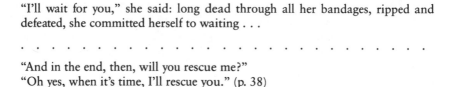

> "I'll wait for you," she said: long dead through all her bandages, ripped and defeated, she committed herself to waiting . . .
>
> . . . . . . . . . . . . . . . . . . . . . . . . . . . . . . .
>
> "And in the end, then, will you rescue me?"
> "Oh yes, when it's time, I'll rescue you." (p. 38)

That Jane's "abandon" is born of "abandonment" points to the association of "passion" with "suffering" that is practically a defining characteristic of love in the Western world, especially for a woman.[16] James's attraction to Jane's pain is consistent with his role as "possessor"—"and when I saw your tears I knew that I would have you, I knew that you were mine" (p. 39); and his terms betray the sinister potentials of their positions.

The novel Jane is writing, the highly stylized, conventionalized "story of she," is an old tale which is crafted from the discourses of the past in a way that calls attention to the pastiche. By means of its "romantic accoutrements" (p. 245) and compelling imagery of drowning ("waterfall," "currents," "floods"), Jane justifies surrender: "waters closed over their heads . . . lost" (p. 37). Though she blames the "lying poets" for "disguising," "excusing," "purifying," "dignifying" truths that are ugly and cruel (p. 93), she is quite capable of enlisting their devices herself to hide from aspects of her situation too harsh to face: abandonment, abandon, adultery, betrayal, faithlessness. But as artfully and elegantly as

Jane portrays the lovers in these sections, Drabble suggests that such stylization masks patterns of domination and subordination, patterns encoded in the custom, law, and literature of our culture—in "conventions." Moreover, Drabble's metafiction shows Jane's reliance on convention making her "conventional," making her (like Atwood's "edible woman") the subject of another's discourse, a "she" instead or an "I."[17]

But that literary convention may encompass more complex attitudes is suggested by Jane's evocation of the paradox and hyperbole of Petrarchan and metaphysical Renaissance love poetry:

> . . . the ways in which they knew and did not know each other, seemed to her to possess a significance that she could hardly bear: such hesitant distance in so small a space, such lengthy knowledge and such ignorance. (p. 36)

These lines contain allusions to Donne ("one small room an everywhere") and to Marlowe ("infinite riches in a little room"). The dialogue that follows James's claim that he'd "have died" if Jane had refused him—" 'it can't be true,' 'of course it's true,' he said, lying there on his back" (p. 36)—recalls the "true and not true" of Shakespeare's *Troilus and Cressida,* with its self-conscious, self-parodic Petrarchanism. Probably James would not have died had Jane refused him—that he is "lying there" suggests more than a physical posture—and Jane herself "lies" in this opening section when she tells him she no longer writes, though she also says this lie "might have been true" (p. 25)—and indeed, it *is* true to the convention she has evoked, which requires her helplessness. Jane's choice of the name "Bianca" for her baby, significant for one who sees her own name (Jane Gray, the martyr) as a symbol of her fate, is also involved with a lie, for she tells her mother that "Malcolm chose it" (p. 42); and it is a "lie" in another sense, in that "Bianca," together with "Gray," is a contradiction in terms, an oxymoron—"a good pun" (p. 42). Though Jane's first choice, "Viola," which she associates with violation (p. 17), would have been truer to her sense of herself as a victim, "Bianca Gray" comes from a part of her that recognizes the need of a more complex and playful mode, a mode which, moreover, "transgresses" the limits of logical discourse. Oxymoron, pun, hyperbole are, as Tanner suggests, characteristic "language of adultery" in that they "bypass the orthodox rules governing communication and relationships" and "bring together entities (meanings/people) that have 'conventionally' been differentiated and kept apart" (p. 23). They are also, traditionally, the language of love and faith because, though illogical and literally "untrue," they speak to a truth beyond reason. Such figures become appropriate to Jane's sense of the complexity of their relationship—a relationship that encompasses faith and faithlessness, grace and betrayal, sacred and profane—and look forward to the wit and play she will attain.

But Jane is incapable of accepting the consolations of convention for very long. Her impulse to another kind of truth, to the "whole truth," causes her to repudiate the very illusions she has created and to plunge furiously into self-scrutiny and self-accusation, using the first-person pronoun and a language of analytical/psychoanalytical investigation. Her repudiation, in the first sentence of the second section, is startling—"It won't, of course, do"—for, swept along by the compelling style as we have been, it has "done" very well; but we are now asked to withdraw our assent—"Because it's obvious that I haven't told the truth":

> And yet I haven't lied. I've merely omitted: merely, professionally, edited. . . . I have lied, but only by omission. Of the truth, I haven't told enough. (p. 47)

Repudiating the "artistic" mode of the first section, Jane launches into the analytical mode of the second section, an investigation, in the first-person pronoun, of family and social backgrounds, James's and her own. Here she tries to "explain" (p. 70) their love in terms of what she calls "the Freudian family nexus" (p. 137)—her relationships, past and present, with her parents and her cousin Lucy. No elegant, artistic ambiguities are tolerated here: this mode insists, rather, that "lies" and "truth" must be clearly differentiated and that language is adequate to the task.

But this mode does not "do" either, for such counting of cost, reckoning of cause, quantifying of quality are no more adequate to love than they are to grace, for both love and grace are miraculous non sequiturs, effects disproportionate to cause: "do not let me find myself reasons. . . . What I deserved was . . . pain. What I received was grace" (p. 51). And besides, the "end" here—"drowned" (p. 70)—is identical to that of the other mode: "it ends in the same place. . . . And since there is no other way, I will go back to that other story, to that other woman, who lived a life too pure, too lovely, to be mine" (p. 70). The submersion in one attitude produces a swing to its opposite and the analytical mode is repudiated for the artistic in the seesaw pattern of self-revision which continues until nearly the end. Each section qualifies, retracts, adds to the preceding sections, as Jane tries to comprehend the whole.

In the next section of the story of "she," Jane again invokes stylized, conventional images of male–female behavior. Playing the role of "his woman" (p. 71), she "submits herself" to James's "addiction" for cars: "She had thought that she would judge and condemn, but there was no judgment left in her. She wanted to be what he wanted, to do what he said" (pp. 71–72). At the racetrack with James, she delights in feeling that "nothing, nothing at all is expected of me: I am merely a woman, merely an attendant woman . . . a proper woman, at last" (p. 80). While James is racing his car around the track, she enjoys playing the "proper woman" in another way, gathering children to her at a nearby playground. Though "usually she hated the cold muddy park, the grimy squares, the dead end of her freedom, the walled, railed plots and enclosures"— differing in this from Margaret of Roiphe's *Up the Sandbox*—her transfigured state has released her from enclosure: "This place looked different: it was high and open" (p. 81), "absolved and beautified" (p. 86).

But the conventional roles also have other potentials, as suggested by James's rather alarming "then let me kill you" (p. 77), which is, on one level, a sexual invitation but on another level reveals the sadomasochistic possibilities implicit in their stances.[18] Yet the pun also introduces an element of verbal play into their dialogue; again, the "artistic" mode can accommodate multiple perspectives in a way that the "narrative explanation," with its insistence on "fact," cannot:

> "I love you, I love you," he said to her . . . and she believed him; she believed . . . even when she thought that she knew that he was lying. I lie to you because I lie with you—the loveliest of ambiguities, though sadly restricted to one language: untranslatable, and lacking therefore the absolute truth that seemed to inform it. (p. 71)

Jane evokes Shakespeare's Sonnet 138—"When my love swears that she is made of truth / I do believe her, though I know she lies"—to express her sense of the ambiguity that now seems the "truth" of her experience. Still, her desire that "lie" have an "absolute truth" indicates that she has not yet relinquished her belief in an absolute beyond the "broken and fragmented" (p. 47) medium of language.

But the equanimity achieved here, the acceptance of "lies" as a condition of life, is dashed by the first line of the next section—"lies, lies, it's all lies. A pack of lies" (p. 89)—in the seesaw movement which is by this time familiar. Jane now accuses herself of using "analogies" to "deceive" and to "misrepresent," condemning these lies as active "commissions" and all verbal representations as "misrepresentations" which have made their love "unreal" (p. 89). Jane's notion of "truth" now requires a connection with "reality," with "the outside world . . . the breath of coarser air . . . the real air"; and she resolves to give love "a quotidian reality" (p. 90) by telling the stories of Malcolm and Lucy. But the "facts" of her life with Malcolm turn out to be more complicated than she had imagined, for having concluded her apparently straightforward account of the marriage with Malcolm's violent departure, she cannot resist quoting one of his letters from an earlier, happier time—a letter filled with "endearments," "solicitude," "affection," "tenderness" (p. 119), which calls into question her entire interpretation. The point made—that her knowledge of the end of the marriage has determined the pattern remembered and the story told—recalls Anna Wulf's realization, after attempting to record "the truth" of a single day in her relationship with Michael, that a written record is no more than "analysis after the event" (GN, pp. 228–29, 331–68). Jane realizes that even her straightforward account has "betray[ed] the texture of a life" (p. 119), that her "facts" are as fictitious as her fictions.

Besides, this investigation of family relationships only brings her back to "the narrative explanation"—"I wanted James because he was [Lucy's], because I wanted to be her" (p. 137)—a mode she cannot sustain even through the end of this section. Two pages before the end she complains, "I am getting tired of all this Freudian family nexus, I want to get back to that schizoid third-person dialogue" (p. 137). Before she can leave it, though, she feels compelled to relate "one or two more sordid conditions": "Firstly . . . I don't think I could have slept with James if the house I did it in hadn't been technically mine." But she cannot sustain this rationalization the time required to complete it—"What a liar I am. I'd have slept with James anywhere"—and she rejects not only the claim, but the very terms of the claim, "mine" and "thine," as false to her sense of herself as "receiver of free gifts" (pp. 137–38). Her inability to complete this thought—"I began the last paragraph with the word 'firstly,' so I must have been intending to begin this with 'secondly,' but I can't remember. . . ."— testifies to her exhaustion of the analytical mode: "Anyway I'm tired of all this. It has a certain kind of truth, but it isn't the truth I care for (Ah, ambiguity)" (p. 138).

Thus Jane again retreats to the mode that allows "ambiguity," evoking conventional representations of a woman waiting at a window ("helpless, ill with longing"), enlisting Shakespeare and Tennyson ("Mariana at the moated grange" [p. 141]):

> As she sat there, waiting for him. . . . She wondered if other people had ever suffered so. . . . She vainly believed . . . that she was the only woman who had waited as she waited. (p. 139)

The stylization is so extreme as to make her feel that "she [is] taking part in some elaborate delicate ritual" (p. 140), and in fact, her interactions with James in these sections do follow the rules of an "old game," of conventional codes that conventionalize them both. More complex potentials are evoked in her paradoxical sense that "it could not last. But it did not seem to end" (p. 139); " 'He will not come,' she said, but he did come, he continued to come, he continued to put an end to those hours of waiting" (p. 141). The paradox suggested here—of an end which is continual and renewing—is that implied by the pun on "die," a logical impossibility that can be accommodated by the literary, but not the analytical, mode.

But Jane is incapable of sustaining the literary mode either, and the shifts follow one another more rapidly as a "protesting" voice makes itself heard almost immediately:

> At times something in her would attempt to defy this entire subjugation; she would hear within her a mute and reasonable voice, another woman's voice, raised in protestation, asking him what he thought he was doing, where was Lucy, did Lucy know what he was up to, why on earth wasn't he at work like everyone else. (p. 141)

And this voice asserts itself beyond the internal monologue that comprises most of the novel, intruding into the dialogue, as, "stepping dangerously out on to the unmarked squares of real life, of the outer world" (p. 141), she asks James why he never works. The two answers he gives—"So that I can be with you"; and "It's because of the boredom, you know. Because really, I've got nothing else to do" (pp. 141–42)—come from the two discourses of the novel: the first is from the literary and conventional ("the courteous answer of the role that he had for some reason chosen to play"), and the second, from the prosaic and mundane. Though this latter is not "courteous," this is the language the lovers need to learn in order to make their concerns real to each other, to give love "a quotidian reality":

> As the weeks drew on they had learned what questions to ask each other: they had asked each other these things at first out of a merely hopeful faith in the communication value of words, any words, though their hearts were on quite other subjects, inarticulate, inexpressible. But already she was beginning to understand his answers, they were more to her now than representations of speech and symbols uttered as in another language. . . . These things, that had seemed at first beyond the grasp of her imagination, were becoming familiar to her: thin papery structures that they had built between them, faint shadows and airy bridges, would one day perhaps bear the weight of quite ordinary feet. This, in her better moments, was what she hoped. It seemed almost to promise a kind of future. (pp. 150–51)

The discussion of stale bread that follows—which James assures her "matters"—is a humble beginning. And such banalities do seem to create the condition that enables each of them to take further risks, risks associated metaphorically with waterfalls—James hazards the card trick called "the waterfall" and Jane surrenders to orgasm.

Throughout most of the novel Jane needs to keep the literary and analytical discourses separate, relegating them to different pronouns and sections. Only near the end does she risk "some kind of unity" (p. 220), "coming together" (p. 109) when she shifts, for the first time in midsection, from "she" into "I" (p. 242), and remaining in "I" for the rest of the novel—putting all of herself into one pronoun as Anna Wulf puts "all of [her]self into one notebook."[19] It is not only her passion for James that enables her to attain this new unity, but also the near-fatal accident that forces her to develop new strengths in coping with the situation as she awaits his recovery. But before James, it was having a baby that indicated her potential for "coming together" and even made her question the conventional mind/body terms of the dichotomy, since "the bodily level was in many ways more profound, more human, more myself" (pp. 108–109). As she shifts into "I," she quotes a fragment of poetry, perhaps her own—"Jane Gray / Head on the block" (p. 242)—which is her only explicit reference to the historical personage whose name she bears, symbol of the martyrdom she has always seen as her fate. Her new strengths enable her to dissociate herself from the doom implied by this name, to acknowledge that her presentation of herself "as a woman on the verge of collapse" was "a plea for acquittal" (p. 243); having absolved herself of innocence, she can absolve herself of guilt.

## Unfinished and Unpunished: Illimitable Circles

Jane may not approve of the open-ended quality of her story—"It's odd that there should be no ending" (p. 249)—but Drabble's refusal of the end is a repudiation of the *telos* of romance and of "closure which is also a disclosure" and a containment of contradiction and change. Though Jane seeks a conclusion in the conventions of the past and considers killing James or herself or maiming him so badly that she "could keep" him—"I search now for a conclusion, for an elegant vague figure that would wipe out all the conflicts, all the bitterness, all the compromise that is yet to be endured" (p. 247)—"the truth" conforms to neither of these, and she must resign herself to the ongoing and inconclusive quality of her experience:

> There isn't any conclusion. A death would have been the answer, but nobody died. . . .
> A feminine ending?
> Or, I could have maimed James so badly, in this narrative, that I would have been allowed to have him, as Jane Eyre had her blinded Rochester. But I hadn't the heart to do it, I loved him too much, and anyway it wouldn't have been the truth because the truth is that he recovered. (p. 248)

Still, Jane's sense of the world has been so structured by literary conventions and "fictitious heroines" that her own experience seems "inartistic," "immoral," "unserious," by contrast.

> But it's hardly a tragic ending, to so potentially tragic a tale. In fact, I am rather ashamed of the amount of amusement that my present life affords me, and of how much I seem to have gained by it. One shouldn't get away with such things. In a way it makes the whole business seem . . . less serious.
>
> . . . . . . . . . . . . . . . . . . . . . . . . . . . . . .
>
> We should have died, I suppose. . . . It isn't artistic to linger on like this. It isn't moral either. . . . It's odd that there should be no ending. (p. 249)[20]

Jane concludes "gratuitously," "irrelevantly," "immorally," with a description of her trip with James to the Goredale Scar: "and it must be irrelevant because the only moral of it could be that one can get away with anything. . . . I write about it simply . . . because it is so lovely" (p. 252). But, unable to rest with this "sublimely" beautiful scene, she goes on to recount their "ridiculous" gagging on the mixture of Scotch and talcum powder in the hotel room later that night, which she calls "a fitting conclusion to the sublimities of nature" (p. 255)— though it is "fitting" only in that it is so absurdly unfitting, so lacking in the conventional attributes of closure. But she cannot rest there, either, for she cannot resist adding a postscript "formulating that final, indelicate irony . . . if we hadn't had that accident I would quite possibly have died myself of thrombosis" (p. 265). This postscript resists "final formulation" (as Rose says),[21] but more, it suggests that final formulations are never possible, for since the accident which seemed to fulfill Jane's prognosis of doom actually became the means of averting doom (by making her stop taking the birth-control pills that were giving her thrombosis), "the pattern" can never be known; and "perhaps" even now, as Jane suggests, "the pattern is not completed" (p. 249).[22]

Drabble resists imposing a pattern on the events of the novel and allows for the muddle and process still to be lived through. She leaves us with several unanswered questions: What does the future hold? Will Jane stay married to Malcolm? What does it mean that James stays with Lucy? What does Lucy think? They seem to be "a resilient couple" (p. 250), but it is nevertheless difficult for James to spend much time with Jane, for they have managed only this one trip together, to the Goredale Scar. Jane never knows Lucy's view of things—"I did not know how she saw it. . . . I have often wondered" (p. 234)—but she does not inquire too deeply: "I do not understand it. I do not understand it at all" (p. 249).

Jane offers a term for her conclusion—"a feminine ending" (pp. 211, 248). In its most specific sense, a "feminine ending" is an unaccented syllable at the end of a line of poetry, a variation that "gives a sense of movement and an irregularity to the meter."[23] But in the context of the novel, it assumes rich extraliterary—"generic" as well as "generic"—associations. The ending of *The Waterfall* may be seen as "feminine" in that it lacks resolution or closure; in that it is "open"—to interpretation and to process; in that it is unpunishing, "irregular," "immoral." In not limiting or closing, it is like the "illimitable, circular, inexhaustible sea" (p. 221); or like the *texte féminine*, which Cixous describes as "always endless, without ending: there's no closure, it doesn't stop."[24] Drabble, like Cixous, associates liberation with "fluidity, diffusion, duration . . . a giving, expending, dispensing of pleasure without concern about ends or closure,"[25] with a "feminine form" that refuses end or closure.

Still, the novel progresses in certain linear ways, and Jane makes progress in all areas of her life. From her initial state of passivity and isolation, she develops the capacity to act and make connections with others. She sets her house in order, embarks on a successful literary career, saves her children from the worst effects of her nature, makes new friends, and even manages to continue her passionate relationship with James:

> I had found, in James, reciprocation: I had found a fitting, unrejecting object for desire. One is not saved from neurosis, one is not released from the fated pattern . . . but sometimes, by accident or endeavor (I do not know which, in writing this I try to decide which), one may find a way of walking that predestined path more willingly. In company, even: one might find a way of being less alone, and thus confining the dangerous outward spreading of emotion, the dark contaminating stain, which when undirected and unaccepted kills and destroys. My need for James had not saved me from myself, but it had perhaps saved others from me. (pp. 169–70)

In a way, Jane gets it "all"—love, work, children—though she does not get it "all together": the children are Malcolm's, James remains married to her cousin, and James is less than ideal in his disapproval of her new strengths. But though her life seems so strangely disjointed, her luck is sufficient to make her revise her sense of herself as a victim: "It is all so different from what I had expected. It is all so much more cheerful" (p. 251).

Jane finds "deliverance" in the most traditional places, in love and motherhood, but Drabble has reevaluated female sexuality and maternity in a way that challenges traditional hierarchies. In this, she is more hopeful and also more radical than the early Lessing. Whereas sexuality traps Martha Quest in the "cycle of birth" and "cycle of procreation" (PM, pp. 251, 152)[26] symbolized by the Ferris wheel that turns ominously outside her window, and Martha is sickened by her ride on this wheel, Jane "had always liked movement; as a child had been intoxicated by fairground roundabouts . . . wouldn't have minded going around that fatal track with James" (pp. 82–83). Whereas Martha naively believes she can "cut the cycle" and "free" her child from the nightmare of determined behavior merely by giving her away, Jane, strengthened by those same sexual and maternal instincts that Lessing sees as impediments, actually does "break the fatal hereditary chain" (pp. 145, 170),[27] and Drabbles's "illimitable, circular inexhaustible sea" is exhilarating and liberating.

## Impossible Possession

In its refusal of closure or enclosure, the "feminine ending" of *The Waterfall* is an instance of "writing the female body." A more profound instance of *"l'écriture féminine"* is in the punning that extends throughout the novel. Jane's wordplay liberates words such as "do," "make," and "have" from syntax and word order in which they denote possession and product, something one person does to another, and makes them not only describe but also reflect processes of reciprocity and mutuality. Jane describes orgasm as resulting from reciprocity of desire: "He had been as desperate to make her as she to be made. And he had done it: he had made her, in his own image"; "She was his, but by having her he had made himself hers" (p. 159)—the circular structure of the sentences mirroring a process of mutual possession and mutual deliverance: "She was his offspring, as he, lying there between her legs, had been hers" (p. 159). Sexual punning has figured in their conversation just previous to this, which concerned card tricks, sex, poetry, the purpose of each, and the relation of expertise to practice. James deprecates his skill at cards—"the things I do aren't worth doing" (p. 154)—and in the ensuing dialogue, the referent to "it" slips from skill at cards to skill at sex: "If one's going to do it . . . one has to learn to do it well" (p. 155). Jane then compares the symmetry of the waterfall to the rhyme of her verse, claiming that poetry is as "pointless" as card tricks:

> It's no good, you know, rhymes in verse are a trivial matter, as trivial as playing cards, as pointless as fast cars. It's no good, any of it. It doesn't do any good. I try

to justify it, but there isn't any justification, there isn't any meaning. It can't be
important, poetry. (p. 155)

Poetry, like card tricks, doesn't "do" any good; neither makes anything or
makes anything happen; both are without "end" or "justification." These terms
recall Jane's earlier anxieties about unfulfilled goals, when, as a child, she had
been asked the purpose of her marbles: "Do you *do* anything with them?"—a
question that filled her with dismay—"for what, after all, did one do with
things when one had got them" (p. 124):

> I always felt myself, with those marbles, to be on the edge of some discovery, some
> activity too delightful to bear, and yet I could never quite reach it: it always eluded
> me and whatever I did . . . never quite fulfilled the glorious expectation of having
> them. I felt there was always something left undone, some final joyful possession
> of them, some way to have my having of them more completely . . . but the
> moment never happened, it would fade and drop away . . . leading . . . nowhere,
> each time bypassing its rightful end. (p. 125)

"Some joyful possession," some "glorious expectation of having," "some way to
have," has always eluded her—was always "left undone," "its rightful end"
"bypassed." This cluster of words ("do," "have," "possess," "ends") describes
the failure of Jane's efforts—her "doing" and "having"—to achieve "ends," a
failure she relates explicitly to sex—"And so it was with sex" (p. 125). It is this
failure which James sets right:

> And how could I refuse James, who gave me that moment, who gave to me this
> impossible arrival, condemning me, by that gift, to an endless ritual of desire, to
> an endless repetition of phrases and gestures, all redeemed, all beautified to me
> by impossible, impossible possession? (p. 125)

In these terms, what James has given Jane is a way of "doing" which is its own
"justification," which is without goal, without "ends"—that is, "endless." In
this context, Jane's description of their reciprocity—"she was his, but by having
her he had made himself hers"—suggests an "impossible possession" by sub-
verting customary subject–verb order and transforming "have" from something
one person does to another to something two people do with each other,
mirroring, in the circularity of its construction, a process that is endless.[28] Her
wordplay transforms enclosures to openings, limits to limitlessness, endings to
endlessness, and thereby transcends the confines of "an old language."[29] This
discourse mirrors the life-giving, transformative exchange Cixous describes as
resulting from *"jouissance"*—"an 'economy' that can no longer be put in
economic terms," a giving without "measure" or "assurance" that one will "get
back," in order "that there may be life, thought, transformation"; and it
represents a challenge to the phallocentric "opposition, hierarchizing exchange, the struggle for mastery which can end only in at least one death."[30]
Also significant is the figure of speech Jane evokes to confront the most

desolate of possibilities—at the end of the long, sleepless night she spends in the hotel waiting for James's recovery—that her passion, born of "need and weakness," was only a "miraged oasis" (p. 221). That "I" uses metaphor is itself evidence of Jane's "coming together," since metaphor has always been the characteristic mode of "she," and that Jane works through her doubts by developing the metaphor is an affirmation of faith, not only in love, but in poetry:

> We were starving when we met . . . and we saw love as the miraged oasis. . . . Like deluded travelers, we had carefully approached, hardly able to trust the image's persistence. . . . But when we got there. . . . When I got there, the image remained, it sustained my possession of it, and the water was not sour. . . . Nor were the leaves green merely through the glamor of distance . . . they remained green to the touch, dense endless foresting boughs, an undiscovered country . . . miles of verdure, rivers, rushes, colored birds, miles with no sign of an ending, and perhaps, beyond them all, no ending but the illimitable, circular, inexhaustible sea. (p. 221)

Standing behind the first-person pronoun, Jane recombines and redefines the cluster of words relating to limits, boundaries, and possession in an evocation of undiscovered country with "no sign of an ending," beyond which is the illimitable, inexhaustible sea—an image which, she insists, "sustains possession." The passage rings changes on the novel's water imagery, transforming the waterfall to the more forceful, compelling, and encompassing sea, endless and limitless. The "illimitable, circular, inexhaustible sea" reverses the traditional meaning of water in the "novel of adultery" from a symbol of "thalassic," regressive surrender to a symbol of liberating *jouissance*. This is the same "ocean" Cixous associates with female libido to suggest energies not confined by "boundaries" or "limits," the sexuality inscribed in the *texte féminine*.[31]

But "feminine ending" refers to literary convention as well as to female anatomy, and Drabble's use of this term in some sense reinstates the value of the literary mode which she has so scrutinized. In fact, though the "poetic" is exposed as "lying" and limiting, it turns out to be more adequate in the end than the analytic—as, in moments of crisis, Jane turns to figures to express "what cannot be explained":

> There is one thing that I can find no way to explain, and that I must recount in amazement, in gratitude . . . he made the new earth grow, he made it blossom. . . . He changed me forever and I am now what he made. I doubt, at times, I panic, I lose faith; but doubt, as they say, is not accessible to unbelievers. (pp. 245–46)

Her final summation of their experience enlists metaphor and bawdy pun ("made") in expression of what there is "no way to explain."

But the "truth" is not contained in either "poetic" or "analytic" discourse. By juxtaposing the two discourses without privileging either, Drabble exposes the inadequacies of literary convention while also demonstrating that a factual account is no more "objective" or free of distortions. The "truth" is in a mode which has elements of both but is different from either and which encompasses multiple and heterogeneous perspectives, and it is in the exploratory and revisionary *processes* that go into making this mode. Evidence of Jane's "coming together" in the final sections is not her attainment of a univocal tone or single perspective but, rather, in her attainment of a complex, ironical, equivocal mode that combines irreverence and play with a sense of the solemnity of events. When, for example, James protests at being made the object of literary exploitation, she "persuades" him "by a little casuistry" that the "very good sequence of poems" she wrote while he was in hospital was "an act of affirmation . . . like his reunion with his car, and he accepted the analogy, though I daresay it would not bear inspection" (pp. 250–51). Jane's humoring of James, this gentle recognition of his limits, this wit on the deadliest of subjects, shows her new capacity for play—in fact, it shows the same sort of "mixture of wit and common sense" that she admires in the adulterous Galsworthy cousins, who rejoiced that their shared surname proved such a convenience in their adulterous affair (p. 252). That "what's in a name" turns out not to be doom but a cheerful convenience suggests a view of life and of language in which "analogy," metaphor, pun, and even "casuistry" are not "lies," but enabling constructions.[32]

Jane had once wished to write "a poem as round and hard as a stone," but she realized that such a poem "would say nothing" (p. 69). Rather than a story which is closed, completed, contained, Drabble offers an unfinished tale of unpunished passion, elusive of final formulations, subject to uncertainties and contradictions—"an event seen from angles" (p. 47) both serious and playful; which—as Barthes describes the writerly text—"is ourselves writing before the infinite play of the world . . . is traversed, stopped, plasticized by some singular system."[33] Jane never does find "the source" of Malcolm's "note," the referent or real thing to which words refer; she experiences no "final vision" or "final revelation" (p. 196), "no sudden light" (p. 233). She finds her "truth," rather, in an equivocal medium, "broken and fragmented" (p. 47), "merely a likeness," open to "confusion" and "paradox" (p. 52), and above all, in the process of her struggle with that medium. But the release from the absolute is a release from "the end" she anticipated—from the *telos* her story was tending to, the conclusion that would have doomed her. This release from the fixed and the final is liberating, for as Barthes suggests, to refuse "to assign . . . an ultimate meaning to the text (and to the world as text) liberates what may be called an anti-theological activity, an activity that is truly revolutionary, since to refuse to fix meaning is, in the end, to refuse God and his hypostases—reason, science, law."[34] In its cheerful subversion of the tradition that has defined women so disastrously, *The Waterfall* transforms "an old story" to "something new."

How any feminist could appreciate this novel—and nearly every feminist cited in this chapter does—is no mystery. Our tradition-bound hearts persist in the illusion that a passionate love can release us from isolation, sweep us away to a sea of love; our modern minds know better. In articulating a female space that realizes the revolutionary potentials of *jouissance, The Waterfall* holds out the possibility that love need not bind and destroy—the possibility of an "impossible possession" that allows us possession of another, by another, while also granting us possession of ourselves.

# VII

## MARGARET LAURENCE'S
## *THE DIVINERS*
### CHANGING THE PAST

> This is the use of memory:
> For liberation—
>
> > T. S. Eliot, "Little Gidding,"
> > *Four Quartets*[1]

> Now I am rampant with memory.
>
> > Margaret Laurence, *The Stone Angel*[2]

I begin with this line from *The Stone Angel,* with its reference to the memory rampage that inspires ninety-two-year-old Hagar's odyssey into her past, because memory is crucial in all Laurence's work and especially in *The Diviners,* and because Laurence singled out this line to be printed on the front of the program for her funeral, in a service she outlined shortly before her death.[3] When I began work on *The Diviners,* Laurence was still alive, and I had no idea, as I began tracking allusions to *The Tempest* through *The Diviners,* that this would be her last novel, as *The Tempest* was Shakespeare's last play— though she seemed to know.[4] When she died on January 5, 1987, articles and tributes appeared in newspapers throughout Canada commemorating her as "a great literary genius," "one of the country's greatest writers," "one of the best loved Canadian writers."[5] As far as I know her death went unnoticed by newspapers in the United States, except for the occasional, perfunctory obituary.

Outside Canada, Laurence continues to be known—when she is known at all—as a "regional" writer, sometimes as a "prairie writer." It is certainly true that her writing gives voice to what she has called Canada's "cultural being," "roots," and "myths,"[6] and *The Diviners,* the last novel of the five-volume Manawaka series which occupied the last decade of her writing career (1964– 74), articulates personal quest in relation to the search for Canadian past.[7] But in *The Diviners* Laurence writes against wider and older traditions, reworking epic quest, Shakespearean romance, and *Kunstlerroman* in a re-vision of central myths of Western culture—the "fortunate fall," paradise, and the idea of the artist. Laurence draws on Joyce's *A Portrait of the Artist as a Young Man* and Shakespeare's *The Tempest* for her portrait of the artist as a young woman, and on T. S. Eliot's *The Waste Land,* which similarly draws on *The Tempest*— and for the same reasons Laurence does—for its concern with the uses of the past.

Yet far from uncritically accepting the values of these works, Laurence's "diviner" artist provides an alternative to Joyce's "artificer" and her reworking of the fortunate fall suggests that paradise is a process, the "doing of the thing."[8] Moreover, Laurence's re-visions of these central myths establishes a new genealogy, a line of descent which is antipatriarchal and delegitimizing—or relegitimizing of those who have been disempowered by gender and race, conferring possession on the "dispossessed." Laurence shows power passing from a stepfather (the disreputable Christie) to a stepdaughter (the disobedient, unchaste, and unsilent Morag), and thence to a daughter (Pique), the dark-skinned and illegitimate child of Morag's adulterous union with a Métis or "half-breed" (Jules): power passes through a female line to a female "inheritor" (p. 452) in a genealogy evermore "adulterate." The novel created a furor in rural Canada, its explicit sex scenes provoking attempts to ban it from school libraries,[9] and though the sexual prudery of provincial Canada seems absurdly stupid the subversive implications of *The Diviners*—its challenge of sexual, social, and racial hierarchies—are real.

### Metafiction as Re-Vision

Morag Gunn is a writer who—like Anna Wulf, Jane Gray, Isadora Wing, and Joan of *Lady Oracle*—uses her fiction to make her way in the world and to make sense of the world; as Morag says, "If I hadn't been a writer I'd have been a first class mess" (p. 4). Like these protagonists, Morag is also a reader, though what she reads is not nineteenth-century fiction centering on love and marriage, but Shakespeare, Milton, and Donne (pp. 178, 191): Morag reads—as Laurence writes against—works which center on male experience and are at the heart of a male-defined and male-dominated canon. *The Tempest,* with its celebration of European colonialism and its one bland and subordinate female character,[10] and *Portrait,* which registers women only as idealizations or sexual objects, seem odd and unlikely models for the development of a strong female protagonist. The epic quest, which concerns a young man's search for his father as part of his search for himself, seems similarly inapplicable, for identification with the father usually interferes with female development, since (as Mary Anne Ferguson suggests), women "must assume their husband's name" as well as their husband's home.[11] But Laurence shows Morag engaged in a quest for the father and a home[12] and shows her maturing from an identification with "Prospero's Child" (the name of a novel Morag writes) into the power of Prospero himself—though not without first reworking the notion of power from its usual sense of domination and control, power *over* others, to mean empathy and connectedness *with* others.

Orphaned young and adopted by Christie, the town "scavenger," Morag is first shown in relation to a stepfather and, later, in relation to a daughter. Christie is a splendid mentor who teaches her qualities unbecoming to a lady—a disrespect of respectability gained from his long acquaintance with the town's "muck"; more than a little of his rage, that side of herself she will come to recognize as "the black Celt"; and a skepticism concerning the value of any authority—" 'you don't want to believe everything them books say' " (p. 83). He also teaches her never to "say sorry" (p. 209) or to make herself a "doormat" (p. 107). Morag disowns Christie and spends years trying to pass as "normal" (as she says; p. 81) before finally coming to recognize him as "my father to me" (p. 396) and to know her "home" as "Christie's . . . country. Where I was born" (p. 391). In the second part of the novel, we see her as an adult and parent engaged in making a home for herself and her daughter, a home on a farm purchased from her earnings as a writer, to which she takes "title." The novel concludes with Morag ready to "set down her title," ready to write the novel we have just read; and the links between "title" as deed to property and "authorship"—an "author" is one who "gives existence to something, a begetter, *father* . . . or founder"—suggests connections between gaining authorial authority and staking a claim.[13] Morag's authority authorizes her, in Laurence's conflation of epic pattern and *Kunstlerroman*, to originate a new order.[14]

Christie is Morag's mentor in other important ways, in that it is he who gives her a past and teaches her the power of the creative imagination. Since her parents died when she was a child, Morag's past is a blank, and, according to the book of *Clans and Tartans of Scotland* which Christie consults, Clan Gunn is "undetermined" (p. 48). But Christie gives Morag a heritage with his stories of Piper Gunn, a "great tall man" with "the strength of conviction," and Piper's "woman Morag," and their adventures conquering and settling a new land. Part legend, part history, but mainly spun "wholecloth" "out of his head—invented" (p. 367), these tales of derring-do are the sort more customarily associated with boys than with girls. Christie's stories provide Morag with inspiration for her first literary creations, and her adaptations are significant, for what minimal gender differentiation Christie introduces, Morag (at age nine) obliterates, appropriating the hero's powers for her heroine—as Laurence herself does. Christie describes Piper as having "the strength of conviction" and "his woman Morag" as having "fine long black hair," but Morag gives Morag *"the power and the second sight and the good eye and the strength of conviction"* and makes her unafraid "of anything" (pp. 51–52); Christie gives Morag "the warmth of a home and the determination of quietness," but Morag has her Morag make not a home but a chariot which is a means of transport for Piper, herself, and their girl child throughout the new land (p. 85).[15] Identifying with male action and potential, Morag has more freedom than heroines usually have; as Carolyn Heilbrun suggests, women may gain by "look[ing] at the male protagonists who have until now stood as models for human action and say[ing]: that action includes me."[16]

Though at first glance *The Diviners* does not seem to have much in common with *The Golden Notebook,* Morag contemplates problems of recalling and reconstructing like those which concern Anna Wulf. She tries to remember "what really happened" (*"I don't even know how much of that memory really happened and how much of it I embroidered later on"* [pp. 17–18]) and to understand the relation of language to memory (*"I used to think words could do anything. Magic. Sorcery. Even miracle. But no. only occasionally"* [p. 5]). She ponders the meaning of photographs, and her "memorybank movies" imply an idea of the artist like Anna's, as "projectionist," and also recall Anna's question—" 'What makes you think that the emphasis you have put on it is the correct emphasis?' " (GN, p. 619). And though Laurence does nothing so spectacular with point of view as Lessing does, her use of italics to mark shifts from third- to first-person pronoun is a way of rendering the interplay of subjective and objective and the movement of the mind in interpreting and revising: *"I am remembering myself composing this interpretation"* (p. 8). This self-reflexivity has not been much noticed, but it is crucial. Marge Piercy misses it so completely that she misses the point of Laurence's metafiction: "Would Morag's life be wildly different if she made clothes rather than novels? . . . the creative process of Morag's novels is worked into the narrative in a perfunctory way."[17] The "creative process" is, on the contrary, "worked into the narrative" so profoundly that all Morag's efforts to recover and recall the past are part of it.

Morag attempts to "reconnect . . . time lost and time continuing" and transmit something of value to the future, in Peter Brooks's terms—though Laurence's line of descent is hardly the patriarchal line Brooks describes.[18] The circular return on which the novel is structured—in which present alternates with past until, in the final section, past becomes present—enables the replaying of past to a more successful outcome, allows repetition in order for there to be an escape from repetition, in order for there to be change or progress. (In fact, Laurence describes her writing in terms similar to these—as an "attempt to come to terms with the past" "in order to be freed from it.")[19] The circular structure demonstrates the interaction of past and present: the past has made Morag and Pique what they are, but Morag's remembering transforms the past—"a popular misconception is that we can't change the past—everyone is constantly changing their own past, recalling it, revising it" (p. 60)—in a way that enables her to make new terms with the present. Laurence's symbol of time, the river that flows both ways—its current pulling one way and the breeze rippling its surface the other way—suggests a similar interdependence of past and present. The backward and forward movement allows transformation and release, as Morag learns to let go of the pain of the past, of her guilt about the way she has raised her daughter, and to let go of her daughter as well, sending her on her way with the best of what she has gleaned from experience.

## Laurence's Portrait of the Artist as a Woman

For her portrait of the artist as a young woman, Laurence draws on Joyce's *A Portrait of the Artist as a Young Man.* Laurence does not specifically refer to Joyce's *Portrait,* as she does to *The Tempest,* and Joyce's Stephen Dedalus, epitome of the Modernist artist, that "monstrously isolated, monstrously narcissistic, pedestalled paragon" that so appalled Lessing (GN, p. xii), seems an unlikely model for Laurence's Canadian, female, and feminist artist: but the numerous parallels she suggests make Joyce's *Kunstlerroman* a primary intertext. Both Morag and Stephen need to be ruthless to escape the provincial communities that claim them, and they develop similar defenses to do this (Morag's last name is "Gun," after all). Morag, like Stephen, turns her back on the claims of others, refusing—as he does—to return home except for a funeral (Prin's) and death (Christie's). But whatever problems Stephen has in freeing himself from his environment, Morag experiences more radical alienations from self, suffering the self-divisions and self-doubt that are part of growing up female and that leave her more vulnerable, although finally more involved with others. Morag can never be as ruthless as Stephen because she forms a tie of a sort that Stephen does not—to a child. In her relation to her daughter she must reconcile the conflicting claims of self and other, of mother and artist—conflicts at the heart of the female *Kunstlerroman*.[20]

The earliest memories of Morag and Stephen show young minds acquiring knowledge through sense impressions and language. Both are nearsighted children who develop interest in language to compensate for their visual handicaps, and with both, the fascination with words ("what means?" Morag asks repeatedly) prefigures a vocation as "wordsmith" (p. 25). But whereas nearsightedness is little more than a physical inconvenience for Stephen, it strikes to the heart of Morag's self-esteem: though she is not particularly vain, she is sufficiently savvy to know, by her first year of high school, that wearing glasses means a girl's "life is over" (p. 123). Morag and Stephen learn similar ways of defending themselves against the authority of elders and the pressure of peers: they learn to conceal their intelligence and never to "apologize."[21] But whereas Stephen turns his sense of difference into a conviction of his superiority, Morag remains more dependent on the opinions of others: "work like hell. . . . Although not letting on to the other kids . . . [they] would be dead set against you" (p. 120). Though for both, education is the means of escaping stifling circumstances, Morag remains divided between impulses to conform and to rebel and is less certain of her course. And whereas girls exist for Stephen only as objects to be idealized or lusted after, boys are to Morag a constant presence and threat:

> Boys are generally mean. Those girls who have a hope of pleasing them, try.
> Those who haven't a hope, either stay out of their way or else act very tough and
> try to make fun of them first. (p. 68)

By the time she is twelve, she has learned how to stand in a way that "shows off her tits" but also leaves her ready to "slug with her closed fist" (p. 61)—a posture that does not leave her the freedom to do much else.

Both Stephen and Morag find their ways out of town at the earliest opportunity, but Morag comes to learn the value of what she has left behind. Morag, like Laurence, leaves only to realize that she has taken the town with her—"the town inhabits you" (p. 227); "the whole town was inside my head, for as long as I live" (p. 353)—whereas *Portrait* ends with Stephen poised for flight. Joyce, too, spends his life trying to understand the place he has fled, and has Stephen return in *Ulysses* in search of a father and home; but in *Portrait* we are so locked in Stephen's perspective that Dublin and its inhabitants remain shadowy, unreal—Stephen's grandiose intention "to forge . . . the uncreated conscience of [his] race" notwithstanding (*Portrait*, p. 253). Though Joyce may be said to have forged the consciousness of a people in *Ulysses* and *Finnegan's Wake*, it is *The Diviners* more than *Portrait* that gives a clear and generous rendering of a community.

The difference in their conceptions of art is suggested by the figure each writer uses to symbolize the artist. Stephen sees in Dedalus, the "artificer" who escaped the labyrinth of the Minotaur and constructed a means of flight, a symbol of the art he aspires to in order to escape the Ireland he despises; and adapting the terminology of his Jesuit fathers, he declares himself "a priest of eternal imagination" who will "transmute the daily bread of experience into the radiant body of everliving life" (*Portrait*, p. 221). Morag develops the skills of a diviner—insight or intuition or "some other kind of sight" (p. 4)—in order to "fathom" (a term which occurs in the novel; p. 44) what goes on in people's minds. Since water is a traditional symbol for consciousness, "divining" is an apt symbol for what Morag tries to do in her writing: to fathom people and the processes that make them what they are. Whereas Stephen is concerned with escape arts that will allow him to flee Dublin and become a creator with power like God's, Morag is concerned with qualities of insight and understanding that will enable her to understand Manawaka and give its people life.

Morag compares her skills to those of Royland, the professional diviner— "He was divining for water. What in hell was she divining for?" (p. 102)—and wonders if her gift, as mysteriously conferred as his, may be as mysteriously taken away (p. 452). Her divining is, like his, related to water in that she spends time "river-watching" (p. 3), contemplating the river she lives by. She also—like a soothsayer or seer—watches birds, though she observes them for information about seasons and life cycles (pp. 404, 411), for natural rather than for supernatural significances. Yet her skills as diviner may actually give her a kind of "second sight" in that they help her to understand the future and achieve a kind of equanimity, an equanimity symbolized by her epiphany of a "Great Blue

Heron" (p. 357). Whereas Stephen's epiphanies of a hawklike man and a birdlike girl beckon him to flight, affirming his singular "genius" and voyeuristic sexual identity (*Portrait,* pp. 171–72), Morag's heron teaches a "serenity" which is empathetic and connected: its "sweeping serene wings" and "the soaring and measured certainty of its flight" signify "certainty," "mastery" even in the face of extinction—"not only . . . individual death, but probably . . . the death of its kind" (p. 357). Laurence's use of "diviner," then, draws on its full range of meanings: water finder, reader of omens, one who has skill in the reading of character and events, seer, soothsayer, prophet. The artist–diviner looks into "the river of now and then" to fathom life, time, and the passing of generations, and, through her understanding of the past, gains faith in the future.

But Laurence's diviner has skills which are more than natural, powers which suggest a Joycean analogy of the artist to God, for in giving life to stories that would otherwise die, the artist–diviner performs acts almost of resurrection. In her first novel, *Spear of Innocence*—which is, like *The Diviners,* "an old story" about a woman who "lights out for the city" (p. 225)—Morag seeks ways of expressing an "inchoate" character; and this problem mirrors Laurence's, for though Laurence's protagonist is not "inchoate," many in *The Diviners* are. Laurence gives voice to those who cannot speak for themselves—outcasts, "unmentionables," half-breeds and poor; those for whom living is so difficult that many prefer not to. Most of Jules' family—Lazarus, Piquette, Val, Paul— "die before their time" (p. 430); Prin buries herself in her mound of flesh; Lachlan MacLachlan, the newspaper editor, and Niall Cameron, the undertaker, find oblivion in drink, giving up the "battle in the mindfield, the minefield of the mind" (p. 399); Royland's wife "drowned herself" (p. 241); Eva lives on but is "beaten by life" (p. 113). Morag's husband, Brooke, also denies life in refusing Morag a child and insisting that she remain one. The contradictory associations of his first and last names, "Brooke" and "Skelton," suggest the life-and-death struggle that most of Laurence's characters wage: "How could you be born and dead at the same time?" (p. 44), Morag wonders; "Dead when born? . . . What is *dead,* really? Do you know when you are?" (p. 76).

Not introspective or educated, "not very verbal people" (p. 155), the characters in this novel do not have language to speak their experience. "Loners and crazies" (p. 301), they express their pain and rage in cries like Lazarus's "dere mine dere, dem" (p. 159) as he rushes into the burned shack to claim the charred remains of his daughter and grandchildren; or Christie's wild "rant[ing] in his sorrow like the skirling of the pipes in a pibroch" (pp. 162, 394); or Jules's drunken sleepwalking and "sleepfighting" (p. 280); or Piquette's "shrieking her pain aloud in public places" (p. 158); or the barely audible name Brooke whimpers in his nightmares. The one painting of Dan McRaith's which is described, *The Dispossessed,* is of a woman with "mouth open in a soundless cry that might never end" (p. 378)—"a sad cry, like the cry of my people" (p. 47), as Christie translates the Gaelic motto of his clan, "The Ridge of Tears." Lazarus "snarls his pain" (p. 338), and even those who have the power of eloquence lose it at the last: Christie, "who told the tales, who divined with the garbage" (p. 394), is reduced to a "growl" by his illness (p. 395), and Jules, who turned pain into song, is silenced by cancer of the throat. Though Morag manages to communicate with Christie at his death, that " 'you've been my father to me' " (p. 396), he reveals little of himself, taking his past and his secrets to the grave. As Morag tells the undertaker,

> "No one knew him all that well. . . . He lived nearly all his life in this town, and everyone knew him to see him, and they all called him Christie, but nobody knew him, to speak of, or even to speak to, much, if it comes to that." (p. 398)

"Most didn't" know Prin, either (p. 254). Jules's family remains, similarly, a blank, "mysterious. People in Manawaka talk about them but don't talk *to* them. They are dirty and unmentionable" (p. 69); and Lazarus dies "a stranger in the place where he lived his whole life" (p. 338), a town that " 'never knew one damn thing about him' " (p. 267). Even Morag has difficulty speaking her deepest feelings: the last time she sees Jules, she cannot find "any way of talking to him any differently, now"—"He contained his own pain" (pp. 444–45). All in this novel are locked into themselves;[22] as in *The Waste Land*, "each locked in a prison, each confirms a prison."[23]

As diviner, then, the artist speaks for those who cannot speak for themselves—fathoms the unfathomable, communicates the incommunicable, mentions the "unmentionable." In this, her art has affinities with Christie's "gift of the garbage-telling" (pp. 74–75) (as Morag suggests when she wonders "which was Morag [scavenger or diviner] . . . or were they the same thing?" [p. 212]); and her powers, like his, derive from knowledge of "muck." "Muck" has several meanings, as Christie uses it, but it refers generally to that side of life which is disowned, disavowed by the respectable community. Garbage is muck: the Nuisance Grounds is filled with "heaps of old muck" in various stages of decomposition and decay—"rusty," "moth-eaten," "moulded," "rotten," "broken," "cracked," "worn-out" (p. 71)—and it is called "Nuisance Grounds" "because all that awful old stuff and rotten stuff is a nuisance and nice people don't want to have anything to do with it" (p. 36); " 'They put it in [bins] and that's the end of it to them' " (p. 76). But muck is "no more dirty than what's in their heads" (p. 39); indeed, it *is* "what's in their heads"—the unconscious, the repressed, the "junkyard of memory," in Hagar's term (p. 190), the underground reservoirs plumbed by the diviner. People are muck (" 'I *am* muck, but so are they,' " Christie declares [p. 39]), common in their elements, "skin and bone and the odd bit of guts" (pp. 30, 39–40, 90–91), and in their ends and origins: " 'one man's muck is every man's muck' " (p. 46). And muck is a source of knowledge and power for Christie as it will be for Morag, as she, too, comes to know the value of muck: " 'By their garbage shall ye know them' " (pp. 39, 75). Laurence uses "muck" as Drabble uses "shit" in *The Middle Ground*, to symbolize the buried past which the artist transmutes to "gold."

Making the arrangements for Christie's funeral, Morag asks the new undertaker what became of the old undertaker, and, when told that Niall Cameron drank himself to death, she recalls Christie's joke, *"Who buries the undertaker? Whoever will undertake it"* (pp. 114, 399). In an odd way, the answer to this riddle is that it is the artist who "undertakes the undertaker," in "undertaking" the story of Niall Cameron and other buried lives. But this "undertaking" is also in some sense a resurrection: Lazarus is "born again" in Jules's songs (as these songs suggest, "the dead don't always die" [pp. 345, 428]); Jules's songs live on in Pique's songs; and all are made to live in *The Diviners*. Whereas Joyce's "artificer" is "like God" in creating a world from which he then withdraws, Laurence's artist–diviner is a "divinity" who (like the prophet in Eliot's poem) breathes life into the dust—or muck; who confers life by telling the tales of those whose stories would otherwise die.

Whereas Stephen's artist is "like the God of creation . . . within or behind or beyond or above his handiwork, invisible, refined out of existence, indifferent, paring his fingernails" (*Portrait*, p. 215), Laurence's artist remains compassionately involved with her creation. The conception of art and the artist that emerges from *The Diviners* suggests an aesthetic which is implicated in and includes the processes of its own creation. Unlike Joyce's Modernist aesthetic, which views art as separate and apart from the processes that create it, Laurence's aesthetic is—as DuPlessis describes that of women's *Kunstlerromane*—"both fabricated from and immersed in . . . temporal, social, and psychic conditions," "immersed in human relations," and "charged with the conditions of its own creation." *The Diviners* provides what DuPlessis terms a "poetics of domestic values—nurturance, community building, inclusiveness, empathetic care"; a poetics which resolves the dichotomy between "artisanal" works and "high art" and contests the Modernist ideal of exile and alienation (WBE, pp. 97, 103).

## Paradise Lost and Regained

Besides being his last play and only totally original plot, *The Tempest* is also Shakespeare's version of the "fortunate fall": Prospero, whose name means "I make to prosper," recreates a world, recovers what is lost, restores the creatures of this world to themselves. In both Shakespeare's play and Laurence's novel, art is the means of redemption and art is compared to magic, and in both works, the future is represented by a daughter. But whereas in *The Tempest*, Prospero's daughter, Miranda, need merely be "chaste, silent, and obedient"—a chaste receptacle for heirs, obedient to father and husband, and stunningly silent—in *The Diviners*, Morag is disobedient, unchaste, and vocal, and her daughter, Pique, child of her adulterous union with a half-breed, is an artist in her own right.

Laurence grafts *Tempest* allusions onto a pattern of loss and recovery which is her version of the fortunate fall, and suggests, in her reworkings, a sense like Shakespeare's and Milton's that redemption involves the loss of fragile innocence and a recreation from painful experience, and that this process requires faith. (That Laurence no more values a "cloistered virtue" than Milton does is clear from her portrayal of the innocents of this novel, the childish Prin [pp. 205, 250] and Bridie [p. 373]).[24] But Morag's powers are considerably more attenuated than Prospero's, not sanctioned by providential plan, and faith is more difficult for her.

Morag lives through a series of losses and recoveries, losing paradise and regaining it, then losing it again to rebuild it on firmer ground. With her parents' death, she is expelled from an Edenic childhood—"the metallic clink of the farm gate being shut. Closed" (p. 17)—which she recreates imaginatively as a "garden of the mind" (p. 227). Life with Christie initiates her prematurely into adult experience, and though she later sees this as "both fortunate and unfortunate" (p. 257), she is, as a child, overwhelmed by it. As soon as she can, she leaves Christie and Manawaka for the big city and makes "a proper marriage," imagining (like Martha Quest) that this will free her from her past. The man she marries, Brooke Skelton, is Christie's antithesis not only in that he is respectable, but also in that his idealization of innocence is antithetical to Christie's acceptance of "muck." Brooke is English, and his desire that Morag be a virgin—virgin territory—recalls Prospero's obsessions with Miranda's chastity: and Morag associates Brooke with Prospero in her novel *Prospero's Child*. His emphasis on the subordination of women is also, like Prospero's, consistent with his attitude toward the dark-skinned inhabitants of the New World.[25]

Initially, Brooke's ideal of innocence coincides with Morag's desire to lose her past. Though she knows that she has always "known things"—about Eva's aborting herself, about the aborted child buried in the dump and the burned shack in the valley—she imagines that she can conceal "what she was really like": "I feel I don't have a past, as if it was a blank" (pp. 194–98). She pretends to be a virgin and resolves never to show him the Black Celt (p. 227). But as she outgrows Brooke's ideal of her, her darkness and past reassert themselves as an irresistible impulse to speak Christie's language—"the loony oratory, salt-beefed with oaths, the stringy lean oaths with some protein in them, the Protean oaths upon which she was reared" (pp. 255–56). The chapter which describes the marriage, "Halls of Sion," begins with Morag waking out of a dream—"*Jerusalem*. Jerusalem? Why? Gone. What had she meant by it?" (p. 169)—a dream which fades as she reaches for it, just as their false paradise dissolves: "What had Morag expected . . . marrying Brooke? Those selfsame halls?" (p. 253).

As her English professor, Brooke represents the literary tradition Morag reveres, but as she herself becomes a writer, her authority comes into conflict with his. Though this destroys their marriage, her writing becomes the means of regaining the self she has suppressed to be with Brooke, the means of "regaining paradise"—which is why the publisher's representative who arrives at the Vancouver boardinghouse where she takes refuge after leaving Brooke seems like "an angel of the Lord . . . come to explain how paradise can be regained" (p. 297). Her writing is also a means of exploring the questions of innocence and experience that her marriage has raised. Morag's first novel, *Spear of Innocence,* which portrays innocence as damaging (p. 225), is a repudiation of Brooke's ideal of her, and her second novel, *Prospero's Child,* is further repudiation of the person she was in the marriage, the child wife in awe of male authority. Morag describes this novel, in a letter to a friend, as having "certain parallels with *The Tempest,*" "which may be presumptuous" but is "the form the thing seems to demand":

> It is called *Prospero's Child,* she being the young woman who marries His Excellency, the Governor of some island in some ocean very far south, and who virtually worships him and then who has to go to the opposite extreme and reject nearly everything about him, at least for a time, in order to become her own person. (p. 330)

Morag allies herself definitively with her past and her "darkness" when she flees Brooke and becomes pregnant by Jules, a "half-breed" who, like herself, grew up on the margins of Manawaka society and who represents—as Sherrill Grace suggests—not only "her immediate Manawaka past, but the historical Indian and French roots of Canada" (p. 69). Her departure from the "doll's house" occurs in the middle, with the rest of the novel a writing beyond this ending. As in contemporary versions of the "two-suitor convention," the husband represents the restrictions of patriarchy and the lover represents freedom;[26] and Jules provides Morag a way out of her marriage and beyond the bounds of her society, for in bearing a child with dark skin, she burns her bridges back to the respectable world. Her adulterous liaison with Jules is a defiance of the patriarchal rule of chastity: following *The Tempest* parallels through, Miranda gets together with Caliban.

No longer a child or a child–wife but a parent, Morag realizes that "if she is to have a home, she must create it" (p. 291). The identification of the home she makes, the farm at McConnell's Landing, with "some kind of garden" (p. 406) associates the recovery of home with regaining paradise. And that this home is near a small town like the one she fled, a place which is "different, but . . . the same" (p. 354), suggests that regaining paradise requires coming to terms with the past. The home Morag makes for herself and her daughter is "different" from both Edens she has lost—different from the imaginary Eden of her childhood and the fool's paradise of her marriage: it is a new order wrested from adult experience and pain.

### Christie as Fool and Mentor

Accepting her past and experience, Morag comes to understand what Christie has always known: the value of "muck." But Christie knows more than "muck": he is, as his name and frequent oaths suggest, a "Christly" character who, like Shakespeare's fools, is licensed to speak truth because he is an outsider,[27] and who—like them—veils his truths in paradoxes and riddles.

Christie plays the fool deliberately and defiantly when he comes up against representatives of respectable society, shocking them by offering a buffoonery that caricatures the behavior they expect of him. When Morag asks why he acts so loony, he explains he is " 'only showing them what they thought they would be expecting to see, then, do you see?' She does not see" (p. 38). Underlying his mockery is a knowledge of the townspeople gained from long experience of their garbage, a knowledge that they suspect and fear. Christie expresses his fool-wisdom in logically impossible, self-contradictory statements—" 'You have to work hard at it . . . to be such a bloody flop as I stand before you. . . . Although that's not the truth of it, neither. It's all true and not true.' " And his paradox expresses "the truth" of the situation, that he is and is not a "flop": he is, according to the standards of the world, but is not according to the standards that matter—an insight he buttresses by reference to Shakespeare:

> *Oh what a piece of work is man.* Who said that? Some brain. . . . Oh what a piece of work is man oh what a bloody awful piece of work is man    enough to scare the pants off when you come to think of it    the opposite is also true. (p. 88)

The association of paradox with Shakespeare is appropriate, since it is the mode not only of Shakespeare's fools but of Shakespeare himself, whose genius has been described by more than one critic as "complementarity," "ambivalence," a capacity to see both sides of a question.[28]

Similarly, when Christie reassures Morag that it was all right for her to leave him and Manawaka (" 'it's a bloody good thing you've got away from this dump' ") and she asks, " 'Do you really think that, Christie?' " he answers with a paradox: " 'I do. . . . And also I don't. That's the way it goes.' " Again, his illogic suggests a truth—that Morag's leaving Manawaka has been both good and bad: good in that she has escaped what is bad about the town, bad in that she has lost something of value by leaving. Christie continues, offering his one bit of prophecy: " 'It'll all go along with you, too. That goes without saying.' 'You mean—everything will go along with me?' 'No less than that, ever,' Christie says" (p. 207). As is characteristic of prophets and jesters, his utterance is ambiguous: does the "it" which will "go along" with her mean good luck, or Manawaka, or both? In fact, "it" comes to mean both, in that Morag's taking Manawaka "along with her" will be her means to good fortune. Later in the novel, Morag herself has picked up his habit of paradox,[29] when, arranging for Christie's funeral, she expresses her sense that Niall Cameron "did and didn't, both" want to go on living, and develops this insight with a reference to Shakespeare: "to be or not to be—that sure as death is the question. The two-way battle in the minefield. The minefield of the mind" (p. 399).

Christie's Piper Gunn tales similarly express a sense of the complexity of things—not that the tales are complex in themselves, but that Christie's free-wheeling adaptations fabricate a past which becomes "real" though fictional: "the myths are my reality" (p. 390), as Morag says. Christie gives Morag a personal past with his tales of the heroism of her father, Colin, in the Battle of

Bourlon, and he gives her a heritage with the Piper Gunn stories. Culling from such disparate sources as James Macpherson's Ossianic Poems and *The 60th Canadian Field Artillery Battery Book,* he conjures spirits "who probably never lived in so-called real life but who live forever" (p. 418), conjuring when "the spirits are in him" and "when the spirit moves him" (pp. 47–48), truly "inspired." But his skepticism about what "them books say" (p. 83) extends even to those authorities he most trusts: he says of the Battle of Bourlon, "it was like the book [the *Field Artillery Book*] says, but it wasn't like that, also" (p. 90). This skepticism of official versions is a quality he shares with Jules, also an outsider, who knows that Dieppe "wasn't the way the papers told it" (p. 164) and, when confronted with the history books's versions of the Métis rebel Riel, knows that "the books lie" (p. 147). What Prin reveals, when she surfaces for a rare moment of lucidity to tell the truth of the Battle of Bourlon—that it was Christie who rescued Colin and not Colin who rescued Christie—impugns the "truth" of Christie's tales generally; but Morag later comes to realize that "it doesn't matter a damn" whether they happened or not (p. 350).

From believing Christie's tales, Morag comes to disbelieve them and then to "believe in them again, in a different way" (p. 367)—a movement which replicates other patterns of loss and recovery, difference and sameness, in the novel. Though young Morag once sought the certainties her daughter now seeks, Morag has, as we meet her in the present episodes, a sense of complexity like Christie's. To Pique's questions about "the truth" of Christie's stories and Jules's songs, whether they "really happened," Morag says, in language like Christie's:

> "Some did and some didn't, I guess. It doesn't matter a damn.
> Don't you see?"
> "No," Pique said, "I don't see. I want to know what really happened."
> Morag laughed. Unkindly, perhaps.
> "You do, eh? Well, so do I. But there's no one version. There just isn't." (p. 350)

She has come to accept the uncertain status of Christie's tales—stories "real and . . . imagined" (p. 249) about "those who have never been and yet would always be" (p. 244)—and this sense of complexity informs her attitudes generally ("things remained mysterious" [p. 4], "ambiguity is everywhere" [p. 402]) and makes her humble about judging:

> *Whatever is happening to Pique is not what I think is happening, whatever that may be. What happened to me wasn't what anyone else thought was happening, and maybe not even what I thought was happening at the time.* (p. 60)

Morag understands that the past, the present, and the self in its "many versions" (p. 396) are constructs of the fictionalizing imagination, fictions that are constantly being revised. That *"everyone is constantly changing their own past, recalling it, revising it"* makes all knowledge provisional: *"What really happened? A meaningless question"* (p. 60). These realizations are related to her profession as writer: "a daft profession. Wordsmith. Liar, more likely. Weaving fabrications. Yet, with typical ambiguity, convinced that fiction was more true than fact. Or that fact was in fact fiction" (p. 25); "What is a true story? Is there any such thing?" (p. 144). That the tales lead back not to "real things" but to other tales suggests a postmodern sense of referentiality, a sense of the truth of fiction and the fiction of truth.

## The Doing of the Thing

In the letter which describes her novel *Prospero's Child,* Morag speculates about Prospero's need of "grace," wondering if he will be able to keep his "strength" after he dismisses his spirits:

> I've always wondered if Prospero really would be able to give up his magical advantages once and for all as he intends to do at the end of *The Tempest.* That incredibly moving statement, "What strength I have's mine own, Which is most faint—" If only he can hang onto that knowledge, that would be true strength. And the recognition that his real enemy is despair within, and that he stands in need of grace, like everyone else. (p. 330)

Her suggestion that his "enemy" is "despair" indicates a sense that this is her "enemy" also—which explains why, in her earliest stories, Morag gave her character Morag "the strength of conviction."

But faith is more difficult for Morag than for Prospero because it is unsanctioned by belief in God or an afterlife. The world Morag inherits does not resemble a paradise or inspire much confidence in the future: she has a sense, rather, of "doom all around" (p. 27), of the present as "nightmare" (p. 106) and the future as "apocalypse" (p. 4). As she says in one of her imaginary exchanges with Catharine Parr Trail, the pioneer woman she conjures and argues with, "the evidence of your eyes showed you Jerusalem the Golden," "the evidence of my eyes, however, does little to reassure me" (p. 171). Laurence's affirmations occur in the *absence* of God, and Morag's revelations are not of a transcendent, providential pattern, but are a pattern-making: her "grace" is a process, a creation and recreation.[30]

Morag's resolutions are worked out in terms that recall *The Tempest.* She wonders if the home she has made is an "island":

> *I've made an island. Are islands real? . . . Islands are unreal. No place is far enough away. Islands exist only in the head. And yet I stay. All this . . . may be a fantasy. But I can bear to live here until I die, and I couldn't elsewhere.* (p. 356)

These speculations are answered by her vision of the "Great Blue Heron," which, in the "soaring and measured certainty of its flight" (p. 357), symbolizes the equanimity she aspires to. This vision leads to a realization like Stacey's, "that here and now was not, after all, an island. Her quest for islands had ended some time ago, and her need to make pilgrimages had led her back here" (pp. 356–57). Morag's "quest for islands" has ended, both in the sense that she has dispelled the illusion that the "British Isles"—England or Scotland—are home and she now knows that home is Canada; and in the sense that she has ceased to "insulate" herself, to make herself an island—a metaphor which recalls Donne's. Morag's "here and now" is "not an island" (p. 357) because it represents a connection with a human community and with the past—so that unlike Prospero, she does not have to leave this place to return to society. The last section of the novel is the first section to conclude with Morag *not* moving on to a new place—though her daughter, Pique, does move on.

That Morag has attained a measure of faith is indicated by her dismissal of her "spirit," Catharine Parr Traill, in terms that again recall *The Tempest:* "So farewell, sweet saint—henceforth, I summon you not" (p. 406). Catharine Parr Traill was a Canadian heroine who raised nine children, tilled the fields, *and* managed to write books,[31] whom Morag has conjured to make herself feel inadequate; but she has learned, as she says, to "stop feeling guilty that I'll never be as hard-working or knowledgable or all-round terrific as you were" (p. 406). Having dismissed her spirit, Morag's powers are, like Prospero's, "her own": though in a sense her powers have always been "her own" in a way that Prospero's are not. Whereas Shakespeare suggests that Prospero's purposes are in harmony with Providence, Laurence gives no indication that Morag's are. Whereas Prospero redeems the creatures of his world, Morag can only recreate the stories of those she writes about, making her characters relive symbolically but not actually. Though Prospero requests applause as a sign of his power, Morag has no way of knowing whether she has pleased, no idea how her books are received or understood. Yet she has attained sufficient self-assurance to risk confronting the most desolate of possibilities, that her work has been for nothing:

> At least Royland knew he had been a true diviner. There were the wells, proof positive. . . . Morag's magic tricks were of a different order. She would never know whether they actually worked or not, or to what extent. . . . In a sense, it did not matter. The necessary doing of the thing—that mattered. (p. 452)

She must resign herself to the ephemeral and uncertain consolation of process, the "doing of the thing," knowing that what has been created will need to be recreated. This sense of life more resembles Virginia Woolf's than Shakespeare's—and Woolf is the one woman writer Laurence refers to in this novel: "a woman, if she is to write, Virginia Woolf once said . . . must have a room of her own" (pp. 293–94).[32]

Morag contemplates the possibility that her skills as diviner may be as mysteriously taken from her as Royland's were, and even wonders "was this, finally and at last, what Morag had always sensed she had to learn from the old man?"—that "the gift, or portion of grace, or whatever it was, was finally withdrawn, to be given to someone else." This is, as he tells her, " 'not a matter for mourning,' " for divining is " 'not something that everybody can do, but . . .

quite a few people can learn to do it' " (pp. 451–52). She can resign herself to losing her gift because she knows that it will pass to somebody else—as it does pass from Christie to Morag to Pique. Laurence's vision of the artist stresses not the development of individual talent or the imposition of self on experience, but a letting-go of self and a wise resignation to processes beyond one's control, a sense of continuity and community, of the involvement of self with all. Realizing that she cannot control or even understand the processes that shape people and events, Morag learns to let go, not only of her "gift" and her books, but of the people in her life—and not only of men (Brooke, Jules, Dan McRaith), but of her daughter. She has learned—like Anna Wulf, and like Prospero—to let them go "free," in a gesture corroborating the movement of narrative toward release. In fact, Laurence describes her writing in terms like these: "Perhaps this is all one can do with one's characters—try to set them free."[33]

The novel began with Morag unable to accept Pique's setting out on her own; it ends with her reconciled to her departure—"Let her go. This time, it had to be possible and was" (p. 440). She has come to understand her part in her daughter's life, to accept "the hurts" she has "unwittingly inflicted upon Pique," and to accept Pique's forgiveness as well:

> Morag had agonized over these often enough, almost as though, if she imagined them sufficiently, they would prove to have been unreal after all. But they were not unreal. Yet Pique was not assigning any blame—that was not what it was all about. (p. 441)

The test of what Morag achieves is in what she passes on to Pique, and Pique sets out at the end in possession of knowledge it has taken Morag a lifetime to acquire. Part of what she understands is not to "assign blame." Pique forgives the sins of her elders (as the younger generation does in Shakespearean romance) because she understands that the processes which make people what they are reach back to an unknowable past—an understanding which, like many others, goes back to Christie: " 'Nobody can't help nothing . . . so best shut up about it' " (p. 209).[34] She leaves "on some kind of search" (p. 237), headed for her uncle's farm, the place of her father's people, to help make a new community, on a quest which is "different [from] . . . but the same" as Morag's (p. 422): it is "the same" in that she, too, seeks a father and home, but is "different" in that she seeks the past rather than fleeing it. Pique even takes something of the paradoxical wisdom of Morag and Christie, in her knowledge that "It will and it won't" go well for her (p. 440). Thus personal past intersects with cultural heritage, and Pique is "the inheritor" of her mother's and father's traditions and of old and new worlds. Whereas the men in the novel—Jules, Brooke, Dan—are all determined *not* to be like their fathers (pp. 141, 219, 354), Pique does not repudiate Morag: in a way that is rare in contemporary women's fiction, this mother leaves her daughter "a place to stand" (in the words of the novel's epigraph).

Dispossessed, but also in possession—of herself and the past—Pique takes the past with her in the form of art. The songs she has composed combine the

Scottish legend and history of Christie's tales (via Morag's stories of Christie) with the Métis legend and history of Lazarus's stories (via Jules's songs). This mixture of genres and forms—song, oral history, history, family lore—is appropriate to her lineage, which represents a combination of Métis (themselves a mixture of Indian and French) with Scotch and Irish. This mélange also exemplifies Laurence's transgression of generic boundaries, her combination of fiction, history, legend, autobiography, and song,[35] of marginal and mainstream, canonical and noncanonical, traditional and revisionary.

### The River that Runs Both Ways

The first short story Morag ever showed anyone was praised for not "opting for an easy ending"—by which her reader meant she didn't marry the protagonist off (pp. 122, 124)—and *The Diviners* may be similarly described. Though the novel makes gestures toward closure, ending with a death (Jules's) and departure (Pique's), Morag's ending is not "easy" or conventional. She ends alone, a "maverick," living in an isolated place by a river, known by the town as the local crazy woman. But Laurence's sense of process makes any ending provisional: whereas the end of *Portrait* stresses the sharp break and final accomplishment, Laurence's vision precludes finality. Thus Morag describes her terms with life—"I've worked out my major dilemmas as much as I'm likely to"—and immediately qualifies this:

> Now that I read that over, I wonder if it's true. The calm plateau still seems pretty far off to me. I'm still fighting the same bloody battles as always, inside the skull. Maybe all there is on that calm plateau is a tombstone. (p. 289)

Throughout, this sense of process prohibits a resting place: Morag's "Rites of Passage" (the title of the long fourth chapter) is a process extending over an entire lifetime rather than a single initiation from adolescence into adulthood (as Morley points out [1981]; p. 125).

Laurence, like Lessing, describes her work as "an attempt at something new" (Gadgetry or Growing," pp. 54–55). And for Laurence, as for Lessing, change is accomplished not by dramatic ends and new beginnings, but by a gradual movement through each stage. Morag uses Anna Wulf's metaphor for change when she compares herself to "a snake shedding its skin"—"another shed skin of another life" (p. 172); and Morag's definition of knowing—" 'You sometimes see things suddenly, and then you know you've known them a long time' " (p. 271)—recalls Anna's sense of learning as "knowing, on deeper and deeper levels, what one knew before' " (GN, p. 239). As in *The Golden Notebook,* ends work back to beginnings, and *The Diviners* ends with the protagonist ready to write the novel we have read; in the same way that Lessing's novel opens and closes on similar scenes, on conversations between Anna and Molly, so too does Laurence's novel begin and end with Morag contemplating the river that "flows both ways" (p. 3).

The river's paradoxical movement suggests that the way back is the way forward and alludes to time that is both subjective and objective: time that is subjective—memory—moves backward, while time that is objective moves forward.[36] This "apparently impossible contradiction" (p. 3) is the central paradox of the novel, part of the pattern of repetition of sameness within difference, or difference within sameness, and part of the larger pattern of loss and recovery on which the novel is structured.[37] But the circular return represents not a "nightmare repetition" but a fruitful intertwining of ends and beginnings, a sense of the past as nourishing, feeding, and renewing the present and future—a sense like that symbolized by the Ouroboros, the serpent swallowing its tail, figure for "the continuity of life" and "continual return, within a cyclic pattern."[38] Pique's journey continues this circular return, for she, too, travels back to the past in order to make a new future. This backward and forward movement dramatizes that we *can* change the past by imaginatively recreating it, and that by changing the past, we can transform present and future. The line with which Laurence concludes *The Diviners*—"*Look ahead into the past, and back into the future, until the silence*" (p. 453)—is the line with which she concluded her funeral service.

Laurence's "use of" memory, then, is "for liberation." So, too, does she use the literary tradition "for liberation," making Morag actor, writer, director, and epic hero. She allows her to found a new order and assume the powers of Prospero—powers which have been, however, considerably redefined, reenvisioned as an acknowledgment of the *limits* of power, a relinquishing of individuality, rationality, and control, and the attainment of a difficult humility and involvement with others. In her appropriation of male canonical authors, Laurence reworks epic quest, *Bildungsroman*, and Shakespearean romance, and her reworkings are as bold and original as Milton's adaptation of classical epic to his Christian vision, Wordsworth's adaptation of Milton's *Paradise Lost* to his autobiographical *Prelude,* or Joyce's adaptation of *The Odyssey* to his epic of modern life, *Ulysses.*

# VIII

## MARGARET ATWOOD'S
## *LADY ORACLE*
### GOING OFF GOTHICS

> You can't change the past. . . . Oh, but I
> wanted to; that was the one thing I really
> wanted to do.
>
> Atwood, *Lady Oracle*[1]

> A woman with an eating obsession is
> searching for the memory of things past. For
> in that past and in its hidden, troubled
> memory is the possibility of liberation from
> the unseen conflicts and ambivalence that
> keep her from moving into her own
> development and from the re-creation of
> herself she urgently requires. . . . At the heart
> of a disordered relation to food there is a
> disorder in memory.
>
> Kim Chernin, *The Hungry Self*[2]

> How, then, can one return into the cave, the
> den, the earth? Rediscover the darkness of all
> that has been left behind? Remember the
> forgotten mother?
>
> Luce Irigaray, *Speculum of the Other
> Woman*[3]

Joan Foster (née Joan Delacourt, alias Louisa Delacourt) is a junk-fiction junkie
who is "hooked on plots" (p. 342) as she was once addicted to junk food, a
closet writer of Costume Gothics which she admits are "trash of the lowest
order"—"worse than trash, for didn't they exploit the masses, corrupt by

distracting, and perpetuate degrading stereotypes of women as helpless and persecuted? They did and I knew it, but I couldn't stop" (pp. 33–34). "An escape artist" herself (p. 367), Joan is expert at fabricating escape for others, making it "available for them at the corner drugstore, neatly packaged like the other painkillers" (p. 34); and though she defends her Gothic romances as "necessary" for the many women incapable of devising "escapes of their own," she also hides this writing behind an assumed name. Joan's Gothics take an unexpected turn, however, when, after her trip through the looking glass, she returns from "the other side" with fragments which become the basis of a long poem, "Lady Oracle," a bizarre and troubling work which seems like "a Gothic gone wrong" (p. 259); and though she more nearly acknowledges this writing as her own, publishing it under her name, she again finds a way of disowning it by insisting that it was "dictated by powers beyond [her] control" (p. 250). Whereas Anna Wulf, Jane Gray, and Morag Gunn use their writing to achieve self-knowledge and power, Joan uses hers to avoid knowing herself or the past, thereby entrenching herself more firmly in the situation she seeks to escape.

What is the point of this portrait of the artist as degraded seer, this "oracle" who is so bemired in the worst tendencies of her world that she can heal neither self nor society? Oracular knowledge is notoriously enigmatic, and some critics have claimed that *Lady Oracle* raises more questions than it resolves, accounting for its ambiguities by calling it "parody."[4] But to call it "parody" is to trivialize it: presumably Atwood was serious about the two years she spent writing it, more time than she took with any of her other novels.[5] *Lady Oracle* does include parody of literary trends and vogues, the publishing market, the way women writers get reviewed, the cults that form around poetesses (especially red-headed or suicidal poetesses); it is a marvelously imaginative *jeu d'esprit* which has been variously described as "a roman à clef in which Atwood mocks the manners and mores of the Toronto literary scene and uses 'her fiction to pay off old scores' "[6] and as "a wonderfully complicated Gothic–comic–murder mystery with feminist overtones."[7] Primarily, of course, it parodies Gothics:[8] Atwood calls it "anti-Gothic romance" and says she uses "the components [of Gothics] and then pulls them inside out, as you would a glove" (Dembo, p. 379), demonstrating what she calls "the perils of Gothic thinking," the irrelevance of "Gothic sensibility" (p. 253) to "real-life" problems.[9] But aside from the fact that Gothics are a popular form with women, what accounts for Atwood's interest in them? What is the point of the parody?

Joan is addicted to writing Gothics as she was once addicted to eating and as—according to Janice Radway—many readers are addicted to reading them:[10] "I couldn't stop," she says of both eating and writing (pp. 34, 78). What we know of her "standard Costume Gothic" suggests that it follows the standard formula: "she was in peril, my eternal virgin on the run. . . . The house was after her, the master of the house as well, and possibly the mistress. Things were closing in on her" (p. 146). Their covers "feature gloomy, foreboding castles and apprehensive maidens in modified nightgowns, hair streaming in the wind . . . toes poised for flight" (p. 33); their stories feature "the hero in the mask of a villain, the villain in the mask of a hero, the flights, the looming death, the sense of being imprisoned" (p. 259). There is also the "other woman," perhaps a former wife, murdered or vanished in mysterious circumstances and associated with a dark secret; there is the maze, a place of danger and mystery which the heroine must somehow penetrate;[11] and—from these inauspicious materials—always the "happy ending [and] true love" (p. 259). One can understand Joan's addiction to happy endings, but beyond this, what do Gothics have to do with her life—her overeating? Her mother? Why do they provide the relief they do, and why do they cease providing this relief? What makes these questions particularly difficult is that Joan offers us no help with them: her dissociation from self is so complete that she hasn't a clue what her story is about.

To complicate matters, *Lady Oracle* seems in several ways to parody feminist quest fiction of the sort that Atwood herself has written. It includes many of the same elements: woman seeks freedom from the past, from constraints associated with an oppressive mother and husband; and though Joan's trip through the looking glass is not quite the harrowing descent into madness taken by Jane Gray, Anna Wulf, or Martha Quest, it is a comparable plunge into the irrational. If the novel is not quite a *Kunstlerroman* in ways that *The Golden Notebook, The Waterfall,* and *The Diviners* are, still, Joan is a woman writer who experiments with various genres and speculates about forms; and that Joan's "Lady Oracle" bears the same name as Atwood's novel implies correspondences between Joan's writing and Atwood's. Joan is also, like other protagonists of contemporary women's fiction, a reader; her expectations have been shaped by romance fiction and fairy tales (Snow White, the Little Mermaid, the Lady of Shallott)[12] and by films—named after Joan Crawford, she fantasizes herself as Moira Shearer in *The Red Shoes* and even as a Fellini whore. Besides the doomed women she identifies with are the menacing mythological figures Atwood invokes, whose power is associated with subterranean caves: the Gorgons (three monstrous women, one of whom was the Medusa), the Demeter–Persephone–Hecate triad and the Artemis–Selene–Hecate triad. But if Atwood is writing against the tradition, suggesting that Gothics, romances, fairy tales, myths, and movies ill equip her protagonist for life, does Joan accomplish what the protagonists of feminist *Kunstlerromane* do and write her way through to "something new"—to (in her own term) "a fresh beginning, a new life" (p. 342)? Or, since Joan's "Lady Oracle" is "a Gothic gone wrong," might Atwood's *Lady Oracle* be a feminist *Kunstlerroman* gone wrong?

"Escape artist" Joan goes to great lengths to get free—twice by changing her identity and once by staging her own death, disappearing into Lake Ontario and reemerging on "the other side" (of the Atlantic), hoping to be "free at last, the past discarded" (p. 3), "to get rid of it entirely and construct a different one" (p. 157). But her efforts to escape leave her at the end (which is also the beginning) feeling that "nothing had changed" (p. 7), "the new life . . . hadn't materialized" (p. 342): "Why did every one of my fantasies turn into a trap?" (p. 367). As final scene returns to first scene, she ends, as she began, on her balcony in Terremoto, "waiting for something to happen, the next turn of events (a circle? a spiral?)"—"caged on [her] balcony," "waiting to change" (p. 342).

That the Gothic formula has brought her in a circle, leaving her trapped by those trappings that promised escape, suggests the dead-end quality of the genre. Gothics provide Joan a means of "containment," functioning for her, as they do for women generally, to contain ambivalences and conflicts regarding "the significant people in their lives—mothers, fathers, lovers."[13] "Contain yourself" is a frequent injunction of her husband, Arthur, and Joan uses the Gothic formula, with its predictable pattern and unvarying ending, to keep herself within bounds and prevent "transgression," to avoid "making a spectacle" of herself—a "specifically feminine danger" (as Mary Russo terms it), and one which involves "loss of boundaries."[14] Working within a conventional fictional form enables Joan to maintain conventional bounds in her life, to be Arthur's docile, obliging wife. Deploring her "tendency to spread, to get flabby, to scroll and festoon"—to overflow boundaries and expand to take up space— Joan aspires to "a neat and simple" form (p. 3). She enlists the Gothic formula to the same end that Anna Wulf uses her notebooks, to divide and control, fearing that "if I brought the separate parts of my life together (like uranium, like plutonium, harmless to the naked eye, but charged with lethal energies) surely there would be an explosion" (p. 242).

But though Gothics contain Joan's "lethal" energies, they also contain her creative energies; devised as escape, they become a prison, locking her into a fixed, fruitless relationship to the past, a past become "dead . . . irretrievable" (p. 149), or—in a central metaphor of the novel—become a "snarl": "My life was a snarl, a rat's nest of dangling threads and loose ends" (p. 326) (Joan returns from her first trip through the looking glass with "a single long red line that twisted and turned back on itself, like a worm or a snarl of wool" [p. 124]). For Gothics may allow her to take refuge in "those receding centuries" (p. 179), but they offer only a futile recycling of the past, a repetition of the same elements to the same end; they cannot help her "undo the tangle that [her] life had become" (p. 324) or "unravel . . . the past" (p. 217).

But the return to the beginning may be a "spiral" rather than a circle. In the novel as a whole, episodes set in the past alternate with episodes set in the present, until, in the last section, past becomes present—a circular return which suggests not dead end and finality but repetition in order that there may be escape from repetition.[15] For despite her efforts to "contain" herself, Joan changes, and her inability to finish her last Gothic and its inability to "contain" her are evidence of that change. Atwood contrasts two "female forms," one which fixes and one which is fluid, and renders her protagonist's development as a repudiation of the former and celebration of the latter: Joan's Gothic romances may lock her in repetition, but Atwood's *Lady Oracle* allows release.

## Gothic Horrors

Atwood's novel offers a brilliant exposé of escape fiction—how it provides escape, what from and what to. Like Martha Quest and other "hungry heroines" of contemporary women's fiction, Joan turns to reading because she is starved, deprived of maternal nurturance and of what Phyllis Chesler terms the maternal "legacy of power and humanity" that women are denied in a culture that devalues women.[16] Gothic romances, like other romance forms and popular women's fiction, satisfy women's "emotional malnutrition" (in Madonne Miner's term)[17] and provide "emotional gratification": in creating "that perfect union where the ideal male, who is masculine and strong yet nurturant too, finally recognizes the intrinsic worth of the heroine," they allow the reader the feeling of being "cared for" and "reconstituted affectively" (Radway, pp. 59, 97). As a girl, Joan spent summers "eating and reading trashy books" (p. 167), "reading trashy books and eating chocolates" (p. 169), and as an adult, she turns to writing Gothics with the same compulsiveness: "As long as I could spend a certain amount of time each week as Louisa, I was all right. . . . But if I was cut off, if I couldn't work at my current Costume Gothic, I would become mean and irritable, drink too much and start to cry" (p. 238). But junk fiction, like junk food and the packaged painkillers at the corner drugstore, offers only short-term relief; Radway describes it as a "tranquilizer or restorative agent" (p. 62) whose "short-lived therapeutic value . . . is finally the cause of its repetitive consumption" (p. 85).

Tania Modleski accounts for the popularity of Gothics in terms of their ability to contain "conflicts and anxieties" generated by "the structure of the Western family, with its unequal distribution of power" (p. 81), inequities which leave the girl feeling "anger at the domineering father" and "at the mother for allowing herself to be a victim" (p. 66). Gothics alleviate women's "fears of and confusions about masculine behavior" (p. 60): Atwood herself suggests that they are "consumed in such great quantities by women because secretly they think their husbands are trying to kill them."[18] Typically, the heroine either suspects the man of having killed his first wife or fears that her relationship with him will be a repetition of one which occurred in the past (Modleski, p. 76):

> The heroine comes to a mysterious house, perhaps as a bride, perhaps in another capacity, and either starts to mistrust her husband or else finds herself in love with a mysterious man who appears to be some kind of criminal. . . . She tries to convince herself that her suspicions are unfounded, that, since she loves him, he must be trustworthy and that she will have failed as a woman if she does not implicitly believe in him. Often, but not always, the man is proven innocent of all wrongdoing by the end of the novel, and the real culprit is discovered and punished. (p. 59)

When the villain turns hero—especially when his transformation is inspired by love of the heroine—female anxiety about male behavior is relieved: the formula thus allows expression and also repression of suspicion of men (p. 66).

But primarily, Gothics help women to deal with their ambivalence toward mothers, "to convince women that they will not be victims the way their mothers were" (pp. 83, 69). Modleski notes that the protagonist often feels a strong identification with a woman from the past, either the remote or the recent past—a woman who may have been a former wife and may have "died a mysterious and perhaps violent or gruesome death" (p. 69). This woman threatens to engulf her: "the heroine has the uncanny sensation that the past is repeating itself through her," "the sensation of actually being possessed, the feeling that past and present are not merely similar but are 'intertwined' "; she may feel "suffocated—as well as desperate and panic stricken in her inability to break free of the past" (Modleski, pp. 69, 170). This is "the rival female" of Joan's fiction, who, "like all such women . . . came to a bad end" (*Lady Oracle*, p. 175), the "other woman" onto whom terror of women is projected. Claire Kahane suggests that "the Gothic fear" is "the fear of femaleness itself, perceived as threatening to one's wholeness, obliterating the very boundaries of self," "committing women to an imprisoning biological destiny" (pp. 346–47): at the "forbidden center of the Gothic" is "the spectral presence of a dead—undead mother, archaic and all-encompassing" (p. 336). The castle itself is, according to Kahane, "the maternal legacy," "the female body" (p. 343). Norman Holland and Leona Sherman similarly associate the imprisoning house with the mother, "mother . . . as sexual being, as body, as harboring a secret," "a woman with a sexuality [which is] her secret."[19]

This, then, is the menacing secret at the heart of the claustrophobic castle—the mother, who represents entrapment, engulfment, and whose repression is the *basis* of the structure, as indeed it is the basis of Western thought, as Irigaray demonstrates in *The Speculum of the Other Woman* (pp. 295–309): an ancient, terrifying pain and rage so long repressed that it is unspeakable. Kahane argues that the terror in Gothics derives from fear of the repressed: citing Ellen Moers's description of Gothics as giving "visual form to the fear of the self,"[20] she suggests that "what was once veiled in the pre-Freudian darkness is now unveiled and even more terrifying for being seen" (p. 343). This explains why the question "What have you seen?" recurs throughout modern Gothics: what is "seen," or not seen, what is veiled and then partially unveiled, glimpsed fitfully and frighteningly—is the mother and the doom she represents. "What do you see?"—a question to be asked of an oracle—is the question that inspires Joan's trip through the looking glass, where she discovers a powerful and frightening woman in a cave, a woman she later identifies with her mother.

Kahane notes that "in modern Gothics the spectral mother typically becomes an embodied actual figure" and that "she, and not some threatening villain, becomes the primary antagonist" (p. 343). Her terms apply to *Lady Oracle*, where the mother is both actual and spectral and is certainly antagonistic. Atwood's awareness that the mother is the animating force behind the Gothic formula is suggested by what happens to Joan's Gothics after her mother dies: when Joan returns home after her mother's death, she discovers that she and her father, formerly conspirators, now have nothing to say—"she'd held us together, like a national emergency, like the Blitz." As her "mother's house disintegrates" (p. 212), so does Joan's relationship with the father, and so, too, does her writing: "the old plots no longer interested me. . . . I did try . . . but the hero played billiards all the time and the heroine sat on the edge of her bed, alone at night, doing nothing" (p. 203). It is the menace of the mother that drives the daughter to the father–rescuer: without her presence the structure disintegrates.

Modleski accounts for other elements of Gothics in terms of anxieties that result from the typical family power structure. She explains their "strong element of paranoia" as originating in what William Meissner terms the "paranoid family dynamic":[21]

> The paranoid usually comes from a family whose power structure is greatly skewed: one of the parents is perceived as omnipotent and domineering, while the other is perceived . . . as submissive to and victimized by the stronger partner . . . the paranoid patient tends to introject these images of his/her parents and . . . internalizes the dynamics of the parental interaction . . . enact[ing] within the self the war between victim and victimizer. When the internal battle becomes too painful to be tolerated, one of these elements gets projected onto the external environment—usually the aggressive introject, for . . . aggressive impulses are tolerated best . . . when we believe we are the victims of another's hostility. (Modleski, p. 66, paraphrasing Meissner, p. 575)

Modleski suggests, however, that this family structure is not really "skewed," since "an imbalance in the power structure—with the male dominant—is considered the ideal familial situation in our culture." And since the aim of our socialization process is to get the child to identify with the parent of the same sex, "the female is more likely than the male to retain the (feminine) 'victim' introject and to deny (project) feelings of aggression and anger" (p. 66). The sense of menace that pervades Gothic fiction, then, the sense that "things are closing in," expresses " 'normal' feminine" paranoia (p. 81).

The "need for an enemy" may be (according to both Modleski and Meissner) a necessary step in "the process of separation–individuation" that any child undergoes, since "being able to project an enemy" allows the individual to establish "boundaries of the self" as well as to deny "intolerable ambivalent feelings, especially aggressive ones." But since "to find out that the enemy is indeed the 'father' would only increase the 'boundary confusion' the paranoid is struggling to eliminate," Gothics deflect anger onto an enemy which is not the father; thus "the attempt to find an enemy and the attempt to exonerate the father . . . [are] part of the same project" (Modleski, pp. 74–75). "Only after the heroine has obtained 'absolute proof' of the man's innocence can 'oedipal conflicts' be resolved and reconciliation with the father become possible; only then can identification with the victimized 'mother' be broken; and only then can the lover be accepted" (pp. 76–77). Only when the lover–husband is proved not guilty—when the villain turns hero—can the heroine's fears about marriage be alleviated.

The Gothic formula thus alleviates woman's ambivalences about the victim mother and the frightening men in her environment, enabling her imaginatively to achieve separation from the mother so that she may herself become a wife. It reinforces the "family romance," making the daughter the mother and then making her into *her* mother.[22] This is the "central plot" of patriarchy, in a term from *Lady Oracle* (p. 375), according to which the original triad (consisting of father, mother, and daughter) becomes a dyad (consisting of wife and father): three becomes two by the elimination of one—and we shall see Atwood's play with these terms. That it is the mother who is eliminated while the father–husband is exonerated and elevated to hero–rescuer suggests what kind of a situation woman must adjust to: no wonder that the mother turns menacing, having been villainized and obliterated, and no wonder that the daughter's anxieties need alleviating, as she is bamboozled into denying the mother even as she is in the process of *becoming* her. And the situation allows no change— daughter becomes mother and has a daughter who in turn becomes a mother, and so on. As Modleski says, "Gothics testify to women's extreme discontent with the social and psychological processes which transform them into victims" (p. 84), yet they also enable women to live with this discontent, "to come at least partially to terms with the ambivalent attitudes towards significant people in their lives" (p. 67). Gothics make an unacceptable situation acceptable and assure that it remain unchanged, and are thus deeply conservative. This is (as Kahane suggests) "the real Gothic horror—the heroine is compelled to resume a quiescent, socially acceptable role or to be destroyed" (p. 342).[23]

## Family Plots and Lost Legacies

Joan's family background—a mother all too present and a father all too absent—leaves her with precisely that constellation of anxieties that the Gothic formula is suited to alleviate. Both mother and father have been trapped by an accidental pregnancy: she is in a "tomb" (p. 201); he is "in a cage" (p. 154). But whereas the mother remains trapped, the father is allowed some outlets, first in war and then in a career. While he is away, Joan's mother fictionalizes him according to her needs: "Nice men did things for you, bad men did things to you"—categories which reveal her sense of herself as victim and which later become Joan's. Upon his return, he "brought nothing and did nothing, and that remained his pattern. Most of the time he was simply an absence" (p. 73)—an absence which allows Joan's fantasies wide range. Accepting her mother's categories, she imagines him as "healer and killer" (p. 325)—he had "killed people and brought them back to life again, though not the same ones" (p. 154)—and projects this division onto all men:

> Every man I'd ever been involved with . . . had had two selves: my father . . . the Royal Porcupine and his double, Chuck Brewer; even Paul, who I'd always believed had a sinister other life I couldn't penetrate . . . Arthur. . . . (pp. 325–26)

Joan endows her father with omnipotence and omniscience—"he was a con-
jurer of spirits, a shaman" who knew "the truth about life" (p. 81)—powers
which make him an ideal model for the Gothic hero–villain.

Joan's mother, Frances Delacourt, bears a striking resemblance to Lessing's
Mrs. Quest, prototypical "bad mother" of contemporary women's fiction. Both
have been trapped by accidental pregnancy; both resent their daughters; both
insist on observing social proprieties, however inappropriate (Mrs. Delacourt
gives dinner parties to advance her husband's career, parties which he assures
her "didn't matter one iota to his career" [p. 78]); and both cherish photographs of the "true love" who got away: Mrs. Quest has a dead war hero and
Mrs. Delacourt has the "white-flanneled man," perhaps a fiancé, perhaps Joan's
real father. Neither understands why she is so unhappy, what went wrong, since
(as Joan says) her mother had "done the right thing, she had devoted her life to
us, she had made her family her career as she had been told to do, and look at
us" (pp. 199–200). "Aggressive and ambitious," though "perhaps" not "aggressive or ambitious enough" (p. 71), Joan's mother pours all her energies into
her home and turns it into a "plastic-shrouded tomb" (p. 201), "static and
dustless and final" (p. 74). But it is her daughter, "embodiment of her own
failure and depression, a huge edgeless cloud of inchoate matter which refused
to be shaped into anything for which she could get a prize" (p. 71), who bears
the brunt of her dissatisfaction: because Joan cannot possibly "justify her
[mother's] life the way she felt it should have been justified" (p. 199), she is made
to feel guilt for her very existence, knowing that the only way she could please
her mother would be "to change into someone else" (p. 56).

Only after her death does Joan become curious about her mother's point of
view and wonder "what had been done to her to make her treat me the way she
did" (p. 201). Looking in the photograph album, she is stunned by the "evidence of her terrible anger":

> In all the pictures of the white-flanneled man, the face had been cut out, neatly as
> with a razor blade. The faces of my father also were missing. There was only my
> mother, young and pretty, laughing gaily at the camera, clutching the arms of her
> headless men. . . . I could almost see her doing it, her long fingers working with
> precise fury, excising the past. (p. 201)

We know little of Joan's mother's childhood, but what we do know suggests that
(as with Mrs. Quest) behind this bad mother is another bad mother: "Her
parents had both been very strict . . . she'd run away from home at the age of
sixteen and never gone back" (pp. 71–72). Joan is right to suspect that "some
tragedy lurked there" (p. 201), and it is more than a "personal" tragedy: it is a
generalized nightmare produced by a system that cages and cripples women, a
social system that colludes with women's reproductive system to assure that
they become mothers and then become *their* mothers.

The vicious and futile circularity of this process is emphasized by Atwood's
use of the looking glass. If, as D. W. Winnicott argues, the mirror replaces the
mother's gaze as confirmation of the infant's existence—when the girl "studies

her face in the mirror she is reassuring herself that the mother-image is there"[24]—then what Joan sees in the mirror is not herself, but a mother who is herself gazing into a three-sided mirror which gives her back a reflection that dismays her; what Joan finds in the mirror is "a vortex, a dark vacuum" (p. 363) conferring not existence but nothingness, for the mother cannot give what she does not have. As Joan's mother gazes into her mirror, watching her image change through the years, the past "turned into the present and betrayed her, stranding her in this house, this plastic-shrouded tomb from which there was no exit" (p. 201). Locked into processes as inexorable as time, she will also imprison her daughter in these processes—Joan later has a three-sided mirror of her own. The three sides are associated with the three-headed monster (p. 70) Joan dreams of in connection with her mother, a figure with rich mythological resonances: besides Cerberus, the three-headed dog who guards the gate of hell (himself the issue of a terrifying monster woman), there are the Gorgones, three formidable winged women with serpents for hair, one of which is the Medusa, with her power to turn men to stone. There is also the triple-faceted goddess of the moon, Artemis, Selene, and Hecate—and Hecate, a Fury terrible in her repressed, underworldly powers, is a particularly apt figure for both Joan and her mother.[25]

Joan's matrophobia is so extreme that she eradicates all traces of her mother in order to eliminate any chance of becoming her: "I never told Arthur much about my mother. . . . I invented a mother for his benefit" (p. 41). But the mother becomes more powerful for being repressed, her hold made stronger for being unacknowledged. She haunts Joan in dreams and visions: "All this time I carried my mother around my neck like a rotting albatross. I dreamed about her often, my three-headed mother, menacing and cold" (p. 238); "I wanted to forget the past, but it refused to forget me" (p. 239). *Lady Oracle* is one of those "maternal death-bed" fictions described by Judith Kegan Gardiner in which "the daughter 'kills' her mother in order not to have to take her place";[26] though it lacks an actual deathbed scene, many of Joan's efforts are directed at burying the mother.

For if Joan sees her mother as a monster, she also sees herself as a monster, since the strategies she develops to resist her—duplicity and obesity—confirm her sense of her own monstrosity and thereby cement her more firmly to her. Her dishonesty leaves her feeling that she is a "duplicitous monster," "doggedly friendly and outgoing" on the surface but filled with "hatred and jealousy" (pp. 100–102). Her obesity makes her physically monstrous, and though she sees this as "victory" (p. 78) in their "war" (p. 73), it actually confirms her mother's victory, as she realizes when she becomes thin and her mother goes to pieces: "Making me thin was her last available project . . . she had counted on me to last her forever . . . she was frantic" (p. 136). Besides, though it serves some positive functions—it is proof that she exists, is solid against her discovery that she was "an accident" (pp. 82–83)—it makes her desperately unhappy: "It was only in relation to my mother that I derived a morose pleasure from my weight; in relation to everyone else . . . it made me miserable. But I couldn't stop" (p.

78). Her obesity provides "insulation" or "cocoon," but it also makes her grotesque, as is clear from the role she is forced to take in the children's dance, when, longing to dance the part of a winged butterfly ("I knew the addition of the wings would make all the difference" [p. 47]), she is forced into the costume of a mothball, more appropriate to her appearance as "a giant caterpillar" or "a white grub" (p. 48). As a fat girl, Joan gets none of the star roles: "I knew this even when I was ten. If Desdemona was fat who would care whether or not Othello strangled her? Why is it that the girls Nazis torture on the covers of the sleazier men's magazines are always good-looking?" (p. 53) Joan might well ask why, if a "heroine" is a woman who is strangled and tortured by men, anyone would want to be one; but she only knows that her obesity makes her so miserable that she cannot imagine prolonging social contact (though she would have liked to go to college, and that she would have liked to study "archeology or perhaps history" [p. 103] suggests that she has some sense of the importance of the past.)

Atwood suggests a relation of eating disorders to the mother of the sort analyzed by Kim Chernin and others.[27] Joan's obesity is evidence of what Chernin calls "a profound mother/daughter separation struggle"; it masks a rite of passage that "fails to accomplish a rite's essential purpose—to move the individual from one stage in the life cycle to the next" (1985, pp. xiii–xiv). Though Joan and her mother reverse the usual relationship, where the daughter strives to be thin against the fleshliness of the mother, they are actually allied in their repudiation of the flesh, for though Joan has plenty of flesh, her obesity is a repudiation of sexuality like her mother's, who, betrayed by her body, makes war on the physical by means of artificial encasings, plastics, and cosmetics (p. 74). In this way, as in others, Joan's attempts to resist her mother cement her more firmly to her: though she escapes her mother's house, as her mother escaped her own mother's house, she cannot work herself free.

It is Aunt Lou who provides a partial break in the cycle—Aunt Lou, who is warm, "soft, billowy, woolly, befurred" (p. 95), and who, in her work (writing public-relations material for a sanitary-napkin company), helps young women accept their bodies: it is she who represents an acceptance of the physical and provides the nurturance Joan's mother could not. She offers Joan a way out of her situation by willing her money on condition that she lose weight; and when Joan begins writing, it is her name, Louisa Delacourt, that she takes, in expression of her childhood fantasy that Aunt Lou be her "real mother" (p. 95).

But Joan's repudiation of her mother is a repudiation of her past and herself, of the maternal legacy that might empower her—a loss which leaves her passive, masochistic, unable to love or to become a mother herself: "I wanted children, but what if I had a child who would turn out like me? Even worse, what if I turned out to be like my mother?" (p. 238). It leaves her stuck in what Joan terms "frenzied cycles" (p. 238), in what Chernin terms a "repetitive round" that prevents a "rebirth to the next stage of the life cycle" (1985, p. 174). *Lady Oracle* writes what Adrienne Rich terms "the great unwritten story," "the essential female tragedy"—"the loss of the daughter to the mother, the mother to the daughter."[28]

## The Nightmare Repetition

The strongest evidence of the mother's hold on Joan is her marriage to Arthur. Joan thinks she is attracted to Arthur because he resembles her father—he is mysterious, inaccessible, and lends himself to embellishment in Gothic terms:

> Heroes were supposed to be aloof. His indifference was feigned, I told myself. Any moment now his hidden depths would heave to the surface; he would be passionate and confess his long-standing devotion. I would then confess mine and we would be happy. (p. 219)

But the real secret of his appeal is his similarity to her mother. Arthur takes over her mother's words and phrases, becoming a standard against which she can never measure up, telling her she is without "discipline" (p. 107) or "goals," that she should "exercise [her] intelligence constructively" (p. 235) and "make something of [her]self" (p. 24). Joan cannot please him any more than she could her mother: "I wanted to turn into what Arthur thought I was, or what he thought I should be" (p. 235), "to do something he would admire" (p. 26); but "no matter what I did, Arthur was bound to despise me. I could never be what he wanted" (p. 275). As with her mother, she is made to bear the burden of another person's unhappiness: "His depressions made me feel miserable, because they made me feel inadequate. The love of a good woman was supposed to preserve a man from this kind of thing. . . . Therefore I was not a good woman" (p. 237)—though actually, Joan is exactly what Arthur wants, since her ineptness allows him to feel superior.[29]

Joan's relationship with Arthur further replicates her relationship with her mother in requiring her duplicity: "I didn't want Arthur to understand me: I went to great lengths to prevent this" (p. 240). Since she never tells him anything important, she can remain "outwardly serene" (p. 241):

> The other wives . . . wanted their husbands to live up to their own fantasy lives . . . they wanted their men to be strong, lustful, passionate . . . but also tender and worshipful. They wanted men in mysterious cloaks who would rescue them from balconies, but they also wanted meaningful in-depth relationship. . . . I felt my own arrangement was more satisfactory . . . why demand all things of one man? (pp. 240–41)

But this duplicity infantalizes her, since it requires that she not only present herself but actually experience herself as a bumbling incompetent incapable of keeping part-time jobs or completing courses ("for the simple reason that I never really took them" [p. 33]). Though Joan does not "die for love," as she might have in another age, her relationship with Arthur kills a part of her—the exuberant, creative side.

Or, rather, it drives it underground, for her writing gives her a way of expressing that other side. After she marries Arthur, writing becomes "really important," but "the really important thing was not the books themselves. . . . It was the fact that I was two people at once, with two sets of identification papers" (p. 238). Having two identities enables her to imagine her life as "more than double . . . triple, multiple" (p. 274), and to imagine that she has eluded the entrapment of her mother. But though she has escaped her mother's house, she has actually exchanged one confinement for another, for she has slotted herself into a stifling marriage and fixed herself there by means of the formulaic repetition, in her fiction, of the "central plot" of patriarchy—"true love and happy endings." Besides, by assuming a fictitious identity, she has fulfilled her mother's wish that she be "someone else." Again, Joan's efforts to work free only entrench her more deeply.

And again, her duplicity leaves her feeling . . . duplicitous. Her division of herself into selfless wife—serene, passive, compliant—and secret writer—devious, plotting, scheming—condemns her to silence and invisibility while also making her feel like a "monster"; and she expresses this sense of herself in dreams and visions (pp. 238, 370). Joan's division replicates the angel–monster dichotomy that pervades fiction and myth—evident, for example, in the Gothics she writes, which split woman into the ideal heroine and the sinister rival, and in the story of Snow White, which functions, as Goddard notes, "as an intertext of *Lady Oracle*" (p. 31). Joan tries to "pass" for Snow White, to make herself the "heroine of a life that *has no story*" (as Gilbert and Gubar describe Snow White),[30] while within her, the Wicked Queen rages: "I was not serene, not really. I wanted things, for myself" (p. 282).

The two sides of Joan, the passive–acquiescent and the active–aggressive, correspond to female accommodations which Mary Russo describes as "purity and danger": "the cool, silent, and cloistered" versus the "lewd, exuberantly parodistic"; the "negation, silence, withdrawal, and invisibility" versus "the bold affirmations of feminine performance, imposture, and masquerade" (p. 213). But both adjustments threaten to obliterate her, as Joan senses in the nightmarish visions she has of shrinking to nothingness (and being obliterated) or of swelling to monstrous proportions (and being obliterated). The former is expressed in her recurrent dream of hiding behind a door, locked into a small space, making herself smaller and smaller: "I would back into the farthest corner of the cubicle and wedge myself in, press my arms against the walls, dig my heels against the floor. They wouldn't be able to get me out" (pp. 238–39). The latter is expressed by the Fat Lady, who recurs at times of stress like a hangover from a bad drug trip, the repressed become monstrous: she "descended on me . . . hovered around me like ectoplasm, like a gelatin shell, my ghost, my angel; then she settled and I was absorbed into her. Within my former body, I gasped for air. . . . Obliterated" (p. 353).[31] "The female freak" is a powerful admonition for the woman writer, who feels freakish because she violates fundamental cultural norms; as Grace Stewart suggests, when a woman insists on "her independence as an artist, she turns into a gorgon," "a monster . . . or a Medusa."[32]

Each of Joan's personalities requires the other but each also cancels the other out: "It was true I had two lives, but on off days I felt that neither of them was completely real" (p. 242). Each side necessitates while also negating the other— in the same way that the Wicked Queen, an artist and plotter, annuls Snow White's ideal virtue and that Snow White's virtue similarly annuls the queen's subversive energies (Gilbert and Gubar, p. 39). But as different aspects of the same personality, they come to the same end, as Gilbert and Gubar's suggestive account (which seems to have been influenced by Atwood's novel, which they cite; p. 57) makes clear: the queen, "finally, in fiery shoes that parody the costumes of femininity . . . will do a silent terrible death-dance out of the story" in an ending like that of doomed ladies of legend and myth "from the abused Procne to the reclusive Lady of Shallott" who have been "told that their art . . . is an art of silence." It is then Snow White's turn to become queen, "to be imprisoned in the looking glass from which the King's voice speaks daily. There is, after all, no female model for her in this tale except the 'good' (dead) mother and her living avatar the 'bad' mother" (pp. 42–43). And indeed, Joan suspects where all plots lead: "I just drifted around, singing vaguely, like the Little Mermaid in the Andersen fairy tale. . . . She'd become a dancer, though, with no tongue. Then there was Moira Shearer, in *The Red Shoes* . . . both of them had died" (p. 241)—a story she moralizes, "You could dance, or you could have the love of a good man" (p. 368).

In the same way that Joan divides herself, she perceives divisions elsewhere— two kinds of love, two kinds of men, two kinds of mothers, "two kinds of people: fat ones and thin ones" (p. 239). Such divisions also annihilate her, for like all binary oppositions, they disadvantage the female. This is evident in Joan's acceptance of Arthur's stereotypically "masculine" standards over her own; and Arthur's standards are identical to Paul's, for whatever the differences between these men—one's a radical and the other's a reactionary—they form the same kind of relationship with Joan. Paul is "tidy," "a systematic man, no loose ends" (p. 169); "he found my lack of order charming, but not for long" (p. 170); Arthur is "fastidious" and has an aversion to "messes" (p. 189); he wants Joan to be "disciplined" (p. 170) and "constructive" (p. 235). And she agrees— "I should have gone to finishing school and had a board strapped to my back and learned . . . self-control" (p. 6). Though both despise the feminine, both insist that she be "feminine" and that she be domestic as well: Arthur insists that she cook, and Paul urges her to sew: " 'I can't sew,' I said, but he would merely say, 'Later you will sew.' " (p. 178).

Joan accepts these masculinist standards and condemns herself for falling short of them, denigrating her own unruliness, untidiness, excessiveness: "For Arthur there were true paths, several of them perhaps, but only one at a time.

For me there were no paths at all. Thickets, ditches, ponds, labyrinths, mor-
asses, but no paths" (p. 189). She imagines herself failing the trials Paul has
passed:

> Details would distract me, the candle stubs and bones of those who had gone
> before; in any labyrinth I would have let go of the thread in order to follow a
> wandering light, a fleeting voice. In a fairy tale I would be one of the two stupid
> sisters who open the forbidden door and are shocked by the murdered wives, not
> the third, clever one who keeps to the essentials. (p. 170)

But Joan will learn, threading her way through the labyrinth, that apparently
"distracting" details turn out to be "essentials": that opening "the forbidden
door" (as she does in her last Gothic) will reveal "the murdered wives" that are
the forbidden secret of patriarchy, and that reading the "bones of those who had
gone before" will guide her through the maze.

Ultimately, Joan does learn—not sewing, exactly, but a version of it, weaving
imaginative constructs, spinning tales, "Costume Gothics" in which clothes play
a central part (p. 175). Atwood transforms the associations of sewing with
domesticity and confinement to associations with strength. Indeed, both significances are available in the myths of the culture: clothes are "paraphernalia of
'woman's place'" and "symbols of female imprisonment";[33] and weaving,
according to Freud (in a passage glossed by Irigaray; pp. 112–17), is one of
woman's "few contributions" to civilization, one which is linked to her "genital
deficiency" and to male terror of that deficiency.[34] But weaving also has mythological associations with female knowledge and power. The three fates who
spin, weave, and cut the thread of life are female and (as Gilbert and Gubar
note) reside in a "cave of power" (p. 95); Ariadne gives Theseus a thread which
guides him out of the labyrinth and saves him (though not herself). Sewing,
weaving, spinning are associated with "subversively female self-expression" (in
Marianne Hirsch's term; p. 68); Nancy Miller describes a subversive women's
writing as "arachnology."[35]

## "One and Three"

Joan's admission "I wanted things, for myself" (p. 282) marks the beginning
of the end of her equilibrium. This realization is prompted by her recollection of
the statue of Diana of Ephesus, symbol of female bounty (p. 282), and a version
of Artemis, one member of the triple goddess. Joan's realization that she no
longer identifies with her, that she is "not serene, not really" (p. 282), seems to
conjure the powerful woman who bursts forth from behind the glass, disrupting
Joan's strategies of containment and bringing with her the bizarre and disturbing "Lady Oracle."

Joan comes across this woman accidentally when, having tired of "the old
sequence of chase and flight, from rape or murder," she seeks "something new,
some new twist" (p. 242) and turns to automatic writing to find it—an idea

inspired by Leda Sprott, a sort of spiritual guide who once assured her that she had "powers" (p. 122). Joan's heroine, Penelope, is placed before a "table with a mirror on it . . . [with] a candle in front of the mirror"; gazing at the flame, she is drawn into the mirror and asked, "Tell us what you see." At this point Joan "comes up against a blank wall: I hadn't the least idea what Penelope would see or hear next"; whereupon she, too, lights a candle and sets it "in front of my dressing-table mirror"—"a three-sided one, like my mother's." Staring at the candle, with its three flames reflected in the three sides of the mirror, she finds herself suddenly "descending. . . . I was going to find someone. I needed to find someone," and emerges from the experience with the feeling that "there had been a figure, standing behind me" (pp. 244–45). Each time she repeats the experiment, she has the feeling that she is descending a long narrow passage and "the certainty that if only I could turn the next corner or the next . . . I would find the thing, the truth or word or person that was mine, that was waiting for me" (p. 247).

The "other woman" breaks through in bits and pieces, fragments "gnomic" and "chthonic" (p. 261), that Joan gradually pieces together into the poem "Lady Oracle." Returning from "the other side," she finds the word "bow" written on the page before her, and the meanings of "bow" she finds in the dictionary—"cringe, stoop, kneel . . . submit, yield, defer" (p. 246)—associate this woman with the victimization of the mother: she "bows," "she kneels, she is bent down. . . . Her tears are the death you fear" (pp. 247–48). But Joan incorporates the word "bow" into her poem as "prow" ("who is the one standing in the prow, who is the one voyaging"), thereby transforming submission to control, obedience to "authority." Each time she repeats the experiment, she returns with images of a woman increasingly powerful:

> She lived under the earth somewhere, or inside something, a cave or a huge building; sometimes she was on a boat. She was enormously powerful, almost like a goddess, but it was an unhappy power. This woman puzzled me. She wasn't like anyone I'd ever imagined, and certainly she had nothing to do with me. I wasn't at all like that. I was happy. Happy and inept. (p. 248)

Though initially, Joan denies that this woman has anything to do with her, insisting that "Lady Oracle" comes from a source beyond herself, she gradually acknowledges her as her "reckless twin" (p. 274). It is appropriate that this quest take Joan through the mirror, for it was in the mirror—the mother–mirror that failed to give her back herself—that she lost herself. The mirror—which has traditionally represented entrapment for women, signifying (in Irigaray's terms) "specular duplication, giving man back 'his' image and repeating it as the 'same' " (p. 54)—becomes, in Atwood's novel, a means of exploration, as Joan journeys through the looking glass to find her mother, her self.[36]

The subterranean cave where this mysterious woman dwells is another of those images associated with female debilitation which Atwood makes over into a symbol of creative power. The cave symbolizes the womb, the anatomy that is woman's destiny, as well as female submergence in immanence, as Simone de

Beauvoir describes it in *The Second Sex* (pp. 77–78) in a passage glossed by Gilbert and Gubar: woman "destroyed by traditional female activities—cooking, nursing, needling, knotting . . . buried in (and by) patriarchal definitions," in "enclosure without any possibility of escape" (p. 94). The cave is also the physical, material world which Western philosophy associates with the female; thus, in Irigaray's reading of Plato's parable of the cave, it is associated with the repression of the female and also with female menace.[37] But there is another tradition of the cave, the tradition Gilbert and Gubar draw on in *Madwoman:* the home of the Sybil of Cumae, with her prophetic speech, a "place of female power, the *umbilicus mundi,* one of the great antechambers of the mysteries of transformation" (Gilbert and Gubar, p. 95).

The question of the identity of Lady Oracle is repeated—"Who is the one . . ." "Who is the one . . ." (p. 247)—and the answer offered by this "oracle" is equivocal:

> She is one and three
> The dark lady       the redgold lady
> the blank lady       oracle
> of blood, she who must be
> obeyed       forever
> Her glass wings are gone
> She floats down the river
> singing her last song. (p. 252)

The three-sidedness associated with the mother is now associated with Joan, for Joan is "three" in that she is "redgold," "dark," and "blank": "redgold" in appearance, dark in her sinister potential, and "blank" in that each side cancels the other out and leaves her unknown to herself. Also, Joan has three selves (the formerly fat girl, the compliant wife, and the feisty woman writer) and three guides (her mother, Aunt Lou, and Leda Sprott, her spiritual guide). In myth and legend, three is an ambiguous number, associated with powers both sinister and benign: there are three monsters and three-headed monsters—the triple goddess (Graves's "White Goddess"), Diana, Venus, and Hecate (spring, summer, and winter), a version of which is the story of Demeter, Persephone and Hecate, a mother–daughter myth signifying the loss of the daughter to the mother and the mother to the daughter[38]—but there are also three Graces, three Fates, three members of the Trinity.

The publication of "Lady Oracle" releases a potential of Joan into the world, a side she recognizes as her "dark twin":

> It was as if someone with my name were out there in the real world, impersonating me, saying things I'd never said but which appeared in the newspapers, doing things for which I had to take the consequences: my dark twin, my fun-house mirror reflection. She was taller than I was, more beautiful, more threatening. (p. 279)

Though Joan discovers that she likes the attention, she fears this twin's murderous potential—"She wanted to kill me and take my place" (p. 279). Just as Joan's dark twin "Lady Oracle" seems like a fun-house-mirror reflection of herself, Joan's "Lady Oracle" seems like a distorted reflection of a Gothic:

> It was upside-down somehow. There were the sufferings, the hero in the mask of a villain, the villain in the mask of a hero, the flights, the looming death, the sense of being imprisoned, but there was no happy ending, no true love. (p. 259)

Whereas Gothics follow a fixed formula, "Lady Oracle" is "uneven in tone and unresolved" (p. 250); whereas Gothics conform to strict expectations—of readers, writers, publishers—everything about "Lady Oracle" is surprising. If Gothics, with their happy endings and true love, reflect the way Joan wishes her life were, "Lady Oracle" is, for all its bizarre mixture of Rod McKuen and Kahlil Gibran (p. 251), closer to the way her life actually is—"a very angry book" (p. 264) about "modern love and the sexual battle" (p. 260) which gains her "Women's Libber fans" (p. 318).

The publication of "Lady Oracle" releases new potentials of Joan and one transgression leads to another, as Joan embarks on an adulterous affair with the "Royal Porcupine" (Chuck Brewer), now become her man in a cape with a touch of the Byronic (p. 283). Like the publication of "Lady Oracle," this affair releases a "shadowy twin," a "reckless twin":

> This was the beginning of my double life. But hadn't my life always been double? There was always that shadowy twin, thin when I was fat, fat when I was thin, myself in silvery negative, with dark teeth and shining white pupils glowing in the black sunlight of that other world. (p. 274)

Though Joan finds this release exhilarating—"the Royal Porcupine had opened a time space door to the fifth dimension . . . and one of my selves plunged recklessly through" (p. 274)—she also finds it terrifying. The collapse of boundaries unleashes paranoia: malevolence seems to "flow" toward her (p. 325) in the form of anonymous phone calls and dead animals appearing on her doorstep. When the Royal Porcupine shaves his beard and emerges as an ordinary person in jeans and a T-shirt, turning "gray and multi-dimensional and complicated like everyone else" (p. 300), yet another of Joan's divisions collapses. Joan is threatened with further conflation when Fraser Buchanan threatens to reveal that all three of her selves are one, and she finds herself entangled in a blackmail plot in addition to the political plot in which she is involved with Arthur's friends, Sam and Marlene. The far-fetched quality of these interlinking plots, like the coincidences in the novel (Marlene has turned up again from Joan's days in Brownies, just as Leda Sprott turned up as the woman who married Joan and Arthur), is the narrative correlative of the "snarl" her life has become, of the past closing in ("everything catches up to you sooner or later," as Leda tells her [p. 230]), leaving Joan "trapped in the nightmare" of her past (p. 255). Appalled by this "rat's nest of dangling threads and loose ends" ("I couldn't possibly have a happy ending" [p. 326]), she plots her death as a way of assuming control of her life—"Pull yourself together, I told myself. You've got to get out" (p. 280).

Joan seeks a new plot—this time, definitive: "hooked on plots" as she is (p. 342), a plot is the only means of escape she can imagine; and plot similarly takes over the latter part of Atwood's novel, becoming increasingly oppressive. But Joan's plot doesn't quite work, for though she escapes to Italy, she not only leaves a "loose end" but brings the past with her: "My own country was embedded in my brain, like a metal plate left over from an operation" (p. 342). Having spent her life fleeing, she now feels lonely "on the other side" and needs to make contact with the past, to send a message. Her understanding that she will need to return to Canada to rescue Marlene and Sam, who have been arrested for murdering her, is the beginning of a recognition that her life is involved with others and that she cannot ditch the past without diminishing herself.

## Of Mothers and Monsters

In Part 5 the past has caught up with and become the present and the action has come full circle; we are again with Joan in Terremoto, wondering why her plot has failed to free her and why her Gothic plot is also failing: "something was blocking it" (p. 348). That "something" is Joan's increasing sympathy for the wife, Felicia, which follows from her reevaluation of the mother/wife: "sympathy for Felicia was out of the question, it was against the rules, it would foul up the plot completely" (p. 352); Felicia "would have to die; such was the fate of wives. Charlotte would then be free to become a wife in her turn" (p. 348). Moreover, Felicia is described in terms that suggest Joan's identification with her—her "extravagance . . . her figure that spread like crabgrass, her hair that spread like fire, her mind that spread like cancer or pubic lice." Though urged to "contain [her]self," "she couldn't contain herself, she raged . . . like a plague" (p. 351). Far from containing herself, Felicia seems to explode in all directions: "tiny electric sparks jumped from the ends of her hair" (p. 351); and though Joan tries to kill her, she keeps coming back—she and the fat lady.

Besides, Joan has begun to sympathize with Felicia *on account of* her "extravagance" and to be repelled by Charlotte's purity, though "purity" was a quality she had admired—"I was getting tired of Charlotte, with her intact virtue and her tidy ways"; she wants to punish her with fleshly afflictions, have her "fall into a mud puddle, have menstrual cramps, sweat, burp, fart" (p. 352). Joan's shifting allegiances provide the opening wedge for the return of the Fat Lady, embodiment of excess and the repressed, "a creature composed of all the flesh that used to be mine and which must have gone somewhere," a figure associated, like the menacing female of Gothics, with the house itself: "Below me in the foundations of the house . . . it was digging itself out, like a huge blind mole, slowly and painfully shambling up the hill to the balcony" (p. 353).

The next installment of Joan's Gothic manages to kill off Felicia, in circumstances that suggest Joan's identification with her—"drowned in an unfortunate accident" from which "they never recovered [the] body" (p. 354). But Felicia keeps on returning—and this time she returns *as* the fat lady, as "an enormously fat woman" with "damp strands of red hair straggling down her bloated face," her hair smelling "of waterweed" (pp. 354–55); and as Joan, Felicia, and the Fat Lady become one, so too does the Gothic hero Redmond turn into Arthur. As boundaries break down—between selves, between reality and fantasy—Joan's paranoia intensifies, and she becomes convinced that "someone is trying to kill me" (p. 358). This paranoia triggers a series of revealing images as she fantasizes her future on the white-slave market, fattened and caged like "one of those Fellini whores": "I didn't want to spend the rest of my life in a cage, as a fat whore, a captive Earth Mother for whom somebody else collected the admission tickets" (p. 362). The Earth Mother–whore, encased in flesh, in a cage, represents Joan's worst fears about female destiny—woman bound by the flesh, held captive for sex and procreation and on display.

Atwood moves back and forth among various modes in this final section, as "actual" events and conscious reflections alternate with hallucinatory visions in an extended meditation and metafiction which is the means of resolution. The image of the captive mother leads, appropriately, to the appearance of the mother. Hearing someone prowling around outside, Joan stares out the window:

> It was only my mother. She was dressed in her trim navy-blue suit with the tight waist and shoulder pads. . . . She was crying soundlessly, she pressed her face against the glass like a child, mascara ran from her eyes in black tears. . . .
>
> She stretched out her arms to me, she wanted me to come with her; she wanted us to be together.

Joan's initial impulse is to join her:

> I began to walk towards the door . . . could she see I loved her? I loved her but the glass was between us, I would have to go through it. I longed to console her. Together we would go down the corridor into the darkness. (p. 362)

But she pulls back, realizing that merging with the mother will bring about her own obliteration. She emerges from this vision knowing that "it had been she standing behind me in the mirror, she was the one who was waiting around each turn, her voice whispered the words" (p. 363). It had been the mother beckoning with the promise of an answer, she who is the "oracle," but her revelation, like that of the Lady of Shallott, is "tragic": "She had been the lady in the boat, the death barge, the tragic lady with flowing hair and stricken eyes, the lady in the tower. . . . How could I renounce her?" (p. 363) Joan now realizes that her mother has so strong a hold on her because in "renouncing" her, she has "never let her go": "What was the charm, what would set her free?" (p. 363) In asking what will set her free, Joan is also asking what will free her (Joan), and the "charm" is suggested within these lines: to "love," to "console"—to acknowledge rather than deny, yet also to realize "I would never be able to make her happy. Or anyone else" (p. 363). To embrace her is also to release her, to free her and free herself.

These insights disrupt the Gothic formula completely: "I'd taken a wrong turn somewhere" (p. 366). Yet Joan keeps trying to force it back on track: "I saw now what was wrong, what I would have to do. Charlotte would have to go into the maze" (p. 364), though it is not clear whether the maze contained "death, or . . . the answer to a riddle, an answer she must learn in order to live" (p. 365). As Charlotte tries to thread her way through the maze, the "ball of knitting wool" she fastens "at the entrance" tangles around her feet and trips her (pp. 365–66)—just as Joan is tripped when, back on her balcony, she cuts her feet dancing on the glass broken by her attempt to join her mother through the glass door that separated them. She generalizes her maimed feet to the plight of all women:

> You could dance, or you could have the love of a good man. But you were afraid to dance, because you had this unnatural fear that if you danced they'd cut your feet off so you wouldn't be able to dance. Finally you overcame your fear and danced, and they cut your feet off. The good man went away too, because you wanted to dance. (p. 368)[39]

In this scenario, the choice between "either–or" narrows to "neither–nor." But this worst-possible case seems to generate another and opposing possibility, as, wondering "how could I escape now, on my cut feet?" (p. 369), Joan has a vision of herself as a monster—not encaged and displayed, but charged with "volcanic" energy:

> A female monster, larger than life, . . . striding down the hill, her hair standing on end with electrical force, volts of malevolent energy shooting from her fingers. . . .
>
> Maybe my mother didn't name me after Joan Crawford after all, I thought; she just told me that to cover up. She named me after Joan of Arc, didn't she know what happened to women like that? They were accused of witchcraft, they were roped to the stake, they gave a lovely light; a star is a blob of burning gas. (pp. 370–71)

With the glass shattered, repressed female energies break through, explosive, transfigurative, transforming Joan into a witch—or a star.

The Gothic form is further disrupted when Joan, having got her heroine into the maze—a heroine changed from Charlotte to Felicia—finds

> four women. Two of them looked a lot like her. . . . The third was middle-aged, dressed in a strange garment that ended halfway up her calves, with a ratty piece of fur around her neck. The last was enormously fat. She was wearing a pair of pink tights and a short pink skirt covered with spangles. From her head sprouted two antennae, like a butterfly's, and a pair of obviously false wings was pinned to her back. (p. 375)

" 'Who are you?' she asked. 'We are Lady Redmond. . . . All of us' "; " 'There must be some mistake,' Felicia protested, 'I myself am Lady Redmond' " (p. 376). At the center, the heroine, having shifted shapes from Charlotte to Felicia and now become Joan, proliferates into four: the Fat Lady, Aunt Lou (good mother rather than bad mother), and two of Joan—who is, after all, "double." Felicia/Joan's realization that "she was trapped here with these women" suggests an understanding of women's imprisonment in "the central plot"; and this, like Joan's sympathy with the wife/mother, implies a growing sense of solidarity with women, a solidarity that cannot be accommodated by Gothics.

What happens in "the central plot" explodes "the central plot" of patriarchy and supporting plots such as Gothics. The women tell Joan that " 'the only way out . . . is through that door' " (p. 376). Opening it, she finds Redmond, waiting to murder her as he has his other wives, ready "to replace her with . . . the next one, thin and flawless": " 'Don't touch me,' she said." But at this point, "cunningly, he began his transformations." According to the formula, Redmond should now change from villain to hero–rescuer, but instead, he shifts shapes through all the men in the novel—Joan's father, Paul, Fraser Buchanan, the Royal Porcupine, Arthur—and then turns back into the Gothic hero (" 'Let me rescue you' ") before revealing himself in his final form: death (p. 377). Rather than exonerating the hero so that the heroine can join with him, Joan's version exposes his menace as real, part of "the central plot" of patriarchy in which girl grows into woman to be replaced by "the next one." The maze is the "secret center" Joan has consistently fled, the female repressed by patriarchal culture and on whose repression the whole edifice depends; penetrating it, she transforms it to a place of new birth,[40] a space in which boundaries dissolve and burst, selves shift and conflate, and all are revealed as one—or three or four. These may not be "the magic transformations" (p. 47) young Joan hoped for, but they do allow "something new."[41]

More boundaries dissolve when Joan hears a knock at the door and realizes "I would have to face the man who stood waiting for me, for my life" (p. 377)— but what she finds behind the door is a harmless journalist, over whose head she breaks an actual bottle. Though she claims "I knew who it would be," she has no more idea who he is than she has had of any of the men in her life: "I'd never seen him before . . . he was a complete stranger" (pp. 377–78). One hopeful sign is that when she visits him in the hospital, where her smashed bottle has landed him, she is attracted to him as "the only person who knows anything about me. Maybe because I've never hit anyone else with a bottle, so they never got to see that part of me. Neither did I, come to think of it" (pp. 379–80). For the first time Joan is drawn to a man for what he knows about her, rather than for what she and he can keep hidden. And what he knows is her rage, a potential of herself that Joan can now acknowledge. Joan can now even accept the mess she's made, and the last line of the novel—"But then I don't think I'll ever be a very tidy person"—contrasts to the first, which expressed her desire for a neat and simple form that would contain her "tendency to spread, to get flabby, to scroll and festoon."

Like Anna Wulf, who learns not to be a victim by locating the terrifying principle within, Joan's discovery of the mother/monster within is a reclamation of power; and like Lessing, Atwood narrates this story metafictionally. Learning not to be a victim means going off Gothics, a misogynist form which, maligning and obliterating the mother and bamboozling the daughter into taking her place, dooms woman to confinement in the family plot, deprives her of her energies, and isolates her from other women. As Joan moves from entrapment in conventional roles to an acceptance of her multiplicity and power, Atwood's novel moves, Houdini-like, from gloomy confinement to a bursting of boundaries, her fictional form providing the release that Gothics could not.

### Maternal Metafictions: A Happy Ending

Atwood originally intended Joan to commit suicide,[42] and when Joan reads about the world's response to her death, she is struck by its "plausibility":

> I'd been shoved into the ranks of those other unhappy ladies, scores of them apparently, who'd been killed by a surfeit of words. There I was, on the bottom of the death barge . . . my name on the prow, winding my way down the river. Several of the articles drew morals: you could sing and dance or you could be happy, but not both. Maybe they were right. . . . I began to feel that even though I hadn't committed suicide, perhaps I should have. They made it sound so plausible. (p. 346)

Joan's images rehearse the plots of patriarchy: woman imprisoned "in the tower . . . weaving away, looking in the mirror," "the curse, the doom" (p. 346). Joan has come perilously close to enacting several of them, but she survives death by water, does not lose her head or her feet (though she cuts them). and does not topple downward—which she fantasizes as the Fat Lady's end—though neither does she grow wings.[43] Joan has tried to live out the family romance but has failed because, try as she may to repress the mother, she is forced to confront and accept her, and in some sense become her—not in the old death-bound way but in a way that releases her. Her terms with the mother are made symbolically, imagistically, since her mother is dead and Joan is not given to introspection: all this is worked through metafictionally, in what Joan calls "a pretty weird story" (p. 378); but like *The Golden Notebook, Lady Oracle* is a work which speaks through its form.

One might view Joan's development as a progress from fragmentation to integration, as a "quest for unified selfhood," as Rubenstein reads it (pp. 99, 91); or one might read it as a discovery of multiple potentials, as Goddard (p. 25) and Hite do. Or one could argue that unity and multiplicity are the same, or at least that they do not exclude one another—since "three is one." What is important is that Joan, like Anna Wulf and Jane Gray, breaks the hold of the dualistic categories that have trapped her and forges a third term. Three is a key number in the novel: associated with the powerful woman who breaks through the looking glass and with Joan herself ("one and three" [p. 252]), it refers also to the domestic triad of mother, father, and child. But in Atwood's revision of the family romance, three *remains* three rather than contracting to two. The mother is not eliminated so that the daughter can join the father: rather, daughter joins with mother—joins with her but also sets her free and remains free herself, either to join or not join with a man, as she chooses. Nor is the daughter eliminated by merging with the father: no one of the three is engulfed by the other. Thus one remains one yet is also three—or four or more.

At the end, Joan achieves some understanding of the way Gothics functioned in her life—"I won't write any more Costume Gothics. . . . I think they were bad for me" (p. 379)—and is left contemplating new forms. Her long poem "Lady Oracle" has accommodated more of her, though, like Gothics, it is backward-looking, what the Royal Porcupine calls "rearview mirror" (p. 268), "a leftover from the nineteenth century" (p. 266). She thinks about writing "a real novel, about someone who worked in an office and had tawdry, unsatisfying affairs," but she feels that this would require her to relinquish her longing for "happy endings" (p. 352); she thinks "maybe I'll try some science fiction. The future doesn't appeal to me as much as the past, but I'm sure it's better for you" (p. 379).[44] That Atwood herself has gone on to write science fiction in *The Handmaid's Tale* and social realism in *Life Before Man* and *Bodily Harm* suggests, perhaps, that *Lady Oracle* freed her of certain retrograde fantasies in the same way that Joan's "Lady Oracle" released her.

If Joan's "Lady Oracle" is a "Gothic gone wrong," Atwood's *Lady Oracle* is "a Gothic gone right"—not simply in writing beyond the Gothic ending of "true love" and "happy endings," but in recycling the materials of Gothics, women's fear of mothers and men, and reworking the conventions of Gothics, with their disastrous implications for women, to happier ends. Like "Lady Oracle," *Lady Oracle* looks back, but it uses the "rearview mirror" to negotiate a new present. *Lady Oracle* "contains," as all narrative must, but its metafiction includes commentary on narrative as containment (as Nancy Miller describes "arachnology," it is women's writing that attends to the representation of women's writing; p. 271) and it contains more of the protagonist than the conventional forms she has confined herself to, accommodating the female energies and eccentricities, scrolls and festoons, excluded and denied by patriarchal formulae. Atwood, like Drabble, associates "loose ends" with "female form";[45] this is what Hite calls "representation with a difference" (p. 165).[46]

Perhaps this is a "self-begetting novel" which concludes with the protagonist ready to write the novel we have just read, or perhaps not; but whatever it is, it transforms female anxiety of authorship to the authority of authorship[47]—"the old silent dance of death become a dance of triumph, a dance into speech, a dance of authority" (in Gilbert and Gubar's terms; p. 44)—as Joan not only survives, but survives with a new story. Atwood's new myth takes images conventionally associated with female doom—clothing, sewing, mirrors, confinement—and transforms them into symbols of power. It transforms claustrophobia to a discovery of power in caves and transforms the female arts from those of doomed cave dwellers into weaver women associated with oracular knowledge, effecting what Gilbert and Gubar term (in another context) "a subversive transfiguration of those female arts . . . into the powerful arts of the underground Weaver woman, who uses her magical loom to weave a distinctively female tapestry" (p. 102). It transforms the mother from a menace into a source of new energy, into a symbol of female insurgence like Cixous's laughing Medusa, as Atwood writes not only beyond the romance and the family romance, but also beyond earlier feminist fiction with its matrophobia, working through to an acceptance and empowerment of mothers that also empowers the daughter. The mother's story may remain "unspeakable" (as Hirsch says of the maternal plot), and Atwood may tell it only from the daughter's perspective,[48] and at that, only metafictionally: but Atwood dramatizes the involvement of one story with the other and points the way to a different form for both.

Atwood herself enlists the weaver's art in a text which is splendidly textured, its "interwoven narrative layers" doubling back on themselves (in Rubenstein's term; p. 100) in "an eternal braid of narrative within narrative" (in Godard's term; p. 17).[49] Intricately wrought, it works like a poem, or like an arachnology, its images and metaphors resonating intertextually with fairy tale and myth, concealing its powerfully subversive statement in a delicate weave. For if the Medusa represents, as Freud claims, "terror of castration that is linked to the sight of something"[50]—or, rather, that is linked to the sight of "nothing," to the missing female genitals that remind the male of the precariousness of his own (as Irigaray suggests, "Woman's castration is defined as her having nothing you can see, as her *having* nothing" [p. 48]); and if—as Freud claims—woman is given a model for weaving by "the pubic hair that conceals the genitals," "a wrapping that . . . serves to hide the difference of the sexes from the horrified gaze of the little boy, and the man" (Irigaray, pp. 112, 115)—then what is concealed and revealed by the weaver's art (which is, as Irigaray reminds us "at least double" [p. 116]) is that "nothing" which men fear. This "nothing" (which Irigaray associates with the repression of the female and her rage at the system that annihilates her) is

> a nothing threatening the process of production, reproduction, mastery, and profitability, of meaning, dominated by the phallus—that *master signifier* whose law of functioning erases . . . a *heterogeneity* capable of reworking the principle of its authority . . .

a "nothing" which "might cause the ultimate destruction, the splintering, the break in their systems of 'presence,' of 're-presentation' and 'representation' " (Irigaray, p. 50). What Atwood's arachnology allows is precisely this splintering, this break—a fissure which, releasing the female energy repressed by patriarchy, explodes "the central plot" of patriarchy.

# Part III
# Postfeminist Fiction

# IX

## WHATEVER HAPPENED TO FEMINIST FICTION?

> We were discussing the increasing feeling of
> despair that we are all suffering from . . . we
> were all using the word "disillusioned." Then
> someone pointed out that if what one had
> held in the past was an "illusion" then it was
> very healthy, even important, to be
> "disillusioned". . . . If on the other hand what
> one had held before was vision . . . then what
> the present political climate was doing was
> "disvisioning" . . . [but] there was no word
> . . . for "disvisioning." No word to describe
> the experience of having had a real vision, a
> true vision of possibility and then having that
> taken away from you.
>
> Sara Maitland, "Futures in
> Feminist Fiction"[1]

Feminist metafiction held out "visions of possibility." Forged from women's efforts of self-definition in the face of change, it devised narrative strategies that rendered the process of change and played an actual part in transforming psychic and social structures, in raising the consciousness and expectations of a generation. Its formal innovations were also ideological critiques and its critiques extended to more than gender; they were fundamentally concerned with the systems—social and political, linguistic and epistemological—of which gender ideology is but a part. But novels of the eighties—even by Lessing, Atwood, and Drabble—no longer envision new possibilities.

Feminism was, of all the protest movements of the sixties, in some sense the most radical, its effects the most lasting. But postfeminist backlash is also real; more than media hype, it is evident in current social policies, in fiction and film, and, most tellingly, in the attitudes of the young. Had I finished this book closer to when I began it, in the early eighties, it might have had a happier ending, and it is sadly anticlimactic to conclude with this discussion of postfeminism. But times have changed since the seventies—the swing to the right, the consolidation of power into multinational corporations, the world recession—have created a mood epitomized by Maggie Thatcher's oft-reiterated pronouncement "There is no alternative."

## Dismembering and Disremembering

Margaret Drabble describes the early eighties in terms of public irresponsibility and private self-indulgence, social unrest and conspicuous consumption, and the dimming of "the great social dream":

> These were years of inner city riots, of race riots . . . of rising unemployment and riotless gloom . . . of a small war in the Falklands (rather a lot of people dead), and of the Falklands Factor in politics. . . .
>
> .  .  .  .  .  .  .  .  .  .  .  .  .  .  .  .  .  .  .  .  .  .  .  .  .  .  .  .  .
>
> An ageing film star became President of the United States of America and his wife bought a lot of new clothes. The heir to the throne of England married a kindergarten assistant and she bought a lot of new clothes. Much attention was paid to these new clothes by the media of the Western world, to the derision, bewilderment, envy, curiosity or ignorance of various non-Western nations.[2]

As Thatcher dismembered the welfare state in England and Reagan dismantled public programs in the United States, as private fulfillment was elevated to practically a moral imperative, we entered what Barbara Ehrenreich terms "a moral climate that endorsed irresponsibility, self-indulgence and an isolationist detachment from the claims of others—and endorsed these as middle-class virtues and even as signs of 'health.'"[3]

A reinvigorated individualism, both in the United States and in the United Kingdom, destroys the notion of collective responsibility and blames the victim—or victims, for there are many victims—of the cuts of health, welfare, and educational programs. The sociobiology that emerged in the seventies, a new version of an old biological determinism, provides "scientific" justification for New Right policies, implicitly relieving government of the responsibility for social change:[4] the "long-cherished notion of progress dies . . . survival of the fittest seems to be the new-old doctrine. . . . People have short memories" (RW, p. 172). In the United States the "Moral Majority" favors aggressive defense and a return to an idealised past when men were men and women were women—a nostalgia which Doane and Hodges call "frighteningly antifeminist."[5] In TV and film, a new image of the male—more aggressive, "super-cool, super-detached"—emerges;[6] and what Susan Jeffords terms the "remasculinization of America"—the idealization of male heroics, male bonding, and "the masculine" in representations of the Vietnam War in fiction, film, and journalism—reinforces the polarization of gender.[7] Fear that the blurring of gender roles might weaken an already emasculated military makes feminism a threat to national security. As in the fifties, so in the eighties—the retreat to the family makes the family the source of stability and value. And again, when the family is seen as the basis of social order, control of female sexuality becomes crucial: hence the current controversy over reproductive rights. Similarities between the fifties and eighties are striking—nostalgia (often nostalgia *for* the fifties), the reassertion of traditional roles, the polarization of male and female, the sentimentalization of domesticity, the shrunken sense of alternatives.

Popular works such as Sylvia Hewlett's *A Lesser Life: The Myth of Women's Liberation in America,* Nicholas Davidson's *The Failure of Feminism,* and Cowan and Kinder's *Smart Women, Foolish Choices* tell us that the women's movement is dead and also that it is responsible for women's problems today—messages that are not entirely consistent but seem to have wide appeal.[8] The bad news is reinforced by newspaper and magazine coverage. The term "postfeminist" resurfaced early in the decade, making a comeback from 1919, when Susan Bolotin's 1982 *New York Times* article, "Voices from the Post-Feminist Generation," described young women's aversion to feminists as "man-hating," masculine, lesbian, militant, "not chic," and hairy-legged.[9] A notorious 1986 *Newsweek* cover story, "Too Late for Prince Charming," reasserted the old bind for women by demonstrating what slim chances college-educated women have of getting married, claiming that forty-year-olds have a better chance of being "killed by a terrorist."[10] A cover of *Time* (November 1989) pictures a woman, hewn grimly from wood, carrying a briefcase in one hand and a baby in the other, with the caption, "In the '80s they tried to have it all. Now they've just plain had it."[11] What is missing from mainstream media discussion of these issues is, as Elayne Rapping points out, "the role of social forces and political activity. Never once is it suggested that this is anything but a women's problem, one she must handle."[12] Women's problems are depicted as negotiating for position and privilege within established institutions, families and corporations, with no sense that these institutions should themselves be changed. Women's magazines reinforce the message that a woman can "have it all" if she exercises enough, stays thin, dresses fashionably, and consumes avidly, and if she fails, she can blame only herself, since it is rarely suggested that opportunity may be "related to economic, political, or social factors beyond the control of the individual" (Sidel, p. 99).

Though feminism has always had a bad press, in the eighties backlash came from within, from those very women who pioneered it. Friedan's *The Second Stage* (1981) and Jean Bethke Elshtain's *Public Man, Private Woman* (1981), both of which valorize the family and urge a separation of private from public life, signal what Judith Stacey calls a "new conservative feminism" which "attempts to fortify the family . . . [and] return it to its prefeminist status as an ahistorical essence."[13] Such discussions reinforce sociobiology in isolating analyses of the family from an understanding of culture and, like sociobiology, undo the major intellectual contribution of feminism: the understanding of the individual as connected to social and historical processes. In fact, a major tendency of the eighties has been to dismantle the syntheses accomplished by sixties and seventies feminism.

If "re-vision"—and words such as "rewriting," "re-naming," "rescripting," "remembering," "rediscovering," "recovering," "reconstructing," "restructuring"—epitomized the feminist project of the sixties and seventies, "dis" seems to be the characteristic prefix for activity in the eighties: "disvision," "disillusion," "dismember," "dissever," "dismantle," "disremember." Feminism is divided, not only in itself but from a larger constituency. Alison Light expresses the "feeling that feminism is now somehow adrift, unanchored and cut off in crucial ways from the everyday texture of women's lives" ("Feminist Criticism in the 1990s," in Carr, p. 25). Cora Kaplan describes the loss of the dialectical relationship between feminism as a social movement, feminist criticism and feminist fiction: feminism is "cut off . . . from what women are actually writing and from a political movement" ("Feminist Criticism Twenty Years On," in Carr, pp. 19, 21). One of the most disturbing divisions is that between academic feminism, with a theoretical discourse engaged in increasingly subtle deconstruction of such categories as "individual" and "community," and political activity directed at *changing* individuals and communities; feminist writing can no longer claim to be activism, since most of it is barely comprehensible.[14] Though some applaud the diversity of the current scene,[15] others lament the loss not so much of consensus as of a popular base. It is not surprising to find metaphors of dismemberment recurring in current fiction.

Even those who once identified with feminism now reject the term, recoiling from it as from the "F word" and expressing doubts about what the women's movement has accomplished. In a 1985 *New York Times Magazine* article, "How to Get the Women's Movement Moving Again," Friedan describes women's

> disillusionment with male-defined careers, a faintheartedness about "having it all," a rebellion against superwoman standards, a sense of malaise or guilt or regret about prices paid . . . and a recurring theme of "not wanting to be like a man."[16]

The women interviewed by Anita Shreve in her study of women in consciousness-raising groups fifteen years later, *Women Together, Women Alone*, are skeptical about the changes feminism has wrought, even though, as Shreve notes, all "are living lives richly dependent upon the fruits of feminism."[17] They speak of their exhaustion trying to maintain a family and job, of continued inequity in relationships, of increased isolation from other women, of "antiwoman feeling from other women," of lack of child care and fear that the right to abortion will be lost. Many also lament the reversion to standards of appearance that require at least as much time, energy, and cost as fashions did in the fifties (pp. 224–25 and *passim*). As the protagonist of Atwood's *Cat's Eye* says, "Party dresses have come back, bows and flamenco ruffles, straplessness and crinolines, puffed sleeves like marshmallows: everything I thought was left behind forever. And miniskirts too, as bad as ever."[18] The protagonist of Anne Roiphe's *Lovingkindness,* a novel about an eminent feminist historian whose daughter joins an orthodox Yeshiva, marvels at "our daughters' " regression:

> We are the ones who freed women from the beauty parlor, from waxing their legs, from doing their nails, from feeling that their worth lay in conformity to some model. . . . We were the ones who said you shouldn't squeeze your stomach into a merry widow, you shouldn't have to mince around in uncomfortable shoes . . . but look at our daughters. They diet. . . . They gorge and they binge and they hate themselves.[19]

"We underestimated the problem," she concludes. "There is something in the air that makes women unable to accept their shape."

Though Roiphe explains this "something" in sociobiological terms—"the roar of biology, the odors of sexuality" (p. 155)—it seems, rather, to be related to the revulsion against the feminine so pronounced in contemporary culture. The "containments" exploded in seventies fiction and fashion have been reasserted with a vengeance, and the intensity of young women's desire to fit them is evident in the eating disorders—anorexia and bulimia—that have become epidemic. As always, women's magazines prescribe regimens, though their regimens are even more extreme than in the fifties—liposuction, eyelid surgery, nose alteration, breast enlargement or reduction (Sidel, p. 97). Whereas the protagonist of Fay Weldon's 1967 *The Fat Woman's Joke* rebelled against such standards by asserting her right to obesity, the protagonist of Weldon's 1983 *Life and Loves of a She-Devil* literally cuts herself down to size, hacking six inches from her femur and remolding her burgeoning body to the containments of femininity: "Since I cannot change the world, I will change myself,"[20] she says, expressing the despair many young women feel of making anything beyond their own private terms.

Even those who continue to identify with feminism do so privately, rather than publicly or collectively, "in their own way," seeing their actions as meaningful on a personal, rather than a political, level. The women Shreve interviewed expressed isolation and confusion as pronounced as that of women in the fifties and early sixties, "a sense . . . of operating in a vacuum" (Shreve, p. 215). Friedan also notes a similarity between the eighties and the fifties; she describes "the new generation,"

> each thinking she is alone with her personal guilt and pressures, trying to "have it all," having second thoughts about her professional career, desperately trying to have a baby before it is too late . . . and maybe secretly blaming the movement for getting her into this mess, almost as isolated, and as powerless in their isolation, as those suburban housewives afflicted by "the problem that had no name" whom I interviewed for *The Feminine Mystique* over twenty years ago. (1985, p. 89)

The difference, of course, is that between the fifties and eighties, the women's movement occurred. "The problem" is no longer without a "name" since there are terms and vocabulary to explain it, but women deny or forget them because they fear feminism. In a 1987 review essay in *Feminist Studies,* "Second Thoughts on the Second Wave," Deborah Rosenfelt and Judith Stacey define postfeminism as "an emerging culture and ideology that simultaneously incorporates, revises, and depoliticizes many of the fundamental issues advanced by Second Wave feminism."[21] "Postfeminist" is not necessarily "antifeminist"; nor does the term imply that feminism is dead; rather, like "postmodernist" or "postrevolutionary," it acknowledges that a change has occurred—that there has been a shift in consciousness about women; but it also acknowledges that it is no longer possible to feel as hopeful about change as it was in the seventies.

I use the term "postfeminist" because it describes an attitude and a phenomenon. To use the term is not to endorse the attitude; nor will not using it make the phenomenon go away. There is no doubt that feminism has produced real changes: more women are working, though most continue to work in low-status, low-income, dead-end jobs, and few have made it into the upper echelons of management and the professions (Sidel, p. 180). Many young women have higher expectations. As a 1989 *Time* cover story, "Women in the Nineties," observes, the same young woman who insists that she is "not a feminist" will say in the next breath that "she certainly plans on a career as well as marriage and three kids" (p. 81). But there is an enormous distance between the kind of work young people imagine themselves doing and the kind of work actually available to them (Sidel, p. 181), and their fantasies, ungrounded in reality as they are, may actually be counterproductive of real change.

As in the fifties, women are again the victims of contradictory messages— they should achieve in the workplace and take control of their lives, but should above all be sexy, seductive, deferential, dress fashionably, consume endlessly, and make themselves marketable (Sidel, p. 102): young women have got the mixed message, which is why they are confused. Despite the rhetoric of career, success, and independence, Sidel notes "a curious strain of passivity, of not quite being in control," evident in the carelessness about birth control that accounts for the shockingly high incidence of teenage pregnancy in the United States (double that of England, Canada, and France; p. 127). Though teen pregnancy is discussed as though it were the individual's fault, actually, young women are responding quite accurately to their situations, to "inadequate life options and . . . societal ambivalence about women's roles" (p. 129).

And yet the vast majority of young women assume that the women's movement is irrelevant to them—Sidel notes that of the young women she interviewed, only one admitted to being a feminist, while several energetically professed not to be (p. 5). Since feminism has not enlisted the support of the young and not mobilized them politically, since years under Reagan and Thatcher seem to have killed any notion of collective action, we are living through a version of backlash like that which occurred after the first wave of feminism in this century. We can only hope that this one will not last three decades.

As long ago as *The Golden Notebook,* Lessing contemplated the possibility of backlash when Anna predicted, " 'The generations after us are going to take one look at us, and get married at eighteen, forbid divorces, and go in for strict moral codes and all that, because the chaos otherwise is just too terrifying' ";[22] in *The Summer Before the Dark,* the protagonist is doubtful that her daughter's generation will do better than her own, despite its rhetoric of change—a perspective reiterated more disturbingly in *The Good Terrorist* by a mother who is appalled at her daughter's regressions. In this novel, as in Roiphe's *Lovingkindness,* mothers are bewildered to see their daughters drift from bad to worse, amazed at how little they have managed to teach them; "feminism is not an inherited trait," as Roiphe's protagonist says (p. 222), watching her daughter drift through drugs, punk, promiscuity to anchor, finally, in an orthodox Yeshiva. Not that postfeminist backlash can be reduced to a matter of generational revolt: it has sources in larger social phenomena—in the turn toward conservatism, the commitment to profit, the social irresponsibility of the eighties. But Lessing's observations are—as usual—prophetic.

In TV and film, one notes a retreat from the strong positive female characters of seventies films to "the either/or film"—either professional success or love *(Broadcast News),* either sex or motherhood *(The Good Mother),* (Sidel, p. 107)—and savage caricatures of single career women (as in *Fatal Attraction, Working Girl, Presumed Innocent).* Eighties novels that dramatize the costs of a career similarly reinforce the old choice between career and motherhood. In Marianne Wiggins's *Separate Checks,* the protagonist, Ellery, is recovering from a breakdown precipitated by a mother who is a successful writer and the novel ends in an unexpected and gratuitous recuperation of the family. In Mary Gordon's *Men and Angels,* the protagonist, a happy mother and wife, takes a job and brings tragedy home. Alison Lurie's *The Truth about Lorin Jones* equates professional success with personal failure. Polly, a failed artist who is writing a biography of a successful artist who turns out to have been ruthless in her personal relations, confronts the problem of what "truth" to tell about Lorin Jones: if she celebrates her as a great artist, she'll gain acceptance by the artistic establishment and become successful herself, but then she will become selfish like Lorin Jones and become a bad mother as well; if she portrays her as a victim of patriarchy, as she'd originally intended, she'll gain acceptance by the lesbian community—portrayed by Lurie with more than a touch of homophobia. Caught between unacceptable alternatives in her professional life, Polly opts for private fulfillment and runs off with Lorin Jones's former lover.[23] Raskin's *Hot Flashes* similarly reiterates "the old story" when the protagonist becomes involved with her dead friend's ex-husband. This novel concludes, "I look up and see Max. He is moving toward me like a mirage, shimmering, quivering, an oasis in the hot, empty desert. He has his hands upon me. He is giving me a transfusion of strength"[24]—an ending worthy of Harlequin romance. "How to save your own life" turns out to be—find a new man; though in eighties fiction, the scarcity of men seems to dictate a sort of tasteless recycling of dead women's ex-husbands and ex-lovers.

Judging by the long runs on best-seller lists enjoyed by Atwood, Godwin,

Tyler, and others, women's fiction is widely read. But it has shrunk in its concerns. In a 1984 *New York Times* article, "Whatever Happened to Feminist Fiction," Elinor Langer asks, "Where are the partisans of yesteryear—the housewives-in-transition of Marilyn French's *Women's Room,* the rebellious feminists of Alix Kates Shulman's *Burning Questions,* the questing commu-nards of Marge Piercy's *Small Changes?*" and describes a fiction that focuses on "character and relationship" and hardly acknowledges the world, let alone challenges it: in seventies fiction "the world was an obstacle to be challenged. Now it has been left behind."[25] A glance at reviews in *The New York Times Book Review* and *The Women's Review of Books* in the late eighties corrobo-rates Langer's analysis, revealing a women's fiction focused on the personal and praised for such qualities as "sweetly romantic nostalgia."[26] As Langer says, this "shift from resistance to respectability" (p. 1) may be evidence of the success of the women's movement, since it suggests that the woman writer has arrived. But it also takes us full circle back to a fiction which is "narrow," "timid," "complacent," and focused on the personal, as Ellen Moers charac-terized women's fiction in 1963.[27]

What strikes me about works by well-known, widely read writers like Anne Tyler, Mary Gordon, Ann Beattie, Anita Brookner, Bernice Rubens, Sue Miller, Ellen Gilchrist, Anne Lamont, Rosellen Brown, Jill McCorkle, Marianne Wig-gins, and Alice Hoffman is the privatization and depoliticization of their con-cerns, the sentimentalization of the family, the resignation to things as they are. Even the feisty feminist writers of the seventies, Piercy and Shulman, participate in this retreat. Piercy's latest novel, *Summer People* (1989), like Shulman's *In Every Woman's Life* (1987), offers a small, circumscribed canvas, focuses on character and relationship, and reduces sexual politics to soap opera. Most of these writers do not envision much possibility of change; in eighties fiction, women accommodate themselves to what is—"we make do," as the protagonist of Atwood's *Cat's Eye* says (p. 93).

Far from opening up new possibilities, postfeminist fiction tends to nostalgia, and in this, too, it resembles postwar fiction. Whereas seventies protagonists celebrated liberation from the forms of the past, the protagonist of *The Hand-maid's Tale* suffers what she calls "attacks of the past";[28] the protagonist of Raskin's *Hot Flashes* admits to "yearn[ing] with surprising nostalgia for the times when we each had a young family that folded like a fist protectively around us" (p. 53); and the protagonist of Sue Miller's *The Good Mother* "yearns . . . to be . . . in a family."[29] Not surprisingly, this is a fiction which is narratively less experimental than feminist metafiction.

Metafictions no longer allow the protagonist the power of the pen to restruc-ture her world. When a character is a writer, as in Brookner's *Hotel du Lac,* Fay Weldon's *Life and Loves of a She-Devil,* Lessing's *Diary of a Good Neighbor,* she writes romances to make a living or to accommodate herself to what cannot be changed. No longer is the writer endowed with special vision: in Raskin's *Hot Flashes,* Sukie, the author of several successful seventies novels, is dead, leaving a record of sorrow and confusion in the journal discovered by her friends; in *The Radiant Way* writers are "a tertiary, terminal bunch" (p. 230). Fiction is no longer a means of revising the world, charting new ground, making new "blueprints."

Metafictions by Anita Brookner and Marianne Wiggins, far from issuing into new futures, reaffirm the hold of the past. In Wiggins's *Separate Checks*, "Going off Booze" is the story of Belle, who, exploited first by her father, a famous artist, and then by her lover, a famous writer, retaliates by shooting the lover: and though her act is a strike at the patriarchal plots that have enmeshed her, it also destroys her. In *Hotel du Lac* (1984), for which Brookner won the prestigious Booker prize, Edith writes romances (as Atwood's Joan does) to maintain a life of anonymity and invisibility, defending her fiction (as Joan defends hers) on the grounds that women "prefer the old myths."[30] Edith's fiction—and this also is like Joan's—originates in her relation with an unhappy mother: "She comforted herself, that harsh disappointed woman, by reading love stories, simple romances with happy endings. Perhaps that is why I write them" (p. 104). But Edith ends, as she began, "anonymous, and accepting her anonymity" (p. 62), incapable of finding voice or visibility, locked into an unresolved relationship to the past, to her mother, to herself—and here the parallel with *Lady Oracle* ends: writing is a means of containing her aversion to the female, of curbing her ambitions and resigning herself to a misery which is barely understood.[31]

Women's fiction of the eighties denies or forgets the syntheses of the seventies and, losing sight of the connections between individual and collective, participates in the dismembering and disremembering of the decade. Recent novels by Atwood and Lessing are marked by disturbing disjunctions. *Cat's Eye* repudiates the feminist terms that might make sense of the tale it tells. Lessing's *The Diary of a Good Neighbor* denigrates "women's lib" (as it is called) even while celebrating women; in *The Good Terrorist,* the disjunctions in Alice's personality, suggested by the oxymoron "good terrorist," leave her furiously at odds with herself; and *The Fifth Child* disjoins innate self from culture in a way that prohibits the possibility of change, individual or collective. While I do not see Lessing's recent fiction as representing a decline of her talents, as some readers do, I do find her "new, upsetting phase" (to use a term from *The Good Terrorist*) disturbing.[32] Also disturbing are the disjunctions between the science fiction and the social realism—between the utopian optimism of the former and the bleakly restricted possibilities of the latter. Lessing's science fiction still offers the vision and commitment of the early Lessing: the Canopus novels remain vitally concerned with change and insist that we make "the effort of imagination necessary to become what we are capable of being."[33] But when Lessing returns to earth and to social realism—as she does in the Jane Somers novels (*The Diary of a Good Neighbor* and *If the Old Could*) and in *The Good Terrorist* and *The Fifth Child*—she no longer asks us to imagine a better world. Only within a framework of fantasy can she envision the possibility of change, but Atwood does not envision it even there, for her science fiction, *The Hand-maid's Tale,* is dystopic, a cautionary tale against change for the worse which holds out little hope of change for the better.

Early in the decade, Drabble and Atwood wrote novels that begin from positions of postfeminist disillusionment but work through to affirmations of new possibilities, but later in the decade, Atwood's *Cat's Eye* (1988) and Drabble's *Radiant Way* (1986) express unqualified disillusionment. Drabble's *The Middle Ground* (1982) begins in a spirit of repudiation, with the pro-tagonist " 'bloody sick of bloody women,' "[34] having lost faith in "freedom" or "progress," no longer sure what sort of change is desirable; but Kate ends at the center of a "circle" of family and friends, a circle encompassing people from various classes, countries, and races, and representing harmony and in-clusiveness while also accommodating change—"Nothing binds her, nothing holds her" (p. 257). In Atwood's *Bodily Harm,* Rennie is a disillusioned journalist who "once . . . had ambitions, which she now thinks of as illu-sions,"[35] who has written a successful piece ("Burned Out") on the failure of the movement (p. 87); but her experience of "bodily harm" enables her to reconnect her personal experience with the political and to connect with other women. Rennie ends with new compassion and commitment—"changed," "a subversive," determined to "report" (p. 265).

I will look briefly at Lessing's 1984 *Diary of a Good Neighbor* to show what I mean by postfeminist disconnections. I'll then look at Atwood's *Handmaid's Tale,* which expresses a similar dimming of vision, before turning to the most recent works of Atwood and Drabble, *Cat's Eye* and *The Radiant Way.* In both, the search for the past comes to "nothing"—and the word "nothing" recurs in both, as do images of dismemberment. Drabble's novel, however, persuades us that the disjunctions derive not from the author's own failure to remember or connect, but from "inassimilable material" (RW, p. 158)—an England more deeply divided than ever before and social problems intractable to the solutions of the past.[36]

## Nostalgic Retrenchments: Lessing's Good Neighbor

Though *The Diary of a Good Neighbor* is moving and effective in its depiction of the aged, underlying its mellowness is a resignation, a sense that reality is both intolerable and unchangeable. This resignation is evident in Jane Somers's acceptance of romantic fictions that earlier Lessing protagonists re-pudiated. Just after Jane meets Maudie, the ninety-two-year-old woman she befriends, and sees the poverty she lives in, she feels ashamed of working at a glamor magazine, *Lilith;* but she soon realizes that Maudie loves this sort of magazine, just as she loves Jane's beautiful clothes. Whereas Martha Quest and Anna Wulf repudiated romantic and nostalgic distortions, Jane delights in the stories by which Maudie reconstructs her past, accepting even the clichés and the "coy, simpering" *persona* of Annie Reeves, another old woman (pp. 168,

171, 172–73). She defends romance novels on the grounds that "truth is intolerable" and people need "escape"[37] and defends the romantic novel she writes, *The Milliners of Marleybone*, on the grounds that "Maudie would love her life, as reconstructed by me" (p. 244), a "reconstruction" in which powerful men "value" and "cherish" women (p. 244) rather than exploit them, as they have Maudie.

But though *The Diary of a Good Neighbor* contains an apologia for romantic novels, it is not itself a romantic novel, and Lessing's qualification of her protagonist's belief in romance by her own graphic realism makes for an interesting complexity. Of the two kinds of writing that Jane tries as ways of representing Maudie's life, she may approve of the romantic—"I know only too well why we need our history prettied up. It would be intolerable to have the long heavy *weight* of the truth there, all grim and painful" (p. 141)—but she uses, in her diary, *The Diary of a Good Neighbor,* a realistic record of that grim, painful truth.

Elsewhere, however, the juxtaposition of perspectives makes for confusion rather than complexity. These novels celebrate women's relationships, women's work, older women—even as they denigrate "women's lib."[38] These are novels in which "Chloe likes Olivia"; in fact, the only real love in *Diary of a Good Neighbor* is between women—between Jane and Joyce, Jane and Vera, Jane and Maudie. Jane's friendship with Joyce is based on their work together, on a wordless communication—"Joyce is the only person I have talked to in my life. And yet for the most part we talk in smiles, silences, signals, music without words" (p. 64)—and on laughter: "those sudden fits of laughing, music without words, that are among the best things in this friendship of ours" (p. 67). Jane also communicates wordlessly with Vera in a "shorthand" which similarly grows out of shared work (p. 105); and Maudie's happiest memories are of working with women—at the milliner's workshop, "singing and larking and telling stories" all the while she is being exploited by a lecherous boss and roughed about by her "man" (pp. 90–93). Jane observes, again and again, that it is women who do the work while men are given the credit and authority. Women run *Lilith* while pretending that their incompetent male bosses do, and in the caring professions, the "home help" hold together their own homes as well as the homes they professionally care for; in the hospital, "it is the nurses who monitor the changes of need, of mood, of the patients, and the doctors who appear from time to time, issuing commands" (pp. 241–43). This "freemasonry of women" "keep[s] things together" (p. 199) and forms the fabric of society.

Yet when Joyce feels that she has "no choice" but to sacrifice her life to a husband who does not particularly want her, to leave everything and follow him to America, Jane asks, "Well, women's lib . . . what do you have to say to that? What, in your little manifestoes, your slamming of doors in men's faces, your rhetoric, have you *ever* said that touches this? As far as I am concerned, nothing . . . of—whatever the power men have that makes Joyce say, I have no choice" (p. 69); "women's lib thoughts" "aren't the point; they never were the point, not for me, not for Joyce" (p. 66). This seems perversely obtuse, for as Lessing doubtless knows, "the point" of "women's lib" "manifestoes" is precisely this question of "the power men have" that makes Joyce feel she has "no choice." And Jane's response seems to be Lessing's, for in these novels the ills and inequities of the world are attributed to innate human nature and "the human condition" (p. 223). Just as Jane's two nieces, Kate and Jill, are inexplicably different, so Joyce has "no choice" because of *what she is*—"It is not a question of will, but of what you are" (p. 11).

Yet what the novel actually demonstrates is that men have the power they have because women give it to them, acting against their own interests by overrating "romance" and underrating their ties to other women and to work. Following "her man," Maudie gave up the chance to work in Paris as a milliner at a job she would have loved (p. 92), just as, following her husband to America, Joyce leaves behind work, friends, and home—choices that both women regret; similarly, Phyllis's marriage to Charlie takes her away from work she loves to raise a family she does not particularly want. And part of the reason women give men this power is that they are brainwashed by romance novels and glamour magazines: magazines like *Lilith* actually *produce* the situation that necessitates the escape they then provide. In a flash of rare insight, Jane glimpses this—"at this very moment a million girls tapping away at their typewriters . . . are dreaming . . . not of women's lib and emancipation—but of *I love you* and a wedding dress. . . . Why? For one thing, because of the efforts of *Lilith* and her sisters" (p. 454). But neither Lessing nor Jane follows this out, to connect the powerlessness of women with the social structures that disempower them.

Similarly, there is a discrepancy between Jane's view of aging as part of an inevitable "human condition" (p. 223) and the suggestions throughout the novel that age is to some extent socially constructed. What Jane observes—that *Lilith*'s "images of women" exclude old women, that old people are invisible on the streets, that old people are better off surrounded by family (p. 222) and were better off in workhouses than in "homes" where they "go mad of boredom" (p. 227)—suggests that aging is made worse by socially imposed isolation and inactivity and supports a view like de Beauvoir's, that age is "not solely a biological, but also a cultural fact."[39] There is a flash of the old Lessing when Jane expresses indignation at being thought "neurotic" for taking an interest in Maudie: "What has happened that, for someone like me, well off, middle class, and in possession of my faculties, to undertake such tasks without any necessity for it means that I am wrong-headed? Sometimes I look at the thing one way, and sometimes another: first, that I am mad, and then that the society we live in is" (p. 221). But Jane, unlike Anna or Martha, does not really see the world as "mad" nor is she much outraged that what she spends on hot water could transform Maudie's life.

There is also the question of Kate, Jane's loser of a niece. Lessing has analyzed the disaffection of the young in social terms in *The Four-Gated City* and *Shikasta,* accounting for it in terms of a world so absurd and brutalizing that it offers young people nothing to connect to; but here, Kate fails where her sister,

Jill, succeeds because they are "innately" different. In *If the Old Could,* young Kate and old Annie Reeves both become burdens on Jane: the author of *The Golden Notebook,* who insisted that we see things in relationship to one another, would have seen these two as related symptoms of a larger cause, as waste products of a system that devalues young and old alike by viewing them in terms of production which make them "redundant." But the Lessing who is Jane Somers no longer sees life whole or as capable of being changed.

## Atwood's "Reduced Circumstances"

In the late eighties, Atwood published two powerful, haunting (and best-selling)[40] novels, one focusing on the collective future and the other on the personal past. *Cat's Eye* (1989) is a "retrospective" concerning an artist's search for her past, and *The Handmaid's Tale* (1986) is a dystopia in the tradition of Orwell's *1984* and Huxley's *Brave New World,* which, of all eighties novels, most explicitly confronts the implications of backlash for women. Despite the apparent dissimilarities of these works, they are similar in their skepticism about social systems, social relations, and social solutions and in their resignation to what Offred calls "reduced circumstances" (p. 8).

In Atwood's "future history," a coup blamed on Islamic terrorists—the president assassinated, Congress machine-gunned—is followed by implementation of a regime designed by "social engineers," sociobiologists, and market researchers. The Republic of Gilead is a Christian fundamentalist theocracy which, threatened by a drastically declining birth rate, has institutionalized control of the female population "for breeding purposes." Females, forbidden property or employment, are made the wards of their husbands or male next of kin, and the new order purges itself of dissidents: "unwomen" (feminists), homosexuals, abortionists. "It's logical, logical," Atwood said in an interview in *Vogue:* "There's not a single detail in the book that does not have a corresponding reality, either in contemporary conditions or historical fact."[41]

As a "handmaid," a "sexual vessel" or "ambulatory chalice" (p. 136), Offred occupies a lowly position in the hierarchy, and we share her bewilderment and disorientation as she tries to piece things together. It is not clear that she ever does see the whole picture. Certainly, she is no "hero"—she is more like a "good German" than a freedom fighter; and in this she is contrasted with her friend Moira, a rebel and lesbian separatist whose courage she does not share but needs to believe in: "I don't want her to be like me. Give in, go along, save her skin. . . . I want gallantry from her, swashbuckling, heroism" (p. 248). Offred identifies herself with the many people who, in "the time before," tried to survive by "lying low," who "lived by ignoring":

> Ignoring isn't the same as ignorance, you have to work at it . . . there were stories in the newspapers . . . but they were about other women. . . . How awful, we would say, and they were, but they were awful without being believable. . . . We

were the people who were not in the papers. We lived in the blank white spaces at
the edges of print. It gave us more freedom. (pp. 56–57)

Such "freedom," Atwood suggests, is illusory, for Gilead, like Nazi Germany,
has been brought into existence by just such "ignoring."

Offred is contrasted not only with Moira but also with her mother, a feminist
who was active in "Take Back the Night" protests, rallies against pornography
and for abortion, and who harangues her daughter for being "a backlash":
"You don't know what we had to go through just to get where you are . . . how
many women's lives, how many women's *bodies,* the tanks had to roll over" (p.
121). Their relationship epitomizes the relation of feminists to postfeminists,
and though the narrator is condescending about her mother's feminism, it is the
complacency of her generation that has allowed the new regime: "History will
absolve me," says the older woman, and it has.

But feminism also is a target of Atwood's satire. After participating in the
orgiastic "birth ceremony," the narrator thinks, "Mother . . . wherever you may
be. . . . You wanted a women's culture. Well, now there is one. It isn't what you
meant, but it exists" (p. 127). Of course, Gilead is not really a women's culture;
it only looks like one, because though women live and work together, sharing
traditional female activities, celebrating female values, "there's no doubt who
holds the real power" (p. 136). Atwood is suggesting that the sentimentalization
of women may have reactionary implications and that separatism also is a form
of "ignoring": "If Moira thought she could create Utopia by shutting herself in
a women-only enclave she was sadly mistaken. Men were not just going to go
away. . . . You couldn't just ignore them" (p. 172). The implication is that
Gilead has been brought about partly because feminism has lost sight of the
larger issues and failed as an effective force in society.

As in Orwell's *1984* and Huxley's *Brave New World,* the authoritarian and
repressive society of the future makes us long for the world of the present. The
restrictions of Gilead make today's "rules" seem like freedom: "I remember the
rules. . . . Don't open your door to a stranger. . . . Don't go to a laundromat,
by yourself, at night," and in one of her many nostalgic "attacks of the past" (p.
53), the narrator "think[s] about laundromats. What I wore to them . . . what I
put in them. I think about having such control." "Now we walk down the same
streets . . . and no man shouts obscenities at us, speaks to us, touches us. No
one whistles" (p. 24). These meditations suggest that as bad as our society is, it
is, when compared with the repressions of a totalitarian regime, "free," for "freedom, like everything else, is relative" (p. 231). Laundromats represent freedom,
as do short dresses, high heels, open toes, makeup—"When I think: I used to
dress like that. That was freedom" (p. 28). The effect of the contrast is to make us
yearn for the abuses of the present, long for a time when we had the privilege of
displaying ourselves as sexual objects, miniskirted, high-heeled, open-toed,
exposed to the harrassments of men—as for the loss of a precious freedom. As
one of the "Aunts" (the older women at the "Indoctrination Centers") says,
"There's more than one kind of freedom. Freedom to and freedom from. In the

days of anarchy, it was freedom to. Now you are being given freedom from" (p. 24).

But this is the aspect of *The Handmaid's Tale* that I find most troubling: to reject Gilead leaves us no alternative but to endorse the old system—our system. Offred recalls "how we used to think, as if everything were available to us, as if there were no contingencies, no boundaries, as if we were free to shape and reshape the ever-expanding perimeters of our lives" (pp. 225–26). *"As if we were free"*: Atwood's conditional raises the possibility that we were (are) not free. If we are, why hasn't the "freedom to" allowed us to imagine more various shapes for our lives? Why, for example, do our ideas of ourselves always seek the well-worn ruts of "falling in love" (pp. 225–26)—as Offred reflects, and as her own plot demonstrates. Atwood critiques the bogus freedoms our society allows and acknowledges the restrictions it imposes, but a regime that forbids all personal relationships makes ours look good.

Despite her reservations, Atwood implies that our society is preferable not only to Gilead, but to any planned society that can be imagined. Even feminist utopias have their horrors—and Gilead illustrates several of them—for as the Commander says, "Better never means better for everyone. It always means worse, for some" (p. 211). "Consider the alternatives," says one of the Aunts; "You see what things used to be like" (p. 118); and Atwood seems to concur that these are "the alternatives"—a "free society," with its risks and abuses, or a planned society, which would probably incur worse. But in the words which conclude *Surfacing*, "There ought to be other choices":[42] indeed, there *have* to be other choices, for the alternatives allowed by the future are not likely to be a "free" or a "planned" society, but a choice of how society will be planned and who will do the planning. Might there not be a kind of "freedom" that Atwood is not seeing, a "freedom to" do or be in ways that are qualitatively different from—other than—anything that we, conditioned as we have been by this society, with its impoverished sense of possibilities, can envision? Underlying Atwood's critique lurks distrust of society, as though there were some truer, more essential state or self: society is finally something she would dispense with, if she could, rather than recognize as the condition of our existence. Though I admit to finding *The Handmaid's Tale* more interesting than the straightforward utopias of LeGuin and Piercy, I can't help thinking there is something this novel misses, some way of imagining a better world that might liberate better potentials in us—even if it is only in the gestures toward the unimaginable made by her earlier fiction.

### Cordelia Absent

*Cat's Eye* is a disturbing tale of female cruelty, of events that allow a male reviewer to say (with some justice) that "the protagonist" has been "emotionally crippled, but not by men. Women have done the damage" "more than a man could."[43] Atwood's protagonist, Elaine Risley, an artist who has attained some notoreity as a "feminist" painter—a category she eschews—returns to Toronto to attend a retrospective of her work. "Retrospective" is what the novel is also, as Elaine, stalking the streets of Toronto "like a tracker" (p. 9), sets out in search of her past, looking for Cordelia, her childhood nemesis, tormentor, and "best friend": "There are things I need to ask her. Not what happened . . . because . . . I know that. I need to ask her why" (p. 434). "What happened" is revealed as a nightmarish tale of girls' inhumanity to girls, of events that nearly destroy Elaine psychologically and physically. "Why" is what I would like to know also—why Atwood tells this tale and why she tells it now.

Elaine has spent her first eight years living like a nomad, in campsites and motels, on account of her father's profession as an entomologist. When her family moves to Toronto she looks forward to having girlfriends—she has read about them in books (p. 29)—but she is "alien" in their world, not used to girls and their "unspoken rules" (p. 50). She must learn a new language, new customs—the appropriate moves for wearing skirts (p. 81), the meaning of "cold wave" and "chintz" (p. 51), the importance of clothes, possessions, and houses. Her guides are her new friends, Grace Smeath and Carol Campbell, their mothers, and above all, the Eaton Catalogue, which, though used for toilet paper in the wilderness, must now be viewed with "reverence," as the girls spend hours cutting out ladies and surrounding them with "cookware, furniture" (p. 57).

Atwood's account of growing up female in Toronto in the forties and fifties is a grim satire of provincial society. At first "the world of girls and their doings" is manageable, easier than the world of boys. It is a world Elaine

> can be part of . . . without making any effort at all. I don't have to keep up with anyone, run as fast, aim as well. . . . I don't have to think about whether I've done these things well, as well as a boy. All I have to do is sit on the floor and cut frying pans out of the *Eaton's Catalogue* with embroidery scissors, and say I've done it badly. Partly this is a relief. (p. 57)

When Cordelia comes on the scene, however, she makes this world a hell. Elaine is made to realize that, by contrast with Cordelia's family, which has egg cups and a cleaning lady, her own family is "not rich" (p. 76) and that, compared to Cordelia's sisters, Perdita and Miranda, with their "extravagant, mocking," mannerisms (p. 76), she lacks social graces. But worse, Cordelia becomes ringleader to Grace and Carol in bullying Elaine, convincing her that she is inadequate, abnormal, "nothing," a word Elaine comes to "connect with [her]self"—"*What do you have to say for yourself?* Cordelia used to ask. *Nothing.* I would say . . . as if I was nothing" (pp. 43, 211, 124). Cordelia's reign of terror climaxes in events so traumatic that Elaine represses them for years: at one point the girls shut her in a hole underground in Cordelia's backyard (p. 113); at another they make her go down the ravine under an old bridge, where she slips into the icy river and nearly freezes.

When Cordelia reenters her life a year later, the two girls begin to change places, Cordelia losing power and Elaine gaining it. Elaine does well in school and has boyfriends, while Cordelia flunks out, has no boyfriends, and becomes more and more unhinged. We—and Elaine—learn more about Cordelia's past: we learn that she dug that hole in the backyard to find refuge from a father she never could please—"Nothing she can do or say will ever be enough, because she is somehow the wrong person" (p. 264)—hence the Shakespearean names with which he burdens his girls, Cordelia, Perdita, and Miranda, all daughters who redeem fathers. The last times Elaine sees Cordelia, it is Cordelia who has become the supplicant, and what she asks is significant; she asks Elaine to make "some connection to her old life" (p. 274) and to free her from the loony bin, to " 'get me out' " (p. 376)—requests for remembrance and release which Elaine denies.

Elaine comes to realize, through a portrait she has painted of Cordelia and specifically through the eyes of the painting, that it is she who is strong and Cordelia who is weak:

> I had trouble with this picture. . . . I wanted her about thirteen, looking out with that defiant, almost belligerent stare of hers. *So?* But the eyes sabotaged me. They aren't strong eyes; the look they give the face is tentative, hesitant, reproachful. Frightened.
> Cordelia is afraid of me, in this picture.
> I am afraid of Cordelia.
> I'm not afraid of seeing Cordelia. I'm afraid of being Cordelia.
> Because in some way we changed places, and I've forgotten when. (p. 239)

Since so much of this relationship still remains unclear, Elaine feels an increasing urgency to confront her; stalking the streets of Toronto, she convinces herself that Cordelia will materialize at any moment, around any corner. Indeed, the name "Cordelia" suggests that she will reappear, since, at the end of *King Lear,* Cordelia, unjustly banished, returns to redeem Lear; but then, the name is so perversely inappropriate in other ways that it is not surprising that she defeats this expectation as well, remaining absent, "nothing"; in Atwood's novel, "nothing" really does "come of nothing." When Cordelia fails to appear at the retrospective, Elaine's disappointment is enormous: "I've been prepared for almost anything; except absence, except silence" (p. 435). Once, at an earlier art show Elaine had with a group of women artists, she was made to realize how few female friends she had (p. 368); now, at the retrospective, where she jealously measures herself against the younger women artists and Cordelia fails to appear, her relations with women remain unchanged.

So why tell this tale? Because these things happen, are part of life—which is the not very helpful explanation Elaine offers: "It's the kind of thing girls of this age do to one another, or did then" (p. 124). In an interview, Atwood is a bit more illuminating, explaining that "unlike the 'cops and robbers' friendships of boys, those of girls are more likely to be intricate and baroque and tangled relationships in which you aren't sure whether you love the person or hate the person." She refers to girls' "exclusion and inclusion tactics . . . whispering, plots, little secret gangings-up-on"; "Most girls . . . grow up blocking those years out of their consciousness because of society's 'collective agreement' that they are not important":

> We are told that the early years were very, very important. And then we have a whole cult of romance and sex . . . so the later period becomes important. The in-between time I think we've forgotten because it's been indicated to us that it's not important, that how you relate to little girls is not really the concern of a mature person.[44]

So if Atwood is illuminating an aspect of female development that is generally neglected, her portrayal is effective—little girls *do* behave this way, and so do grown women. But is it too much to ask *why?*

Atwood implies that Cordelia, Grace, and Carol are doing what comes "naturally." A melodramatic *Macbeth*-like rhetoric of evil, images of poison and deadly nightshade, and an association of the three girls with the three witches suggest that evil is innate, transsocial and corroborated by some principle of malevolence in the universe, "malice blowing around" (p. 407); when Elaine returns to the schoolyard that has been the scene of so much pain, "the light under the trees thickens, turns malevolent. Ill will surrounds me" (p. 420)—another allusion to *Macbeth* (III.ii.50). This is a tale not of human evil, however, but of female evil, from which males are generally absent and exempt, in which there is so much fear and loathing of the female "blowing around," a misogyny so pronounced and so unprocessed that it is impossible to say whether it is Elaine's, society's, or Atwood's.

Elaine's initiation into society is an initiation into a world of girls and women, a world of houses, Eaton's catalogs, possessions, pretentiousness, bigotry—all epitomized by Mrs. Smeath, lying on her couch with her bad heart and her "smug and accusing smile" (p. 354). Atwood associates the oppressiveness of society with an ailing, aging female, the type of joy-killing old woman familiar from Griswold in *Bodily Harm,* Auntie Muriel in *Life Before Man,* the Aunts in *The Handmaid's Tale,* the Gorgon-like landladies throughout her novels. "There's something strange and laughable about older unmarried women" (p. 82), and the girls joke about their teachers' underwear—especially Miss Lumley's—and about other "unspeakable female things" (p. 241). When Elaine learns about the curse, she recoils from "grown-up women's bodies," "alien and bizarre, hairy, squashy, monstrous," though she uneasily suspects that "whatever has happened to them, bulging them, softening them . . . may happen to us too" (p. 97) and worries that whatever category Miss Lumley was in might include her (p. 85). She despises the "extra flesh wobbling" of adolescent girls (p. 219) and when first confronted with a female model in art school is "afraid of turning into that"—"there is a lot of flesh to her, especially below the waist; there are folds across her stomach, her breasts are saggy and have enormous dark nipples . . . the massiveness of her body makes her head look like an afterthought" (p. 284)—an image that recalls Spenser's Duessa and

Milton's Sin. Females in this novel are identified with a stifling society, the mysteries of the flesh, and malevolence—the world, the flesh, and the devil.

If Atwood is suggesting that a misogynist society turns little girls misogynist, neither she nor Elaine seems to notice the *connection* between female "nature" and the social structures that shape women, though at several points the existence of such structures is suggested. Elaine observes that "married women didn't have jobs" (p. 82); that the professors at her art school are men, while the students are girls who don't aspire to be artists themselves (p. 290); and she tells the young journalist interviewing her, in search of "stories of outrage," that of course she never had a female mentor, there weren't any (p. 94), stating this as a fact of life. Elaine observes, another fact of life, that "women are hard to keep track of. . . . They slip into other names, and sink without a trace" (p. 239)—though again, she merely states this, with no curiosity as to *why*.

Elaine's response to her aversion of the female is to make herself an honorary male. She excuses boys for calling women "bitch" and "broad" on the grounds that "they're prove-it words boys need to exchange, to show they are strong and not to be taken in"; "I don't think any of these words apply to me. They apply to other girls" (p. 251). She feels proud to be allowed in on their talk, privileged to hear women called "cow," "bag," "discard," sure that she is "an exception" (p. 294). She admits to sharing men's fear of women:

> The truth is that I would be terrified to get into bed with a woman. Women collect grievances, hold grudges and change shape. They pass hard, legitimate judgments, unlike the purblind guesses of men, fogged with romanticism and ignorance and bias and wish. Women know too much. . . . I can understand why men are afraid of them. (p. 399)

As Elaine grows older, her fear of older women turns to fear of younger women—the "alarmingly young" girls on the sidewalks "make me feel out-moded" (p. 118); of a young woman at the gallery she thinks, "Probably she's out to get me. Probably she'll succeed" (p. 92); and the young painter at the retrospective who views her work with a "past-tense admiration" that "rele-gates her to the dust heap," she sees as "post everything, she is what will come after *post*. She is what will come after me" (pp. 434–35).

The real reason she prefers men is that they are safer. Boys are innocent and "alien" (p. 347), like her brother, or "largely invisible," like the fathers of her friends (p. 100). Elaine does realize at one point that "there is more to [fathers] than meets the eye," that though "invisible in daytime . . . [they] come out at night" and have "real, unspeakable power"—a power she observes when she sees Cordelia cringe before her father (p. 175). But Atwood does not investigate this; she locates power in what's closest, most obvious—in the females that loom large and terrifying: it is female, not male, power, that has Elaine spooked. This sort of confusion is understandable in a child, commonplace in men, but inexcusable in Margaret Atwood.[45] Moreover, Elaine conflates the self-right-eous, menacing women of her childhood with feminists she later meets:

I avoid gatherings of these women, walking as I do in fear of being sanctified, or else burned at the stake. I think they are talking about me, behind my back. They make me more nervous than ever, because they have a certain way they want me to be, and I am not that way. They want to improve me. At times I feel defiant: what right have they to tell me what to think? *Bitch,* I think silently. *Don't boss me around.* (p. 399)

What is odd about *Cat's Eye* is the way it flirts with a feminist analysis, suggests it as a possibility, but then withdraws it, as though refusing so generalized an interpretation of events which Atwood implies are personal and idiosyncratic. "I am not Woman and I'm damned if I'll be shoved into it" (p. 399); " 'I hate party lines, I hate ghettoes' " (p. 94), Elaine insists, and she repeatedly refuses feminist readings of her art—of paintings of her mother and brother (pp. 160–61, 429–30) and, most notably, of *Fallen Women,* which she describes as being

about men, the kind who caused women to fall. I did not ascribe any intentions to these men. They were like the weather, they didn't have a mind. . . . Fallen women were women who had fallen onto men and hurt themselves. . . . *Fallen Women* showed the women, three of them, falling as if by accident off a bridge. . . . Down they fell, onto the men who were lying unseen, jagged and dark and without volition, far below. (p. 282)

Disclaiming "intention," volition, causality itself, Elaine insists on the randomness, the arbitrariness, of the events she portrays.

Perhaps one reason Elaine cannot accept feminist readings of her art is that she so thoroughly trivializes feminism, reducing it to a protest against leg-shaving and men, her stereotypes replicating postfeminist caricatures of hairy-legged man-haters. Of her consciousness-raising group, she says, "Things are being overthrown. Why, for instance, do we shave our legs? Wear lipstick? Dress up in slinky clothing? Alter our shapes? What is wrong with us the way we are?" "What is wrong with us the way we are is men"; "But I am on shaky ground, in this testifying against men, because I live with one"; besides, "I have not suffered enough, I haven't paid my dues, I have no right to speak" (pp. 360–61). At another point she says,

Pain is important, but only certain kinds of it; the pain of women, but not the pain of men. Telling about your pain is called sharing. I don't want to share in this way; also I am insufficient in scars. I have lived a privileged life. . . . Whatever [Jon] did to me, I did back, and maybe worse. (p. 398)

The blindness of this is extraordinary: Elaine *has* suffered, she does have scars, though they have been inflicted by Cordelia, rather than Jon. But her reductive view of feminism prevents her from seeing the connections between her suffering at the hands of Cordelia and Cordelia's suffering at the hands of her father and the conditions that feminism addresses. This is a tale of women warped and diminished by social circumstances which refuses the terms that would make sense of it, for Elaine never does see the connection between her childhood suffering and the world she grows up into: a world which turns girls into women by bamboozling them into reverence of the Eaton Catalogue, forcing them into simpering, affected postures, confining them to houses and possessions, turning them sour and mean like Mrs. Smeath or brutalized and brutalizing like Cordelia; a world which, by repressing the female, makes her dangerous. Though Atwood intuited such connections in her earlier fiction, *The Edible Woman* and *Lady Oracle,* she now seems to have forgotten them and attributes little girls' cruelty to some innate tendency of human—actually, female—nature. The novel takes place within a consciousness that neither asks the meaning of things nor connects one thing with another—and this means that other things don't add up: Cordelia, for instance. The woman who puts on weight and moves back with her parents, who reinvents herself as an actress but then is institutionalized for trying to kill herself, remains a series of discontinuous images in Elaine's consciousness, a consciousness so uncurious that it doesn't even inquire what went on in the meantime: "I should ask her things: what has she been doing, for these years we've skipped? What about her acting, what became of that? . . . What exactly has been going on, to bring her where she is? But all of this is beside the point" (p. 376). "What exactly has been going on, to bring her where she is" is precisely "the point": there is history, there is a social reality, that might account for the events of this story, and though Atwood hints at their existence, she disallows them as explanation of the cruelty she depicts.

At the end, on the plane returning home to Vancouver, Elaine has a final epiphany of loss when she sees "two old ladies" laughing and playing cards together:

> They seem to me amazingly carefree. . . . They're rambunctious, they're full of beans; they're tough as thirteen, they're innocent and dirty, they don't give a hoot. Responsibilities have fallen away from them, obligations, old hates and grievances: now for a short while they can play again like children, but this time without the pain. This is what I miss, Cordelia: not something that's gone, but something that will never happen. Two old women giggling over their tea. (p. 446)

This loss is not of an experience "that's gone," or even of an experience "that will never happen," but of an experience that could never have happened and could never happen, given the confines of this world and of Elaine's consciousness. As effective as this novel is—and it is unprecedented in its depiction of the cruelty of little girls and, like everything Atwood writes, hauntingly evocative—it is, in its severance of personal from political and its unprocessed misogyny, a novel of its time. Elaine may scoff at the term "postfeminist" when it is applied to her art—"the obligatory *post-feminist*" [p. 238]—but this does not make the term any less appropriate to Atwood's novel.

The images of dismemberment that pervade the novel—the bodily parts that litter the studio where Elaine is staying, the "body parts" men reduce women to (p. 294), the "body parts missing" from "the Greek and Roman things" (p. 289),

"women's bodies . . . with other women's heads glued onto them" from the
Eaton's catalogs (pp. 417, 147), the mannequin at the art show, sawn apart and
reassembled, "a violent dismemberment," "her head tucked upside-down
under her arm" (pp. 365–66)—these point to the radical dismemberment I
sense at the heart of this novel: the severance of personal drama, or psycho-
drama, from social context, of woman from woman, and the denial of connectedness between individual consciousness and collective. Atwood can hardly
be accused of sentimentalizing women, as Lessing does in *Diary of a Good
Neighbor,* but she has similarly dead-ended in terms of envisioning new possibilities.

## The Closing of the Circle: Drabble's Not-So-Radiant Way

The social reality missing from *Cat's Eye* is present in abundance in Drabble's *The Radiant Way,* which offers a panorama of English society—north and
south, working-class, middle-class, professional and business classes. Spanning
the first half of the eighties, from New Year's Eve 1979 to the spring of 1985,
the novel takes England through 1984, the year of George Orwell's dreaded
dystopia; and "1984" is repeatedly referred to, as is "brave new world," grim
portents in a work which asks what the future holds.

All three protagonists—Alix Bowen, Liz Headleand, and Esther Breuer—are
concerned with making connections, not the least of which is connections with
one another. The three women meet at Cambridge in 1952 and go on meeting
regularly in the years that follow, over lunches, dinners, on walks. "Narratives,
in the past, related the adventures of the famous and the wealthy. . . . Liz, Alix
and Esther were not princesses. They were not beautiful, they were not rich. But
they were young, and they had considerable wit" and "they had choices"—
"choices" which Drabble locates specifically in postwar England, in "the brave
new world of Welfare State and County Scholarships, of equality for women":
"they were the elite, the chosen, the garlanded of the great social dream" (p. 88).

By focusing on three women, Drabble is able to explore three ways of
understanding, interpreting, and responding to the world. From the start, their
differences are pronounced: Liz would like "to 'make sense of things, to
understand.' By things she meant herself. Or she thought she meant herself."
Alix would like " 'to change things.' By things she did not mean herself. Or
thought she did not mean herself." Esther would like " 'to acquire interesting
information. That is all' " (p. 85). Liz becomes a psychotherapist and asks
questions about the self; Alix contemplates "the social structure" (p. 72) and
does part-time social work, teaching English literature to delinquent girls and
working on a government study of women offenders (p. 153); Esther, in search
of interesting information, becomes an art historian. The three women are
differentiated in terms of their interests and intelligences, and this represents a
major break not only with nineteenth-century fiction, but also with contemporary novels of female friendship (e.g., Mary McCarthy's *The Group,* Alice

Adams's *Superior Women*) in which women are differentiated in terms of their attitudes toward men. Though marriage is important to them—Liz and Alix marry romantically and disastrously just out of college, but then make more lasting second marriages—their main efforts are directed to something other than romance.

We meet them in their forties, living in London. Liz is the most obviously successful of the three, "an accomplished woman" who has achieved a brilliant career, marriage, a family, and a house in Harley Street. Like many seventies protagonists, her ambition is fuelled by matrophobia, "the dread of reliving her mother's unending, inexplicable, still-enduring loneliness" (p. 31), a mother she has left ("long mad, imprisoned, secret, silent, silenced") in a cold, dark flat in the north, having somewhat unscrupulously turned her over to the care of a sister less successful than she at escaping their dismal background. As a psychotherapist, Liz is interested in what makes and motivates people—"what a mystery it is, the way we carry on" (p. 31)—and her career so far has seemed to confirm the assumption on which her practice is based, that knowledge makes progress.

Though Alix is the least ambitious of the three women in terms of what she does (her part-time social work barely supports a life above the poverty line), she is the most ambitious intellectually: "She aspired to a more comprehensive vision. She aspired to make connections." She has a sense that their lives are part of a master network, that there was a pattern, if only one could discern it" (pp. 72–73). One of the "connections" she aspires to is that between past and present, her own and England's; for, like Liz, she sees the past as a means of understanding the present. She tries to relate her Cambridge education to the present, asking what is the relevance of "the tradition," the value of Shakespeare or Blake, to the delinquent girls she teaches; and her thoughts are filled with quotes and misquotes, as she contemplates the relevance of the English tripos to her own crises and England's. In a poignant scene, Alix tries to get her students to see the connections between a Blake poem and their lives; she fails, for most "never suspected that poetry could mean anything about anything real" (p. 212), and the program is cut by Thatcher in any case, "the civilizing effect of classes in English Language and Literature" being "open to dispute" (p. 185).

If Liz represents the "personal" and Alix the "political," Esther's response is a sort of combination of the aesthetic and scholarly. Though Esther claims, "I am not ambitious, I do not seek answers to large questions," she, too, is interested in making connections: she has a sense that "all knowledge" might be "omnipresent in all things . . . one could startle oneself into seeing whole by tweaking unexpectedly at a . . . corner of the great mantle" (p. 83)—an approach that has yielded some "brilliant connections" and gained her success as an art historian in spite of her refusal to commit herself to serious projects.

Though none of these women is a writer, their ways of interpreting and ordering reality offer analogues to narrativizing which make the novel interestingly self-reflexive. Esther's belief that the whole may be seen in the part illuminates Drabble's investigation of representative women, families, and professions as a way of envisioning the whole of British society. Liz's interest in the personal past as a way of understanding the present provides a version of what the novelist does as she tries to make sense of the individual life, to construct the "sequence" of events which determines their "consequence" (the pun is Drabble's; p. 385). Above all, Alix's aspiration to a "comprehensive vision" of the whole of which we are "but a part," her desire to understand the "threads of a vast web, a vast network, which was humanity itself" (pp. 72–73), illuminates Drabble's narrative technique: by filtering events through dozens of perspectives, scattering the interest over myriad consciousnesses, *The Radiant Way* thwarts identification with the striking individual and emphasizes pattern, connection, community.

The brilliant opening scene of the novel—the glittering, "upmarket" New Year's Eve party thrown by Liz and Charles Headland at their Harley Street house—represents the high point of Liz's personal accomplishment and the achievement of a certain kind of community as well. From all over London their guests assemble—young and old, men and women, Left and Right, art and science—"representatives of most of the intersecting circles that make up society" (p. 27): "the communal celebration draws them. . . . They need one another"; they gather "in the hope of a new self, a new life, a new redeemed decade" (p. 1). Liz has worked a Cinderella-like transformation of her life— from rags to riches, margin to center, from obscurity to the blazing lights of Harley Street; and, as the novel opens, she is at the height of her powers, "host in the house of [her]self," the center of a circle—"children of heart and imagination" "moved and circled and wheeled around" (p. 14). Besides marking the end of a decade—"a portentious moment, for those who pay attention to portents" (p. 1)—this party celebrates (or so Liz thinks) her twenty-year marriage to Charles, "a sign that they had weathered so much and were now entering a new phase," "a portent . . . a symbol . . . a landmark in the journey of their lives" (p. 6); for "the Headlands of Harley Street" (p. 18) are "a powerful couple who . . . represented a solidity, a security, a stamp of survival on the unquiet experiments of two decades" (p. 9).

The party does turn out to be a landmark, but not of what Liz anticipated, as in the course of the scene, she comes to realize what everyone else already knows: that Charles is about to leave her for Lady Henrietta Latchett, "the most boring woman in Britain" (p. 42). As Liz takes in this new information, as she processes messages she has been ignoring, pieces together the situation, and tries to respond in a way that allows her to save face, she is shaken by her slowness to read the signals; for as a psychotherapist, she depends on her powers of knowing: "She would have liked to have thought that she had known always, that there was no moment of shock, that knowledge had lain within her . . . that she had never truly been deceived. . . . But no" (p. 39). The scene puts the reader through a process of misreading like Liz's, for only when we reach its end can we see that nothing meant what it seemed to; and this makes an important point—that things change meaning according to the turn of events.

The question of change on a personal level mirrors the question of change on the collective level—of transformation, renewal, progress for England. The marriage and household are microcosmic, and their dissolution at the beginning of the novel and the beginning of the decade marks the end of a dream of unity, of transcending barriers, not only for individuals but for England. In the sixties Liz and Charles "led a charmed life . . . the times were on their side" (p. 18), "heady days" for the Headleands (p. 176). In the seventies their marriage unravels a bit, though it retains "an abiding unity" (p. 142), or so Liz thought. But Charles, once an idealistic young filmmaker who worked for social reform, has capitulated professionally and personally. Charles's television series *The Radiant Way* was a genuine attempt to bring about "the Brave New World . . . a forward-looking, forward-moving, dynamic society, full of opportunity, co-operative, classless . . . everything would get better and better all the time" (p. 176). But Charles has "come full circle" (p. 115) in his women as in his work, turning from the eccentric "ill-born, ill-bred, brilliant" Liz (p. 118) to the empty but titled Lady Henrietta Latchett—a paradoxical reversal, since Lady Henrietta so closely resembles "the dead wood to which, as a younger man, he had taken the axe" (p. 118). Charles has abandoned social commitment and has taken an appointment in New York, a position "quasi-ambassadorial in dignity" (so he thinks; p. 116), "to monitor the collapse of empires," "to read the writing on the wall" (p. 173).

Charles's defection unsettles Liz alarmingly. Her "self-definition" (p. 18) is bound up in her marriage in ways that surprise her, and she experiences an "unmaking of the fabric" of her being, "a negation, a denial, an undoing of past self, of past knowledge . . . of past certainties" (p. 143). Liz now feels "false, false, false" (p. 171), a wounded healer who does not know and cannot cure herself (pp. 125, 137, 144). The patterns that have defined her are destroyed, and this opens a space for memory which makes her aware of something nagging, "something that she did not wish to know, something she needed to know" (p. 132), "something irresolute, unresolved, undiagnosed" (p. 138). She embarks on a quest for lost knowledge, resolving to "turn back in order to leap forwards," to confront "the blank, dark backward nothingness of her own unknowing" (pp. 140–41). As a psychotherapist, Liz is committed to the "proposition that effort will be rewarded," that "knowledge will restore health and life" (p. 145). To doubt this is to doubt her life's work, which (like most human endeavor) depends on the assumption that effort leads to enlightenment and is "consequential."

After her mother's death, Liz finds some of what she seeks when, going through her mother's possessions, she turns up newspaper clippings and a copy of an old childhood reader, *The Radiant Way*. The reader triggers recollections of her child-molester father, memories of "Guilt. Shame. Infantile sexuality" (p. 386); but this "shabby little mystery" (p. 389) is so disappointingly banal and accounts for so little that it leaves her with a sense of "the unsatisfactory nature of knowledge. The anti-climactic nature of knowledge" (p. 388). Liz draws back at a crucial moment—"She would remember no more. She would no longer gaze at the past" (p. 389)—asking "What did it matter who her father was? *What does it matter who I am?*" (p. 385).

Whereas Liz is concerned with questions of personal identity, Alix thinks politically. She is drawn to her second husband, Brian, partly because of his working-class origins but mainly because of "a sense of [his] not being afraid," of his being "connected": lying in his arms, she feels she is "healing the wounds in [her] own body and in the body politic"; making love with him gives her "a basic, reassuring, comforting continuity. . . . He was alive in his body, and that was a rare thing" (pp. 168–69). But Brian, who is in some ways the most attractive character in the novel, is being made "redundant," losing his job teaching literature in an adult-education program—it "made no sense" (p. 170). These are "bad times" for Brian and Alix (p. 265). The closest of the characters to events of the eighties, they are vulnerable in their work to cuts in welfare spending and vulnerable in themselves because they care. Moreover, their marriage is in trouble, and the problem is political, for Brian is being drawn to the militant left just as Alix is losing faith in any sort of political action; and Alix finds herself increasingly attracted to Brian's oldest friend, Otto, whose moderate positions (evidenced by his involvement in the Social Democratic Party) more resemble her own. As with Liz and Charles, rifts between man and woman reflect larger divisions in the social fabric.

As Liz undergoes a crisis of confidence in reason and progress generally, Alix undergoes a crisis of confidence in the political assumptions that have been the guiding lights of her life. At another "portentious moment" in the novel, a long scene which takes place on the eve of 1984, Alix's car breaks down as she is returning home from visiting her dying ex-mother-in-law; stuck by the side of the road in the rain, she reflects that the year is dying, the car is dying, various of her own and Brian's relatives are dying—aged, ailing, bodies which are analogues for the body politic. "At the darkest hour of the longest darkest night of the year" (p. 282), Alix confronts the chasm that has opened between her and Brian, and her reflections take the form of a catechism: did Brian believe that a Labour government "would have halted this process of deterioration?" "Yes." "Did she?" "Not really. No." "So Alix believed the process was inevitable, and that unemployment would continue to rise, violence to increase?" "Sort of. Yes." Alix (like Liz) is left "in a false position" (pp. 282–85). Though she agrees with Brian that "the cause of all this pain, this grinding, this deep misery, was the economic system itself," "her common sense, her rational being, her education all scream out in protest against the folly of" Brian's new militancy, "the vacuous pointlessness of the slogans" of his "new-found . . . chums": "So sat Alix Bowen and many thousands like her . . . [hearing] the terminal struggle of warring factions in her own land. . . . Was the country done for, finished off, struggling and twitching in the last artificially prolonged struggles of old age?" (pp. 342–43) Alix succumbs to the fear she has spent her life resisting: "There is no hope of a peaceable life . . . of a society without fear. Fear grows, flourishes, is bred, blossoms, flames. . . . I am defeated. . . . We are defeated" (p. 337).

She and Brian return to the depressed northern city from which they came, and Alix takes a job with a "famous poet," cataloging the papers and editing the letters of this "disillusioned old monster," consoling herself that "it is, like all her jobs, a dead-end job, but at least it is not socially useful. . . . She has had enough, for the time being, of trying to serve the community. . . . The community does not want her, and she does not at the moment much care for the community" (p. 392). So "Alix sits and reads of dead aspirations. But the poems live. . . . They are high art, and good." Alix does not find the connections she has sought—she "thought of all these things. They made no sense, these blocks. They did not make a building, but she would continue patiently, persistently, to line them up and to look at them. . . . She would compel them" (pp. 170–71); but they remain "inassimilable material" (p. 158), not to be compelled. Like Liz, she has come round to a position which is "unsatisfactory"; like Charles, her reversals are paradoxical—"So this is where my privileged education has brought me, thinks Alix. . . . Paradoxical"; "I have been driven into paradox. . . . I have not chosen it. I have been driven into it. It is not satisfactory. But what else can I do?" Her position is, however, as she says, "not yet finalized" (p. 393).

*The Radiant Way* is a political novel: its characters think politically, see all issues politically, fall in and out of love on account of politics. But its politics are bleak. Events of the eighties put an end to the hope of progress or unity; the defeat of the miners' strike leaves England "divided as never before" and the Labour movement in ruins. Alix withdraws from politics; Esther leaves Britain; so does Otto, convinced that "the whole thing has been an unmitigated, irreversible disaster" (p. 391). Given the analogy between the body and the body politic, the gruesome decapitations that loom closer to the lives of the three women (one of Alix's students, Jilly, is decapitated, and the murderer turns out to reside in Esther's apartment building) imply that England itself is a body without a head. Esther, wandering through "a landscape of nightmare, an extreme, end-of-the world, dreamlike parody of urban nemesis," reflects "one day they would rebuild . . . but when? There was a lot to flatten first" (p. 244). The question recalls that of *The Waste Land,* but Drabble offers no suggestion that destruction will issue into new creation. Nor does she hold out much hope for individual reform as a means of social progress. Nor does she make claims for the civilizing powers of art or the imagination, Alix's capitulation to "high art" notwithstanding.

This novel documents the end of the "great social dream," of belief in "the civilizing force of . . . English," the ideal that inspired the 1944 Education Act. Yet it is named for a reader, and nearly all its characters are readers, people for whom literature is vitally important—Alix carries on a running argument with "Dr. Leavis" (p. 323), Brian becomes a teacher because of his love of English literature (p. 163), and even Mrs. Abelwhite, Liz's mother, has a library of

Victorian novels. Moreover, Drabble's numerous allusions to Shakespeare, nineteenth- and twentieth-century novels, to mythological figures (the Medusa, the Gorgons, the Minotaur) function as an elaborate system of intertextuality, a medium through which we read the events of the novel; and the term "intertextuality" actually appears (p. 157). But these intertexts yield no answers: the master plots—the Biblical-epic pattern of loss and recreation, the Freudian account of individual development, the Leavisite notion of literature as civilizing and ennobling—all lack explanatory force; all are anachronistic, irrelevant, "faint, feeble echoes" (p. 63) from "another world of reference, an older . . . world" (p. 43), "ill-remembered, confused, shadowy" (p. 63). Moreover—and this is what is different—their loss is viewed more in sorrow than in celebration, in a tone more elegiac than exhilarating.

Among the discredited myths is the ideal of the writer as a figure of knowledge and power. Near the end of the novel, a young woman at the Twelfth Night party, surveying the crowd, points out the new class of media people, those who "mediate," interpret, produce our reality: " 'Look around this room and see if you can point to a *single person* in it who is engaged in primary or secondary production?' " " 'These are the experts' "; " 'Tertiary. All. A tertiary, terminal bunch' "; " 'Now writing books . . . is that tertiary production? Or merely unproductive production, would you say?' " (p. 320). "Unproductive production," terminal, tertiary: the several writers in the novel, far from being moral centers, tend to be ineffectual, and male—dissociated, like Stephen, or parasitical, like Pett Petrie; Brian, the best of them, gives up writing.

The novel begins with a fall and fragmentation, and numerous references to paradise, gardens, Edens (pp. 92, 85, 259, 238, 386) suggest the question of recreation and the analogy of England to the New Jerusalem, a topos which resonates through the English tradition from Chaucer, Shakespeare, Milton, and Blake through John Mortimer's *Paradise Postponed* and Drabble's *Jerusalem the Golden*. Drabble enlists Shakespeare's *Tempest* as her primary intertext, as aware as Laurence was of its significance as a version of the fortunate fall. In the opening scene, Liz feels possessed of an almost preternatural power and, like Prospero, "summons these people up"—"at her command, patterns would form and dissolve and form again" (p. 8)—conjuring the party, as she has her life, from the dismal materials of the past, creating light and life and sociability from terror and blankness. The novel closes on a pastoral scene, a spring day which the three women spend walking in the Sussex countryside, at the end of which "perhaps they all, briefly, sleep, and dream" (p. 395) ("We are such stuff / As dreams are made on," *Tempest*, IV.i.156–57). In the middle of the novel, when Liz asks Stephen what he would do if he were "in charge of this wretched country," he replies, in terms that echo The Tempest, " 'I would abolish the Royal Family. And after that, all privileges, all titles, all honours, all degrees. I would take degree away' " (p. 264). This is Stephen's "brave new world," as it was Shakespeare's Gonzalo's; and when we recall that Huxley took his title *Brave New World* from *The Tempest*—from Miranda's exclamation "Oh brave new world" (V.i.183)—the line resonates further. But Drabble's title is, like

Huxley's, ironic: if *The Radiant Way* is not as dystopic as Huxley's *Brave New World* or Orwell's *1984* or Atwood's *The Handmaid's Tale*, neither is it infused with the radiant hope of Shakespeare's *Tempest*. In the final scene, "The sun is dull with a red radiance. It sinks . . . hangs in the sky, burning. . . . The sun bleeds, the earth bleeds" (p. 396).

Liz's ability to dissociate herself from her past and society, to enjoy her dinner though the world is mad (p. 265), is a postfeminist adjustment. Alix, too, abandons hope of making connections, though reluctantly, concluding that "there is no hope, in the present social system, of putting anything right. The only hope is in revolution, and Alix does not think revolution likely." But if political revolution is unlikely, another sort of "revolution" is not only likely but inevitable—"the revolution of the world," the revolution that has returned Alix's Bard to eminence ("Time has passed him by, and by its natural revolution, has caught up with him again" [pp. 392–93]): things continue to continue, the wheel grinds on, and though its processes are "not yet finalized," neither are they susceptible to volition or comprehension. The circle of harmony and community with which this novel opens (and with which *The Middle Ground* concludes) has been replaced by processes "circular, continuous, endlessly repetitive" (p. 353), like those cycles which entrapped Martha Quest in the "nightmare repetition."[46]

Like Shakespeare, who, in a passage from *Cymbeline* that haunts Alix during her dark night of the soul, refuses to "play in wench-like words with that which is most serious" (p. 267), Drabble in *The Radiant Way* seems to "turn on" her own aesthetic structures: "Was Shakespeare, as she had always expected, in these late plays turning on his own art with a sardonic, elegiac, disenchanted wit?" (p. 267)[47] She calls into question the structures on which narrative is based, refuses the forms that make "narrative sense" (p. 383)—that the quest for self and self-knowledge matters, that effort leads to enlightenment, that reason makes progress, that knowledge is power. Her narrative offers, rather, anticlimax, the disruption of causality, and an unsettling repetition, at crucial points, of the word "nothing" (pp. 45, 200, 218, 311, 317, 323, 341, 355, 372). If there is a pattern, it is of "anticlimax" and inconsequence: stories are begun—a possible romance between Liz and Stephen—which lead nowhere; characters appear, only to disappear. Charles misreads the writing on the wall, but it does not much matter. Liz is "exposed to feel what wretches feel" (pp. 127–28), but it does not much matter; she continues her private practice and is made prosperous by a government she disapproves of, and this in spite of the fact that she has more or less demolished the moral and intellectual underpinnings of her profession, having demonstrated that self-discovery is "inconsequential."

An exchange between Alix and Esther epitomizes the resignation with which the novel concludes: " 'You would have expected us to have marched forward into the new light by now? The rational, radiant light?' asked Esther. 'Well. Yes, I would,' said Alix. 'Wouldn't you?' 'I suppose I would have expected a little better,' said Esther. 'A *little* more light.' She sighed" (p. 331).[48] When, at the end of *Cat's Eye*, Elaine looks out the window of the plane on her way back to Vancouver, she describes the stars as "echoes of light, shining out of the midst of nothing. It's an old light, and there's not much of it. But it's enough to see by" (p. 446). Old light, dead light, dim light, reflected light, a "disvision." Drabble's gloom, however, seems less like a projection of her own solipsistic disillusionment and more earned from her depiction of contemporary conditions. Of all these writers, she holds out the longest, pushes the farthest, and though she abandons hope of change, she is still passionately engaged with the question of change, still using fictional form as a probe, and still compassionately involved with her world.

*The Radiant Way* brings this study full circle—the search for the past is no longer revitalizing; the great social dream has faded. I wish that this novel had a different ending and I wish that this book had a different ending. One can hope that the fiction of minority women may take over from where white women's fiction left off: certainly, Morrison's *Beloved* is remarkable in the eighties, for its delving the past as a means to change and its focus on "reconstruction" from the nightmare of the past. We may be sure, at any rate, that changes are in the making—as they were thirty years ago, as they always are—that are even now making a new beginning: that this last turn is not the last round, that processes are "not yet finalized."

# NOTES

## I. Introduction

1. T. S. Eliot, *The Sacred Wood* (London: Methuen, 1932), pp. xv–xvi.

2. "When We Dead Awaken: Writing as Re-Vision," *On Lies, Secrets, and Silence: Selected Prose, 1966–1978* (New York: Norton, 1979), pp. 33–49, 35 (hereafter LSS).

3. For these descriptions of metafiction, see Linda Hutcheon, *Narcissistic Narrative: The Metafictional Paradox* (New York: Methuen, 1984), pp. 1, 6–7; and Patricia Waugh, *Metafiction: The Theory and Practice of Self-Conscious Fiction* (London: Methuen, 1984), pp. 2, 34.

4. Margaret Laurence describes herself as being "90% in agreement with Women's Lib"; "Face to Face," Margaret Atwood, *Margaret Laurence,* ed. William New (Toronto: McGraw-Hill Ryerson, 1977), pp. 33–40, 36. She says that the women's movement gave her "a much-needed sense of community"; "Ivory Tower or Grassroots? The Novelist as Socio-political Being," *A Political Art: Essays and Images in Honor of George Woodcock,* ed. William H. New (Vancouver: University of British Columbia Press, 1978), pp. 15–25, 24, 23 (hereafter NASB).

5. *The Golden Notebook* (New York: Bantam, 1973), 1971 introduction, pp. viii–ix.

6. In "Women Who Write Are Women" (*New York Times Book Review,* December 16, 1984), Elaine Showalter cites reasons why women writers have dissociated themselves from feminism (pp. 1, 31, 33).

7. Interview by Gillian Parker and Janet Todd, *Women Writers Talking,* ed. Janet Todd (New York: Holmes and Meier, 1983), pp. 161–95, 168.

8. "Margaret Drabble: Cautious Feminist," interview by Diana Cooper-Clark, *Atlantic Monthly* (November 1980), pp. 245–46, 69–75, 75, 70.

9. "An Interview with Margaret Atwood" by Betsy Draine (1981), *Interviews with Contemporary Writers,* ed. L. S. Dembo (Madison: University of Wisconsin Press, 1983), pp. 366–81, 373.

10. "Paradoxes and Dilemmas, the Woman as Writer" (1973), in *Woman as Writer,* ed. Jeanette L. Webber and Joan Grumman (Boston: Houghton Mifflin, 1978), pp. 178–87, 179, 185.

11. Margaret Atwood, *Second Words: Selected Critical Prose* (Boston: Beacon, 1982), introduction, pp. 11–15, 15 (hereafter SW); "A Conversation: Margaret Atwood and Students," moderated by Francis X. Gillen, *Margaret Atwood: Vision and Forms,* ed. Kathryn VanSpanckeren and Jan Garden Castro (Carbondale: Southern Illinois University Press, 1988), pp. 233–43, 241. She defines "politics" as "not just elections" but "everything that involves who gets to do what to whom," "who is considered to have power. . . . And . . . what you feel free to say to someone"; "Using What You're Given," interview with Margaret Atwood by Jo Brans; *Margaret Atwood: Conversations,* ed. Earl G. Ingersoll (Willowdale, Ontario: Ontario Review Press, 1990), 149.

12. James Vinson, ed., *Contemporary Novelists* (London: St. James Press, 1972), p. 373.

13. "The Small Personal Voice," in Paul Schleuter, *A Small Personal Voice: Essays, Reviews, Interviews* (New York: Vintage, 1972), pp. 3–21, 6–7 (hereafter SPV); "Doris Lessing at Stony Brook: An Interview by Jonah Raskin," in Schleuter, pp. 61–76, 71.

14. Margaret Atwood, "The Curse of Eve—Or What I Learned in School," in *Second Words,* pp. 215–28, 219–21. For an account of the rise of "English literature" in connection with ideologies that were "imperialist, nationalist . . . sexist, elitist," see

Alan Sinfield, *Literature, Politics, and Culture in Postwar Britain* (Berkeley: University of California Press, 1989), pp. 182, 201, n. 1, and chapters 4 and 6.

15. Unpublished interview with David Leon Higdon, September 1979; quoted in Joanne V. Creighton, *Margaret Drabble* (London: Methuen, 1985), p. 15.

16. "Interview with Margaret Drabble," by Iris Rozencwajg, 1974, *Women's Studies* 6 (1979), pp. 335–47, 337.

17. Penny Boumelha discusses realism as the means by which women writers have "staked a claim" outside the traditional female sphere; "Realism and the Ends of Feminism," in *Grafts: Feminist Cultural Criticism,* ed. Susan Sheridan (London: Verso, 1988), pp. 77–91, 77, 80. Ann Barr Snitow suggests that "the realist novel has always been the novel of . . . first phase . . . 'how-to' manuals for groups gathering their identity through self-description"; "The Front Line: Notes on Sex in Novels by Women, 1969–1979," *Signs* (1980), pp. 5, 4, 702–18, 705. As Rita Felski notes, a glance at the catalogs of such publishing houses as Virago and The Women's Press reveals realist writing as "the mainstay of feminist publishing"; *Beyond Feminist Aesthetics: Feminist Literature and Social Change* (Cambridge: Harvard University Press, 1989), p. 15.

18. Jerome H. Rosenberg, *Margaret Atwood,* Twayne's World Authors Series (Boston: Twayne Publishers, 1984), p. 6.

19. "Books that Mattered to Me," in *Margaret Laurence: An Appreciation, Journal of Canadian Studies,* ed. Christl Verduyn (Peterborough, Canada: Broadview Press, 1988), pp. 239–49, 239. In her memoirs, *Dance on the Earth* (hereafter DOE), she describes her intoxicated sense, in high-school English classes, that "doors were opening in my mind" (Toronto: McClelland and Stewart, 1989), p. 77.

20. Interview with Roy Newquist, in Schleuter, SPV, pp. 45–60, 49. Lessing attended a Roman Catholic convent school in Salisbury from age seven to thirteen, then transferred to Girls High School in Salisbury but withdrew a year later and returned home, claiming eye trouble. She then proceeded to read, voraciously, "books ranging from Balzac, Stendhal, Dostoevsky, and Tolstoy to Ellis," for the next four years (Mona Knapp, *Doris Lessing* [New York: Frederick Ungar, 1984], p. 6), after which she moved back to Salisbury at age eighteen to take a job as a switchboard operator and typist: "I could have been educated—formally, that is—but I felt some neurotic rebellion against my parents who wanted me to be brilliant academically. I simply contracted out of the whole thing and educated myself" (Newquist, p. 49).

21. Margaret Drabble, *The Radiant Way* (London: Weidenfeld and Nicolson, 1987), p. 87 (hereafter, RW). She describes Leavis's influence "and that of the Great Tradition, and all that it stood for," as "enormous" (letter to Gayle Greene, July 11, 1989).

22. Francis Mulhern, *The Moment of "Scrutiny"* (London: New Left Books, 1979), p. 28; see also *Re-Reading English,* ed. Peter Widdowson (London: Methuen, 1982), pp. 51–52 and *passim.*

23. George Lukács, "The Ideology of Modernism," in *The Meaning of Contemporary Realism* (1963), trans. John and Necke Mander (London: Merlin Press, 1969), pp. 17–46, 19; *Studies in European Realism* (New York: The Universal Library, 1964), 1946 preface, pp. 1–19, 9.

24. Terry Eagleton paraphrases this argument in Lukács's article in the *New Hungarian Quarterly* 13, 47 (Autumn 1972); *Marxism and Literary Criticism* (Berkeley: University of California Press, 1976), pp. 29–30 and p. 79 n.10.

25. Remark to BBC interviewer, quoted in Creighton, 1985, p. 25; "An Interview with Margaret Drabble," 1979, by Joanne V. Creighton, in *Margaret Drabble: Golden Realms,* Living Author Series No. 4, ed. Dorey Schmidt (Edinburg, TX: Pan American University, 1982), pp. 18–31, 18.

26. While she was in the process of writing *The Radiant Way,* Drabble told Creighton that she was fascinated by the problems of writing a modern *Middlemarch* (June 19, 1984; Creighton, 1985, p. 109).

27. Showalter notes that "from the moment of the novel's publication, feminist readers felt passionately involved in Dorothea's fate, and the strength of their horror and anger at the novel's substitution of marriage for work is a measure of Eliot's power in posing the Woman Question"; "The Greening of Sister George," in *Nineteenth-Century Fiction* 35 (1980), pp. 292–311, 306.

28. Margaret Drabble, *The Ice Age* (New York: Knopf, 1977), p. 260.

29. *Ramparts* (February 1972), p. 54.

30. John Hannay, interview with Margaret Drabble, quoted in Hannay, *The Intertextuality of Fate: A Study of Margaret Drabble* (Columbia: University of Missouri Press, 1986), p. 13.

31. Bernice Lever, "Literature and Canadian Culture: An Interview with Margaret Laurence," in New (1977), pp. 24–32, 27.

32. "Interview with Margaret Atwood," *Cosmopolitan*, August, 1987, p. 34.

33. Virginia Woolf, *A Room of One's Own* (New York: Harcourt, 1957), p. 101.

34. Rachel Blau DuPlessis, *Writing Beyond the Ending: Narrative Strategies of Twentieth-Century Women Writers* (Bloomington: Indiana University Press, 1985); hereafter WBE.

35. Wendy Mulford, "Notes on Writing," in *On Gender and Writing*, ed. Michelene Wandor (London: Pandora Press, 1983), pp. 34–35. Cf. Marge Piercy: "It was not, of course, a mainstream that had produced me, a tradition to which I was a natural heir. I would never be a gentleman"; "Through the Cracks," in *Partisan Review* 41 (1947), pp. 202–16, 204.

36. Roland Barthes, *S/Z* (New York: Hill and Wang, 1974), p. 135 and *passim*. Catherine Belsey elaborates Barthes's discussion of realism as "the accomplice of ideology," describing it as a closed, fixed system which appears realistic "precisely because it reproduces what we already seem to know" (*Critical Practice* [London: Methuen, 1985], pp. 73, 46–47, 52).

37. For Lévi-Strauss's association of "the emergence of symbolic thought" with the requirement that "women, like words, should be things that were exchanged," see Nelly Furman, "The Politics of Language: Beyond the Gender Principle?" in *Making a Difference: Feminist Literary Criticism*, ed. Gayle Greene and Coppélia Kahn (New York: Methuen, 1985), pp. 59–79, 60.

38. Dee Preussner, "Talking with Margaret Drabble," in *Modern Fiction Studies* 25, 4 (Winter 1979–80), pp. 563–77, 570.

39. Parker and Todd, pp. 163–64. Drabble says of Woolf, "She was very unfashionable here in the fifties and sixties, and I just never read a word, and now I *feel* as though I've been influenced but I can't have been" (Rozencwajg, p. 336); "she didn't influence my formative years. She's certainly influenced me since" (Parker and Todd, p. 164).

40. Letter to Gayle Greene, December 3, 1986.

41. Margaret Laurence, *The Diviners* (Toronto: Bantam, 1975), pp. 293–94. Laurence describes Woolf as "a writer whose perceptions helped shape my view of life, as did her brand of feminism," but who "in a profound way" did not "speak to my life": her novels are "immaculate and fastidious in ways that most people's lives are not" (DOE, p. 130).

42. As Frank Lentricchia suggests, the notion of tradition "as an entity, a static thing, or a completed process," as timeless or transcendent, obscures the *process* of tradition making and blunts the critical edge of writing; *Criticism and Social Change* (Chicago: University of Chicago Press, 1983), pp. 124, 142.

43. The term "something new" occurs in *Martha Quest* (New York: New American Library, 1964), pp. 53, 141, 216 (hereafter MQ); *Landlocked* (New York: New American Library, 1966), p. 117; and *The Golden Notebook*, pp. 61, 353, 472–73, 479 (hereafter GN); "the nightmare repetition" is from *A Proper Marriage* (New York: New American Library, 1970), pp. 77, 95 (hereafter PM).

44. Annette Kolodny, "A Map for Rereading: Or, Gender and the Interpretation of

Literary Texts," *New Literary History* 3 (Spring 1980), pp. 451–67, 465. Showalter also describes feminist criticism's "tasks of revision and rediscovery" ("Literary Criticism," *Signs* 1, 2 [1975], pp. 435–60, 437); Sandra Gilbert refers to "the revisionary imperative" as an "attempt to reform 'a thousand years of Western Culture' "; "What Do Feminist Critics Want? A Postcard from the Volcano," *ADE Bulletin* 66 (1980); rpt. Elaine Showalter, *The New Feminist Criticism: Essays on Women, Literature, Theory* (New York: Pantheon, 1985), pp. 29–45, 32.

45. "Artists and critics are clearly part of the same literary movement, stimulated by the energies released and identified by the women's movement, coming out of the same cultural matrix, and engaged in the same tasks of revision and rediscovery" (1975, p. 437).

46. Cora Kaplan, "Feminist Criticism Twenty Years On," in *From My Guy to Sci-Fi: Genre and Women's Writing in the Postmodern World,* ed. Helen Carr (London: Pandora, 1989), pp. 15–23, 17–19.

47. Margaret Atwood, *Surfacing* (New York: Fawcett, 1972), pp. 66–67.

48. Gail Godwin, *The Odd Woman* (New York: Warner, 1974), pp. 29, 50 (hereafter OW).

49. Margaret Drabble, *The Waterfall* (New York: Fawcett, 1977), p. 138.

50. Marilyn French, *The Women's Room* (New York: Jove Publications, 1977), p. 29.

51. Marge Piercy, *Braided Lives* (New York: Fawcett Crest, 1982), p. 12 (hereafter BL). Blanche H. Gelfant describes the "hungry woman" "in fiction written by women about women," the woman who "believes that books will give her power, and so she reads compulsively—looking for ways to change her life"; "Sister to Faust: The City's 'Hungry' Woman as Heroine," in *Women Writing in America: Voices in Collage* (Hanover, NH: University Press of New England, 1984), pp. 205–224, 207–208.

52. Adrienne Rich, "Motherhood: The Contemporary Emergency and the Quantum Leap," in LSS, pp. 259–73, 260. Cf. Mary Daly, *Beyond God the Father: Towards a Philosophy of Women's Liberation* (Boston: Beacon Press, 1973): "Women have had the power of naming stolen from us" (p. 8). Carol P. Christ refers to the "role of language in articulating and shaping women's experiences of new being"; *Diving Deep and Surfacing* (Boston: Beacon Press, 1980), p. 81.

53. See Grace Stewart, *A New Mythos: The Novel of The Artist As Heroine, 1877–1977* (Montreal: Eden Press, 1981), p. 181.

54. Elaine Tyler May describes these "perplexing" trends; "Explosive Issues: Sex, Women, and the Bomb," in *Recasting America: Culture and Politics in the Age of Cold War,* ed. Lary May (Chicago: University of Chicago Press, 1989), pp. 154–70, 155.

55. *Once a Feminist: Stories of a Generation,* ed. Michelene Wandor (London: Virago, 1990), pp. 38, 91.

56. "The State of Fiction: A Symposium," in *The New Review,* vol. 5, no. 1. (Summer 1978), p. 18. The protagonist of Judith Grossman's *Her Own Terms* accounts for herself in terms of the 1944 Education Act: " 'Without that . . . I should have been a—secretary in an estate-agent's, with a beehive hairdo' " (New York: Ivy Books, 1988, p. 206).

57. Betty Friedan, *The Feminine Mystique* (New York: Dell, 1983), *passim* (hereafter FM).

58. Marge Piercy, *Small Changes* (New York: Fawcett Crest, 1973), p. 29.

59. Sue Kaufman, *Diary of a Mad Housewife* (New York: Bantam, 1970), pp. 50–51, 267.

60. Sheila Ballantyne, *Norma Jean the Termite Queen* (Harmondsworth: Penguin, 1986), p. 120.

61. Erica Jong, *Fear of Flying* (New York: Signet, 1973), pp. 14, 154. Cf. Adrienne Rich: the girl who turns "to poetry or fiction looking for *her* way of being in the world" "comes up against something that negates everything she is about: she meets the image

of Women in books written by men . . . but precisely what she does not find is . . . herself" ("Re-Vision," in LSS, p. 39).

62. Edna O'Brien, *Girls in Their Married Bliss, The Country Girls Trilogy* (New York: New American Library, 1968), p. 531.

63. Alix Kates Shulman, *Memoirs of an Ex-Prom Queen* (New York: Bantam, 1972), pp. 24, 285, 293.

64. Erica Jong, *How to Save Your Own Life* (New York: Signet, 1977), p. 236.

65. Toni Morrison, *Sula* (New York: New American Library, 1973), p. 52. Nancy K. Miller distinguishes between the "euphoric text" and the "dysphoric text"; *The Heroine's Text: Readings in the French and English Novel, 1722–1782* (New York: Columbia University Press, 1980), p. xi. See also DuPlessis, pp. 1–19.

66. Henry James compares the "happy ending" to the "course of dessert and ices" that follows "a good dinner," "a distribution at the last of prizes, pensions, husbands, wives, babies, millions . . . and cheerful remarks"; "The Art of Fiction" (1888), in *The Art of Fiction and Other Essays* (New York: Oxford University Press, 1948), pp. 3–23, 7.

67. Stephen Heath, *"Touch of Evil,"* *Screen* 16, no. 2 (1975), pp. 91, 16, 1, 49; in Rosalind Coward and John Ellis, *Language and Materialism: Developments in Semiology and the Theory of the Subject* (London: Routledge and Kegan Paul, 1977), p. 49. Leo Bersani also refers to "strategies for containing (and repressing)"; *A Future for Astyanax: Character and Desire in Literature* (Boston: Little Brown, 1976), p. 63.

68. Belsey, *Critical Practice*, p. 80. Nancy K. Miller discusses the laws of probability and possibility that govern closure as a kind of "contract" between writer and reader; "Emphasis Added: Plots and Plausibilities in Women's Fiction," in *PMLA* 96, no. 1 (January 1981), pp. 36–48, 36. However, critiques of realism are often somewhat reductive about nineteenth-century fiction, describing it as simpler, less self-conscious, and more monolithic than it was. See, for example, George Levine, *The Realistic Imagination: English Fiction from Frankenstein to Lady Chatterley* (Chicago: University of Chicago Press, 1981); D. A. Miller, *Narrative and Its Discontents: Problems of Closure in the Traditional Novel* (Princeton: Princeton University Press, 1981); and Margaret Homans, *Bearing the World: Language and Female Experience in Nineteenth-Century Women's Writing* (Chicago: University of Chicago Press, 1986).

69. Alice Walker, *Meridian* (New York: Washington Square Press, 1977), p. 117. This ending persists in contemporary women's fiction—in O'Brien's *Girls in Their Married Bliss*, Muriel Spark's *The Driver's Seat*, Joan Didion's *Play It As It Lays*, Judith Rossner's *Looking for Mr. Goodbar*, Bernice Rubens's *Go Tell the Lemming*, Joyce Carol Oates's "Where Are You Going?" and Lessing's *The Grass Is Singing* and "To Room 19."

70. Fanny Bryant, *Ella Price's Journal* (Berkeley: Ata Books, 1972), p. 84.

71. As Carolyn G. Heilbrun suggests, in *Writing a Woman's Life* (New York: Norton, 1988), pp. 42–43.

72. Barbara Raskin, *Loose Ends* (New York: Bantam, 1973), pp. 312–13.

73. Alan Friedman, *The Turn of the Novel* (New York: Oxford University Press, 1966), pp. xiii, 187.

74. Marianna Torgovnick, *Closure in the Novel* (Princeton: Princeton University Press, 1981), p. 205.

75. Margaret Drabble, *The Realms of Gold* (New York: Knopf, 1975), p. 351.

76. Peter Brooks and others have compared narrative to psychoanalysis: the goal of narrative, as of psychotherapy, is to redescribe reality, to come up with a new story. Narrative re-collects, re-members, re-tells, in order for there to be an escape from repetition, in order for there to be change or progress; *Reading for the Plot: Design and Intention in Narrative* (New York: Vintage, 1985), pp. 98, 235, 285. See also Roy Schafer, "Narration in the Psychoanalytic Dialogue," in *On Narrative*, ed. W. J. T. Mitchell (Chicago: University of Chicago Press, 1981), 25–49. It is not surprising that

this function assumes special importance in fiction that is explicitly concerned with change, as I argue in "Feminist Fiction and the Uses of Memory," *Signs* 16, no. 2 (Winter 1990), pp. 1–32.

77. Introduction, *The Voyage In: Fictions of Female Development,* Elizabeth Abel, Marianne Hirsch, and Elizabeth Langland, eds. (Hanover, NH: University Press of New England, 1983), p. 8. Mary Anne Ferguson, "The Female Novel of Development and the Myth of Psyche," in Abel (1983), pp. 228–43, 228. Carol Pearson and Katherine Pope describe woman's journey as "circuitous, labyrinthine"; *The Female Hero in American and British Literature* (New York: R. R. Bowker, 1981), pp. 77–78; see also Annis Pratt, *Archetypal Patterns in Women's Fiction* (Bloomington: Indiana University Press, 1981), p. 11. Women "voyage within," as the title of Abel's anthology suggests, or "dive deep and surface," as Carol P. Christ's title suggests.

78. Hélène Cixous, "The Laugh of the Medusa," in *Signs* (Summer 1976), rpt. Elaine Marks and Isabelle de Courtivron, eds., *New French Feminisms: An Anthology* (Amherst: University of Massachusetts Press, 1980), pp. 245–64, 247, (hereafter LM).

79. Stephen Jay Gould, *Time's Arrow, Time's Cycle: Myth and Metaphor in the Discovery of Geological Time* (Cambridge: Harvard University Press, 1987). For the association of the linear with the West and the cyclic with the East, see Samuel L. Macey, *Patriarchs of Time: Dualism in Saturn-Cronus, Father Time, the Watchmaker God, and Father Christmas* (Athens, GA: University of Georgia Press, 1987), pp. 165–66; for biblical history as linear, see M. H. Abrams, *Natural Supernaturalism* (New York: Norton, 1971), pp. 32–37. Gould, like Richard Morris (*Time's Arrows* [New York: Simon and Schuster, 1984]) and Mercea Eliade (*The Myth of the Eternal Return* [Princeton: Princeton University Press, 1954] and *Images and Symbols: Studies in Religious Symbolism* [New York: Sheed and Ward, 1961], pp. 72–73), identifies the cyclic with the archaic and the linear with the modern and Western.

80. Julia Kristeva, "Women's Time," in *Signs* 7, no. 1 (1981), pp. 13–35, 16–17. Others who associate cyclic patterns and structures with the "female" include Sydney Janet Kaplan, *Feminine Consciousness in the Modern British Novel* (Chicago: University of Illinois Press, 1975), p. 10; Susan Gubar, "The Representation of Women in Fiction," in *Selected Papers from the English Institute,* New Series, no. 7 (1981), ed. and intro. Carolyn G. Heilbrun and Margaret R. Higonnet (Baltimore: Johns Hopkins University Press, 1981), pp. 19–59, 31; Josephine Donovan, "Toward a Women's Poetics," in *Tulsa Studies in Women's Literature* 3, no. 1/2 (Spring/Fall 1984), pp. 99–110, 102–103; Robbie Pfeufer Kahn, "Women and Time in Childbirth and during Lactation," in *Taking Our Time: Feminist Perspectives on Temporality,* ed. Frieda Johles Forman with Caoran Sowton (Oxford: Pergamon Press, 1988), pp. 20–36, 25; and Jean Wyatt, who associates the circle with the extended family that emerges as a challenge to patriarchal family arrangements in novels by Louisa May Alcott, Marilyn Robinson, Alice Walker, and E. M. Broner; *Reconstructing Desire: The Role of the Unconscious in Women's Reading and Writing* (Chapel Hill: University of North Carolina Press, 1990).

81. Irma Garcia, "Femalear Explorations: Temporality in Women's Writing," in Forman, pp. 161–82, discusses women writers' "refusal to accept time's linearity" (p. 163). DuPlessis analyzes Richardson's refusal of linearity, her challenge of narrative sequence, chronology, and causation as part of her female poetics (WBE, p. 151); Gillian Beer describes the "narrative politics" of Woolf's rejection of linearity; "Beyond Determinism: George Eliot and Virginia Woolf," in *Women Writing and Writing about Women,* ed. Mary Jacobus (New York: Barnes and Noble, 1979), pp. 80–99, 90, 97.

82. *Time and the Novel: The Genealogical Imperative* (Princeton: Princeton University Press, 1978), pp. 13, 6–7. Tobin relates assaults on linearity in twentieth-century fiction wherein the line is replaced "by such wild divergencies as the double cycle, the circle, the spiral, and the Mobius strip" to the "generalized drift away from all authority" (pp. 27, 211).

83. Erika Ostrovsky describes it as "unending annihilation and creation"; "A Cos-

mogony of O: Wittig's *Les Guérillères*," in *Twentieth-Century French Fiction: Essays for Germaine Bree*, ed. George Stambolian (New Brunswick, NJ: Rutgers University Press, 1975), pp. 241–51, 247. Carl Jung, in *Mandala Symbolism* (Princeton: Princeton University Press, 1972), describes the circle or mandala as "the psychological expression of the totality of the self" (p. 20). This is consistent with the symbolism Wyatt describes, of "the preoedipal illusion of completion . . . a unity without beginning or end that seemed to be the truth of things before the self began to emerge from primary identification with the mother." Torgovnick suggests that the circular structure is "one of the most common of closural patterns" and it may signify growth or stasis or nothing at all (pp. 13, 199–200); only in combination with particular content does it assume particular meaning.

84. Monique Wittig, *Les Guérillères* (Boston: Beacon, 1985), p. 114.

85. Héléne Cixous, "Castration or Decapitation?" in *Signs* 7, no. 1 (Summer 1981), pp. 41–55, 53. This same sense of the dual potential of circles turns up in a contemporary Soviet writer, Lidia Ginzburg, "Notes of a Blockade Survivor" (*Neva*, no. 1, [1984], 84–108), where the circle symbolizes both "consciousness locked within itself" and the writing which breaks through the blockage—"To write about the circle is to break the circle"—much as it does in the *Kunstlerromane* I discuss. I am indebted to Sally Pratt for this observation and for this translation.

86. Irigaray, *This Sex Which Is Not One*, trans. Catherine Porter, (Ithaca: Cornell University Press, 1985), "Questions," pp. 119–69, 134–35; "The Power of Discourse and the Subordination of the Feminine," pp. 68–85, p. 68. Irigaray is referring to the shape of her own *Speculum of the Other Woman*. She also describes women's speech as involving "a different economy," "one that upsets the linearity of a project, undermines the goal-object" ("This Sex Which Is Not One," in *This Sex*, pp. 23–33, 29–30), and in terms of fluids or streams, "without fixed banks . . . without fixed boundaries" ("When Our Lips Speak Together," in *This Sex*, pp. 205–18)—terms that are germane to Drabble's *The Waterfall*.

87. Alice Jardine defines gynesis as "the putting into discourse of 'woman'" ("Gynesis," in *Diacritics* [Summer 1982], pp. 54–65, 58) but notes that "'woman' does not necessarily mean the biological female in history," but rather "those *processes* that disrupt symbolic structures in the West"; *Gynesis: Configurations of Woman and Modernity* (Ithaca: Cornell University Press, 1985), p. 42. See also Abel (1983), p. 184, and WBE *passim*.

88. Ellen Moers, *Literary Women: The Great Writers* (Garden City, NY: Anchor Press, Doubleday, 1977), pp. 389ff.

89. Steven G. Kellmann, "The Fiction of Self-Begetting," *Modern Language Notes* 91 (December 1976), pp. 1243–56, 1245.

90. *The Madwoman in the Attic: The Woman Writer and the Nineteenth-Century Literary Imagination* (New Haven: Yale University Press, 1979), pp. 43–46.

91. Heilbrun notes that women writers usually deny their women characters the strengths that they themselves have (p. 55). Atwood speculates that Austen and Eliot never made protagonists writers because "they felt themselves, as woman writers, to be so exceptional as to lack credibility" ("The Curse of Eve," SW, p. 219). See also Gilbert and Gubar, p. 69.

92. Marilyn French, *Her Mother's Daughter* (New York: Summit Books, 1987), p. 427. For the significance of journals in women's lives, see Suzanne Juhazs, "Towards a Theory of Form in Feminist Autobiography," in *Women's Autobiography*, ed. Estelle C. Jelinek (Bloomington: Indiana University Press, 1980).

93. All four of these writers have children—which is a departure from the pattern set by the Brontës, Austen, Eliot, and Woolf—and all make motherhood a central fictional focus. Atwood, however, is the only one who has stayed with the father of her children, Graeme Gibson, an they are unmarried. Laurence married, at twenty-three, an engineer, Jack Laurence, had two children, and remained married for thirteen years, but the

marriage came apart over her writing (DOE, pp. 128, 159). After their separation she retained custody of the children but never remarried. Lessing married, at nineteen, Charles Wisdom, a civil servant; she divorced him four years later, leaving their two children with him; she was married to Gottfried Anton Lessing, a German refugee and Marxist, for four years, had a son with him, left him to come to London in 1949, bringing their son with her; and did not remarry. Just out of college, in 1960, Drabble married Clive Swift, an actor, but they separated after twelve years of marriage and she retained custody of their three children. She is now married to biographer Michael Holyroyd; they keep separate residences.

94. Robin Morgan begins her 1970 anthology *Sisterhood Is Powerful* with the statement "This book is an action." Introduction, *Sisterhood Is Powerful: An Anthology of Writings from the Women's Liberation Movement* (New York: Vintage, 1970), p. xv. For this sense among minority women writers, see Chapter IX, n. 14.

95. Dale Spender, *For the Record: The Making and Meaning of Feminist Knowledge* (London: The Women's Press, 1985), p. 99. Sheila Rowbotham, *Woman's Consciousness, Man's World* (Harmondsworth: Penguin, 1973), describes women as "immigrants into alien territory" (p. 31).

96. The term is Gilbert and Gubar's. *The Norton Anthology of Literature by Women: The Tradition in English* (New York: Norton, 1985), p. 1678.

97. Lorna Sage describes Lessing as a "demystifier" or "critical observer of social processes and systems"; *Contemporary Writers: Doris Lessing* (London: Methuen, 1983), pp. 11, 24. Susan Lardner describes her as "an exile, a philosophical hobo, temperamentally restless"; "Angle on the Ordinary," in *New Yorker* (September 19, 1983), pp. 140–54, 140.

98. "In the Heart of Literary London," by David Plante, *New York Times Magazine* (September 11, 1988), pp. 42ff, 80.

99. Morris Dickstein, *Gates of Eden: American Culture in the Sixties* (New York: Penguin, 1989), pp. 35–36.

100. Teresa de Lauretis, "The Technology of Gender," in *Technologies of Gender* (Bloomington: Indiana University Press, 1987), pp. 1–30, 25.

101. Wallace Martin, *Recent Theories of Narrative* (Ithaca: Cornell University Press, 1986), p. 69. Walter L. Reed describes the novel as "inherently anti-traditional," "suspicious of its own literariness," "oppos[ing] the forms of everyday life, social and psychological, to the conventional forms of literature"; *An Exemplary History of the Novel: The Quixotic versus the Picaresque* (Chicago: University of Chicago Press, 1981), pp. 3–4.

102. See Robert Alter, *Partial Magic: The Novel as a Self-Conscious Genre* (Berkeley: University of California Press, 1975). Carla L. Peterson discusses "the debate over book reading and, most particularly, novel reading" that took place within the nineteenth-century novel; *The Determined Reader: Gender and Culture in the Novel from Napoleon to Victoria* (New Brunswick: Rutgers University Press, 1985), p. 19.

103. Julia Kristeva defines "intertextuality" in "Breaching the Thetic: Mimesis," *Revolution in Poetic Language,* Leon S. Roudiez ed. and intro. (New York: Columbia University Press, 1984), pp. 57–61, 59–60. See also *Desire in Language: A Semiotic Approach to Literature and Art* (New York: Columbia University Press, 1980), introduction, p. 15.

104. If we accept Brian McHale's distinction between Modernist and postmodernist fiction as the difference between epistemological and ontological concerns, they are more Modernist than postmodernist; *Postmodernist Fiction* (New York: Methuen, 1987), pp. 9–10.

105. *The Other Side of the Story: Structures and Strategies of Contemporary Feminist Narratives* (Ithaca: Cornell University Press, 1989), p. 2. See also Patricia Waugh, *Feminine Fictions: Revisiting the Postmodern* (London: Routledge, 1989), p. 169. As Linda Anderson suggests, "Juxtaposing stories with other stories or opening up the

potentiality for multiple stories . . . frees the woman writer from the coercive fictions of her culture that pass as truth" and points to "an imagined elsewhere, unacknowledged alternatives, other stories waiting silently to be told." Ed. *Plotting Change: Contemporary Women's Fiction* (London: Edward Arnold, 1990), pp. vii–viii.

106. *Literature against Itself: Literary Ideas in Modern Society* (Chicago: University of Chicago Press, 1979), pp. 239, 20. Graff, however, seems oblivious that his injunctions have any relevance to feminist fiction.

107. Mary Jacobus, "The Difference of View," in *Women Writing and Writing about Women*, ed. Jacobus (New York: Barnes and Noble, 1979), pp. 10–20, 14. As Irigaray says, "If we keep on speaking the same language together, we're going to reproduce the same history. Begin the same old stories all over again" ("When Our Lips Speak Together," p. 205). As Audre Lorde asserts, *"the master's tools will never dismantle the master's house";* "The Master's Tools Will Never Dismantle the Master's House," in Moraga and Anzaldúa, pp. 98–101, 99.

108. Kristeva, though skeptical of *l'écriture féminine*, maintains that women's experience of *jouissance*—pleasures repressed by patriarchal culture—and her access to the preoedipal "semiotic" can be the source of subversive energy and an alternative discourse (1984, especially Part I, "The Semiotic and the Symbolic").

109. As critics of Franco-feminist positions have pointed out, the assumption that the female body provides access to a prelinguistic authenticity, a place outside discourse and ideology, implies an essentialism which is hardly less reactionary than Anglo-American empiricism. See Ann Rosalind Jones, "Writing the Body; Toward an Understanding of *l'Écriture féminine*," in Elaine Showalter, *The New Feminist Criticism: Essays on Women, Literature and Theory* (New York: Pantheon, 1985), pp. 361–77; and Felski, pp. 33–40.

110. For differences between Anglo-American and French feminism, see Margaret Homans, "'Her Very Own Howl': The Ambiguities of Representation in Recent Women's Fiction," in *Signs* 9, no. 2 (1983), pp. 186–205, 186–87; Toril Moi's critique of Cixous and Irigaray, in *Sexual/Textual Politics* (New York: Methuen, 1985), pp. 119–26, 138–40, 142–49, Jardine, 1985, *passim;* Elaine Marks, "Women and Literature in France," in *Signs* 3, no. 4 (1978); Greene and Kahn, pp. 25–26. Betsy Draine provides a useful summary of this debate; "Refusing the Wisdom of Solomon: Some Recent Feminist Literary Theory," in *Signs* 15, no. 1 (Autumn 1989), pp. 144–70.

111. Elaine Showalter, "Feminist Criticism in the Wilderness," in *Critical Inquiry* 8, no. 2 (1981), pp. 179–205, 184–85.

112. Belief in referentiality is itself—as Jane Gallop puts it—"politically conservative, because it cannot recognize that the reality to which it appeals is a traditional ideological construction"; *"Quand nos lèvres se parlent:* Irigaray's Body Politic," in *Romantic Review* 74, no. 1 (January 1983), p. 83.

113. Mary Jacobus, "The Question of Language: Men of Maxims and *The Mill on the Floss*," in *Writing and Sexual Difference, Critical Inquiry*, ed. Elizabeth Abel (Winter 1981), pp. 8, 2, 207–23, 210. As Toril Moi says, "There is no *other space* from which we can speak" (p. 170).

114. Waugh suggests that the popularity of such novels as *Fear of Flying* and *Kinflicks* meant that "the more subversive (though less ostentatious) reexamination of plot and construction and subjectivity" by less explicitly feminist writers was "ignored or misrepresented by the literary establishment" (1989, p. 26). One might add that the subtler and more subversive forms of feminist fiction were overlooked even by feminist critics, whose definitions, like Felski's, are based on the simpler forms. Thus, Chikwenye Okonjo Ogunyemi describes a "protest literature" which portrays "the struggle of a victim or rebel" with "a patriarchal institution," leading "to female victory in a feminist utopia or a stasis signifying the failure to eliminate sexism" ("Womanism: The Dynamics of the Contemporary Black Female Novel in English," in *Signs* [1985], pp. 11, 1, 63–80, 64–65); Deborah S. Rosenfelt describes a "progress from oppression, suffering, vic-

timization, through various stages of awakening consciousness, to active resistance, and finally . . . to some form of victory, transformation or transcendence of despair" ("Feminism, Postfeminism, and Contemporary Women's Fiction," in *Tradition and the Talent of Women,* ed. Florence Howe [Urbana: University of Illinois Press, forthcoming]). Feminist fiction as I define it is a more complex form than this.

115. Annette Kuhn distinguishes between two types of "cultural practice, one which tends to take processes of signification for granted and one which argues that the meaning production is itself the site of struggle" and defines a "feminist signifying practice" as one where "the ideological character of the signification process is regarded as itself something to be challenged"; *Women's Pictures: Feminism and Cinema* (London: Routledge and Kegan Paul, 1982), pp. 17–18.

116. Barthes contrasts the "readerly" mode of realism, which is "product" and "can only be read," with the "writerly" text, which invites the reader into the process of production and which, as process and capable of being "written" or "produced," is capable of accommodating change (*S/Z*, pp. 4–5).

117. Josette Feral describes the woman writer as "borrowing forms and structures from the established discourse . . . in order to disrupt them"; "The Power of Difference," in *The Future of Difference,* ed. Hester Eisenstein and Alice Jardine (New Brunswick: Rutgers University Press, 1985), pp. 88–94, 93; Toril Moi describes a " 'deconstructive' form of writing as one that engages with and thereby exposes the duplicitous nature of discourse" (p. 9); DuPlessis discusses "feminine aesthetic" as "strategies born in struggle with already existing culture" (DuPlessis and Members of Workshop 9, "For the Etruscans: Sexual Difference and Artistic Production—The Debate over a Female Aesthetic," Eisenstein, pp. 128–56; rpt. Showalter, 1985, pp. 271–91, 275); Jardine refers to "a new kind of feminist hermeneutics . . . capable of self-reflection on its own complicity with inherited systems of representation" (1985, p. 63). Homans describes contemporary women's novels as "simultaneously appropriating and rejecting the dominant discourse" (1983, p. 205) and does refer to actual texts by women, though not to the texts I discuss.

118. DuPlessis describes feminist aesthetic in terms of the absence of telos, the preference of process over product ("Etruscans," p. 287); Jane Marcus also suggests a "Penelope aesthetic" characterized by process which "does not separate art from work and daily life"; "Still Practice, A/Wrested Alphabet: Toward a Feminist Aesthetic," in *Tulsa Studies,* pp. 79–97, 84ff.

119. Drawing on discussions of female identity in terms of boundary fluidity by Nancy Chodorow (*The Reproduction of Mothering: Psychoanalysis and the Sociology of Gender* [Berkeley: University of California Press, 1978]) and others, Judith Kegan Gardiner suggests that "the processual nature of female identity illuminates diverse traits of writing by women"; "On Female Identity and Writing by Women," in Elizabeth Abel, ed. *Critical Inquiry, Writing and Sexual Difference* 8, no. 2 (1981), pp. 347–61, 349. Elizabeth Abel, "[E]merging Identities: The Dynamics of Female Friendship in Contemporary Fiction by Women," *Signs* 6 (1981), pp. 413–35, posits "a theory of influence to balance Bloom's," a theory which is more consistent with women's "flexible ego boundaries and relational self-definition" and is characterized by a "willingness to absorb literary influence instead of defending the poetic self from it" (pp. 432–33). DuPlessis describes the "looping back" of female quest plots in terms of "the 'bisexual oscillation' " between oedipal and preoedipal and a "loop[ing] backward to mother–child attachments" (WBE, p. 37).

120. Lee Edwards, *Psyche as Hero: Female Heroism and Fictional Form* (Middletown, CT: Wesleyan University Press, 1984).

121. Joanne S. Frye, *Living Stories, Telling Lives: Women and the Novel in Contemporary Experience* (Ann Arbor: University of Michigan Press, 1986), pp. 16, 36, 55.

122. Nina Baym, "Melodramas of Beset Manhood: How Theories of American

Fiction Exclude Women Authors," in *The New Feminist Criticism: Essays on Women, Literature, Theory,* ed. Elaine Showalter (New York: Pantheon, 1985), pp. 63–80, 71. See also Quentin Anderson, "The Emergence of Modernism," in *Columbia Literary History of the U.S.,* ed. Emory Elliott (New York: Columbia University Press, 1988), pp. 695–714, 701 (hereafter CLH).

123. Bernard Bergonzi, *The Situation of the Novel* (Pittsburgh: University of Pittsburgh Press, 1970), p. 42; "The heroes of American novels are defiant solitaries, preserving their precious innocence and freedom" (p. 81). Bergonzi cites Leslie Fielder, Richard Poirier, and R. W. B. Lewis. Lionel Trilling also describes the "resistance" of American writers "to looking closely at society"; "Manners, Morals, and the Novel" (1947), in *The Liberal Imagination* (New York: Doubleday, 1953), pp. 199–215, 206–207.

124. Charles Molesworth, "Culture, Power, and Society," in CLH, pp. 1023–44, 1037–38.

125. Toni Morrison has said that "avoiding politics, avoiding social implications, is de rigueur in this country [in "mainstream" novels] and there's some sort of feeling that if any novel is political then it's propaganda or it's harangue and it's somehow not art." Interview by Kay Benetti, American Audio Prose Library, May 1983, New York City.

126. Sylvia Plath, *The Bell Jar* (New York: Bantam, 1981), p. 199; Anne Richardson Roiphe, *Up the Sandbox* (New York: Simon and Schuster, 1970), p. 99; Johanna Davis, *Life Signs* (New York: Dell, 1973), p. 169.

127. Though it does seem paradoxical that the more communally oriented traditions of England and Canada produced writers more reluctant to identify with organized feminism than American women writers have been, this may be because the movement originated in the United States and only later moved to England and Canada: Atwood and Drabble came to it later and more circumspectly, and with a certain disdain for its bandwagon potentials. Thus, the protagonist of Drabble's *The Middle Ground* (New York: Bantam, 1980) is appalled at "the commercial exploitation of Women" and mentions (though not by name) the "best-selling angry feminist novel" that characterized "woman's lot" as " 'shit and string beans' " (p. 33)—French's *Women's Room.*

128. See WBE, p. 156. DuPlessis quotes Alice Walker, *Interview with Black Women Writers,* ed. John O'Brien (New York: Liverright, 1973), p. 192. Morrison says, "If anything I do, in the way of writing novels . . . isn't about the village or the community . . . then it is not about anything . . . the work must be political"; "Rootedness: The Ancestor as Foundation," in *Black Women Writers, 1950–1980,* ed. Mari Evans (New York: Doubleday, 1984), pp. 339–45, 344. For community in Afro-American fiction, see Susan Willis, "Black Women Writers: Taking a Critical Perspective," in Greene and Kahn, pp. 211–37, 212–19; and *Specifying* (Madison: University of Wisconsin Press, 1987).

129. Marshall enlists circle imagery in a way similar to that of the *Kunstlerromane* I discuss, to suggest forces that confine her protagonist by connecting her to the Barbadian community, but which are also potentially liberating. Selina's task is to transform the "ruinous circle" and "oppressive round" of the past into a liberatory form which allows release; and she forges a new form in her dance, "the life cycle." In the pattern characteristic of feminist fiction, change is accomplished by a return to the past, as Selina sets out at the end for Barbados in order to make a new future. *Brown Girl, Brownstones* (Old Westbury, NY: The Feminist Press, 1981), pp. 263, 310.

130. *New Review,* pp. 31–32. Toni Morrison says, "It seems to me there's an enormous difference in the writing of black and white women" (interview with Claudia Tate, *Black Women Writers at Work,* ed. Claudia Tate [New York: Continuum, 1983], pp. 117–31, 122). Chikwenye Okonjo Ogunyemi calls black women's fiction "womanist" rather than "feminist" and describes its politics as "more complex than white sexual politics, for it addresses more directly the ultimate question relating to power: how do

we share equitably the world's wealth and concomitant power among the races and between the sexes?" (p. 68). Her sense of feminist fiction, however, is based on the simplest form of feminist fiction.

131. David Jeffrey, "Biblical Hermeneutic and Family History in Contemporary Canadian Fiction: Wiebe and Laurence," in *Mosaic* 11, no. 3 (Spring 1978), pp. 87–106, 87. Patricia Morley, *Margaret Laurence* (Boston: G. K. Hall, Twayne, 1981), also describes this "concern for community" in Canadian literature, where the individual traditionally finds greatest freedom in an alliance with the social order (pp. 146–47). Dick Harrison contrasts the American frontier myth, which is "dependent on the individual in relative isolation," with the Canadian Garden myth, which assumes "a tradition of law and order"; "Cultural Insanity and Prairie Fiction," in *Figures in a Ground: Canadian Essays on Modern Literature Collected in Honour of Sheila Watson,* Diane Bessai and David Jackel, eds. (Saskatoon, 1978), p. 148; in Morley, p. 278.

132. Interview with Margaret Atwood, in *Eleven Canadian Novelists,* Graeme Gibson (Toronto: Anansi, 1973), pp. 5–31, 14. "In Canada in the 1950's there was no context for writers. We did a lot of inventing" (letter to Gayle Greene).

133. There are many more serious contemporary women novelists than could be included in one study, even a study which attempted to be comprehensive—which this does not (e.g., Zoe Fairbairns, Louise Erdrich, Marian Engels, Mavis Gallant, Jane Rule, Joan Barfoot, Anne Tyler, A. S. Byatt, Penelope Lively, Anita Brookner, Joan Didion, Cynthia Ozick, Anne Beattie, Joan Chase, Marilyn Robinson, Bobbie Ann Mason, Carolyn Chute, Joanna Russ, Margaret Walker, Toni Cade Bambara, Gloria Naylor, Marianne Wiggins, Elizabeth Jolley, Cynthia Proper Seton, Alice Hoffman, Kate Braverman, Diane Johnson, Rosellen Brown, Carolyn See, Rebecca Hill, Mary Wesley, Nadine Gordimer, and Bessie Head, to name only a few). There are very few, however, who try to render that nexus between individual and collective, between consciousness and history, that interests me.

134. Quoted in Randall Stevenson, *The British Novel since the Thirties: An Introduction* (Athens, GA: University of Georgia Press, 1986), p. 183.

135. To list them is to make a point about the extraordinary development of feminist criticism: Sydney Janet Kaplan, *Feminine Consciousness in the Modern British Novel* (1975); Patricia Meyer Spacks, *The Female Imagination* (1975); Elaine Showalter, *A Literature of Their Own* (1977); Anthea Zeman, *Presumptuous Girls: Women and Their World in the Serious Woman's Novel* (1977); Barbara Hill Rigney, *Madness and Sexual Politics in the Feminist Novel* (1978); Anne Z. Mickelson, *Reaching Out: Sensitivity and Order in Recent American Fiction by Women* (1978); Carol P. Christ, *Diving Deep and Surfacing: Women Writers on Spiritual Quest* (1980); Grace Stewart, *A New Mythos: The Novel of the Artist as Heroine, 1877–1977* (1981); Carol Pearson and Katherine Pope, *The Female Hero in American and British Literature* (1981); Annis Pratt, *Archetypal Patterns in Women's Fiction* (1981); Linda Huf, *A Portrait of the Artist as a Young Woman: The Writer as Heroine in American Literature* (1983); Blanche H. Gelfant, *Women Writing in America: Voices in Collage* (1984); Lee Edwards, *Psyche as Hero: Female Heroism and Fictional Form* (1984); Rachel Blau DuPlessis, *Writing Beyond the Ending: Narrative Strategies of Twentieth-Century Women Writers* (1985); Catherine Rainwater and William J. Scheick, eds. *Contemporary American Women Writers: Narrative Strategies* (1985); Shari Benstock, *Women of the Left Bank: Paris, 1900–1940* (1986); Joanne S. Frye, *Living Stories, Telling Lives: Women and the Novel in Contemporary Experience* (1986); Mary V. Dearborn, *Pocahontas's Daughters: Gender and Ethnicity in American Culture* (1986); Esther Kleinbord Labovitz, *The Myth of the Heroine: The Female Bildungsroman in the Twentieth Century* (1986); Bonnie St. Andrews, *Forbidden Fruit: On the Relationship between Women and Knowledge in Doris Lessing, Selma Lagerlof, Kate Chopin, Margaret Atwood* (1986); Thelma J. Shinn, *Worlds within Women: Myth and Mythmaking in Fantastic Literature by Women* (1986); Roberta Rubenstein, *Boundaries of*

the Self: Gender, Culture, Fiction; Coral Ann Howells, *Private and Fictional Worlds* (1987); Hazel V. Carby, *Reconstructing Womanhood: The Emergence of the Afro-American Woman Novelist* (1987); Charlotte Spivack, *Merlin's Daughters: Contemporary Women Writers of Fantasy* (1987); Marleen Barr, *Alien to Femininity: Speculative Fiction and Feminist Theory* (1987); Patricia S. Yaeger, *Honey-Mad Women: Emancipatory Strategies in Women's Writing* (1988); Sandra M. Gilbert and Susan Gubar, *No Man's Land: The Place of the Woman Writer in the Twentieth Century* (1988); Olga Kenyon, *Women Novelists Today: A Survey of English Writing in the Seventies and Eighties* (1988); Gilbert and Gubar, *No Man's Land*, vol. 2, *Sexchanges* (1989); Michael Awkward, *Inspiriting Influences: Tradition, Revision, and Afro-American Women's Novels* (1989); Rita Felski, *Beyond Feminist Aesthetics: Feminist Literature and Social Change* (1989); Molly Hite, *The Other Side of the Story: Structures and Strategies of Contemporary Feminist Narratives* (1989); Patricia Waugh, *Feminine Fictions: Revisiting the Postmodern* (1989); Niamh Baker, *Happily Ever After? Women's Fiction in Postwar Britain, 1945–1960* (1989); Flora Alexander, *Contemporary Women Novelists* (1989); Nicola Beauman, *A Very Great Profession: The Woman's Novel, 1914–39* (1989); Jean Wyatt, *Reconstructing Desire: The Role of the Unconscious in Women's Reading and Writing* (1990); Amy Ling, *Between Worlds: Women Writers of Chinese Ancestry* (1990).

## II. Women Writing in the Twentieth Century

1. Julia Kristeva, "Women's Time," in *Signs* 7, no. 1 (1981), pp. 13–35, 32.

2. John Holloway, "The Literary Scene," in *The New Pelican Guide to English Literature: The Present,* ed. Boris Ford (Harmondsworth: Penguin, 1984), pp. 417–49, 124.

3. Ellen Moers, "Angry Young Women," in *Harper's* (December 1963), pp. 227, 89–97, 88–89.

4. Ellen Moers, *Literary Women: The Great Writers* (Garden City, NY: Anchor Press, Doubleday, 1977), p. xvii.

5. Elaine Showalter, *A Literature of Their Own: British Women Novelists from Bronte to Lessing* (London: Virago, 1978), p. 35.

6. Carolyn G. Heilbrun cites 1973 as a "turning point" because there seemed to be a lifting of the prohibition against anger and anger is necessary to finding voice; *Writing a Woman's Life* (New York: Norton, 1988), pp. 12–13, 15.

7. E.g., Toni Morrison's *The Bluest Eye,* Maya Angelou's *I Know Why the Caged Bird Sings,* Joan Didion's *Play It As It Lays,* Alison Lurie's *Real People,* Anne Richardson Roiphe's *Up the Sandbox* (1970), Alice Munro's *Lives of Girls and Women,* Fay Weldon's *Down among the Women,* Renata Adler's *Speedboat,* Joyce Carol Oates's *Wonderland* (1971), Dorothy Bryant's *Ella Price's Journal,* Elizabeth Ayrton's *Two Years in My Afternoon* (1972), Rita Mae Brown's *Rubyfruit Jungle,* Barbara Raskin's *Loose Ends,* May Sarton's *As We Are Now,* Rhoda Lerman's *Call me Ishtar,* Johanna Davis's *Life Signs,* Blanche Boyd's *Nerves* (1973), Beryl Bainbridge's *The Bottle-Factory Outing,* Angela Carter's *Fireworks,* Lois Gould's *Final Analysis,* Sue Kaufman's *Falling Bodies,* Penelope Mortimer's *Long Distance,* Tillie Olsen's *Yonnonidio: From The Thirties,* Munro's *Something I've Been Meaning to Tell You,* Kate Millett's *Flying* (1974), Lisa Alther's *Kinflicks,* Lurie's *The War between the Tates,* Kay Boyle's *The Underground Woman,* E. M. Broner's *Her Mothers,* Gayl Jones's *Corregidora,* Judith Rossner's *Looking for Mr. Goodbar,* Marianne Hauser's *The Talking Room,* Verena Steffan's *Shedding* (1975), Atwood's *Lady Oracle,* June Arnold's *The Cook and the Carpenter,* Alice Walker's *Meridian,* Marge Piercy's *Woman on the Edge of Time,* Weldon's *Remember Me* (1976), Drabble's *The Ice Age,* Erica Jong's *How to Save Your Own Life,* Didion's *A Book of Common Prayer,* Munro's *The Beggar Maid,* Gould's *A Sea Change,* Leslie Marmon Silko's *Ceremony,* Weldon's *Words of Advice,* Marilyn

French's *The Women's Room* (1977), Weldon's *Praxis,* Sally Gearhart's *The Wanderground,* Russ's *The Two of Them* (1978), Kate Braverman's *Lithium for Medea,* A. S. Byatt's *The Virgin in the Garden,* Jayne Anne Phillips's *Black Tickets,* Zoe Fairbairns's *Benefits* (1979). In addition to these are eight novels by Iris Murdoch (*A Fairly Honourable Defeat,* 1970; *An Accidental Man,* 1971; *The Black Prince,* 1973; *The Sacred and Profane Love Machine,* 1974; *A Word Child,* 1975; *Henry and Cato,* 1976; *The Sea, The Sea,* 1978; *Nuns and Soldiers,* 1980); six by Muriel Spark (*The Driver's Seat,* 1970; *Not to Disturb,* 1971; *The Hothouse by the East River,* 1973; *The Abbess of Crewe,* 1974; *The Takeover,* 1976; *Territorial Rights,* 1978); and three, besides those mentioned, by Lessing (*Briefing for a Descent into Hell,* 1971; *Shikasta,* 1979; *The Marriages between Zones Three, Four, and Five,* 1980).

8. "The Small Personal Voice," in *A Small Personal Voice: Essays, Reviews, Interviews,* ed. Paul Schleuter (New York: Vintage, 1972), pp. 3–21, 14–15 (hereafter SPV).

9. Elizabeth Sifton, interview with Mary McCarthy, in *Women Writers at Work, The Paris Review Interviews,* ed. George Plimpton (New York: Viking Penguin, 1989), pp. 169–99, 189–90.

10. "Women Who Write Are Women," *New York Times Book Review* (December 16, 1984), p. 31; Showalter quotes Mailer's *Advertisements for Myself.*

11. *The Golden Notebook* (New York: Bantam, 1963), pp. 333, 167.

12. Nancy F. Cott, *The Grounding of Modern Feminism* (New Haven: Yale University Press, 1987), p. 218.

13. *Harper's,* vol. XCXXV (October 1962), pp. 115–16; quoted in William Chafe, *The American Woman: Her Changing Social, Economic, and Political Roles, 1920–1970* (London: Oxford University Press, 1972), p. 226.

14. Judith Hole and Ellen Levine, *Rebirth of Feminism* (New York: Quadrangle, 1971), p. 81.

15. See Dale Spender, *For the Record: The Making and Meaning of Feminist Knowledge* (London: The Women's Press, 1985), p. 24.

16. Dee Preussner, "Talking with Margaret Drabble," in *Modern Fiction Studies 25,* no. 4 (Winter 1979–80), pp. 563–77, 568. See Lois Gould's *The Final Analysis* (New York: Avon, 1974), p. 41; Valerie Miner's *Movement* (New York: Methuen, 1982), p. 116; Dorothy Bryant's *Ella Price's Journal* (Berkeley: Ata, 1972), p. 88. Lessing's influence on Drabble's *The Waterfall* and Jong's *Fear of Flying* is discussed in later chapters.

17. *Martha Quest* (New York: New American Library, 1964), p. 10. All references to *The Children of Violence* novels are to the New American Library editions and are referred to as MQ, PM (*A Proper Marriage*), and FGC (*The Four-Gated City*).

18. Grace Stewart, *A New Mythos: The Novel of the Artist as Heroine, 1877–1977* (Montreal: Eden Press, 1981), p. 181.

19. For Woolf's adaptation of Modernist strategies to feminist politics, see Patricia Waugh, *Feminine Fictions: Revisiting the Postmodern* (London: Routledge, 1989), pp. 88–125. Showalter discusses the "deliberate female aesthetic" of Richardson and Mansfield (1977, p. 33); Gilbert and Gubar describe the stylistic innovations of Richardson, Stein, and Barnes as providing what Woolf termed "a woman's sentence," "employing the experimental strategies of male modernists to . . . feminist goals"; *The Norton Anthology of Literature by Women: The Tradition in English* (New York: Norton, 1985), pp. 1240–41; and DuPlessis analyzes Richardson's "lack of a 'story' " as a deliberate part of her "poetics of fiction, given the fact that 'story' for women has typically meant plots of seduction, courtship"; *Writing beyond the Ending* (Bloomington: Indiana University Press, 1985), p. 151.

20. "Approximately" because the first wave of feminism ended shortly after the vote was won, in 1920—the turning of the tide is usually placed at mid-decade, as Barbara Sinclair Deckard suggests (*The Women's Movement: Political, Socioeconomic, and*

*Psychological Issues* [Riverside: University of California, 1983], pp. 285, 295)—whereas Modernism had a longer run, lasting throughout the decade.

21. See Alan Bullock, "The Double Image," in *Modernism,* ed. Malcolm Bradbury and James McFarlane (Harmondsworth: Penguin, 1976), pp. 58–70.

22. Spender, quoted in Randall Stevenson, *The British Novel since the Thirties: An Introduction* (Athens, GA: The University of Georgia Press, 1986), p. 21; D. H. Lawrence, *England, My England* (London: M. Secker, 1924), p. 32; Woolf, "Mr. Bennet and Mrs Brown," *The Captain's Death Bed and Other Essays* (New York: Harcourt, Brace, Jovanovich, 1950), p. 96. "Many . . . were . . . convinced that they were living at the beginning of a new age . . . that they were developing new ways of looking . . . new ways of understanding . . . new forms of expression" (Bradbury and McFarlane, p. 68).

23. For his "consecration of an 'orthodox' tradition," see Gilbert and Gubar (1988, pp. 154–55). Eliot's longing for lost certainties led him to idealize classical, Christian, and Renaissance traditions, and eventually to embrace Anglicanism; Pound and Lawrence were drawn to extreme forms of authoritarianism; and Joyce, to an aestheticism as fanatical as the Catholicism he renounced.

24. See Susan Stanford Friedman's description of Modernist artists' attempts "to fill the gaps left by established church and state"; *Psyche Reborn: The Emergence of H. D.* (Bloomington: Indiana University Press, 1981), p. 207. Victor Turner notes that "where historical life itself fails to make cultural sense in terms that formerly held good, narrative and cultural drama may have the task of . . . *remaking* cultural sense, even when they seem to be dismantling ancient edifices of meaning that can no longer redress our modern 'dramas of living' "; "Social Dramas and Stories about Them," in *On Narrative,* ed. W. J. T. Mitchell (Chicago: University of Chicago Press, 1981), pp. 137–64, 164.

25. Malcolm Bradbury and James McFarlane, "The Name and Nature of Modernism," in *Modernism,* ed. Bradbury and McFarlane, pp. 19–55, 48–49.

26. Lawrence Durrell, interview with Malcolm Cowley, ed. *Writers at Work: The "Paris Review" Interviews* (London: Secker and Warburg, 1963), p. 21; quoted in Stevenson, p. 205; see also Bernard Bergonzi, *The Situation of the Novel* (Pittsburgh: University of Pittsburgh Press, 1970), p. 194.

27. Maurice Beebe, *Ivory Towers and Sacred Founts: The Artist as Hero in Fiction from Goethe to Joyce* (New York: New York University Press, 1964), p. 4.

28. See Lynne Segal, *Is the Future Female? Troubled Thoughts on Contemporary Feminism* (London: Virago, 1987), pp. 206, 69, 57–58.

29. Michelene Wandor, *Once a Feminist: Stories of a Generation* (London: Virago, 1990), p. 3 (hereafter OAF).

30. Fay Weldon, *Down among the Women* (Harmondsworth: Penguin, 1985), p. 118.

31. "Margaret Drabble: Cautious Feminist," interview by Diana Cooper-Clark, in *Atlantic Monthly* (November 1980), pp. 245–46, 69–75, 71; Margaret Drabble, "Doris Lessing: Cassandra in a World under Siege," in *Ramparts* (February 1972), pp. 50–55, 52.

32. As Alicia Ostriker remarks, Prufrock may yearn to be Hamlet, but what woman would want to be Ophelia? "The Thieves of Language: Women Poets and Revisionist Mythmaking," in *The New Feminist Criticism: Essays on Women, Literature, and Theory,* ed. Elaine Showalter (New York: Pantheon, 1985), pp. 314–38, 330. Margaret Laurence's description of her fiction as an "attempt to assimilate the past, partly in order to be freed from it" applies generally to feminist fiction; *Heart of a Stranger* (Toronto: McClelland and Stewart, 1976), p. 14.

33. As I argue in "Feminist Fiction and the Uses of Memory," in *Signs* (Winter 1990).

34. Feminist critics are demonstrating how important women writers were to Modernism (e.g., Sandra M. Gilbert and Susan Gubar, *No Man's Land: The Place of the Woman Writer in the Twentieth Century,* volume 1, *The War of the Words* [New

Haven: Yale University Press, 1988], and volume 2, *Sexchanges* [New Haven: Yale University Press, 1989]; Shari Benstock, *Women of the Left Bank: Paris, 1900–1940* [Austin: University of Texas Press, 1987], pp. 24–34; and Gillian Hanscombe and Virginia L. Smyers, *Writing for Their Lives: The Modernist Women, 1910–1940* [Boston: Northeastern University Press, 1987], p. xvii)—but their work has not been assimilated into mainstream literary histories.

35. David Daiches, *The Present Age in British Literature* (Bloomington: Indiana University Press, 1958), p. 2.

36. Philip Stevick, "Scheherezade runs out of plots, goes on talking; the King, puzzled, listens: an Essay on New Fiction," *Triquarterly* (1973); rpt. in *The Novel Today: Contemporary Writers on Modern Fiction*, ed. Malcolm Bradbury (Totowa, NJ: Rowman and Littlefield, 1977), pp. 186–216, 214–15.

37. Malcolm Bradbury, *The Modern American Novel* (Oxford: Oxford University Press, 1984), pp.. 187–95.

38. Patrick Swinden, *The English Novel of History and Society, 1940–1980* (London: Macmillan, 1984).

39. Robert Boyers, *Atrocity and Amnesia: The Political Novel since 1945* (Oxford: Oxford University Press, 1985), p. 13.

40. There are a few exceptions. Olivia Manning describes "the present age" as "remarkable for the preponderance of women fiction writers of such quality that they have out-faced prejudice"; *New Review* on "The State of Fiction: A Symposium" (Summer 1978, 5:1), p. 52. Julia O'Faolain notes that "an exhilarating side-effect of the women's movement was the freeing of the female imagination," though she adds, "Conspicuous were pert, polemical, feminist novels written, as though on disposable paper panties, to provoke outrage ('raise consciousness')" (p. 57). The most generous—and astute—evaluation is Ian McKewan's: "Women writers seem best placed now to use the novel seriously to open out relatively unexplored areas of individual and social experience" (p. 51).

41. Brian Aldiss, ibid., p. 16; Isabel Colegate, p. 32. It was "a bleak time" (A. Alvarez, p. 15; David Benedicts, p. 21), "a bad time" (John Braine, p. 27).

42. Robert Stepto, "Afro-American Literature," in *Columbia Literary History of the United States*, ed. Emory Elliott (New York: Columbia University Press, 1988), pp. 785–799, 788 (hereafter CLH).

43. Virginia Woolf, "The Leaning Tower," in *Collected Essays* (London: Hogarth Press, 1966), II, pp. 172.

44. Alison Prentice, Paula Bourne, Gail Cuthbert Brandt, Beth Light, Wendy Mitchinson, Naomi Black, *Canadian Women: A History* (Toronto: Harcourt, 1988), p. 218.

45. Elaine Showalter, "Women Writers between the Wars," in CLH, pp. 822–41, 830.

46. Betty Friedan, *The Feminine Mystique* (New York: Norton, 1983), p. 100. See also Alan Sinfield, *Literature, Politics, and Culture in Postwar Britain* (Berkeley: University of California Press, 1989), pp. 203–204.

47. Barbara Miller Solomon also describes a "quality of déjà vu" about the eighties; *In the Company of Educated Women: A History of Women and Higher Education in America* (New Haven: Yale University Press, 1984), p. 209.

48. Susan Bolotin, "Voices from the Post-Feminist Generation," *New York Times Magazine* (October 17, 1982), p. 28ff; Cott, pp. 282, 365, n. 23, cites *Judy* 1, no. 1 (June 1919); *Judy* 2, no. 3 (1919), n.p. The Arthur and Elizabeth Schlesinger Library on the History of Women in America, Radcliffe College, Cambridge, MA; Cott, p. 365, n. 23.

49. Dorothy Dunbar Bromley, "Feminist—New Style," *Harper's*, no. 155 (October 1927), pp. 152–60; in Chafe, pp. 92, 278. Ray Strachey describes "a strong hostility to the word feminism"; *Our Freedom and Its Results* (London: Hogarth Press, 1936), p. 10; cited in Martin Pugh, "Domesticity and the Decline of Feminism, 1930–1950," ed.

Harold L. Smith, *British Feminism in the Twentieth Century* (Amherst: The University of Massachusetts Press, 1990), pp. 144–64, 144.

50. Lillian Hellman, *An Unfinished Woman: A Memoir* (Boston: Little, Brown, 1969), p. 35.

51. See Elizabeth Wilson, "The British Women's Movement," in *Hidden Agendas: Theory, Politics, and Experience in the Women's Movement,* ed. Elizabeth Wilson with Angela Weir (London: Tavistock, 1986), pp. 93–133, 97; and Olive M. Banks, *Faces of Feminism: A Study of Feminism as a Social Movement* (Oxford: Basil Blackwell, 1986), p. 238.

52. Juliet Mitchell, "Reflections on Twenty Years of Feminism," in *What Is Feminism? A Re-Examination,* ed. Juliet Mitchell and Ann Oakley (New York: Pantheon, 1986), pp. 34–48, 35.

53. Michele Barrett and Roberta Hamilton, *The Politics of Diversity* (London: Verso, 1986), p. 8; though for differences between the American and Canadian movements, see their introduction (pp. 1–31).

54. Deborah Rosenfelt describes a specific instance of how the proletarian realism that dominated critical theory of the left in the early 1930s stifled a particular woman writer's talent, analyzing Olsen's inability to finish *Yonnondio* in relation to her difficulties with the injunctions of socialist realism; "From the Thirties: Tillie Olsen and the Radical Tradition," in *Feminist Criticism and Social Change: Sex, Class and Race in Literature and Culture,* ed. Judith Newton and Deborah Rosenfelt, pp. 216–48. James W. Tuttleton, " 'Combat in the Erogenous Zone': Women in the American Novel Between the Two World Wars," in *What Manner of Woman: Essays in English and American Life and Literature,* ed. Marlene Springer (New York: New York University Press, 1977), 271–96, describes male writers' "idealization of the woman" in this period, "the stereotype of the 'womanly woman' " in the role of "life-giving, nourishing, life-sustaining presence ministering to her husband or family" (pp. 292–93).

55. Virginia Woolf, *A Room of One's Own* (New York: Harcourt, 1957), p. 108.

56. Douglas T. Miller and Marion Nowak, *The Fifties: The Way We Really Were* (Garden City, NY: Doubleday, 1977), pp. 152, 147; Banks, p. 203.

57. In Canada, also, "media portrayals of women in the post-war years stressed an all-pervasive stereotype of women as happy homemakers, winsome wives, and magnanimous mothers. Woman's role as consumer was re-emphasized" and she was urged into such occupations as "stenography, homemaking, dressmaking and nursing" (Prentice et al., pp. 306–307).

58. Penelope Mortimer, *The Pumpkin Eater* (Plainfield, VT: Daughters, 1975), p. 149.

59. Marilyn French, *The Women's Room* (New York: Jove Publications, 1977), pp. 113, 99.

60. Sylvia Plath, *The Bell Jar* (New York: Bantam, 1981), p. 128.

61. Alice S. Rossi argued for "a socially androgynous conception of the roles of men and women" ("Equality of the Sexes: An Immodest Proposal" *Dædalus,* no. 93 (Spring 1964), pp. 607–52); rpt. in *The Woman in America,* ed. Robert Lifton (Boston: Houghton Mifflin, 1965). According to Germaine Greer, "The castration of women has been carried out in terms of a masculine–feminine polarity, in which men have commandeered all the energy" (*The Female Eunuch* [New York: McGraw Hill, 1971], p. 6). In *The Dialectic of Sex,* Shulamith Firestone described "the end goal of feminist revolution" as "not just the elimination of male *privilege* but of the sex *distinction* itself" (New York: Bantam, 1972), p. 11. See also Carolyn Heilbrun, *Toward a Recognition of Androgyny* (New York: Knopf, 1973).

62. Sinfield notes that "insistent ideological work" may "witness to uncertainty and confusion" (p. 205). Elaine Tyler May relates the containment of female sexuality in this period, the restrictive fashions and ideology, to anxiety about the bomb. "Explosive Issues: Sex, Women, and the Bomb," in *Recasting America: Culture and Politics in the*

*Age of Cold War,* ed. Lary May (Chicago: University of Chicago Press, 1989), pp. 154–70, 155–56.

63. See Morris Dickstein, *Gates of Eden: American Culture in the Sixties* (New York: Penguin, 1989), p. 40; and Miller and Nowak, Chapter 8, "Intellectuals: The Conservative Contraction," pp. 220–46.

64. Fraya Katz-Stoker describes it as "reflect[ing] the thoroughness with which anticommunism . . . penetrated even literary studies" ("The Other Criticism: Feminism vs. Formalism," in Susan Koppelman Cornillon, *Images of Women in Fiction* [Bowling Green, OH: Bowling Green University Popular Press, 1972], pp. 315–27, 320). Eagleton calls it "a recipe for political inertia and thus for submission to the political status quo" (*Literary Theory: An Introduction* [Minneapolis: University of Minnesota Press, 1983], p. 50). See also Sinfield, pp. 104–105.

65. Philip Slater, *The Pursuit of Loneliness* (Boston: Beacon, 1970), p. 79.

66. Philip Wylie, *A Generation of Vipers* (New York: Rinehart, 1955), p. 201.

67. Jo Freeman, *The Politics of Women's Liberation* (New York: David McKay, 1975), p. 25.

68. Margaret Laurence, *The Fire-Dwellers* (Toronto: McClelland and Stewart, 1984), p. 11.

69. Alix Kates Shulman, *Memoirs of an Ex-Prom Queen* (New York: Knopf, 1972), p. 269.

70. Quoted in Stevenson, p. 82. See Stevenson, Chapter 3, for nostalgia in postwar British fiction.

71. Bergonzi calls Snow "the most deeply backward-looking and nostalgic of living English novelists" (p. 137) and criticizes Powell's complacency about English society (p. 122). See also Holloway, p. 105.

72. Rebecca O'Rourke, "Doris Lessing: Exile and Exception," in Jenny Taylor, ed., *Notebooks, Memoirs, Archives: Reading and Rereading Doris Lessing* (Boston: Routledge, 1982), pp. 206–26, 215–17. See also Elizabeth Wilson, *Only Halfway to Paradise* (New York: Tavistock, 1980), p. 150; and Sinfield, p. 63.

73. Holloway notes that though the working-class novel was much-discussed, "working-class fiction of the fifties recurrently deals, in the end, with one mode or another of *release* from, or evasion of, working class life, rather than with the staple of it" (in Ford, p. 106). Sinfield observes "they aspired to rise in society, rather than to change it" (p. 232). But he also discusses the emergence of the CND as a "focus of left-wing activity" in the period (p. 239).

74. Gerald Graff, *Literature against Itself: Literary Ideas in Modern Society* (Chicago: University of Chicago Press, 1979), p. 222. See also Sinfield, pp. 155–56, 163.

75. See Jenny Taylor, "Introduction: Situating Reading," in Taylor (1982), pp. 1–42, for an excellent discussion of Lessing's intellectual, cultural, and historical backgrounds: As Taylor suggests, Lessing "came to England out of an extraordinary range of displaced histories and mythologies" (p. 21).

76. Besides her first novel, *This Side Jordan* (1960), Laurence published a collection of short stories set in Ghana (*The Tomorrow Tamer,* 1963), a travel memoir describing her experience in Somaliland (*New Wind in a Dry Land,* also 1963; *The Prophet's Camel Bell* in British edition); *A Tree for Poverty: Somali Poetry and Prose,* 1954; and *Long Drums and Cannons: Nigerian Dramatists and Novelists 1952–1966,* 1966, which includes chapters on Wole Soyinka, Chinua Achebe, and Amos Tutuola.

77. Unpublished article by Laurence, quoted in Patricia Morley, *Margaret Laurence: Twayne's World Author Series* (Boston: G. K. Hall and Co., 1981), p. 39; "Ivory Tower or Grass Roots? The Novelist as Socio-political Being," in *A Political Art: Essays and Images in Honor of George Woodcock,* ed. William H. New (Vancouver: University of British Columbia Press, 1978), pp. 15–25, 22.

78. *Doris Lessing Newsletter* 8, no. 2 (1984), p. 3.

79. For women writers' adaptations of the *Bildungsroman,* see *The Voyage In:*

*Fictions of Female Development,* ed. Elizabeth Abel, Marianne Hirsch, and Elizabeth Langland (Hanover, NH: University Press of New England, 1983); and Rita Felski, *Beyond Feminist Aesthetics: Feminist Literature and Social Change* (Cambridge: Harvard University Press, 1989), pp. 133–38.

80. Sheila Ballantyne, *Norma Jean the Termite Queen* (Harmondsworth: Penguin, 1986), pp. 13, 16.

81. Marge Piercy, *Small Changes* (New York: Fawcett Crest, 1973), p. 38.

82. Sue Kaufman, *Diary of a Mad Housewife* (New York: Bantam, 1970), p. 44.

83. Marge Piercy, "Through the Cracks," in *Partisan Review* 41 (1974), pp. 202–16, 215, 208, 207. "There was a blank, the space where concepts and ways of putting things together is now," says Sally Alexander (OAF, p. 86).

84. Adrienne Rich, "Translations," in *Poems Selected and New, 1950–1974* (New York: Norton, 1975), p. 205. Even if one did not belong to a consciousness-raising group, becoming a feminist involved some process of making connections between the personal and political like those described in OAF (pp. 96, 99, 123, 218).

85. "Internally, the movement was a *'teaching* movement,' using an oral tradition— conversation and consciousness-raising groups—and the written word—newspapers, poems, or books—to reveal the world and women in a new light"; Catharine R. Stimpson with Nina Kressner Cobb, *Women's Studies in the United States,* A Report to the Ford Foundation (Ford Foundation, 1986), p. 12. Florence Howe and Carol Ahlum, "Women's Studies and Social Change," in *Academic Women on the Move,* ed. Alice Rossi and Ann Calderwood (New York: Russell Sage, 1973), also call it a "teaching movement" (p. 395); Mary Hughes and Mary Kennedy, *New Futures: Changing Women's Education* (London: Routledge, 1985), call it a "learning experience" (p. 46) and quote Jack Mezirow, "Perspective Transformation," in *Studies in Adult Education* (October 1977), pp. 9, 2, 153–64.

86. In Canada the pattern is similar, though a few years behind: "enrollment of women undergraduates reached its peak in 1930," then "declined throughout the 1930s. . . . The proportion of women in the total graduate enrollment also dropped during this decade, going from 26 percent in 1930 to 20 percent in 1940" (Prentice et al., pp. 241–42). "At the graduate level in Canadian universities . . . the proportion of students who were women (22 percent) was still lower in 1970 than it had been in 1921 (26 percent). . . . In the mid-1960s only slightly more than one in ten university teachers in Canada was a woman, and most were in the faculties of education, nursing, household science, and arts" (p. 329).

87. John Lawson and Harold Silver, *A Social History of Education in England* (London: Methuen, 1973), p. 436. Wilson discusses renewed interest in the education of women in England in the late fifties and early sixties (*Halfway,* pp. 32–36).

88. Margaret Laurence, *Dance on the Earth* (Toronto: McClelland and Stewart, 1989), pp. 4–5.

89. Between 1960 and 1970, the number of women earning master's degrees increased from 21 percent to 30 percent; the proportion of earned doctorates jumped from 10 to 26 in 1,000; and women were moving into fields besides education, languages, literature, and the health professions. Robert L. Daniel, *American Women in the Twentieth Century: The Festival of Life* (New York: Harcourt, 1987), pp. 276–77.

90. Feminism produced dramatic educational reform at a later date, introducing women's-studies courses into the curriculum and integrating the study of women into existing courses. In 1972 the Education Act prohibited sex discrimination in colleges and universities.

91. Audrey Wise sets the beginning of the women's movement in England with the Ford strike, 1968–69, which she sees as an event as important as the Ruskin College conference of 1970 (OAF, pp. 201–202). But what Rowbotham terms the "process of class-transition," brought about by the education of working-class or lower-middle-class women, was also enormously important (OAF, p. 38).

92. Howard R. Bowen, "The Effects of Going to College," in CHE 15 (October 31, 1977), pp. 3–4; cited in Daniel, p. 403. See Mary V. Dearborn, *Pocahontas's Daughters: Gender and Ethnicity in American Culture* (New York: Oxford University Press, 1986), pp. 60–96, on ethnic and immigrant women in relation to education.

93. Myra Marx Ferree and Beth B. Hess, *Controversy and Coalition: The New Feminist Movement* (Boston: Twayne, 1985), p. 8.

94. Modernist journals included *Poetry, The Little Review, Broom,* the *Dial, Blast,* the *Egoist* (which began as a feminist magazine), *Wheels* (edited by Edith Sitwell), the *Criterion,* and *transition.*

95. *The Feminine Mystique* was first in nonfiction on the Bowker Annual list of best-sellers for 1964. It remained on *The New York Times Book Review* best-seller list throughout most of 1963 and 1964. Wilson notes that Friedan's work and *The Second Sex* "must have had a kind of underground influence on hundreds of thousands of women who read them. Both were printed all over the Western world in popular paperback editions that sold out over and over again. Which women read them, which were influenced by them and how, we cannot altogether know. But their yeast must have been working in the doughy femininity of the fifties and early sixties." (*Halfway,* pp. 194–95).

96. Janet Batsleer, Tony Davies, Rebecca O'Rourke, and Chris Weedon, *Rewriting English: Cultural Politics of Gender and Class* (London: Methuen, 1985), pp. 143–45. Prentice et al. discuss the contributions of Canadian women writers in the sixties to the formation of feminist consciousness (pp. 340–42).

97. Lynn Wenzel, "A Decade Later Burning Questions Remain Unanswered," in *New Directions for Women* (May/June 1990), p. 23.

98. Nora Johnson, "Housewives and Prom Queens, 25 Years Later," *New York Times Book Review* (March 20, 1988), p. 1.

99. Barbara Raskin, *Hot Flashes* (New York: St. Martin's Press, 1987), p. 74.

100. Cora Kaplan, "Feminist Criticism Twenty Years On," in *From My Guy to Sci-Fi: Genre and Women's Writing in the Postmodern World,* ed. Helen Carr (London: Pandora, 1989), pp. 15–23, 18–19.

101. Anthea Zeman, *Presumptuous Girls: Women and Their World in the Serious Woman's Novel* (London: Wiedenfeld and Nicolson, 1977), p. 2.

102. Interview with Peter Firchow, *The Writer's Place: Interviews on the Literary Situation in Contemporary Britain* (Minneapolis: University of Minnesota Press, 1974), p. 107.

103. Elizabeth Wilson, "Yesterday's Heroines: on Rereading Lessing and de Beauvoir," in Taylor, pp. 57–74, 57. See also Anna Davin and Anna Paczuska, OAF, pp. 56, 151; and Mary King, *Freedom Song: A Personal Story of the 1960s Civil Rights Movement* (New York: William Morrow and Company, 1987).

104. Jenny Taylor, "Introduction: Situating Reading," in Taylor, pp. 1–42, 5.

105. Catharine R. Stimpson, "Doris Lessing and the Parables of Growth," in Abel et al. (1983), pp. 186–205, 186.

106. Joanne S. Frye, *Living Stories, Telling Lives: Women and the Novel in Contemporary Experience* (Ann Arbor: University of Michigan Press, 1986), p. 167.

107. Laurie Stone, *MS.* (July/August 1987), p. 29.

108. Annis Pratt, introduction, *Doris Lessing: Critical Studies,* ed. Annis Pratt and L. S. Dembo (Madison: University of Wisconsin Press, 1974), pp. vii–ix, viii.

109. Susan Lydon, review of Lessing's *Four-Gated City,* in *Ramparts* (January 1970), pp. 48–50, 48.

110. Erica Jong, *Fear of Flying* (New York: Signet, 1973), p. 100.

111. Jane Marcus, "Invisible Mending," in *Between Women: Biographers, Novelists, Critics, Teachers and Artists Write about Their Work on Women* ed. Carol Ascher, Louise De Salvo, and Sara Ruddick (Boston: Beacon, 1984), pp. 381–95, 391.

112. John Leonard, *Newsday* (March 17, 1988), Part II, p. 8; rpt. *Doris Lessing Newsletter,* "In Person" (Fall 89), pp, 12, 2, 5.

113. Nancy Porter, "Silenced History—*Children of Violence* and *The Golden Notebook,*" in *World Literature Written in English* 12 (November 1973), pp. 161–79.

114. Lisa Alther, "The Writer and Her Critics," in *Women's Review of Books* 6, (October 1988), p. 11.

115. Dee Seligman, in an early issue of *Doris Lessing Newsletter,* quoted in Ellen Cronan Rose and Carey Kaplan, *The Canon and the Uncommon Reader* (forthcoming, University of Tennessee Press).

116. Rachel Blau DuPlessis and Members of Workshop 9, "For the Etruscans: Sexual Difference and Artistic Production—The Debate over a Female Aesthetic," in Eisenstein, pp. 128–56; rpt. Showalter (1985), pp. 271–91, 279–80.

117. Susan Lardner, "Angle on the Ordinary," in *The New Yorker* (September 19, 1983), pp. 140–54, 144.

118. "Cassandra" (1972), p. 50. Drabble also refers to Lessing as "the toughest and the most independent and the most extraordinary . . . the hardest and most uncompromising" of contemporary women writers—"she makes everybody else look like magazine stories" (Rozencwajg, p. 341).

119. John Leonard, "The Spacing Out of Doris Lessing," in *Critical Essays on Doris Lessing,* ed. Claire Sprague and Virginia Tiger (Boston: G. K. Hall, 1986), pp. 204–209, 208.

120. Mary Allen, *The Necessary Blankness: Women in Major American Fiction of the Sixties* (Urbana: University of Illinois Press, 1976), pp. 4, 182. See also Martha Masinton and Charles G. Masinton, "Second-class Citizenship: The Status of Women in Contemporary American Fiction," in *What Manner of Woman: Essays in English and American Life and Literature,* ed. Marlene Springer (New York: New York University Press, 1977), pp. 297–315.

121. Margaret Drabble, "Stratford Revisted: A Legacy of the Sixties," the Gareth Lloyd Evans Shakespeare Lecture (Shipston-on-Stour, Warwickshire: The Celandine Press, 1989), p. 17. As Wilson points out, Drabble was also writing articles in the *Guardian* on "the trials and tribulations of motherhood," and Penelope Mortimer wrote a column in the *Evening Standard*: "some of the novelists themselves became well known media figures . . . sometimes they were exploited as a popular image of liberated womanhood" (e.g, Françoise Sagan, Edna O'Brien, Mortimer, and Drabble) (*Halfway,* pp. 156–57).

122. M. Morris, "Newspapers and the New Feminists: Blackout as Social Control," in *Journalism Quarterly* 50, pp. 37–42; cited in Ferree, p. 75.

123. Rowbotham, OAF, pp. 14–17. Though Audrey Wise sets the beginning in 1968, at the fiftieth anniversary of women's winning the vote—an anniversary which generated considerable press coverage—and the year of the Ford women's strike (OAF, pp. 201–202).

124. Ellen Goodman, "The Doris Lessing Hoax," in the *Washington Post* (September 27, 1984), p. 31; rpt. "Doris Lessing as Jane Somers: The Media Response," in *Doris Lessing Newsletter* 9, no. 1 (Spring 1985), p. 3. Ellen Cronan Rose and Carey Kaplan point out that *The Golden Notebook* was "not immediately acclaimed" in either the United States or England; "The novel's reputation grew slowly, not reaching its present eminence until the seventies"; introduction, *Approaches to Teaching Lessing's The Golden Notebook,* ed. Carey Kaplan and Ellen Cronan Rose (New York: The Modern Language Association of America, 1989), pp. 1–7, 2. Not coincidentally, this growth curve followed that of the women's movement.

125. Letter from John Ciursit to Mary Hurley Moran, September 4, 1981, Mary Hurley Moran, *Margaret Drabble: Existing within Structures* (Carbondale: Southern Illinois University Press, 1983), p. 7. Moran notes that early reviewers "compared her

with ranking contemporary novelists, predicting that she would develop into one of Britain's major writers" (p. 6); she cites "The Little Woman," *TLS* review of *The Garrick Year* (July 23, 1964), p. 645, and *Library Journal,* review of *The Millstone* (May 1, 1966), p. 2361).

126. "An Interview With Margaret Drabble" (1979), by Joanne V. Creighton, in *Margaret Drabble: Golden Realms,* Living Author Series No. 4, ed. Dorey Schmidt (Edinburg, TX: Pan American University, 1982), pp. 18–31, 25–26.

127. Nancy Poland, "There Must Be a Lot of People Like Me," *Midwest Quarterly* 16, no. 3 (1975), pp. 256–57.

128. Joanne V. Creighton, *Margaret Drabble* (London: Methuen, 1985), p. 14.

129. Terry Coleman, "A Biographer Waylaid by Novels," in *Guardian* 15 (April 1972), p. 23; Rosalind Miles, *The Fiction of Sex: Themes and Functions of Sex Differences in the Modern Novel* (New York: Barnes and Noble, 1974), p. 156; both quoted in Lynn Veach Sadler, *Margaret Drabble* (Boston: Twayne, 1986), p. 6.

130. Joyce Carol Oates's review of *The Needle's Eye,* *New York Times Book Review* (June 14, 1972), pp. 1, 23; quoted in Ellen Cronan Rose, *Critical Essays on Margaret Drabble* (Boston: G. K. Hall, 1985), introduction, pp. 1–18; p. 1. Jean Wyatt speaks of Drabble's novels as helping her survive a divorce.

131. Marian Engel, *The Globe and Mail,* Toronto (April 19, 1975), p. 37; rpt. in New, pp. 219–21.

132. Phyllis Gross Kurth, "Wise and Gentle," review of *The Fire-Dwellers,* in *Canadian Literature* 43 (1970), pp. 91–92.

133. *Christian Science Monitor* (June 12, 1969), p. 13.

134. Margaret Atwood, "Face to Face," in *Margaret Laurence,* ed. William New (Toronto: McGraw-Hill Ryerson, 1977), pp. 33–40, 37.

135. Erica Jong, "Blood and Guts: The Tricky Problem of Being a Woman Writer in the Late Twentieth Century," in *The Writer on Her Work,* ed. Janet Sternburg (New York: Norton, 1980), pp. 169–79, 175, 178.

136. John Getlin, "No Fear of Flying," *Los Angeles Times,* pp. E1–2. Since publishers refuse to release publication figures, actual numbers are hard to come by; but presumably this figure, occurring in an interview with Jong, is accurate.

137. Erica Jong, *How to Save Your Own Life* (New York: New American Library, 1977), pp. 14, 255.

138. Interview with Jong by Curt Schleir, *USAir* (April 1989), pp. 86–91, 91.

139. For an especially strong statement of this position, see Lennard J. Davis, *Resisting Novels: Ideology and Fiction* (New York: Methuen, 1987).

### III. Mad Housewives and Closed Circles

1. Joanna Russ, "What Can A Heroine Do? or Why Can't Women Write?" *Woman as Writer,* ed. Jeanette L. Webber and Joan Grumman (Boston: Houghton Mifflin, 1978), pp. 158–63, 159–60.

2. In Alix Kates Shulman, *Memoirs of an Ex-Prom Queen* (New York: Bantam, 1972), p. 55 (hereafter EPQ); Sylvia Plath, *The Bell Jar* (New York: Bantam, 1981), p. 23 (hereafter BJ); Barbara Raskin, *Loose Ends* (New York: Bantam, 1973), (hereafter LE).

3. Betty Friedan, *The Feminine Mystique* (New York: Norton, 1983), p. 290. Elizabeth Wilson describes the fifties and sixties as a time when "it was difficult to know about any oppression of women," when oppression was "invisible" and "silenced"; *Only Halfway to Paradise: Women in Postwar Britain, 1945–1968* (London: Tavistock, 1980), pp. 207, 187.

4. Doris Lessing, *Martha Quest* (New York: New American Library, 1964), p. 10 (hereafter MQ). This question is echoed almost verbatim thirty years later in Colette Dowling's *Cinderella Complex* (New York: Pocket Books, 1981): "She doesn't want to be 'like her mother.' . . . Whom, then, will she be like?' " (p. 198)

5. This sense is corroborated by Anita Shreve's interviews with women in consciousness-raising groups: "She had never really thought beyond college . . . and she had no idea what to do with herself . . . she'd studied English literature"; *Women Together, Women Alone* (New York: Viking, 1989), pp. 62–63.

6. Marge Piercy describes herself similarly, as unable to "imagine a future"; "Through the Cracks," in *Partisan Review* 41 (1974), pp. 202–16, 203.

7. Annis Pratt, *Archetypal Patterns in Women's Fiction* (Bloomington: Indiana University Press, 1981), describes "imagery of maiming, dwarfing, and suffocating" in women's "coming of age" fictions (p. 9). Pearson and Pope discuss the house, cage, and mirror as representing "the limiting and oppressive effects of the traditional female role" (p. 22).

8. Penelope Mortimer, *The Pumpkin Eater* (Plainfield, VT: Daughters; 1975) (hereafter PE); Sue Kaufman, *Diary of a Mad Housewife* (New York: Bantam, 1970) (hereafter DMH); Fay Weldon, *The Fat Woman's Joke* (Chicago: Academy, 1967) (hereafter FWJ); Margaret Laurence, *The Fire-Dwellers* (Toronto: McClelland and Stewart, 1984) (hereafter FD); Anne Richardson Roiphe, *Up the Sandbox* (New York: Simon and Schuster, 1970); Dorothy Bryant, *Ella Price's Journal* (Berkeley: Ata Books, 1982) (hereafter EPJ); Johanna Davis, *Life Signs* (New York: Dell, 1973); Sheila Ballantyne, *Norma Jean the Termite Queen* (Harmondsworth: Penguin, 1986) (hereafter NJTQ). Other novels that might have been discussed in this chapter include Lessing's *The Grass Is Singing, A Proper Marriage* (New York: New American Library, 1964) (hereafter PM), and *The Summer Before the Dark*, all of which grimly illustrate the closed circle of female conditioning; Drabble's *The Realms of Gold*, which contrasts a trapped housewife with a liberated professional woman; Marge Piercy's *Small Changes* (New York: Fawcett Crest, 1973) and Alice Walker's *Meridian*, which write beyond conventional endings of romance and marriage. Marilyn French's *The Women's Room* (New York: Jove, HBJ, 1977) (hereafter WR) is in some sense the paradigmatic madhousewife novel; Anne Tyler's *Earthly Possessions,* published (amazingly) the same year as *The Women's Room* (1977), celebrates domesticity and the circular return. Drabble's *The Waterfall* is the subject of a later chapter.

9. In "Women and the Family" a paper presented at the Ruskin College Women's Conference, Oxford, March 1970 and printed in *Shrew* [February–March 1970]) by Jan Williams, Hazel Twort, and Ann Bachelli (members of the London Peckham Rye group, Women's Liberation Workshop), housework is described in similar terms: "The appropriate symbol for housework . . . is . . . a compulsive circle like a pet mouse in its cage spinning round on its exercise wheel, unable to get off" (*The Politics of Housework*, ed. Ellen Malos [New York: Schocken Books, 1980], pp. 113–18, 114). See also Suzanne Gail: "The thought of all those millions of women performing exactly the same gestures as me, enclosed in their little circular activities, and perhaps with no desire or possibility of ever escaping, depresses me more than I can say" ("The Housewife," excerpted from *New Left Review* 1965–66, in Malos, pp. 105–12, 109).

10. In *Dance on the Earth* (Toronto: McClelland and Stewart, 1989) (hereafter DOE), Margaret Laurence marvels that the first time she described childbirth in her fiction, she did so from the male point of view: "At that point I had borne two children, but women writers had virtually no models in describing birth, or sex, from a woman's view" (p. 6).

11. Michelene Wandor, *Once a Feminist: Stories of a Generation* (London: Virago, 1990), p. 186 (hereafter OAF). As Janet Ree says, "It [the women's movement] just made different things important, and it was the first time I heard women talk about the things that affected their ordinary everyday lives" (OAF, p. 96).

12. John Berger, *Ways of Seeing* (London: BBC and Penguin, 1977), p. 46.

13. Frigga Haug and others, *Female Sexualization: A Collective Work of Memory* (London: Verso, 1987), pp. 129–30.

14. Simone de Beauvoir, *The Second Sex* (New York: Vintage, 1952), p. 758. Carol

Pearson and Katherine Pope, *The Female Hero in American and British Literature* (New York: Bowker, 1981), describe the protagonist's discovery "that she has a separate, heroic self, which conflicts with . . . [what] society has told her she should have" (p. 49). Alicia Ostriker refers to "the divided self" as "probably the single issue women poets since 1960 most consistently struggle with"; "The Thieves of Language: Women Poets and Revisionist Mythmaking," in *The New Feminist Criticism: Essays on Women, Literature, and Theory*, ed. Elaine Showalter (New York: Pantheon, 1985), pp. 314–38, 331.

15. Margaret Drabble, *A Summer Bird-Cage* (Harmondsworth: Penguin, 1974), pp. 183–84. Cf. Sally Alexander: "I think now that there was no way to be a woman and to be intelligent and articulate in the sixties" (OAF, p. 85). Margaret Laurence describes this conflict in her own life (DOW, pp. 38, 128, 158).

16. Novels besides those discussed here also split narratives into "I" and "she": Rosamond Lehmann's *Weather in the Streets,* Ann Quin's *Passages,* Weldon's *Down among the Women,* Emma Tennent's *Bad Sister,* Francine Du Plessix Gray's *Lovers and Tyrants,* Lisa Alther's *Kinflicks,* Nadine Gordimer's *The Burger's Daughter,* and Christa Woolf's *Model Childhood.* See Judith Kegan Gardiner, "On Female Identity and Writing by Women," in Elizabeth Abel, ed., *Writing and Sexual Difference, Critical Inquiry* 8, no. 2 (Winter 1981), pp. 347–61, 357; and Randall Stevenson, *The British Novel since the Thirties: An Introduction* (Athens, GA: University of Georgia Press, 1986), pp. 158–60.

17. Gail Godwin, *The Odd Woman* (New York: Warner Books, 1974), pp. 309–26.

18. In Patricia S. Yaeger's term, *Honey-Mad Women: Emancipatory Strategies in Women's Writing* (New York: Columbia University Press, 1989).

19. Alice Munro, *Lives of Girls and Women* (New York: New American Library, 1971), p. 198.

20. Barbara Sinclair Deckard confirms this figure; *The Women's Movement: Political, Socioeconomic, and Psychological Issues* (New York: Harper and Row, 1983), p. 309. Wilson notes the key role of "the domestic market, where women . . . were the crucial spenders," in Britain's postwar economic recovery (p. 37).

21. "Advertising was big business and grew during the fifties at a faster rate than did the GNP"; Douglas T. Miller and Marion Nowak, *The Fifties: The Way We Really Were* (Garden City, NY: Doubleday, 1977), p. 118. They describe further aspects of consumerism in the fifties—business control of the content of TV and radio, the program to change values from thrift to spending, planned obsolescence, "cold war spending . . . sprawling suburbias" (p. 123).

22. Margaret Atwood, *The Edible Woman* (New York: Warner Books, 1983) (hereafter EW), p. 216.

23. Elaine Tyler May, "Explosive Issues: Sex, Women, and the Bomb," in *Recasting America: Culture and Politics in the Age of Cold War,* ed. Lary May (Chicago: University of Chicago Press, 1988), pp. 154–70, 155–56.

24. Doris Lessing, *The Golden Notebook* (New York: Bantam, 1973), p. 167.

25. Jean E. Kennard, "Convention Coverage or How to Read Your Own Life," in *New Literary History* 13, no. 1 (Autumn 1981), pp. 69–88, 79.

26. Anthea Zeman, *Presumptuous Girls: Women and Their World in the Serious Woman's Novel* (London: Wiedenfeld and Nicolson, 1977), pp. 120–30. Zeman's generalizations are based, however, on only three novels: *Diary of a Mad Housewife,* Martha Wiley Emmett's *A Shadow Backwards,* and Alison Lurie's *War between the Tates.*

27. A. Alvarez, *The Savage God: A Study in Suicide* (New York: Bantam, 1973), p. 20.

28. Though Marjorie G. Perloff approves of this incident, describing Esther as "the New Woman" who "calmly sends [the man] the bill," "an authentic, indeed an exem-

plary heroine of the seventies" (" 'A Ritual for Being Born Twice': Sylvia Plath's *The Bell Jar*," in *Contemporary Literature* 13, no. 4 [1972], pp. 507–522, 521–22), I find it chilling. Elizabeth Hardwick's sense of Esther is closer to mine: she describes her "stifling self-enclosure" as "so extreme that only death—and after that fails, shock treatment—can bring any kind of relief. Persons suffering in this way simply do not have any room in their heads for the anguish of others—and later many seem to survive their own torments only by an erasing detachment . . . neither is she moved to self-criticism or even self-analysis"; *Seduction and Betrayal* (New York: Random House, 1974), p. 108.

29. Alan Sinfield, *Literature, Politics, and Culture in Postwar Britain* (Berkeley: University of California Press, 1989), reads Plath as the site or "point of intersection" of contradictory stories (p. 216) and describes the novel as "fractured by partial consciousness"—marriage is conceived of as the return to the norm, yet the men in the novel are inadequate and sex is unpleasant; he relates these contradictions to Plath's disintegrating relation with Ted Hughes (pp. 219–20).

30. Sinfield cites passages in Plath's journals and letters that point to her political awareness and commitment (pp. 222–23). But I'd say of this novel what he says of her poem "Daddy"—that the connections are not "fully articulated" but are, rather, "struggling into consciousness" (p. 224).

31. Sara Ruddick defines "maternal thinking" as "distinctive ways of conceptualizing, ordering, and valuing" that arise "out of maternal practices," citing specifically humor, humility, "a sense of the limits of one's actions"; "Maternal Thinking," in *Feminist Studies* 6, no. 2 (Summer 1980), pp. 342–67, 359, 350–51. See also *Maternal Thinking: Toward a Politics of Peace* (Boston: Beacon 1989).

32. Rosalind Coward, "The Voice," in *Female Desires: How They Are Sought, Bought and Packaged* (New York: Grove, 1985), pp. 153–58, 158, 154.

33. Lucy is "platinum and elegantly coiffured"; Millie is "brassy . . . and cropped" (pp. 20–21); Mrs. Grot has hair "the colour of a metal refrigerator tray" (p. 19). The women Marian sees shopping in the bargain basement have a "patina of lower-middle income domesticity, that weathered surface . . . that invisible colour that was like a smell, the underpainting of musty upholstery and worn linoleum" (p. 217)—imagery which suggests that people become what they do. I argue this more fully in "Margaret Atwood's *The Edible Woman*: 'Rebelling Against the System,' " in *Margaret Atwood: Reflection and Reality* (Edinburg, TX: Pan American University, 1987), pp. 95–115.

34. Dorothy Van Ghent, *The English Novel: Form and Function, Great Expectations* (New York: Harper and Row, 1953), especially pp. 158–61; also "The Dickens World: A View from Todgers's," in *Sewanee Review* 58 (1960), pp. 419–30. Atwood cites Dickens as one of her favorite authors; "A Conversation: Margaret Atwood and Students," moderated by Francis X. Gillen; *Margaret Atwood: Vision and Forms*, ed. Kathryn VanSpanckeren and Jan Garden Castro (Carbondale: Southern Illinois University Press, 1988), pp. 233–43, 233.

35. Catharine MacKinnon analyzes this relation between woman's alienation in work and her sexual objectification; "Feminism, Marxism, Method, and the State: An Agenda for Theory," in *Signs* 7, no. 3 (1982) pp. 515–44.

36. Margaret Atwood, *Surfacing* (New York: Fawcett, 1972), p. 220. As Atwood says, Marian's "choices remain much the same at the end of the book as they are at the beginning: a career going nowhere, or marriage as an exit from it"; "An Introduction to *The Edible Woman*," *Second Words: Selected Critical Prose* (Boston: Beacon, 1982), pp. 369–70, 370.

37. No wonder that Isabel Archer, who also sets out determined to control events but ends humbled beyond her wildest imaginings, is the literary heroine who most intrigues her (pp. 83, 135), though it is not clear that Sasha ever understands Isabel's real relevance to her.

38. When Martin accuses her, " 'your work . . . isn't earning the money' " (p. 109),

Norma Jean's unusually enlightened therapist points out the wage value of her services (p. 191). In Ballantyne's variation on this convention, therapy becomes part of the process of extending the boundaries—"one that deals with *inner* boundaries" (p. 127).

39. Raskin's *Loose Ends* also expresses a sense of intertextuality with contemporary women's fiction, but of a more adversarial sort. Coco, tormented by the success of other women writers, scans book reviews and new novels, "blocking because all across the nation Didions, Goulds, Kaufmans . . . and Roiphes were selling their novels to the movies" (p. 78). Coco suffers "anxiety of influence" with a vengeance:

> What did it matter if . . . Kate Millett and Germaine Greer conspired to off her? What did it matter if Joyce Carol Oates or Joan Didion or Sylvia Plath . . . or Doris Lessing or Grace Paley or Anaïs Nin . . . or Allison [sic] Lurie or Louis [sic] Gould or Sandra Hochman or Sue Kaufman . . . or Edna O'Brien or Alix Kate [sic] Shulman vetoed Coco's name if it were ever put in nomination for membership in that Mighty Living tradition? (p. 190)

So much for the idea that "thinking back through our mothers" (or "rival sisters," as Coco calls them [p. 67]) is inherently different from thinking back through fathers, as Elizabeth Abel claims; "[E]merging Identities: The Dynamics of Female Friendship in Contemporary Fiction by Women" in *Signs* 6 (1981), pp. 413–35, 432–33; see also Gilbert and Gubar, *No Man's Land: The Place of the Woman Writer in the Twentieth Century,* vol. 1, *The War of the Words* (New Haven: Yale University Press, 1988), p. 199. What is also interesting is that by 1973, this group of writers has assumed the weight of a "Mighty Living Tradition."

40. Ellen Morgan, "Humanbecoming: Form and Focus in the Neo-Feminist Novel," in *Images of Women in Fiction,* ed. Susan Koppelman Cornillon (Bowling Green, OH: Bowling Green University Popular Press, 1972), pp. 183–205, 183.

41. I am indebted to Ann Rosalind Jones for this term.

42. Susan Kress, "Lessing's Responsibility," in *Salmagundi* (Winter–Spring 1980), pp. 95–131, 130.

43. June Arnold's *Applesauce* (1966) and Ursula K. LeGuin's *The Left Hand of Darkness* (1969) are fantasy explorations of "the argument for androgyny"; and in *The Four-Gated City* Lessing similarly turns to the fantastic because she "could no longer say what [she] wanted to say inside the old form" (*Doris Lessing Newsletter* 8, no. 2 [1984], p. 3).

## IV. "Old Stories"

1. Erica Jong, *Fear of Flying* (New York: New American Library, 1973), p. 24.

2. Gail Godwin, *The Odd Woman* (New York: Warner Books, 1974), p. 65.

3. Susan Robin Suleiman, *Subversive Intent: Gender, Politics, and the Avant-Garde* (Cambridge: Harvard University Press, 1990), pp. 120–21.

4. At a 1976 MLA panel chaired by Josephine Donovon, for example, Cheri Register describes how *Fear of Flying* provoked her women's-studies group to discussions of what a feminist novel is (as reported by Lillian Robinson).

5. Jean E. Kennard, "Convention Coverage or How to Read Your Own Life," in *New Literary History* 13, no. 1 (Autumn 1981), pp. 69–88, 79.

6. This is one of many references to *The Golden Notebook:* Anna Wulf similarly assigns herself dreams as a cure. The epigraph to the chapter "Dreamwork"—"What's terrible is to pretend that the second-rate is first-rate" (p. 281)—is also from *The Golden Notebook.*

7. Grace Stewart, *A New Mythos: The Artist as Heroine* (Montreal: Eden Press, 1979), p. 177. For the association of "flying" with "stealing," see Claudine Herrmann, *The Thieves of Language;* Hélène Cixous and Catherine Clément, *The Newly-Born Woman;* Alicia Ostriker in *Stealing the Language;* and Suleiman, p. 122.

8. Cited in Annis Pratt, *Archetypal Patterns in Women's Fiction* (Bloomington: Indiana University Press, 1981), p. 11.

9. Susan Robin Suleiman, *The Female Body in Western Culture: Contemporary Perspectives* (Cambridge: Harvard University Press, 1986), pp. 9–10. Suleiman reiterates this position in *Subversive Intent*, p. 121. Anne Z. Mickelson suggests that Jong's language may be an attempt to "preempt man's power"; *Reaching Out: Sensitivity and Order in Recent American Fiction by Women* (Metuchen, NJ: The Scarecrow Press, 1979), p. 47.

10. Erica Jong, *How to Save Your Own Life* (New York: Signet, 1977), p. 285.

11. George Eliot, *Daniel Deronda* (Harmondsworth: Penguin, 1976), p. 842.

12. Actually, there are more than we realize; as Annis Pratt points out, a surprising number of novels, from the early nineteenth century to the present, center on "the self-sufficient, autonomous woman who chooses not to be married, who happens to remain unmarried, or who finds herself out of the marriage market" (p. 114); but that neither Jane nor most of us know this suggests that such novels did not make it into the canon—which makes the (not very surprising) point that works get canonized which affirm the dominant ideology. Pratt cites works by Edna Ferber, Charlotte Perkins Gilman, Sheila Kaye-Smith, Mary Wilkins Freeman, May Sarton, Sarah Orne Jewett, and Edith Wharton (pp. 115–22). Niamh Baker, in *Happily Ever After? Women's Fiction in Postwar Britain, 1945–60* (New York: St. Martin's Press, 1989), finds "positive images of 'odd' women" in postwar fiction, concluding that "the single state, though characterised by loneliness . . . is viewed with less pessimism" than marriage: "Marriage is disappointment: spinsterhood is hope" (pp. 176, 175). See also Laura L. Doan, *Old Maids and Excellent Women: The Spinster in the Twentieth Century Novel* (Urbana: University of Illinois Press, 1991).

13. W. B. Yeats, Byzantium," l. 8, in *The Collected Poems* (New York: Macmillan, 1964); *The Waterfall* (New York: Fawcett Popular Library, 1976), p. 69.

14. In her response to the responses to her review of Sandra M. Gilbert's and Susan Gubar's *Norton Anthology of Literature by Women* (*New York Times Book Review*, April 28, 1985), Godwin refers to "the achievement of the individual artist" as though it were a "universal" that transcends gender; and (as Carolyn Heilbrun, Nina Auerbach, Myra Jehlen, Nancy K. Miller, and Catharine R. Stimpson point out in their response) she implies that the canon is " 'universal,' unideological, while any reformation of the canon is the work of ideologues."

15. Nancy K. Miller ("Emphasis Added: Plots and Plausibilities in Women's Fiction," *PMLA* 96, no. 1 [January 1981], pp. 36–48, 36) refers to the laws of probability and possibility that govern realist fiction as a "contract"; she discusses Gérard Genette's ideas of "plausibility" and "probability" in "Vraisemblance et motivation," in *Figures II* (Paris: Sueil, 1969), p. 74. See also Pierre Macherey, *A Theory of Literary Production*, trans. Geoffrey Wall (London: Routledge and Kegan Paul, 1978), pp. 48–49.

16. Mickelson comments on this overpatterning: "The symmetrical form of the novel, the careful plotting of characters as either parallel or antithetical to one another" (p. 76) "gives the novel a constricting quality of a *fait accompli* which prevents it from moving toward a more expansive experience. The reader has a feeling of being caged in the author's constrictions" (p. 79).

17. "Becoming a Writer," *The Writer on Her Work*, ed. Janet Sternburg (New York: Norton, 1980) pp. 231–55, 253. Godwin elsewhere expresses a sense of this problem. In *The Finishing School* Ursula De Vane tells Justin, "There are two kinds of people. . . . One kind, you can tell just by looking at them at what point they congealed into their final selves. . . . Whereas the other kind keep moving, changing. . . . You must be constantly on your guard . . . against congealing" (New York: Avon, 1984), pp. 4–5— though the melodramatic resolution of this novel "congeals" to cliché. In *A Southern Family,* Theo issues a last challenge before his suicide to his sister, the novelist: " 'Why don't you write a book about something that can *never* be wrapped up?' " (New York:

Avon, 1987), p. 44.

18. In Godwin's case it is the mother who is the writer, which represents an interesting reversal of the pattern in twentieth-century feminist *Kunstlerromane* described by DuPlessis, where the daughter becomes a writer in order to extend her mother's insights in more permanent form; *Writing beyond the Ending* (Bloomington: Indiana University Press, 1985), Chapter 6. But underlying this difference is a deeper similarity: since Kitty writes pulp fiction rather than "serious" fiction, the mother still represents a principle which the daughter moves beyond.

19.

> In the past year, Cate had read at least three novels about women fleeing into the honesty of the woods. In the first book, the woman fell in love with a bear; in the second, the woman discovered latent artistic impulses; in this book, the woman was, at the moment, down on all fours naked in the forest, rooting and snuffling around, trying to get back to her basic instincts and wondering if she could grow hair over her whole body.

She adds, "But at least these writers are trying to . . . envision new ways to live" and asking "what have we done wrong, and how can we do better next time? I don't knock these writers; how can I? I'm stuck in the same place—between reassessment and what comes next—but I allow myself the right to be impatient with them, all the same" (New York: Viking, 1982), pp. 442–43.

20. This is Kate's term for her knack for transforming the raw materials of life into art; Margaret Drabble, *The Middle Ground* (New York: Bantam, 1980), p. 19.

### V. Doris Lessing's *The Golden Notebook*

1. Doris Lessing, *The Golden Notebook* (New York: Bantam, 1973), pp. 10, 616.

2. She felt that this put her in "a false position" because "the last thing I have wanted to do was to refuse to support women" (p. viii). "I got angry over the reviews of *The Golden Notebook*. They thought it was personal—it was, in parts. But it was also a highly structured book. . . . The point about that book was the relation of its parts to each other. But the book they wanted to turn it into was called *The Confessions of Doris Lessing*"; interview by Roy Newquist, in *Doris Lessing: A Small Personal Voice: Essays, Reviews, Interviews,* ed. Paul Schleuter (New York: Vintage, 1975), pp. 45–60, 51.

3. Review of *The Four-Gated City,* by Susan Lydon, *Ramparts* (January 1970), pp. 48–50. Though Lydon is reviewing *The Four-Gated City,* this description applies equally to *The Golden Notebook.*

4. *Doris Lessing: Critical Studies,* ed. Annis Pratt and L. S. Dembo (Madison: University of Wisconsin Press, 1974), Introduction, p. vii.

5. Rachel Blau DuPlessis, "For the Etruscans," in *The New Feminist Criticism: Essays on Women, Literature, and Theory,* ed. Elaine Showalter (New York: Pantheon, 1985), pp. 271–91, 279.

6. *A Proper Marriage,* p. 62. All references to *Children of Violence* are to the New American editions and are referred to as MQ *(Martha Quest),* PM *(A Proper Marriage),* and FGC *(The Four-Gated City).*

7. Ellen Cronan Rose and Carey Kaplan, *The Canon and the Common Reader* (Knoxville: University of Tennessee Press, forthcoming).

8. Rose and Kaplan point out that the first Lessing scholarship was written by men—James Gindin, Fredrick Karl, Fredrick P. W. McDowell, John Carey, Paul Schleuter—but that after 1971, far more women than men wrote about her: "From 1971 to 1986, 78% of the articles, 88% of the books, 93% of the MLA presentations, and 95% of the dissertations on Lessing in this country were written by women" (pp. 13, 16–17).

9. Louis Kampf, *On Modernism: The Prospects for Literature and Freedom*

(Cambridge: M.I.T. Press, 1967), describes "Lessing's massive novel" as "a significant, and exemplary, attempt to deal with" the central questions of modernism (p. 322), "a very true—and very great—work of art" (p. 326); and Robert Taubman, "Free Women," in *The New Statesman* (April 20, 1962), rpt. *On Contemporary Literature,* ed. Richard Kostelanetz (New York: Avon, 1964), pp. 402–403, calls it "unique in its truthfulness and range . . . the sort of book that determines the way people think about themselves," though he slips in an invidious comparison with de Beauvoir—Lessing "says far more of genuine interest, is less self-conscious and much less boring" (p. 403). And Irving Howe calls it "the most absorbing and exciting piece of new fiction I have read in a decade," but he, too, gets in an invidious comparison: Lessing is "radically different from other women writers who have dealt with the problems of their sex . . . in that she has no use either for the quaverings of the feminist writers or the aggressions of those female novelists whose every sentence leads a charge in the war of the sexes. . . . And Miss Lessing is far too serious for those displays of virtuoso bitchiness which are the blood and joy of certain American lady writers." *The New Republic* 147 (December 15, 1962), pp. 17–20; rpt. Sprague and Tiger, pp. 177–81, 181, 178.

10. Anthony Burgess, *The Novel Now: A Guide to Contemporary Fiction* (New York: Norton, 1967), p. 19.

11. P. W. Frederick McDowell, "The Fiction of Doris Lessing: An Interim View," in *Arizona Quarterly* 21 (1965), pp. 315–45, 329–30. See Mona Knapp, *"The Golden Notebook:* A Feminist Context for the Classroom," in *Approaches to Teaching Lessing's The Golden Notebook,* ed. Carey Kaplan and Ellen Cronan Rose (New York: The Modern Language Association of America, 1989), pp. 108–14, 109–110, for a discussion of McDowell's essay and other sexist criticism of the novel.

12. Walter Allen, *The Modern Novel in Britain and the United States* (New York: E. P. Dutton, 1964), p. 277.

13. Patrick Parrinder, "Descents into Hell: The Later Novels of Doris Lessing," *Critical Quarterly* 22, no. 4 (Winter 1980), pp. 5–25, 14.

14. Frederick R. Karl, *A Reader's Guide to the Contemporary English Novel* (New York: Farrar, Straus, and Giroux, 1971), p. 291.

15. James Gindin, *Postwar British Fiction: New Accents and Attitudes* (Berkeley: University of California Press, 1962), pp. 86, 83–84.

16. Bernard Bergonzi, *The Situation of the Novel* (Pittsburgh: University of Pittsburgh Press, 1970), pp. 200–202.

17. "The Small Personal Voice," in *A Small Personal Voice: Doris Lessing: Essays, Reviews, Interviews,* ed. Paul Schleuter (New York: Vintage, 1975), pp. 3–21, 3.

18. John Holloway, "The Literary Scene," and Gilbert Phelps, "The Post-War English Novel," in *The New Pelican Guide to English Literature: The Present,* ed. Boris Ford (Harmondsworth: Penguin, 1983), pp. 65–125, 417–49.

19. *British Novelists since 1900,* ed. Jack I. Biles (New York: AMS Press, 1987). See also my discussion of literary histories in Chapter 2.

20. Mervyn Jones, "The State of Fiction: A Symposium," in *New Review* 5, no. 1 (Summer 1978) expresses surprise that "over that last ten years, more novels haven't been written employing the *Golden Notebook* technique" and concludes that writers are "unable to take off from the groundwork which she had already attained" because they felt "daunted" (p. 47). As my study demonstrates, *The Golden Notebook* did inspire followers who employed its techniques.

21. Lennard J. Davis, *Resisting Novels: Ideology and Fiction* (New York: Methuen, 1987), p. 157.

22. Ellen W. Brooks, "The Image of Women in Lessing's *Golden Notebook,*" in *Critique: Studies in Modern Fiction* 11 (1973), p. 101.

23. Elayne Antler Rapping, " 'Unfree Women': Feminism in Doris Lessing's Novels," in *Women's Studies* 3 (1975), p. 30.

24. Quoted in Elaine Showalter, *A Literature of Their Own: British Women Novel-*

ists *from Bronte to Lessing* (London: Virago, 1978), p. 311.

25. Alice Bradley Markos, "The Pathology of Feminine Failure in the Fiction of Doris Lessing," in *Critique: Studies in Modern Fiction* 16 (1974), p. 88.

26. Showalter refers to the novel's "aversion to the feminine sensibility" (p. 309); Ellen Morgan, "Alienation of the Woman Writer in *The Golden Notebook*," in Pratt and Dembo, p. 63. Mona Knapp argues that Anna does not "make a breakthrough toward feminist self-consciousness. She remains male-oriented and resents even the physical condition of femaleness"; *Doris Lessing* (New York: Ungar, 1984), p. 60.

27. Catharine Stimpson, "Doris Lessing and the Parables of Growth," in *The Voyage In: Fictions of Female Development*, ed. Elizabeth Abel, Marianne Hirsch, and Elizabeth Langland (Hanover, NH: University Press of New England, 1983), pp. 186–205, 193–94.

28. Jenny Taylor, "Introduction: Situating Reading," in *Notebooks, Memoirs, Archives: Reading and Rereading Doris Lessing*, ed. Jenny Taylor (Boston: Routledge, 1982), pp. 1–42, 9.

29. Joanne S. Frye, *Living Stories, Telling Lives: Women and the Novel in Contemporary Experience* (Ann Arbor: University of Michigan Press, 1986), p. 172.

30. "Disloyal to Civilization: Feminism, Racism, Gynephobia," in *On Lies, Secrets, and Silence: Selected Prose 1966–1978* (New York: Norton, 1979), pp. 275–310, 279.

31. *World Press Review* (July 1981), p. 61; also introduction, p. x, and Lessing's talk in Marin County, California in April 1984.

32. As I argue in "Divided Selves: Women and Men in *The Golden Notebook*," in *The [M]other Tongue: Essays in Feminist Psychoanalytic Criticism*, ed. Shirley Nelson Garner, Claire Kahane, and Madelon Sprengnether (Ithaca: Cornell University Press, 1985), pp. 280–305. Judith Kegan Gardiner also describes empathy as a means to change in Lessing's fiction: "As the book progresses, Anna finds seeing from the other person's perspective and feeling as they do essential to her mental health and to her fiction"; *Rhys, Stead, Lessing and the Politics of Empathy* (Bloomington: Indiana University Press, 1989), pp. 120, 151. Patricia Waugh similarly sees "the solubility of [Anna's] ego boundaries as . . . a source of utopian strength"; "for Lessing, salvation can come only through a profound and full recognition of our relational needs and desires and the attempts to construct a collective world which is not based on the competitive striving of the isolated ego"; *Feminine Fictions: Revisiting the Postmodern* (London: Routledge, 1989), pp. 204, 208.

33. Nancy Chodorow, *The Reproduction of Mothering: Psychoanalysis and the Sociology of Gender* (Berkeley: University of California Press, 1979), pp. 103, 166–67.

34. "The limits of masculinity" is Andrew Tolson's term; *The Limits of Masculinity* (London: Tavistock, 1977); "the confines of masculinity" is Warren Farrell's term in *The Liberated Man, or Beyond Masculinity: Freeing Men and Their Relationships with Women* (New York: Bantam, 1975), pp. 29–31; see also Herb Goldberg, *The Hazards of Being Male* (New York: New American Library, 1976). For literature on men, see James B. Harrison, "Review Essay: Men's Roles and Men's Lives," in *Signs* (Winter 1978), pp. 324–36; and Lois Banner, review essay, in *Signs* 14, no. 3 (Spring 1989), pp. 703–708.

35. Cf. Martha Lifson's discussion of the novel's "non-chronological treatment of time": "The novel works frequently to confuse one's sense of time by slowing it down or speeding it up, or to suggest, by juxtaposing sections of the notebooks, that disparate events occurred simultaneously." "Structural Patterns in *The Golden Notebook*," in *Michigan Papers in Women's Studies* 2, no. 4 (1978), pp. 95–108, 102. Anne M. Mulkeen similarly suggests that the novel's form allows a simultaneous movement back, forward, and within: "Free Women" "moves forward in present time," "but as we take each step forward, we are also asked to explore in depth: to go inward, into the world of Anna's mind . . . to go backwards, through the times and experiences those notebooks attempt to record"; "Twentieth-Century Realism: The 'Grid' Structure of *The Golden*

*Notebook,"* in *Studies in the Novel* 4, no. 2 (Summer 1972), pp. 262–74, 264–65.

36. Roberta Rubenstein's Jungian reading stresses Anna's search for "personal wholeness" and sees Anna's "crackup" as ultimately resolved "into positive integration" (*The Novelistic Vision of Doris Lessing: Breaking the Forms of Consciousness* [Urbana: University of Illinois Press, 1979], pp. 6, 89). See also Mary Cohen, " 'Out of the Chaos a New Kind of Strength': Doris Lessing's *The Golden Notebook*," in *The Authority of Experience: Essays in Feminist Criticism*, ed. Arlyn Diamond and Lee R. Edwards (Amherst: University of Massachusetts Press, 1977), pp. 178–93. Mulkeen argues that "disintegration," which "seems the most all-inclusive movement in the book, [is] set against a structure which calls for unity and interrelationship" (p. 270).

37. As Claire Sprague observes, "A few years ago we were all talking . . . about splits and divisions and fragmentation. . . . Now I'm hearing about diversity, about multiplicity, about protean selves, about incoherence as a potentially positive thing" (quoted by Molly Hite, *Doris Lessing Newsletter* 11, no. 2 [Fall 1987], p. 12). Sprague's revisions of "Doubletalk and Doubles Talk in *The Golden Notebook*," in *Papers on Language and Literature* 18, no. 2 (Spring 1982), pp. 181–97, to "Doubles Talk in *The Golden Notebook*," in Sprague and Tiger (1986), pp. 44–60, illustrate this shift: in the latter, she explores fragmentation as a means to multiplicity and suggests that "doubles and multiples force us to see at least double, force us to question any single view of personality or reality" (p. 55). Frye argues that multiple selfhood offers a way beyond the either–or choice between femaleness and adulthood, autonomy and sexuality (pp. 92–93), and in both *The Golden Notebook* and *The Waterfall*, protagonists choose "an enabling self-fragmentation" (p. 146). Hite suggests that "despite a rhetoric of wholeness informing [Lessing's] encyclopedic novel, the emphasis throughout is on the complexity of experience, its intractability to integration"; "fragmentation, breakage, gaps, and lapses are precisely what allow possibility to emerge"; *The Other Side of the Story: Structures and Strategies of Contemporary Feminist Narratives* (Ithaca: Cornell University Press, 1989), p. 64.

38. Patricia Waugh discusses early feminists' adherence "to a liberal humanist belief in the possibility of discovering a 'true' self," an idea of "becoming a 'person' " which involves throwing off false social roles and discovering an "inner essence," and suggests that this "was a necessary phase," since "for women in the 1960s and early 1970s, 'unity' rather than dispersal seemed to offer more hope for political change"; *Feminine Fictions: Revisiting the Postmodern* (London: Routledge, 1989), pp. 22–23, 25, 13. Cora Kaplan describes her reassessment of subjectivity: "In the early stages of thinking about women and writing I had, in common with other feminists, talked mostly about the ways in which women were denied access to something I have called 'full' subjectivity. . . . In the last few years I have come round to a very different perspective on the problem, drawn from Marxist and feminist appropriations of psychoanalytic and structuralist theories. . . . Rather than approach women's difficulty in positioning themselves as writers as a question of barred access to some durable psychic state to which all humans should and can aspire, we might instead see their experience as foregrounding the inherently unstable and split character of all human subjectivity. . . . The instability of 'femininity' . . . points to . . . the impossibility of a . . . unified and cohered subject" and to a "potentially hopeful incoherence"; "Speaking/Writing/Feminism," in *On Gender and Writing*, ed. Michelene Wandor (London: Pandora Press, 1983), pp. 51–66; 57–59.

39. Roland Barthes, *S/Z* (New York: Hill and Wang, 1974); Julia Kristeva, "The Novel as Polylogue," in *Desire and Language* (New York: Columbia University Press, 1980), pp. 159–209; Catherine Belsey, *Critical Practice* (London: Methuen, 1980), *passim*.

40. Nissa Torrents, "Testimony to Mysticism: Interview with Lessing," in *Doris Lessing Newsletter* (Winter 1980), pp. 4, 2, 12.

41. See Jenny Taylor, "Introduction: Situating Reading," in *Notebooks, Memoirs,*

*Archives,* pp. 32, 34–35; and Claire Sprague, "Dialectic and Counter-Dialectic in the Martha Quest Novels," in *The Journal of Commonwealth Literature* 14, no. 1 (August 1979), pp. 39–52, 40.

42. An early reviewer remarks that the "Chinese box" arrangement of *The Golden Notebook* is "similar to Brecht's 'alienation technique' on the stage" (Jeremy Brooks, "Doris Lessing's Chinese Box," in *Sunday Times* [April 15, 1962], p. 32); quoted in Taylor, p. 1, who adds, "The alienation technique and the use of montage, the way in which the novel 'lays bare the device' of the conditions of its own production, recall not only the work of Brecht but the debates of the Russian Formalists, and the writings of Walter Benjamin." Eagleton summarizes Walter Benjamin's *Understanding Brecht* (London: 1973) in a way that makes clear its relation to Lessing: "The task of theatre is not to 'reflect' a fixed reality, but to demonstrate how character and action are historically produced, and so how they could have been, and still can be, different. . . . Instead of appearing as a seamless whole, which suggests that its entire action is inexorably determined from the outset, the play presents itself as discontinuous, open-ended, internally contradictory, encouraging in the audience a 'complex seeing' "; the audience becomes "collaborator in an open-ended practice, rather than the consumer of a finished object" (*Marxism and Literary Criticism* [Berkeley: University of California Press, 1976], pp. 65–66). See also Rosalind Coward and John Ellis, *Language and Materialism: Developments in Semiology and the Theory of the Subject* (London: Routledge and Kegan Paul, 1977), pp. 36–37.

43. As discussed in Chapter 1; see also Lukács, "The Problems of a Philosophy of the History of Forms" (1920), in *The Theory of the Novel* (Cambridge; MIT Press, 1971), pp. 40–55; and Eagleton, pp. 27–28.

44. For Gramsci on hegemony, see *The Modern Prince* (London: International Publishers, 1957), and Raymond Williams, *Marxism and Literature* (Oxford: Oxford University Press, 1977), pp. 108–14. See also Walter L. Adamson, *Hegemony and Revolution: A Study of Antonio Gramsci's Political and Cultural Theory* (Berkeley and Los Angeles: University of California Press, 1980).

45. Louis Althusser, *For Marx,* trans. Ben Brewster (Harmondsworth: Penguin, 1969; first published in French 1966; reissued London: New Left Books, 1977); *Lenin and Philosophy and Other Essays,* trans. Ben Brewster (London: New Left Books, 1971; first published in French 1968), especially pp. 231–36; see also Pierre Macherey, *A Theory of Literary Production,* trans. Geoffrey Wall (London: Routledge and Kegan Paul, 1978, first published in French 1966).

46. In 1957 Roland Barthes described "myth" as "a conjuring trick" which "transforms history into nature"; *Mythologies,* trans. Annette Lavers (New York: Farrar, Straus, and Giroux, 1972), pp. 142, 129.

47. Antonio Gramsci, "The Study of Philosophy," in *Selections from the Prison Notebooks* (New York: International Publishers, 1976), pp. 322–77, 323.

48. The term is Frank Lentricchia's; *Criticism and Social Change* (Chicago: University of Chicago Press, 1983), p. 76.

49. Fredric Jameson, *The Political Unconscious: Narrative as a Socially Symbolic Act* (Ithaca: Cornell University Press, 1982), pp. 98–99.

50. Roland Barthes, *Writing Degree Zero,* trans. Annette Lavers and Colin Smith (New York: Hill and Wang, 1968), pp. 13, 16.

51. Raymond Williams, *Marxism and Literature* (Oxford: Oxford University Press, 1977), p. 176.

52. Rachel Blau DuPlessis, *Writing beyond the Ending: Narrative Strategies of Twentieth-Century Women Writers* (Bloomington: Indiana University Press, 1985), p. ix.

53. Audre Lorde, "The Master's Tools Will Never Dismantle the Master's House," in *This Bridge Called My Back: Writings of Radical Women of Color,* ed. Cherríe Moraga and Gloria Anza lúa (New York: Women of Color Press, 1981), pp. 98–101, 99.

54. Lessing uses the same image Drabble will use (in *The Waterfall,* p. 139) of a woman waiting at a window, to suggest female bereavement: "waiting, every night . . . staring out the window waiting for a man whom she knew, quite well, would never come to her again" (p. 227).

55. Diana Trilling cites these discussions of "real" as opposed to clitoral orgasms approvingly *(Times Literary Supplement* [October 1978], p. 1165), whereas Showalter cites them as evidence that Lessing has not "confronted the essential feminist implications of her own writing" (1978, p. 311); but neither makes a distinction between Lessing and her protagonist.

56. "The right man" is associated with the "real story" by Rennie in Atwood's *Bodily Harm,* when Rennie looks back to a time when "she had ambitions, which she now thinks of as illusions: She believed there was a right man, not several and not almost right, and she believed there was a real story, not several and not almost real" (New York: Simon and Schuster, 1982), p. 62.

57. "One result of this tendency was the vacuousness of Soviet linguistics from the 1930s to the 1950s" with its view of language as "a superstructural form" (Coward and Ellis, pp. 78–79).

58. As Rubenstein says, Lessing reveals that "objectivity is an aesthetic and epistemological convention; there is only the subjective point of view" (p. 74); "all perception is interpretation; there is no single authoritative view of events" (p. 102). Draine notes, "no longer bound to find *the* truth. . . . Anna is free to present *her* truth, with renewed conviction" (p. 86).

59. Raymond Williams, *The Long Revolution* (London: Chatto and Windus, 1961), pp. 20, 37–38.

60. Sprague suggests that *The Golden Notebook* is "steeped in an awareness of 'dark doubles' " ("Doubletalk," p. 197), that "doubles and multiples force us to see at least double, to question any single view of personality or reality," and that this is more than a revelation of the complexity at the heart of reality; it is a "burst[ing] of the boundaries of twoness" ("Doubles Talk," pp. 55–56). See also Elizabeth Abel, "The Golden Notebook: 'Female Writing' and 'The Great Tradition,' " in Sprague and Tiger, pp. 101–107, who argues that like the women's writing advocated by Cixous, the form of *The Golden Notebook* "dramatically challenges the structure of binary oppositions" (pp. 102, 104).

61. Caryn Fuoroli, "Doris Lessing's 'Game': Referential Language and Fictional Form," in *Twentieth-Century Literature* 27, no. 2 (Summer 1981), pp. 146–65, 164. Fuoroli relates Lessing's "awareness of the problematic nature of language" to her "dissatisfaction with social realism" and suggests that Anna realizes the limits of referential language and comes "to define herself through an intuitive knowledge beyond the confines of social reference. Yet, having done so, she also acknowledges and accepts referential language as a stabilizing force and as a means of communication. No matter how confining this language may be, it is necessary as a means of maintaining personal and social order" (p. 146). Susan Kress notes that "the pressure to deny language is opposed by another, the necessity of forming, of shaping, of 'naming' "; "Lessing's Responsibility," in *Salmagundi* (Winter–Spring 1980), 95–131, 118.

62. Jouve argues that nothing happens "from *inside* the language . . . the process of writing itself is excluded, except as a tool, from the operation that is taking place"; "the prose never really confronts you with the experience of madness" (pp. 114–15).

63. Jean Bethke Elshtain, "The Post-*Golden Notebook* Fiction of Doris Lessing," in *Salmagundi* (Winter–Spring 1980), pp. 95–114, 101.

64. Doris Lessing, *Briefing for a Descent into Hell* (New York: Bantam, 1972), p. 112.

65. DuPlessis suggests that each notebook's "acts of containment are criticized by the presence of the others, for each constructs a reality that tries to exclude the others" (p. 101). Mulkeen describes *"The Golden Notebook* as "completely self-questioning— . . .

only its many juxtaposed, overlapping, and sometimes contradictory viewpoints, taken together, can approximate the 'density of our experience' now" (p. 267). Draine describes the resolution of the novel as a "saving schizophrenia—a state that permits [Anna's] commitment to practical goals, visionary ideals, art, works, altruism, social reorganization, logic, and order, while at the same time allowing her to acknowledge and even honor all that accompanies chaos" ("Nostalgia and Irony: The Postmodern Order of *The Golden Notebook*," in *Modern Fiction Studies* 26, no. 1 [Spring 1980], pp. 31–48, 48.

66. Contrary to Ruth Whittaker's assertion that "*The Golden Notebook* is not a treatise advocating autonomy for women; rather, it is a lament for its seeming impossibility" (*Modern Novelists: Doris Lessing* [New York: St. Martin's Press, 1988], pp. 70–71), Anna does achieve autonomy, though she does so, paradoxically, by submerging herself in the experience of others. Phyllis Sternberg-Perrakis ("*The Golden Notebook:* Separation and Symbiosis," in *American Imago* 38, no. 4 [Winter 1981], pp. 407–28) describes Anna's overcoming the "need to lose herself in symbiotic relationships with others, her massive separation anxiety," and learning "to be alone" (p. 408). But Anna achieves this precisely *because* she first loses herself in a symbiotic relationship with Saul; it is her ability to break down into him that enables her to break away from him.

67. Neither can Anna; as she says of Saul during their breakdown, "I say *he*, taking for granted that I can pinpoint a personality. That there is a *he* who is the real man. Why should I assume that one of the persons he is is more himself than the others? But I do" (p. 591).

68. John Fowles, *The French Lieutenant's Woman* (Boston: Little, Brown and Company, 1969), p. 417.

69. Margaret Drabble, "Doris Lessing: Cassandra in a World Under Siege," in *Ramparts* (February 1972), pp. 50–54, 52.

## VI. Margaret Drabble's *The Waterfall*

1. Margaret Drabble, *The Waterfall* (New York: Fawcett Popular Library, 1977), pp. 47, 53. All references are to this edition.

2. Lynn Veach Sadler, *Margaret Drabble* (Boston: Twayne, 1986), p. 131. The novel reminds Bernard Bergonzi of "women's magazine fiction"; *Contemporary Novelists,* ed. James Vinson (New York: St. Martin's Press, 1976), pp. 373–74.

3. Joanne V. Creighton, "An Interview with Margaret Drabble," Hampstead, September 4, 1970; in *Margaret Drabble: Golden Realms,* Living Author Series No. 4, ed. Dorey Schmidt (Edinburg, TX: Pan American University School of Humanities, 1982), pp. 18–31, 18.

4. Nancy S. Hardin, interview with Margaret Drabble, Hampstead, October 1972; in *Interviews with Contemporary Writers,* ed. L. S. Dembo (Madison: University of Wisconsin Press, 1983), pp. 89–111, 109. Drabble says elsewhere, "I can see why feminists don't like it—because it's about a passionate heterosexual love affair which disturbs everything. It disturbs all one's preconceptions about what's important in life. I think passionate heterosexual love affairs are extremely important. . . . When I wrote that book there was no feminist criticism around . . . and so I was not in any way conscious of any reaction. I don't suppose I would have cared if I had been"; interview by Gillian Parker and Janet Todd, *Women Writers Talking,* ed. Janet Todd (New York: Holmes and Meier, 1983), pp. 161–95, 166.

5. In the lead essay in Schmidt's anthology, "Margaret Drabble's Golden Vision," Nora Stovel describes Drabble as "a social realist [who] has held the mirror up to contemporary society" (p. 14). Ellen Z. Lambert describes Drabble's work as generally "praised for its fine criticism of contemporary English society and . . . sympathetic portrayal of domestic life—love, marriage, and the bearing of children" ("Margaret Drabble and the Sense of Possibility," in *University of Toronto Quarterly* 49 [Spring

1980], pp. 228–51, 228). Even with a novel so obviously self-referential as *The Waterfall*, critics focus on such questions as the character and development of the protagonist. Virginia K. Beards, "Margaret Drabble: Novels of a Cautious Feminist," in *Critique: Studies in Modern Fiction* 15, no. 2 (1973), sees the novel's focus as "exclusively sexual"—as concerning "a female destroyed by her physiology and culture" (p. 43). Marion Vlastos Libby focuses on the novel's "stultifying determinism" ("Fate and Feminism in the Novels of Margaret Drabble," in *Contemporary Literature* 16, no. 2 [Spring 1975], pp. 186, 175–76). Roberta Rubenstein is concerned with questions of style, in her discussion of Drabble's "use of myths and allegories" ("*The Waterfall*: The Myth of Psyche, Romantic Tradition, and the Female Quest"; in Schmidt, p. 139), but she does not address the novel's striking structural features. Joan Manheimer usefully describes the alternating pronouns as "imply[ing] that the development of identity . . . is function of a dialectic between the self as object and the self as subject" ("Margaret Drabble and the Journey to the Self," in *Studies in the Literary Imagination* 11, no. 2 [Fall 1978], p. 139), but she does not investigate the literary/aesthetic implications of the division. Even Joanne V. Creighton, who discusses the novel as "a nontraditional work" which invites consideration "as a fictional construction," is concerned with "the 'real' character Jane" ("Reading Margaret Drabble's *The Waterfall*," in *Critical Essays on Margaret Drabble*, ed. Ellen Cronan Rose [Boston: G. K. Hall, 1985], pp. 106, 116–17).

    6. Julia Kristeva, "Word, Dialogue, and Novel," in *Desire in Language: A Semiotic Approach to Literature and Art,* ed. Leon S. Roudiez (New York: Columbia University Press, 1980), pp. 71, 86.

    7. Review of Lessing's *Stories* in *Saturday Review* (May 27, 1978); cited in Ellen Cronan Rose, "Twenty Questions," in *Doris Lessing Newsletter* 4, no. 2 (Winter 1980), p. 5.

    8. Jane uses the word "comprehend" to mean both "understand" and "include" (pp. 53, 90).

    9. Doris Lessing, *The Golden Notebook* (New York: Ballantine, 1973), p. 660.

    10. Hélène Cixous, "The Laugh of the Medusa," in *Signs* (Summer 1976), rpt. in *New French Feminisms: An Anthology,* ed. Elaine Marks and Isabelle de Courtivron (Amherst: University of Massachusetts Press, 1980), pp. 245–64, 256 (hereafter LM). In this manifesto of *l'écriture féminine*, Cixous argues that a polymorphous female sexuality subverts hierarchies based on a "reigning phallus." Luce Irigaray similarly sees woman's experience of *jouissance* ("pleasure," but more specifically the physical pleasures of sexuality which have been repressed by phallogocentric culture) as revolutionary; *This Sex Which Is Not One* (Ithaca: Cornell University Press, 1985). Julia Kristeva sees both men and women as having access to a prelinguistic *jouissance; Revolution in Poetic Language* (New York: Columbia University Press, 1984).

    11. Tony Tanner, *Adultery in the Novel: Contract and Transgression* (Baltimore: Johns Hopkins University Press, 1979), pp. 69–72.

    12. Gail Godwin, *The Odd Woman* (New York: Warner Books, 1974), p. 302.

    13. Kristeva describes *la mère qui jouit* as a challenge to phallocentrism in *About Chinese Women* (New York: Urigen Books, 1977), especially Chapter 3, "The Virgin of the Word"; and *Desire in Language,* especially "Motherhood According to Giovanni Bellini," pp. 237–70; see also Marks and Courtivron, p. 36.

    14. Tanner, p. 12. Tanner describes adultery as "an act of transgression, a violation of boundaries that leads to instability, asymmetry, disorder" (p. 12) and "threatens the very existence of civilization . . . itself . . . threatening . . . all existing bonds that held together states, armies, families, lovers, friends" (p. 24), for "if rules of marriage, economic rules, and linguistic rules are in some way systematically interdependent, then the breakdown of one implies the possible breakdown of all three" (p. 85). He also calls adultery "the generative form of Western literature as we know it" (p. 12).

    15. My reading of the alternating pronouns takes issue with Ellen Cronan Rose's, though it also owes much to her "Feminine Endings—and Beginnings: Margaret Drab-

ble's *The Waterfall*," in *Contemporary Literature* 21, no. 1 (1980), pp. 81–99. Rose argues that Jane "has divided herself into Jane, the woman (whose experience is liquid and formless), and Jane Gray, the artist (who gives form, order, and shapeliness to that experience)" in her search for a form that "amalgamates feminine fluidity and masculine shapeliness" (pp. 89, 90, 96). She describes Jane's division as representing a split between "the 'I' who meditates on the art of writing and the 'she' who has a love affair," with the "she" representing the "essentially passive sexuality" and "inchoate liquid 'femininity' " which Jane must bring together with the "rational, productive, 'masculine' aspect," the "Apollonian, 'male' " principle of artistic "shaping" expressed by the "I" (p. 92; see also *The Novels of Margaret Drabble: Equivocal Figures* [Totowa, NJ: Barnes and Noble, 1980], pp. 49–70). But I see the "she" sections as exploring problems of artistic shaping and the "I" sections as primarily concerned with the analysis of passion. Jean Wyatt's description of the alternating pronouns as reflecting "the conflict between Jane's desire to live out the intensities of a romantic love story and her desire to understand the truth of her own experience" is closer to my sense of the novel; "Escaping Literary Designs: The Politics of Reading and Writing in Margaret Drabble's *The Waterfall*," in *Perspectives on Contemporary Literature* 2 (1985), p. 38. So, too, is Mary Hurley Moran's description of the third-person sections as "narrated in a heavily cadenced . . . style that draws attention to itself" and Jane's development toward connecting the refined, airtight world of the romance with "the 'coarser air' of ordinary reality"; *Margaret Drabble: Existing within Structures* (Carbondale: Southern University Illinois Press, 1983), pp. 87–89. Joanne S. Frye describes the "she" as enacting "the cultural expectations of femininity" and the I as "claim[ing] narrative agency"; *Living Stories, Telling Lives: Women and the Novel in Contemporary Experience* (Ann Arbor: University of Michigan Press, 1986), pp. 154, 155, 160, 163.

16. That "passion" is derived from "patior" ("I suffer"), a deponent verb whose grammatical form is the passive, suggests that the "passivity" of suffering is inscribed within language.

17. Though Jane's use of convention also involves some fascinating twists. When she describes herself and James as "separated by her condition more safely than by Tristram's sword" (p. 40), the image rings striking changes on the barrier which separated the lovers in medieval versions: Drabble replaces the barren, death-dealing metal of Tristram's sword, symbol of male law and boundary, with the female condition of openness and vulnerability after childbirth, which serves not simply as barrier, but as "prolonged initiation" (p. 40), and which, like the childbirth that imposes it, is generative, has "issue."

18. Such potentials are suggested elsewhere, as in the lovers' dialogue just after James has returned from holiday:

> "I'd have liked to have locked you up in here . . . to put you under a
> stone, to make sure you'd stay where I wanted you."
> "Cruel, you are," she said, smiling.
>
> . . . . . . . . . . . . . . . . . . . . . . . . . . . . . .
>
> "You had to sit here and wait for me. You had to sit here and
> miss me. I hope you were sad enough . . . the sadder the better. . . ."
> [She was] amazed at his acceptance of her dreadful tribute.
> "I like it," he said, "it's what I want." (pp. 174–75)

19. Manheimer describes this shift as signifying "Jane's increasing maturity" (p. 139); Rose notes that the shift "signals the unification of the divided self who is Jane Gray" ("Feminine Endings," p. 92); Rubenstein similarly suggests that it signals the end of "the inner division that has plagued Jane and forced her to split her story into two perspectives" (in Schmidt, p. 152).

20. Drabble said that she originally intended Jane to die, but "as I neared the conclusion, my heart softened." Lecture, Los Angeles, March 8, 1990.

21. Rose, "Feminine Endings," p. 96; and *Equivocal Figures*, p. 66.

22. Creighton describes the novel as "full of 'unresolved ambiguities'— . . . gaps or spaces, disharmonies or tensions" which do not fit "into traditional novelistic or psychic resolution and unity" and suggests that "remission from the heavily-orchestrated endings of women's stories, lives, and books is exactly what [Jane's] story is about" (in Rose [1985], pp. 117, 115). Skoller observes that Drabble's "reconstitution" "is not resolution or synthesis but invention that renders the work and the world as incomplete" ("The Progress of a Letter: Truth, Feminism, and *The Waterfall*," in Rose [1985], p. 122). See also Lorna Irvine's excellent discussion of Drabble's avoidance of endings as an affirmation of life, futurity, and "personal and cultural continuity" ("No Sense of an Ending: Drabble's Continuous Fictions," in Rose [1985], pp. 73–86).

23. William Flint Thrall and Addison Hibbard, *A Handbook to Literature* (New York: The Odyssey Press, 1960), p. 200.

24. Hélène Cixous, "Castration or Decapitation," *Signs* 7, no. 1 (Summer 1981), p. 53. It is significant that Drabble refers to *The Waterfall* as "the most female of all my books" ("Say a Good Word for the Curse," *Good Housekeeping* [English edition] [February 1978], p. 51; in Rose, "Feminine Endings," p. 81).

25. Marks and Courtivron, introduction, pp. 36–37, n. 8.

26. *A Proper Marriage* (New York: New American Library, 1964), pp. 251, 152 (hereafter PM).

27. Drabble describes herself as "happier in a more traditional domestic life" than Lessing and therefore as "having more faith in ordinary structures and democratic processes than she does"; Dee Preussner, "Talking with Margaret Drabble," in *Modern Fiction Studies* 25, no. 4 (1979–80), p. 569.

28. Irigaray defines "a feminine syntax" as one in which "there would no longer be subject or object . . . [and which] would preclude any . . . establishment of ownership, thus any form of appropriation"; "Questions," in *This Sex* 119–69, 134.

29. Probably such wordplay combines conscious and unconscious processes. Tanner cites Freud's discussion of "joke work" as exploiting "the double-sidedness and duplicity of speech"; *Jokes and Their Relation to the Unconscious*, in *The Standard Edition of The Complete Psychological Works of Sigmund Freud*, vol. 8, ed. James Strachey (London: Hogarth Press, 1960), pp. 169–72. Tanner calls literature "a complex kind of 'joke-work' . . . the profoundest kind of play work," both "basic responses on the part of man at finding himself irreversibly involved in language"; in both, "purposive intention and the processes of the unconscious meet" (pp. 334–35). Coward and Ellis, citing Kristeva's *Revolution in Poetic Language*, describe "the influx of unconscious processes" (p. 149) as allowing for the expression of repressed material; Barthes describes "the text that discomforts . . . [and] unsettles the reader's historical, cultural, psychological assumptions"; *The Pleasure of the Text*, trans. Richard Miller (New York: Hill and Wang, 1975), p. 14.

30. LM, p. 264. Cixous describes this "exchange" in paradoxical terms that similarly recall Drabble's: "The woman arriving over and over again does not stand still; she's everywhere, she exchanges, she is the desire-that-gives. . . . She comes in, comes-in-between herself me and you, between the other me where one is always infinitely more than one and more than me, without the fear of ever reaching a limit; she thrills in our becoming. And we'll keep on becoming!" (pp. 263–64).

31. Not "inscribed . . . within boundaries . . . without ever inscribing or discerning contours," female sexuality is like the sea: "We are ourselves sea, sand, coral, sea-weed, beaches, tides, swimmers, children, waves. . . . We know how to speak them all" (LM, pp. 259–60). Irigaray describes "feminine" style in similar terms—as *"fluid,"* as "resist[ing] and explod[ing] every firmly established form, figure, idea or concept" ("The

Power of Discourse," in *This Sex,* pp. 68–85, 79); as "continuous . . . unending" ("The 'Mechanics' of Fluids," in *This Sex,* pp. 106–18, 111); "These movements cannot be described as the passage from a beginning to an end. These rivers flow into no single, definitive sea. These streams are without fixed banks, this body without fixed boundaries" ("When Our Lips Speak Together," in *This Sex,* pp. 205–18, 215). In *Diving Deep and Surfacing: Women Writers on Spiritual Quest* (Boston: Beacon, 1980), Carol Christ notes that water imagery is recurrent in contemporary women's fiction. One thinks of the sea in Lessing's *Landlocked* and *The Summer Before the Dark;* the lake in Atwood's *Surfacing* and *Lady Oracle;* the oceans, rivers, streams, and pools in Iris Murdoch's *The Nice and the Good, The Sea, the Sea, Nuns and Soldiers, The Good Apprentice;* the lake, floods, and rains in Marilynne Robinson's *Housekeeping.*

32. Whereas Jane's poetry expresses only the pain of her experience, her fiction accommodates its multifacetedness. In her loneliness after Malcolm's departure, she "was writing [poetry] more copiously, more fluently, than . . . ever . . . before," and she uses an image uncannily like Cixous's (LM, p. 261)—"The ink was pouring on to the sheets like blood" (p. 115). Once she starts loving James, she stops writing poetry because, as she says, "I did not know how to write about joy, I could find no words, no patterns for the damp and intimate secrets of love" (p. 115); but on the basis of his accident, she writes "a very good sequence of poems" (p. 250). Jane's fiction, however—and Drabble's—encompasses "misery" as well as "joy" (pp. 114–15), pleasure and pain, "wetness" and wounds.

33. *S/Z* (New York: Hill and Wang, 1974), p. 5.

34. Roland Barthes, *Image-Music-Text* (London: Fontana, 1977), p. 147.

## VII. Margaret Laurence's *The Diviners*

1. T. S. Eliot, "Little Gidding," in *Four Quartets, The Complete Poems and Plays: 1909–1950* (New York: Harcourt, Brace and Company, 1952), p. 142.

2. *The Stone Angel* (New York: Bantam, 1981), p. 3.

3. Service for Jean Margaret Wemyss Laurence, Bloor Street United Church, Toronto, January 9, 1987. Thanks to Greta Coger for sending me a copy of this service, and for sending me articles on Laurence's death in Canadian newspapers and journals.

4. Eleanor Johnston, "The Quest of *The Diviners*," in *Mosaic* 11, no. 3 (Spring 1978), quotes Laurence as saying, "I don't think I'll ever write another novel. It's not because I don't want to. I just have this knowledge, it's a sort of a Celtic second sight" (pp. 116–17).

5. E.g., *The Globe and the Mail, The Montreal Gazette* (January 6, 1987).

6. Clara Thomas describes Laurence as "predominantly engaged in writing out of the experience of Canadians and in their accustomed speech patterns"; "The Chariot of Ossian: Myth and Manitoba in *The Diviners*," in *Journal of Canadian Studies* 13, no. 3 (Fall 1978), pp. 55–63, 62. Laurence describes herself as trying to convey a "strong sense of place and of our own culture . . . to give Canadians a . . . sense of who they are, where they came from, and where they may be going . . . by forging our myths and giving voice to our history, to our legends, to our cultural being"; Bernice Lever, "Literature and Canadian Culture: An Interview with Margaret Laurence," in *Critical Views on Canadian Writers: Margaret Laurence,* ed. William New (Toronto: McGraw-Hill Ryerson Limited, 1977), p. 27.

7. Margaret Atwood refers to *The Diviners* as "paradoxically . . . the most 'international' of Laurence's books and the most 'national' "; "Face to Face," in New, pp. 33–40, 39. Clara Thomas describes it as concerned with "an entire culture, its myths and legends"; *The Manawaka World of Margaret Laurence* (Toronto: McClelland & Stewart, 1975), p. 131.

8. Margaret Laurence, *The Diviners* (Toronto, New York, London: Bantam, 1974), p. 60.

9. See Patricia Morley, *Margaret Laurence,* Twayne's World Author Series (Boston: G. K. Hall, 1981), pp. 130–31. In *Dance on the Earth* (Toronto: McClelland and Stewart, 1989) (hereafter DOE), Laurence discusses what she calls "the controversy" (pp. 213–17) and describes herself as feeling "extraordinarily damaged" by it (p. 214).

10. *The Tempest* is arguably the most sexist and racist of all Shakespeare's plays. See Lorie Jerrell Leininger, "The Miranda Trap: Sexism and Racism in Shakespeare's *Tempest,*" in *"The Woman's Part": Feminist Criticism of Shakespeare,* ed. Carolyn Ruth Swift Lenz, Gayle Greene, and Carol Thomas Neely (Urbana: University of Illinois Press, 1980), pp. 285–94. Laurence was well aware of Prospero as European colonial: she had read O. Mannoni's *Prospero and Caliban: The Psychology of Colonization* (New York: Praeger, 1964) with a "shock of recognition"; quoted in Jane Leney, "Prospero and Caliban in Laurence's African Fiction," in *The Work of Margaret Laurence,* ed. John R. Sorfleet, *Journal of Canadian Fiction* 27 (1980), pp. 63–80, 68. See also DOE, p. 155. In *This Side Jordan,* "Miranda" is a naively well-intentioned English colonial woman.

11. Mary Anne Ferguson, "The Female Novel of Development and the Myth of Psyche," in *The Voyage In: Fictions of Female Development,* ed. Elizabeth Abel, Marianne Hirsch, and Elizabeth Langland (Hanover, NH: University Press of New England, 1983), p. 228.

12. Michel Fabre, "Words and the World: 'The Diviners' as an Exploration of the Book of Life," in *Canadian Literature* 93 (Summer 1982), pp. 60–78, calls *The Diviners* "as much a pilgrimage along epic lines as a *Bildungsroman*" (p. 60). Thomas suggests that the structure of *The Diviners* is "as complex as that of a classical epic, and one that incorporates many of the traditional epic techniques . . . the stories of heroes and their battles, the lists and heightened descriptions . . . the transposition of the oral into the written—and . . . epic simile" (1975, p. 169). Stephanie A. Demetrakopoulos ("Laurence's Fiction: A Revisioning of Feminine Archetypes," in *Canadian Literature* 93 [Summer 1982], pp. 42–57) refers to Morag as "the feminine counterpart of Odysseus" and describes the novel as "reiterat[ing] the idea of the Fortunate Fall that a redemptive growth and wholeness come from engaging in struggling and taking risks" (pp. 52–53).

13. Edward W. Said, *Beginnings: Intention and Method* (New York: Basic Books, 1975), p. 83.

14. That "Morag" is Gaelic for "Sarah" points to her role in the founding of a new order and to the position of *The Diviners* as the culmination of the Manawaka cycle. Morag/Sarah fulfills the promise left unfulfilled by Hagar, protagonist of *The Stone Angel,* first of the Manawaka novels. The Biblical Hagar bore a son to Abraham, but it was Sarah's child who founded the new dynasty. Laurence's Hagar is, like her Biblical precedent, a "bondswoman" in the sense that she is bound to destructive conventions; she, too, flees to the wilderness and is in an important sense left wandering there; and her legacy to her sons is destructive. But Morag finds a way out of the wilderness and bears a daughter who becomes "the inheritor." See Joan Coldwell, "Hagar as Meg Merrilies, the Homeless Gipsy," in Sorfleet, pp. 92–100, 99.

15. Morag's imaginary childhood playmates similarly suggest her identification with male strengths: contrasted to the conventional heroine Peony, with "curly blonde hair . . . and sweet little rosebud lips," is Morag's "sturdier" "alter ego" Rosa Picardy, who "did brave deeds, slew dragons and/or polar bears. . . . Not for her the martyr's death" (p. 13). Laurence describes her childhood preference for "adventure stories": "I don't think it ever occurred to me that such adventures could never happen to me, a girl" (DOE, p. 64).

16. *Reinventing Womanhood* (New York: Norton, 1979), p. 124. Surprisingly, however, Laurence's novels have not received much attention from feminist critics. Harriet Blodgett praises Laurence for writing from a "feminine point of view . . . without being polemical" and says it was "fortunate chance" that she was born "too early to become a self-conscious participant in the recent women's movement" because this saved her "from the tendentiousness and shrillness of much radicalist [sic] feminine

writing" (p. 5). "The Real Lives of Margaret Laurence's Women," in *Critique: Studies in Modern Fiction* 23, no. 1 (1981), pp. 5–17. More helpfully, Demetrakopoulos sees Laurence as "making a radical change in the whole literary tradition by re-telling from a woman's point of view traditional and archetypal feminine life patterns that have been portrayed hitherto by male authors only" (p. 42); Laurence "re-visions what it means to be a woman," and her heroines are "changing the very structure of characterization in world literature" (p. 55). But Demetrakopoulos stresses "feminine archetypes" (p. 42) in a way that I do not find particularly relevant. Angelika Maesar, "Finding the Mother: The Individuation of Laurence's Heroines" (in Sorfleet, pp. 151–66), also stresses archetypes in a Jungian reading of Laurence's female characters as wresting identity from "the pre-patriarchal form of the Absolute, the Great Mother" (p. 151).

17. "Gritty Places and Strong Women," review of *The Diviners*, in *New York Times* (1974), rpt. *Margaret Laurence*, ed. New, pp. 212–13.

18. Peter Brooks, *Reading for the Plot: Design and Intention in Narrative* (New York: Random House, 1984), pp. 63, 235, 285. Marianne Hirsch, *The Mother/Daughter Plot: Narrative, Psychoanalysis, Feminism* (Bloomington: Indiana University Press, 1989), discusses the "exclusively male" "sexual and psychological model" which Brooks assumes, and asks, "Can this plot pattern accommodate a female subject?" (p. 54). Laurence shows that it can.

19. "A Place to Stand On," in *Heart of a Stranger* (Toronto: McClelland and Stewart, Bantam, 1984), pp. 5, 2, 1.

20. See DuPlessis, pp. 84–104; and Susan Gubar, "The Birth of the Artist as Heroine: (Re)production, the *Kunstlerroman* Tradition, and the Fiction of Katherine Mansfield," in *The Representation of Women in Fiction: Selected Papers from the English Institute*, ed. Carolyn G. Heilbrun and Margaret R. Higonnet (Baltimore: Johns Hopkins University Press, 1981), pp. 19–59.

21. Christie teaches Morag never to say "sorry" (p. 209, 277), and Morag teaches Pique (p. 239). Stephen is repeatedly forced to "apologize"; *A Portrait of the Artist as a Young Man* (New York: Viking, 1960), pp. 8, 78, 143.

22. Theo Quayle Dombrowski ("Word and Fact: Laurence and the Problem of Language," in *Canadian Literature* 80 [Spring 1979] pp. 50–62) interprets silence in the novel as evidence of grace (pp. 53, 55), but I see it as symbolizing isolation and desolation, as it does in *The Stone Angel*.

23. T. S. Eliot, *The Waste Land and Other Poems* (New York: Harcourt Brace, 1958), l. 243. David Blewett, "The Unity of the Manawaka Cycle," in *Journal of Canadian Studies* 13, no. 3 (Fall 1978), pp. 31–39, discerns a movement in the Manawaka cycle "like that of Eliot's *Waste Land* . . . from dryness to water, from spiritual barrenness to rebirth" (p. 36). He notes the prominence of water in the novel—the centrality of the river, the reference to death by water on the first page, Jules Tonnerre's "voice like distant thunder." A deeper correspondence between *The Diviners* and *The Waste Land* is in Eliot's and Laurence's concern with the uses of the past, a concern which explains both writers' allusions to *The Tempest* (as I argue in "Shakespeare's *Tempest* and Eliot's *Waste Land*: 'What the Thunder Said,' " in *Orbis Litterarum* [1979], pp. 34, 289–300).

24. Laurence quotes Milton's *Areopagitica* in her discussion of censorship; "The Greater Evil," *Toronto Life* (September 1984); in DOE, pp. 265–74, 269.

25. Brooke reveals a nasty streak of racism when he finds Morag drinking with Jules: " 'I thought it was supposed to be illegal to give liquor to Indians' "—a remark which precipitates Morag's departure (p. 269).

26. Jean E. Kennard, "Convention Coverage or How to Read Your Own Life," in *New Literary History* 13, no. 1 (Autumn 1981), p. 79.

27. Fabre calls Christie "a clown, jester, a sacred idiot" and "an incarnation of Christ" (p. 62). Blewett refers to him as "one of the greatest fools in modern literature, but for that reason a channel and an image of divine grace" (p. 32) and sees Morag's education as an emulation of his wisdom: "Morag gives up 'everything' in order to

possess the only thing that really matters: but in this way, by becoming a fool, she finally learns Christie's lesson" (p. 36). Patricia Morley describes Christie as a "clown, fool, hero, and religious prophet" like "the fool figures" in Russian novels, "a mystic, whose simplicity and honesty is interpreted by conventional society as stupidity, even madness," a "foolish sage [who] points to the limitations of reason and to a super-rational vision" (pp. 126–27). Nobody notes the Shakespearean resonances, however.

28. "Complementarity" is the term Norman Rabkin uses to describe the coexistence of opposing viewpoints in Shakespeare's plays; *Shakespeare and the Common Understanding* (New York: The Free Press, 1967), p. 22. "Ambivalence" is A. P. Rossiter's term: ". . . two opposed value judgments are subsumed, and both are valid. . . . The whole is only fully experienced when both opposites are held and included in a 'two-eyed' view; and all 'one-eyed' simplifications are not only falsifications; they amount to a denial of some part of the mystery of things." "Ambivalence: The Dialectic of the Histories," in *Discussions of Shakespeare's Histories,* ed. R. J. Dorius (Boston: Heath, 1964), p. 128.

29. Some of Morag's most important insights are paradoxical: her awarenesses of the "apparently impossible contradiction" of the river which "flowed both ways" (p. 3); her realization that "You Can't Go Home Again . . . You have to go home again" (p. 302); her recognition, when she sees Jules after many years, that he is "both older, and younger" (p. 429). She also sees that her notion of Gaelic accents in Christie's language is "perhaps" sentimental, and "perhaps not" (p. 371); that the fiction Pique makes of Jules will be both "more and less true than himself" (p. 449); and that Pique is *"harbinger of my death, continuer of life"* (p. 290).

30. Thomas claims that the Miltonic parallels point to Laurence's belief in "a Miltonic Eternal Providence" (1975, pp. 170–71); Fabre suggests that Morag's divining is the ability "to read the meaning inscribed in the world, in nature, and in events by the hidden hand of God . . . to discern a design or a 'pattern' " (pp. 63–64). But Melanie Mortlock, "The Religion of Heritage: *The Diviners* as a Thematic Conclusion to the Manawaka Series" (in Sorfleet, pp. 132–42), describes Laurence's "modern philosophical religion," her "mythological religion, based on the concept of heritage" (p. 132), in terms closer to my sense of her faith in community and the continuity of generations. Eleanor Johnston, "The Quest of *The Diviners,*" in *Mosaic* 11, no. 3 (Spring 1978), quotes Laurence as saying, "I don't have a traditional religion, but I believe that there's a mystery at the core of life" (p. 108).

31. For Laurence's use of Catharine Parr Traill, see Thomas (1978), p. 58.

32. It is Christie who is Morag's mentor, in this way as others, in giving her a room of her own. When Morag first arrives at the Logans' and sees her room, she feels, "You could be safe in a place like that if it was really yours" (p. 30); she later realizes that it is "really hers, it has always been hers" (p. 51).

33. "Gadgetry or Growing: Form and Voice in the Novel," in Sorfleet, pp. 54–62, 57.

34. Morag expresses a similar awareness with regard to Jules's sister, Piquette (p. 158), and Fan Brady (p. 310); and Royland says of the aunt who raised him, " 'It wasn't really her fault, either. You don't know how it is for other people, or how far back it all goes' " (p. 241).

35. Songs written by Laurence are printed at the end of the novel, and the original edition of *The Diviners* included tapes of these. In "Ivory Tower or Grassroots? The Novelist as Socio-political Being," in *A Political Art: Essays and Images in Honor of George Woodcock,* ed. William H. New (Vancouver: University of British Columbia Press, 1978), pp. 15–25, Laurence says, "fiction may be viewed as history" and "history . . . as fiction. They are twin disciplines, and they include biography and autobiography" (p. 15).

36. Barbara Hehner, "River of Now and Then: Margaret Laurence's Narratives," in *Canadian Literature* 74 (Autumn 1977), pp. 40–57; Leona M. Gom, "Laurence and the Use of Memory," *Canadian Literature* 71 (Winter 1976), pp. 48–58, 48.

37. Brooks (p. 91) relates repetition with re-vision to Tzvetan Todorov's "model of narrative transformation whereby plot . . . is constituted in the tension of . . . difference and resemblance; it is, we might say, the same-but-different"; "Les Transformations narratives" (in *Poétique de la prose* [Paris: Editions du Seuil, 1971], p. 240; English trans. Richard Howard, *The Poetics of Prose* [Ithaca: Cornell University Press, 1977]). The paradoxical intertwining of sameness and difference is suggested in Morag's realization that "it's different" for Pique, "but . . . the same, too" (p. 422); that the farm Dan makes will be "different, but . . . the same" (p. 354) as his father's; that things are both "better" and "worse" now than they were in the past (p. 95); that "You Can't Go Home Again . . . You have to go home again, in some way or other" (p. 320).

38. J. E. Cirlot, *A Dictionary of Symbols* (New York: Philosophical Library, 1962), p. 235. See also Paula Gunn Allen, *The Sacred Hoop: Recovering the Feminine in American Indian Traditions* (Boston: Beacon, 1986), especially pp. 56, 150.

## VIII. Margaret Atwood's *Lady Oracle*

1. Margaret Atwood, *Lady Oracle* (New York: Avon, 1976), p. 6.

2. Kim Chernin, *The Hungry Self: Women, Eating and Identity* (New York: Harper and Row, 1985), pp. 154–55.

3. Luce Irigaray, "Plato's *Hystera*," in *Speculum of the Other Woman* (Ithaca: Cornell University Press, 1985), p. 345.

4. Sherrill Grace asks, "To what end has Atwood created this ornate, elaborate structure . . .? In part . . . for the sheer joy of creation," and concludes that it "is both more and less than it seems—more complicated . . . and less serious. Atwood's mixture of comedy, satire and parody does not allow soul-searching interpretations"; it does "not offer answers or entirely satisfying resolutions (what oracle does?)" *Violent Duality: A Study of Margaret Atwood* (Montreal: Vehicle Press, 1980), pp. 123, 128. Susan Maclean calls the novel "an entertaining but unsettling book, leaving the reader not only with his own mystifying questions but also with the vague suspicion that he has, in some sense, been duped" and suggests that it "illuminates the complexity and elusiveness of Margaret Atwood": "We are still left wondering: what exactly is Atwood up to?" *Lady Oracle: The Art of Reality and the Reality of Art*," in *Journal of Canadian Fiction* 28–9, (1980), pp. 179–97, 179, 186. Brian Vincent calls the novel "a diverting fantasy"; review of *Lady Oracle*, *Quill and Quire* 42, no. 11 (1976), p. 6; quoted in Maclean, p. 196.

5. "*Lady Oracle* is the most rewritten of my books and it took about two years to write. *Surfacing* and *Edible Woman* each took six months, approximately"; Linda Sandler, "Interview with Margaret Atwood," *Malahat Review* 41 (January 1977), p. 15. Atwood reiterates this in *Interviews with Contemporary Writers*, ed. L. S. Dembo (Madison: University of Wisconsin Press, 1983), pp. 366–81; adding that "it was a more difficult book to write [than *Surfacing* or *The Edible Woman*]" (p. 379).

6. Jerome H. Rosenberg, *Margaret Atwood*, Twayne's World Authors Series, Canadian Literature (Boston: Twayne Publishers, 1984), p. 112. Rosenberg cites "Margaret Atwood in Conversation with Jerome Rosenberg," July 31, 1976; Patricia Morley, "The Gothic as Social Realism," in *Canadian Forum* 56 (December–January 1976–77), p. 49; cf. "Letters: Royal Porcupine's Identikit," in *Saturday Night* (January–February 1977), p. 3. Barbara Godard, "My (m)Other, My Self: Strategies for Subversion in Atwood and Hébert," in *Essays in Canadian Writing* 26 (1983), pp. 13–44, notes parallels between the journalist Fraser Buchanan and Fraser Sutherland of *Northern Journey* (p. 22).

7. This is Susan Jaret McKinstry's term, "Living Literally by the Pen: The Self-Conceived and Self-Deceiving Heroine-Author in Margaret Atwood's *Lady Oracle*," in *Margaret Atwood: Reflection and Reality*, Living Author Series No. 6 (Edinburg, TX: Pan American University, 1987), pp. 58–70, 66.

8. Gothic conventions are, as Rachel Blau DuPlessis points out, "comically deflated"; *Writing beyond the Ending: Narrative Strategies of Twentieth-Century Women*

*Writers* (Bloomington: Indiana University Press, 1985), p. 45. Wilfred Cude reads the novel as a diatribe against "gothic escapism"; *A Due Sense of Differences: An Evaluative Approach to Canadian Literature* (Washington, DC: University Press of America, 1980), pp. 155, 152; so does Frank Davey, *Margaret Atwood: A Feminist Poetics* (Vancouver: Talonbooks, 1984), p. 59.

9. J. R. Struthers, "An Interview with Margaret Atwood," in *Essays in Canadian Writing* 6 (Spring 1977), p. 23. Atwood cites Jane Austen's *Northanger Abbey* as a major influence on *Lady Oracle* (p. 26). She says, "What the book is really about . . . is the futility of romance," of people "casting themselves and other people in their own romance" (interview with Anne Tremblay in *The Gazette;* quoted in Elspeth Cameron, "Margaret Atwood: A Patchwork Self," in *Book Forum* 4 [1978], pp. 35–45, p. 40).

10. Janice A. Radway, *Reading the Romance: Women, Patriarchy, and Popular Literature* (Chapel Hill: University of North Carolina Press, 1984), discusses the addictive nature of romance reading, characterizing romance readers as "generally heavy consumers" (p. 60) who have an "intense reliance on these books" (p. 59). Radway discusses readers' "need to arrive at the *ending* of the tale" in order to achieve "the emotional gratification" (p. 59).

11. Cf. Claire Kahane's description: "Within an imprisoning structure, a protagonist, typically a young woman whose mother has died, is compelled to seek out the center of a mystery, while vague and usually sexual threats to her person from some powerful male figure hover on the periphery of her consciousness. Following clues that pull her onward and inward . . . she penetrates the obscure recesses of a vast labyrinthean space and discovers a secret room sealed off by its association with death," the dark secret at the "center of the Gothic structure"; "The Gothic Mirror," in *The (M)other Tongue: Essays in Feminist Psychoanalytic Interpretation,* ed. Shirley Nelson Garner, Claire Kahane, and Madelon Sprengnether (Ithaca: Cornell University Press, 1985), p. 334.

12. Atwood refers to Grimm's fairy tales as "the most influential book I ever read" (in Sandler, p. 14).

13. Tania Modleski, *Loving with a Vengeance: Mass-Produced Fantasies for Women* (New York: Methuen, 1982), p. 83.

14. Mary Russo, "Female Grotesques: Carnival and Theory," in *Feminist Studies, Critical Studies,* ed. Teresa de Lauretis (Bloomington: Indiana University Press, 1986), pp. 213–29, 213.

15. Peter Brooks, *Reading for the Plot: Design and Intention in Narrative* (New York: Random House, 1984), pp. 228, xi, 63, 235, 285.

16. Phyllis Chesler, *Women and Madness* (New York: Doubleday, 1972), p. 18.

17. Madonne M. Miner, "Guaranteed to Please: Twentieth-Century American Women's Bestsellers," in *Gender and Reading: Essays on Readers, Texts, and Contexts,* ed. Elizabeth A. Flynn and Patrocinio P. Schweickart (Baltimore: The Johns Hopkins University Press, 1986), pp. 187–211, 208, 188.

18. Catherine Martens, "Mother-Figures in *Surfacing* and *Lady Oracle:* An Interview with Margaret Atwood," in *American Studies in Scandanavia* 16 (1984), pp. 45–54, 49. Quoted in Molly Hite, *The Other Side of the Story: Structures and Strategies of Contemporary Feminist Narratives* (Ithaca: Cornell University Press, 1989), p. 151.

19. Norman H. Holland and Leona F. Sherman, "Gothic Possibilities," *New Literary History* 8 (1976–79), pp. 279–94, 289, 292.

20. Ellen Moers, *Literary Women: The Great Writers* (Garden City, NY: Doubleday, 1977), p. 107.

21. W. W. Meissner, *The Paranoid Process* (New York: Jason Aaronson, 1978), p. 73.

22. See Hirsch's discussion of Freud's 1908 essay "Family Romances" as "founded on the elimination of the mother and the attachment to a husband/father." Hirsch describes this as the plot of many nineteenth-century novels, fictions which are similarly

based on "maternal repression" in which "it is the mother's absence which creates the space in which the heroine's plot and her activity of plotting can work"; *The Mother/ Daughter Plot: Narrative, Psychoanalysis, Feminism* (Bloomington: Indiana University Press, 1989), p. 57. Joanna Russ detects in Gothics "an echo of the family romance in which the Heroine plays daughter, the Super-Male is father, and the Other Woman/First Wife plays mother"; "Somebody is Trying to Kill Me and I Think It's My Husband: The Modern Gothic," *Journal of Popular Culture* 6 (1973), pp. 666–91, 684.

23. Radway also stresses the conservative implications of romance reading: "While the act of romance reading is used by women as a means of partial protest against the role prescribed for them by the culture, the discourse itself actively insists on the desirability, naturalness, and benefits of that role by portraying it not as the imposed necessity that it is but as a freely designed, personally controlled, individual choice" (p. 208). "In the end, the romance-reading process gives the reader a strategy for making her present situation more comfortable without substantive reordering of its structure" (p. 215). Romances thus "leave intact the very cultural categories, assumptions, and institutions" that drive readers to them (p. 214).

24. D. W. Winnicott, "Mirror-Role of Mother and Family in Child Development," in *Playing and Reality* (New York: Tavistock, 1971; 1985), pp. 111–18, 112. With thanks to Jean Wyatt for referring me to Winnicott.

25. Mark P. O. Morford and Robert J. Lenardon, *Classical Mythology* (New York: David McKay, 1977), p. 141. Atwood describes herself as being "terrified" when she read Robert Graves's *The White Goddess* (New York: Creative Age Press, 1948): Graves placed women "right at the center of his poetic theory," but as "inspirations rather than creators, . . . incarnations of the White Goddess herself, alternately loving and destructive, and men who got involved with them ran the risk of dismemberment or worse" (*Ms. Magazine* [July/August 1987], p. 79). Grace glosses Graves's myth: "Whether as the goddess of the three phases of the moon or as sky, earth, and underworld . . . 'the Triple Goddess' . . . was a personification of . . . woman the creatress and destructress" (p. 146).

26. Judith Kegan Gardiner, "A Wake for Mother: The Maternal Deathbed in Women's Fiction," in *Feminist Studies* (June 1978), pp. 4, 2 146–65, p. 146–47, 149–51. Gardiner discusses Agnes Smedley's *Daughter of Earth,* Jean Rhys's *After Leaving Mr. Mackenzie,* Drabble's *Jerusalem the Golden,* Piercy's *Small Changes,* and Lisa Alther's *Kinflicks.*

27. Chernin, *The Hungry Self* (n. 2, above). In *The Obsession: Reflections on the Tyranny of Slenderness* (New York: Harper and Row, 1981), Chernin explains female eating disorders in terms of rage felt against the mother "directed by the girl at her own body" (pp. 152–53). See also Susie Orbach, *Fat Is a Feminist Issue* (New York: Berkley Books, 1981).

28. Adrienne Rich, *Of Woman Born: Motherhood as Experience and Institution* (New York: Norton, 1976), pp. 225–26, 237.

29. Joan behaves like those protagonists Gardiner describes who, unable to separate from their mothers, seek mothers in men—who turn to men with "futile dependency" and "re-create the personality of the powerless" (p. 153). Roberta Rubenstein notes that "Joan merely transforms her symbiotic needs to Arthur . . . [who] is in important psychological ways a version of her mother"; *Boundaries of the Self: Gender, Culture, Fiction* (Urbana: University of Illinois Press, 1987) p. 89.

30. Sandra M. Gilbert and Susan Gubar, *The Madwoman in the Attic: The Woman Writer and the Nineteenth-Century Literary Imagination* (New Haven: Yale University Press, 1979), p. 99.

31. Joan's fantasies about the return of the Fat Lady may seem fantastic, but they resemble an account by a woman in Wendy Chapkis's *Beauty Secrets: Women and the Politics of Appearance* (Boston: South End Press, 1986): "When I was 130 pounds, I still looked in the mirror and saw a fat person. . . . I did really weird stuff when I met new

people. I never wanted them to know I had been fat. If I would be in a group of people and they would start talking about somebody who was fat, I would freeze. I thought that if I was absolutely quiet, they might not turn and look at me and realize I was fat too" (p. 159).

32. Grace Stewart, *A New Mythos: The Novel of the Artist as Heroine, 1877–1977* (Montreal: Eden Press Women's Publications, 1981), pp. 107, 177–78.

33. This is Gilbert and Gubar's term (p. 85). Joanna Russ discusses the role of the domestic arts in romances, the ways that "Occupation: Housewife is simultaneously avoided, glamorized, and vindicated" (p. 675).

34. Sigmund Freud, "Femininity," in *New Introductory Lectures on Psychoanalysis,* trans. James Strachey (New York: Norton, 1965), p. 132.

35. Nancy K. Miller, "Arachnologies: The Woman, the Text, and the Critic," *The Poetics of Gender,* ed. Nancy K. Miller (New York: Columbia University Press, 1986), pp. 270–95, describes an "arachnology" that would be attentive to the representation of women's writing within women's writings, noting the connection between "the language of textiles" and the "metaphorics of femininity" in contemporary literary criticism (pp. 270–71).

36. Gilbert and Gubar describe the woman writer's journey toward literary autonomy as a "reach[ing] toward the woman trapped on the other side of the mirror/text [to] help her to climb out," to release the "enraged prisoner" caught in "the mirror of the male-inscribed literary text"—an autonomy which is imagined as "monstrous" for woman (pp. 15–16). See also Kahane: "at the center of the Gothic structure" is an "ongoing battle with a mirror image who is both self and other" (p. 337), "a fearsome figure . . . remaining to be acknowledged" (p. 341). Pamela S. Bromberg describes the novel as "exposing the rhetoric and politics of women's entrapment in the mirror of gender"; "The Two Faces of the Mirror," in *Margaret Atwood: Vision and Forms,* ed. Kathryn VanSpanckeren and Jan Garden Castro (Carbondale: Southern Illinois University Press, 1988), pp. 12–23, 23.

37. Wolfgang Lederer, *The Fear of Women* (New York: Harcourt Brace Jovanovich, 1968), associates these cave-dwelling female monsters with fear of women: "Echidna, half a young woman . . . half a snake dwelling in the depths of the earth and eating raw meat, killed all men who happened to come her way. . . . Her daughter Scylla, once a beautiful woman but changed into a monster with six fearful heads and twelve feet, sitting in a cave opposite Mount Aetna . . . the whirlpool Charybdis, the 'sucker down,' a daughter of Mother Earth" (p. 57).

38. Chesler sees this myth as signifying "the inevitable sacrifice of self that biology demands of women" [p. 29]). But for feminists' use of the myth as "an empowering paradigm" of the mother–daughter story, see Garner et al., introduction, pp. 15–29, 23; and Adrienne Rich, *Of Woman Born* (New York: Norton, 1976).

39. Stewart describes the dangers women artists face when they attempt to dance and fly: "They run the risk of cutting, mangling, or infecting their feet so that they can hardly stand alone, not to mention dance. Indeed, the feet and legs of female artists receive inordinate attention" (p. 177).

40. See Sherrill Grace's discussion of W. F. Jackson Knight on mazes as "symbols in an ancient matriarchal earth cult involving . . . initiation into new life" (p. 120). Knight, *Virgil: Epic and Anthropology* (London: George Allen and Unwin, 1967), p. 165, links mazes to the Persephone–Demeter myth as well as to Sibyls and Oracles: "Upon reaching the centre of the maze, the initiate finds the desired wisdom or rebirth . . . mazes are not places where the unwary become lost . . . but places sacred to the worship and wisdom of Mother Earth" (Grace, p. 120).

41. Goddard notes that Joan has "romantic fantasies of metamorphoses" ("the Royal York Hotel is seen as a fairy castle, the Polish Count appears miraculously and takes her to The Golden Egg restaurant") but encounters instead a pattern of failed, thwarted, or inverted metamorphoses: "Joan . . . experiences repeatedly that initial inversion to

moth-ball, moving always thus towards death, not happiness. . . . Joan casts herself . . . as 'Cinderella's ugly sister,' for whom the metamorphosis can never come about. Similarly, Grimm's Frog Prince is inverted since she is 'Princess-for-a-day' but feels 'like a toad.' In Bluebeard's castle, she would be one of the two stupid sisters" (p. 31). The final series of transformations inverts such inversions, as Joan undergoes genuine metamorphoses.

42. "*Lady Oracle* was more tragic to begin with—it was going to start with a fake suicide and end with a real one. As you know, it turned out differently"; in Sandler, p. 14. It is interesting that—like Drabble in *The Waterfall*—Atwood began this novel with a tragic end in mind, but reshaped the old plot in the process of writing.

43. Wings are a recurrent motif in *Lady Oracle*: Joan longs to dance the part of a winged butterfly; the Brownies aspire to Golden Wings (p. 58); "owls . . . meant wisdom" (p. 57); a stuffed owl presides at Joan's marriage (pp. 228, 223); Paul wears a signet ring with "a mythical bird, a griffin or a phoenix" on it (p. 164); Leda, Joan's spiritual guide, bears the name of the woman raped by Zeus in the form of a swan; and in the Fat Lady's last spectacular appearance, she topples from the high wire, her false wings useless. Grace Stewart comments on imagery of birds and flight in women's *Kunstlerromane* as signifying the desire to escape the "polarity between woman and artist" and notes that birds are often "broken, crippled, strangled, or hung" (p. 177). Ellen Moers also discusses bird imagery in women writers (pp. 372–82). In what seems a deliberate elaboration of Joan's fantasies, Angela Carter makes the protagonist of *Nights at the Circus* a winged fat-lady circus performer.

44. Ann McMillan similarly reads Joan's turning to other forms as a sign that she is ready "to create alternatives to the ideal of victimization"; "in writing Gothic fantasy, Joan has shared the guilt of those writers who assure women that conventional female virtues will receive tangible rewards. She has helped to keep the house haunted with romantic fears"; "The Transforming Eye: *Lady Oracle* and Gothic Tradition," pp. 48–64, 63.

45. As Rubenstein says, "Atwood's narratives . . . structurally represent the boundary issues they explore; conclusion without resolution" (p. 16); as Maclean suggests, Atwood does not allow "the solace of neatly packaged endings" (p. 196).

46. Hite argues that Atwood has "created an alternative narrative structure, a structure that in important ways is not modeled on masculine sexuality (as in the 'classic' linear and teleological plot, with its situation, rising action, climax, and denouement) and that resists the masculinist ideologies encoded in the 'classic' structure" (p. 165).

47. Rubenstein describes Joan as "tak[ing] charge of the form and emphasis of her story" (p. 236); as Maclean observes, she "becomes author of her story and writes herself into existence"; according to Goddard, she gives birth to the self and also to a new myth of origins related to the lost tradition of the great goddess, the Great Mother (p. 24).

48. Hirsch suggests that there may be a necessary "conjunction between the maternal and the unspeakable"—that perhaps "maternal discourse can exist in the text only on the condition that it remain fragmentary, incomplete and mediated through the perspective of the daughter–writer" (p. 185).

49. See Naomi Schor, "For a Restricted Thematics: Writing, Speech, and Difference in *Madame Bovary*," in *The Future of Difference: The Scholar and the Feminist*, ed. Hester Eisenstein and Alice Jardine (Boston: G. K. Hall, 1980), pp. 167–92, for "the relationship between the 'textual' and the 'textile' " as "one of the obsessive metaphors of current criticism" (p. 167): "the thread unraveled by Ariadne, cut by the Fates, woven by Penelope, is a peculiarly feminine attribute, a metonym for femininity" (p. 169).

50. Sigmund Freud, "Medusa's Head," in *The Complete Psychological Works*, vol. 18, trans. and ed. James Strachey, p. 273.

## IX. Whatever Happened to Feminist Fiction?

1. Sara Maitland, "Futures in Feminist Fiction," in *From My Guy to Sci-Fi: Genre and Women's Writing in the Postmodern World*, ed. Helen Carr (London: Pandora

Press, 1989), pp. 193–203, 194.

2. Margaret Drabble, *The Radiant Way* (London: Weidenfeld and Nicolson, 1987), pp. 88, 227, 229 (hereafter RW).

3. Barbara Ehrenreich, *The Hearts of Men: American Dreams and the Flight from Commitment* (Garden City, NY: Anchor, 1983), p. 169. Marilyn Power, "Falling through the 'Safety Net': Women, Economic Crisis, and Reaganomics," in *Feminist Studies*, 10, no. 1 (Spring 1984), pp. 31–58; and Wendy Kaminer, *A Fearful Freedom: Women's Flight from Equality* (Reading, Mass.: Addison-Wesley, 1990), chapter 9, for conservatives' assaults on welfare and on civil liberties.

4. See Wini Breines, Margaret Cerullo, and Judith Stacey, "Social Biology, Family Studies, and Antifeminist Backlash," in *Feminist Studies* 4, no. 1 (February 1978), pp. 43–67. For the use of sociobiology by the New Right in England, see Alan Sinfield, *Literature, Politics, and Culture in Postwar Britain* (Berkeley: University of California Press, 1989), p. 149.

5. Janice Doane and Devon Hodges, *Nostalgia and Sexual Difference: The Resistance to Contemporary Feminism* (New York: Methuen, 1987), p. xiii.

6. Ruth Sidel, *On Her Own: Growing up in the Shadow of the American Dream* (New York: Viking Penguin, 1990), pp. 106–108. An article in *The Peninsula Times Tribune* by Christopher Kimball (August 24–26, 1990) announces that 1963 "saw the death of the American man"—associated somehow with the death of John F. Kennedy—but now men "can act like men again," to the "relief and satisfaction of all" (p. 4). Kimball is publisher of *Men* magazine, one of the numerous new "men's magazines"—"reflecting the new interest in men's image and role, the field is suddenly the hottest in magazine publishing" (p. 5).

7. Susan Jeffords, *The Remasculinization of America: Gender and the Vietnam War* (Bloomington: Indiana University Press, 1989).

8. Sylvia Hewlett, *A Lesser Life: The Myth of Women's Liberation in America* (New York: William Morrow, 1986); Nicholas Davidson, *The Failure of Feminism* (Buffalo, NY: Prometheus Books); Connell Cowan and Melvyn Kinder, *Smart Women, Foolish Choices: Finding the Right Man and Avoiding the Wrong One* (New York: Crown, 1985).

9. Susan Bolotin, "Voices from the Post-Feminist Generation," *New York Times Magazine* (October 17, 1982), p. 28ff. (See Chapter 2, n. 48.)

10. "Too Late for Prince Charming," in *Newsweek* (June 2, 1986), p. 55.

11. Claudia Wallis, "Women Face the Nineties," in *Time* (November 1989), pp. 80ff., 81.

12. Elayne Rapping, "Youth Ponder Sexual Politics," in *New Directions for Women* (March/April 1989), p. 10.

13. Jean Bethke Elshtain, *Public Man, Private Woman: Women in Social and Political Thought* (Princeton: Princeton University Press, 1981); Betty Friedan, *The Second Stage* (New York: Summit Books, 1981); Judith Stacey, "The New Conservative Feminism," in *Feminist Studies* 9, no. 3 (Fall 1983), pp. 559–83, 571, 569.

14. For the sense of writing as power among minority women, see Gloria Anzaldúa, "Speaking in Tongues: A Letter to 3rd World Women Writers," and Nellie Wong, "In Search of the Self as Hero: Confetti of Voices on New Years Night: A Letter to Myself," in *This Bridge Called My Back: Writings of Radical Women of Color*, ed. Cherríe Moraga and Gloria Anzaldúa (New York: Women of Color Press, 1981), pp. 165–73, 177–81.

15. Most notably, Catharine R. Stimpson, "Nancy Reagan Wears a Hat; Feminism and Its Cultural Consensus," in *Critical Inquiry* 14 (Winter 1988), pp. 224–43; and Deborah Rosenfelt, who suggests that the dissolution of the feminist myth into multiple stories and multiple narrations may reflect a healthy skepticism about the adequacy of one interpretation of reality and may bring feminist thought into a fruitful political alliance with postmodernism; "Feminism, Postfeminism, and Contemporary Women's Fiction," in *Tradition and the Talents of Women*, ed. Florence Howe (Urbana: Univer-

sity of Illinois Press, forthcoming).

16. Betty Friedan, "How to Get the Women's Movement Moving Again," in *New York Times Magazine* (November 3, 1985), pp. 26ff, 67.

17. Anita Shreve, *Women Together, Women Alone: The Legacy of the Consciousness-Raising Movement* (New York: Viking, 1989), p. 215. For feminism as the "F word," see Shreve, pp. 208–15.

18. Margaret Atwood, *Cat's Eye* (New York: Doubleday, 1989), p. 46.

19. Anne Roiphe, *Lovingkindness* (New York: Warner, 1987), pp. 154–55.

20. Fay Weldon, *The Life and Loves of a She-Devil* (New York: Ballantine, 1983), p. 236.

21. Deborah Rosenfelt and Judith Stacey, "Second Thoughts on the Second Wave," in *Feminist Studies* 13, no. 2 (Summer 1987), pp. 341–61, 341.

22. Doris Lessing, *The Golden Notebook* (New York: Bantam, 1973), p. 510.

23. Alison Lurie, *The Truth about Lorin Jones* (Boston: Little, Brown, 1988). Edmund White notes that the question is really "will Polly end up a lesbian feminist separatist or will she remain unregenerate and heterosexual," and compares the novel, approvingly, to Henry James's *The Bostonians*. "A Victim of the Male Establishment?" in *New York Times Book Review* (September 4, 1988), p. 3.

24. Barbara Raskin, *Hot Flashes* (New York: St. Martin's Press, 1987), p. 377.

25. Elinor Langer, "Whatever Happened to Feminist Fiction?" in *New York Times Book Review* (March 4, 1984), pp. 1, 35–6, cites Sheila Ballantyne's *Imaginary Crimes,* Robb Forman Dew's *Dale Loves Sophie to Death,* Lynne Sharon Schwartz's *Disturbances in the Field,* and Joan Chase's *During the Reign of the Queen of Persia* as examples of this trend, and cites black women writers as exceptions: in their fiction "the world is not so much an option; it is a fact"—"society is present in every thought and feeling of the characters simply because they contain it" (p. 35).

26. *New York Times Book Review* (November 12, 1989), p. 9. Bill Kent praises Mary Higgins Clark's *The Anastasia Syndrome and Other Stories* for being like "the sunny, likable tales that flourished in the 1950s" (*New York Times,* December 3, 1989), p. 82; Nina Auerbach describes Henrietta Garnett's *Family Skeletons* as "lost in beautiful fabrications, cut off from any times at all" (*New York Times Book Review,* June 14, 1987), p. 32; Joan Conarroe describes Joan Chase's *The Evening Wolves* as paying "virtually no attention" "to the outside world; the family exists in a social vacuum, out of time and out of place. There are few references to current events or to public figures" (*New York Times Book Review,* May 29, 1989), p. 11. Richard Rosen puts Emily Listfield's *Variations in the Night* in "that category of anorexic fiction that thinks it's sleek and fashionable when it's really just dangerously thin," "classic minimalist" (*New York Times Book Review,* September 6, 1987), p. 12; Richard Bausch approves of Anne Lamott's "wonderful little novel," *All New People,* with its "elegiac tone" (*New York Times Book Review,* October 22, 1989), p. 8; Alan Cheuse praises Annette Williams Jaffe's *Recent History* "for recreating the dreamy aspects of childhood" and "leading us toward homecoming and reconciliation" (*New York Times Book Review,* August 28, 1988), p. 7; Valerie Sayers laments "another present-tense narrative told in the flat affectless voice of the 80's"; review of Elizabeth Cooke's *Complicity, New York Times Book Review,* February 28, 1988, p. 11.

27. Ellen Moers, "Angry Young Women," in *Harper's* (December 1963), pp. 227, 89–97.

28. Margaret Atwood, *The Handmaid's Tale* (Boston: Houghton Mifflin, 1986), p. 53.

29. Sue Miller, *The Good Mother* (New York: Harper and Row, 1986), p. 308. Rosenfelt also describes this tendency.

30. Anita Brookner, *Hotel du Lac* (London: Triad/Panther, 1985), p. 27.

31. Writing functions similarly in Brookner's 1983 *Look at Me,* to confirm the protagonist's isolation and bond with a dead mother. In an interview, Brookner says, "I

prefer men, because . . . I know about women. . . . There is a certain inborn competitiveness among women which is a little bit murky . . . a woman under the guise of friendship will engage in acts of duplicity"; "Interview with Anita Brookner," in *Novelists in Interview,* ed. John Haffenden (London: Methuen, 1985), pp. 57–75, 67–68. When Haffenden comments on her success "as an academic and as a novelist," she replies, "Those two activities that you've mentioned are outside the natural order. I only ever wanted children, six sons" "instead of being this grown-up orphan with what you call success" (pp. 62–63). Such confidence about what is "inborn" and "natural" is extraordinary, as is Brookner's attitude toward her own writing.

32. Doris Lessing, *The Good Terrorist* (New York: Knopf, 1985), p. 257.

33. "The Small Personal Voice," *A Small Personal Voice,* ed. Paul Schleuter (New York: Vintage, 1972), p. 9.

34. Margaret Drabble, *The Middle Ground* (Toronto: Bantam, 1980), p. 2.

35. Margaret Atwood, *Bodily Harm* (New York: Simon and Schuster, 1982), p. 62.

36. Drabble is addressing the division of the Left in England following the coalminers' strikes in the mid-eighties, but other social divisions have occurred in this decade: both England and the United States have seen a widening gap between rich and poor and the division of the lower classes into those who work and "the underclass"—as Sinfield suggests, "the claim is no longer that everyone is included in the good state" (pp. 305–306).

37. Doris Lessing, *The Diaries of Jane Somers* (New York: Vintage, 1984), pp. 151, 140.

38. For a discussion of the sentimentalization of women and its reactionary implications in contemporary feminist thought, see Lynne Segal, *Is the Future Female? Troubled Thoughts on Contemporary Feminism* (London: Virago, 1988).

39. Simone de Beauvoir, *The Coming of Age* (New York: G. P. Putnam's Sons, 1972), pp. 13, 10.

40. *The Handmaid's Tale* sold "within the first year of its publication well over a million copies." *Cat's Eye* "was a hardcover best seller on *The New York Times* Best Seller List for well over twenty weeks." Letter from Phoebe Larmore, Atwood's literary agent, to Gayle Greene, October 11, 1989. My discussion of *The Handmaid's Tale* was published as a review of *The Handmaid's Tale,* "Choice of Evils," in *Women's Review of Books* (June 1986), pp. 14–15.

41. Le Anne Schreiber, interview with Margaret Atwood, *Vogue* (January 23, 1983), pp. 208 ff, 209.

42. Margaret Atwood, *Surfacing* (New York: Fawcett, 1972), p. 220.

43. Richard Eder, review of *Cat's Eye,* *Los Angeles Times.* Other reviews describe the novel as "a harsh indictment of women as their own worst enemies"; Elayne Rapping, *Guardian* (April 12, 1989), p. 17; "What Little Girls Are Really Made Of," Alice McDermott, *New York Times* (February 5, 1989), p. 1; "Troubling Tale Laments the Lack of Sisterhood," Caryn James, *New York Times* (January 28, 1989), p. 15; "Brilliant New Book Takes Little Girls to Task"; Alison Lurie, *Ms.* (March 1989), p. 38.

44. Camille Peri, "Witchcraft," *Mother Jones* (April 1989), pp. 26ff, 30.

45. As Nina Baym observes, "It seems to be a fact of life that we all—women and men alike—experience social conventions and responsibilities first in the persons of women, since women are entrusted by society with the task of rearing young children. . . . Thus, although women are not the source of social power, they are experienced as such" and are perceived as "entrappers and domesticators." "Such a portrayal of women is likely to be uncongenial, if not basically incomprehensible, to a woman. It is not likely that women will write books in which women play this part"; "Melodramas of Beset Manhood: How Theories of American Fiction Exclude Women Authors," Elaine Showalter, *The New Feminist Criticism* (New York: Pantheon, 1985), pp. 72–73. Guess again.

46. In *Waterland* (London: Picador, 1984), Graham Swift plays on the word "revo-

lution" in the same way that Drabble does: "Though the popular notion of revolution is that of categorical change, transformation—a progressive leap into the future—yet almost every revolution contains within it an opposite if less obvious tendency: the idea of a return" (p. 119); "How it repeats itself, how it goes back on itself. . . . How it goes in circles and brings us back to the same place" (p. 123).

47. I think that Alix is right, as I argued in " 'Excellent Dumb Discourse': Silence and Grace in *The Tempest*," in *Studia Neophilologica* 50 (1978), pp. 173–208.

48. Parts of this discussion of *The Radiant Way* were published as a review of Drabble's *The Radiant Way*, "The End of a Dream," in *Women's Review of Books* (January 1988), pp. 4–5.

# BIBLIOGRAPHY

Elizabeth Abel. "[E]merging Identities: The Dynamics of Female Friendship in Contemporary Fiction by Women." *Signs* 6 (1981), 413–35.

———. *"The Golden Notebook:* 'Female Writing' and 'The Great Tradition,' " in Sprague and Tiger, 101–107.

———, ed. "Writing and Sexual Difference." Special issue of *Critical Inquiry* 8, no. 2 (Winter 1981).

———, Marianne Hirsch, and Elizabeth Langland, eds. *The Voyage In: Fictions of Female Development.* Hanover, NH: University Press of New England, 1983.

M. H. Abrams. *Natural Supernaturalism.* New York: Norton, 1971.

Walter L. Adamson. *Hegemony and Revolution: A Study of Antonio Gramsci's Political and Cultural Theory.* Berkeley: University of California Press, 1980.

Renata Adler. *Speedboat.* New York: Popular Library, 1978.

Flora Alexander. *Contemporary Women Novelists.* London: Edward Arnold, 1989.

Mary Allen. *The Necessary Blankness: Women in Major American Fiction of the Sixties.* Urbana: University of Illinois Press, 1976.

Paula Gunn Allen. *The Sacred Hoop: Recovering the Feminine in American Indian Traditions.* Boston: Beacon, 1986.

Walter Allen. *The Modern Novel in Britain and the United States.* New York: Dutton, 1964.

Robert Alter. *Partial Magic: The Novel as a Self-Conscious Genre.* Berkeley: University of California Press, 1975.

Lisa Alther. *Kinflicks.* New York: New American Library, 1975.

———. *Other Women.* New York: Signet, 1984.

———. "The Writer and Her Critics." *Women's Review of Books* 6, no. 1 (October 1988), 11.

Louis Althusser. *For Marx,* trans. Ben Brewster. Harmondsworth: Penguin, 1969; first published in French, 1966; reissued London: New Left Books, 1977.

———. *Lenin and Philosophy and Other Essays,* trans. Ben Brewster. London: New Left Books, 1971; first published in French, 1968.

A. Alvarez. *The Savage God: A Study in Suicide.* New York: Bantam, 1973.

Linda Anderson. *Plotting Change: Contemporary Women's Fiction.* London: Edward Arnold, 1990.

Quentin Anderson. "The Emergence of Modernism," in Elliott, 695–714.

Maya Angelou. *I Know Why the Caged Bird Sings.* New York: Bantam, 1973.

Gloria Anzaldúa. "Speaking in Tongues: A Letter to 3rd World Women Writers," in Moraga and Anzaldúa, 165–73.

June Arnold. *Applesauce.* New York: Daughters Publishing, 1977.

———. *Sister Gin.* New York: The Feminist Press, 1989.

Carol Ascher, Louise De Salvo, and Sara Ruddick, eds. *Between Women: Biographers, Novelists, Critics, Teachers and Artists Write about Their Work on Women.* Boston: Beacon, 1984.

Margaret Atwood. *Bodily Harm.* New York: Simon and Schuster, 1982.

———. *Cat's Eye.* New York: Doubleday, 1989.

———. "A Conversation: Margaret Atwood and Students," moderated by Francis X. Gillen, in VanSpanckeren and Castro, 233–43.

———. "The Curse of Eve—Or What I Learned in School," in *Second Words,* 215–28.

———. *The Edible Woman.* New York: Warner Books, 1983.

———. "Face to Face," in New, 33–40.

———. "Great Unexpectations." *Ms.*, July/August, 1987, 78ff.

———. *The Handmaid's Tale*. Boston: Houghton Mifflin, 1986.

———. "Introduction to *The Edible Woman*," in *Second Words*, 369–70.

———. *Lady Oracle*. New York: Avon, 1976.

———. "Paradoxes and Dilemmas: The Woman as Writer," in Webber and Grumman, 178–87.

———. *Second Words: Selected Critical Prose*. Boston: Beacon, 1982, "Introduction," 11–15.

———. *Surfacing*. New York: Fawcett, 1972.

———. *Survival: A Thematic Guide to Canadian Literature*. Toronto: Anansi, 1972.

———. "Using What You're Given," interview with Margaret Atwood by Jo Brans, in *Margaret Atwood: Conversations*, ed. Earl G. Ingersoll. Willowdale, Ontario: Ontario Review Press, 1990, 140–51.

Michael Awkward. *Inspiriting Influences: Tradition, Revision, and Afro-American Women's Novels*. New York: Columbia University Press, 1989.

Niamh Baker. *Happily Ever After? Women's Fiction in Postwar Britain, 1945–60*. New York: St. Martin's Press, 1989.

M. M. Bakhtin. "Discourse in the Novel," in *The Dialogic Imagination: Four Essays*, ed. Michael Holquist. Austin: University of Texas Press, 1981.

Sheila Ballantyne. *Imaginary Crimes*. New York: Penguin, 1983.

———. *Norma Jean the Termite Queen*. Harmondsworth: Penguin, 1986.

Olive M. Banks. *Faces of Feminism: A Study of Feminism as a Social Movement*. Oxford: Basil Blackwell, 1986.

Lois Banner. Review essay of literature about men. *Signs* 14, no. 3 (Spring 1989), 703–708.

Marleen Barr. *Alien to Femininity: Speculative Fiction and Feminist Theory*. Westport, CT: Greenwood Press, 1987.

Michele Barrett and Roberta Hamilton. *The Politics of Diversity*. London: Verso, 1986.

Roland Barthes. *Image-Music-Text*. London: Fontana, 1977.

———. *Mythologies*, trans. Annette Lavers. New York: Farrar, Straus, and Giroux, 1972.

———. *The Pleasure of the Text*, trans. Richard Miller. New York: Hill and Wang, 1975.

———. *S/Z*, trans. Richard Miller. New York: Hill and Wang, 1974.

———. *Writing Degree Zero*, trans. Annette Lavers and Colin Smith. New York: Farrar, Straus, and Giroux, 1981.

Janet Batsleer, Tony Davies, Rebecca O'Rourke, and Chris Weedon. *Rewriting English: Cultural Politics of Gender and Class*. London: Methuen, 1985.

Nina Baym. "Melodramas of Beset Manhood: How Theories of American Fiction Exclude Women Authors," in Showalter, 1985, 63–80.

Virginia K. Beards. "Margaret Drabble: Novels of a Cautious Feminist." *Critique: Studies in Modern Fiction* 15, no. 2 (1973), 35–47.

Nicola Beauman. *A Very Great Profession: The Woman's Novel 1914–39*. London: Virago, 1989.

Maurice Beebe. *Ivory Towers and Sacred Founts: The Artist as Hero in Fiction from Goethe to Joyce*. New York: New York University Press, 1964.

Gillian Beer. "Beyond Determinism: George Eliot and Virginia Woolf," in Jacobus, 1979, 80–99.

Catherine Belsey. *Critical Practice*. London: Methuen, 1985.

———. "Re-Reading the Great Tradition," in Widdowson, 121–35.

Walter Benjamin. *Understanding Brecht*, trans. Anna Bostock. London: NLB, 1973.

Shari Benstock. *Women of the Left Bank: Paris, 1900–1940*. Austin: University of Texas Press, 1987.

John Berger. *Ways of Seeing.* London: BBC and Penguin, 1977.

Bernard Bergonzi. *Contemporary Novelists,* ed. James Vinson. New York: St. Martin's Press, 1976, 373–74.

————. *The Situation of the Novel.* Pittsburgh: University of Pittsburgh Press, 1970.

Leo Bersani. *A Future for Astyanax: Character and Desire in Literature.* Boston: Little Brown, 1976.

Eva Bertelson. "The Persistent Personal Voice: Lessing on Rhodesia and Marxism: Excerpts from an Interview with Doris Lessing," London, January 9, 1984. *Doris Lessing Newsletter* 9, no. 2 (Fall 1985), 8–10, 18.

Jack I. Biles, ed. *British Novelists since 1900.* New York: AMS Press, 1987.

David Blewett. "The Unity of the Manawaka Cycle." *Journal of Canadian Studies* 13, no. 3 (Fall 1978), 31–39.

Harriet Blodgett. "The Real Lives of Margaret Laurence's Women." *Critique: Studies in Modern Fiction* 23, no. 1 (1981), 5–17.

Harold Bloom. *A Map of Misreading.* New York: Oxford University Press, 1975.

Susan Bolotin. "Voices from the Post-Feminist Generation." *New York Times Magazine,* October 17, 1982, 28ff.

Penny Boumelha. "Realism and the Ends of Feminism," in Sheridan, 77–91.

Howard R. Bowen. "The Effects of Going to College." CHE 15 (October 31, 1977): 3–4; in Daniel, 403.

Blanche M. Boyd. *Nerves.* Plainfield, VT: Daughters, 1973.

Robert Boyers. *Atrocity and Amnesia: The Political Novel since 1945.* Oxford: Oxford University Press, 1985.

Kay Boyle. *The Underground Woman.* Garden City, NY: Doubleday, 1975.

Malcolm Bradbury, *The Modern American Novel.* Oxford: Oxford University Press, 1984.

————, ed. *The Novel Today: Contemporary Writers on Modern Fiction.* Totowa, NJ: Rowman and Littlefield, 1977.

———— and James McFarlane, eds. *Modernism.* Harmondsworth: Penguin, 1976.

———— and James McFarlane. "The Name and Nature of Modernism," in Bradbury and McFarlane, 19–55.

Kate Braverman. *Lithium for Medea.* Los Angeles: Pinnacle Books, 1979.

Wini Breines, Margaret Cerullo, and Judith Stacey. "Social Biology, Family Studies, and Antifeminist Backlash." *Feminist Studies* 4, no. 1 (February 1978), 43–67.

Pamela S. Bromberg. "Narrative in Drabble's *The Middle Ground:* Relativity versus Teleology." *Contemporary Literature* 14, no. 4 (Winter 1983), 463–79.

————. "The Two Faces of the Mirror," in *Margaret Atwood: Vision and Forms,* ed. Kathryn Van Spanckeren and Jan Garden Castro. Carbondale: Southern Illinois University Press, 1988, 12–23.

Dorothy Dunbar Bromley. "Feminist—New Style." *Harpers* 155 (October 1927), 152–60; in Chafe, 92, 278.

E. M. Broner. *Her Mothers.* New York: Berkley, 1975.

Anita Brookner. *The Debut.* New York: Vintage, 1985.

————. *Hotel du Lac.* London: Triad/Panther, 1985.

————. *Look at Me.* New York: Dutton, 1985.

Ellen W. Brooks. "The Image of Women in Lessing's *Golden Notebook.*" *Critique: Studies in Modern Fiction* 15, no. 1 (1973), 101–109.

Jeremy Brooks. "Doris Lessing's Chinese Box." *Sunday Times,* April 15, 1962, 32; in Taylor, 1.

Peter Brooks. *Reading for the Plot: Design and Intention in Narrative.* New York: Vintage, 1984.

Rita Mae Brown. *Rubyfruit Jungle.* New York: Bantam, 1980.

Rachel Brownstein. *Becoming a Heroine: Reading about Women in Novels.* New York: Viking, 1982.

————. "*The Odd Woman* and Literary Feminism," in Pearlman, 173–91.

Fanny Bryant. *Ella Price's Journal*. Berkeley: Ata Books, 1972.

Alan Bullock. "The Double Image," in *Modernism*, ed. Bradbury and McFarlane, 58–70.

Anthony Burgess. *The Novel Now: A Guide to Contemporary Fiction*. New York: Norton, 1967.

A. S. Byatt. *The Virgin in the Garden*. Harmondsworth: Penguin, 1978.

Hazel V. Carby. *Reconstructing Womanhood: The Emergence of the Afro-American Woman Novelist*. New York: Oxford University Press, 1987.

Helen Carr, ed. *From My Guy to Sci-Fi: Genre and Women's Writing in the Postmodern World*. London: Pandora, 1989.

Angela Carter. *Fireworks: Nine Profane Pieces*. New York: Penguin, 1987.

————. *Nights at the Circus*. London: Picador, 1984.

William Chafe. *The American Woman: Her Changing Social, Economic, and Political Roles, 1920–1970*. London: Oxford University Press, 1972.

Wendy Chapkis. *Beauty Secrets: Women and the Politics of Appearance*. Boston: South End Press, 1986.

Joan Chase. *During the Reign of the Queen of Persia*. New York: Ballantine, 1983.

Kim Chernin. *The Hungry Self: Women, Eating and Identity*. New York: Harper and Row, 1985.

————. *The Obsession: Reflections on the Tyranny of Slenderness*. New York: Harper and Row, 1981.

Phyllis Chesler. *Women and Madness*. New York: Doubleday, 1972.

Nancy Chodorow. *The Reproduction of Mothering: Psychoanalysis and the Sociology of Gender*. Berkeley: University of California Press, 1978.

Carol P. Christ. *Diving Deep and Surfacing*. Boston: Beacon Press, 1980.

J. E. Cirlot. *A Dictionary of Symbols*. New York: Philosophical Library, 1962.

Hélène Cixous. "Castration or Decapitation?" *Signs* 7, no. 1 (Summer 1981), 41–55.

————. "The Laugh of the Medusa." *Signs* (Summer 1976); in Marks and Courtivron, 245–64.

Hélène Cixous and Catherine Clément. *The Newly-Born Woman*, trans. Betsy Wing. Minneapolis: University of Minnesota Press, 1986.

Mary Cohen. "'Out of the Chaos a New Kind of Strength': Doris Lessing's *The Golden Notebook*," in Diamond and Edwards, 178–93.

Joan Coldwell. "Hagar as Meg Merrilies, the Homeless Gipsy," in Sorfleet, 92–100.

Terry Coleman. "A Biographer Waylaid by Novels." *Guardian*, April 15, 1972, 23.

Diana Cooper-Clark. "Margaret Drabble: Cautious Feminist." *Atlantic Monthly*, November 1980, 69–75.

Susan Koppelman Cornillon, ed. *Images of Women in Fiction: Feminist Perspectives*. Bowling Green, OH; Bowling Green University Popular Press, 1972.

Nancy F. Cott. *The Grounding of Modern Feminism*. New Haven: Yale University Press, 1987.

Connell Cowan and Melvyn Kinder. *Smart Women, Foolish Choices: Finding the Right Man and Avoiding the Wrong One*. New York: Crown, 1985.

Rosalind Coward. "Are Women's Novels Feminist Novels?" in Showalter, 1985, 225–39.

————. *Female Desires: How They Are Sought, Bought and Packaged*. New York: Grove, 1985.

————, with John Ellis. *Language and Materialism: Developments in Semiology and the Theory of the Subject*. London: Routledge and Kegan Paul, 1977.

Joanne V. Creighton. "An Interview with Margaret Drabble," in Schmidt, 18–31.

————. *Margaret Drabble*. London: Methuen, 1985.

————. "Reading Margaret Drabble's *The Waterfall*," in Rose, 1985, 106–18.

Wilfred Cude. *A Due Sense of Differences: An Evaluative Approach to Canadian Literature*. Washington, DC: University Press of America, 1980.

David Daiches. *The Present Age in British Literature*. Bloomington: Indiana University Press, 1958.

Mary Daly. *Beyond God the Father: Towards a Philosophy of Women's Liberation*. Boston: Beacon Press, 1973.

Robert L. Daniel. *American Women in the Twentieth Century: The Festival of Life*. New York: Harcourt, 1987.

Frank Davey. *Margaret Atwood: A Feminist Poetics*. Vancouver: Talonbooks, 1984.

Nicholas Davidson. *The Failure of Feminism*. Buffalo: Prometheus Books, 1988.

Johanna Davis. *Life Signs*. New York: Dell, 1973.

Lennard J. Davis. *Resisting Novels: Ideology and Fiction*. New York: Methuen, 1987.

Mary V. Dearborn. *Pocahontas's Daughters: Gender and Ethnicity in American Culture*. New York: Oxford University Press, 1986.

Simone de Beauvoir. *The Second Sex*. New York: Vintage, 1952.

———. *The Mandarins*. Cleveland: World, 1956.

———. *The Coming of Age*. New York: G.P. Putnam's Sons, 1972.

Barbara Sinclair Deckard. *The Women's Movement: Political, Socioeconomic, and Psychological Issues*. New York: Harper and Row, 1983.

Teresa de Lauretis, ed. *Feminist Studies, Critical Studies*. Bloomington: Indiana University Press, 1986.

———. *Technologies of Gender*. Bloomington: Indiana University Press, 1987.

L. S. Dembo. *Interviews with Contemporary Writers*. Madison: University of Wisconsin Press, 1983.

Stephanie A. Demetrakopoulos. "Laurence's Fiction: A Revisioning of Feminine Archetypes." *Canadian Literature* 93 (Summer 1982), 42–57.

Robb Forman Dew. *Dale Loves Sophie to Death*. Harmondsworth: Penguin, 1982.

Arlyn Diamond and Lee R. Edwards, eds. *The Authority of Experience: Essays in Feminist Criticism*. Amherst: University of Massachusetts Press, 1977.

Lore Dickstein. Review of *The Odd Woman*. *New York Times Book Review*, October 20, 1974, 4.

Morris Dickstein. *Gates of Eden: American Culture in the Sixties*. New York: Penguin, 1989.

Joan Didion. *A Book of Common Prayer*. New York: Pocket Books, 1977.

———. *Play It As It Lays*. New York: Bantam, 1972.

Dorothy Dinnerstein. *The Mermaid and the Minotaur*. New York: Harper and Row, 1976.

Laura L. Doan. *Old Maids and Excellent Women: The Spinster in the Twentieth Century Novel*. Urbana: University of Illinois Press, 1991.

Janice Doane and Devon Hodges. *Nostalgia and Sexual Difference: The Resistance to Contemporary Feminism*. New York: Methuen, 1987.

Theo Quayle Dombrowski. "Word and Fact: Laurence and the Problem of Language." *Canadian Literature* 80 (Spring 1979), 50–62.

Josephine Donovan, ed. *Feminist Literary Criticism: Explorations in Theory*. Lexington: University Press of Kentucky, 1975.

———. "Toward a Women's Poetics." *Tulsa Studies in Women's Literature* 3, nos. 1/2 (Spring/Fall 1984), 99–110.

Colette Dowling. *The Cinderella Complex*. New York: Pocket Books, 1981.

Margaret Drabble. "Doris Lessing: Cassandra in a World Under Siege." *Ramparts* (February 1972), 50–55.

———. *The Ice Age*. New York: Knopf, 1977.

———. *Jerusalem the Golden*. Harmondsworth: Penguin, 1976.

———. *The Middle Ground*. New York: Bantam, 1980.

———. *The Radiant Way*. London: Weidenfeld and Nicolson, 1987.

———. *The Realms of Gold*. New York: Knopf, 1975.

———. "Stratford Revisited: A Legacy of the Sixties." The Gareth Lloyd Evans Shake-

speare Lecture. Shipston-on-Stour, Warwickshire: The Celandine Press, 1989.
————. *A Summer Bird-Cage*. Harmondsworth: Penguin, 1971.
————. "There Must Be a Lot of People Like Me." *Midwest Quarterly* 16, 1975, 256–57.
————. *The Waterfall*. New York: Fawcett, 1977.
————. "A Woman Writer," in Wandor, 156–59.
Betsy Draine. "An interview with Margaret Atwood," 1981, in Dembo, 366–81.
————. "Nostalgia and Irony: The Postmodern Order of *The Golden Notebook*." *Modern Fiction Studies* 26, no. 1 (Spring 1980) 31–48.
————. "Refusing the Wisdom of Solomon: Some Recent Feminist Literary Theory." *Signs* 15, no. 1 (Autumn 1989), 144–70.
Rachel Blau DuPlessis. *Writing beyond the Ending: Narrative Strategies of Twentieth-Century Women Writers*. Bloomington: Indiana University Press, 1985.
———— and members of Workshop 9. "For the Etruscans: Sexual Difference and Artistic Production—The Debate over a Female Aesthetic," in Eisenstein and Jardine, 128–56; in Showalter, 1985, 271–91.
Lawrence Durrell. Interview with Malcolm Cowley, *Writers at Work: The 'Paris Review' Interviews*. London: Secker and Warburg, 1963; in Stevenson, 205.
Terry Eagleton. *Literary Theory: An Introduction*. Minneapolis: University of Minnesota Press, 1983.
————. *Marxism and Literary Criticism*. Berkeley: University of California Press, 1976.
Richard Eder. "An Allegory of One Child Too Many," review of Lessing's *The Fifth Child*. *Los Angeles Times,* March 27, 1988, 3.
Lee Edwards. *Psyche as Hero: Female Heroism and Fictional Form*. Middletown, CT: Wesleyan University Press, 1984.
Barbara Ehrenreich. *The Hearts of Men: American Dreams and the Flight from Commitment*. Garden City, NY: Anchor, 1983.
Hester Eisenstein and Alice Jardine, eds. *The Future of Difference*. New Brunswick: Rutgers University Press, 1985.
Mercea Eliade. *Images and Symbols: Studies in Religious Symbolism*. New York: Sheed and Ward, 1961.
————. *The Myth of the Eternal Return*. Princeton: Princeton University Press, 1954.
George Eliot. *Daniel Deronda*. Harmondsworth: Penguin, 1976.
————. *Middlemarch*. Boston: Houghton Mifflin, 1956.
T. S. Eliot. *The Sacred Wood*. London: Methuen, 1932.
————. *The Waste Land*. In *The Complete Poems and Plays, 1909–1950*. New York: Harcourt, 1952.
Emory Elliott, ed. *Columbia Literary History of the U.S.* New York: Columbia University Press, 1988.
Mary Ellmann. *Thinking about Women*. New York: Harcourt Brace Jovanovich, 1968.
Jean Bethke Elshtain. "The Post-*Golden Notebook* Fiction of Doris Lessing." *Salmagundi* (Winter-Spring 1980), 95–114.
————. *Public Man, Private Woman: Women in Social and Political Thought*. Princeton: Princeton University Press, 1981.
Marian Engel. *The Globe and Mail,* Toronto: April 19, 1975, 37; in New, 219–21.
Nora Ephron. *Heartburn*. New York: Pocket Books, 1983.
Mari Evans, ed. *Black Women Writers, 1950–1980*. New York: Doubleday, 1984.
Michel Fabre. "Words and the World: 'The Diviners' as an Exploration of the Book of Life." *Canadian Literature* 93 (Summer 1982), 60–78.
Zoe Fairbairns. *Benefits*. London: Virago, 1985.
Warren Farrell. *The Liberated Man, or Beyond Masculinity: Freeing Men and Their Relationships with Women*. New York: Bantam, 1975.
Richard Feldstein and Judith Roof, eds. *Feminism and Psychoanalysis*. Ithaca: Cornell University Press, 1989.

Rita Felski. *Beyond Feminist Aesthetics: Feminist Literature and Social Change.* Cambridge: Harvard University Press, 1989.

Josette Feral. "The Power of Difference," in Eisenstein and Jardine, 88–94.

Mary Anne Ferguson. "The Female Novel of Development and the Myth of Psyche," in Abel et al., 1983, 228–43.

Myra Marx Ferree and Beth B. Hess. *Controversy and Coalition: The New Feminist Movement.* Boston: Twayne, 1985.

Peter Firchow. "Interview with Margaret Drabble," in *The Writer's Place: Interviews on the Literary Situation in Contemporary Britain.* Minneapolis: University of Minnesota Press, 1974.

Shulamith Firestone. *The Dialectic of Sex.* New York: Bantam, 1972.

Elizabeth A. Flynn and Patrocinio P. Schweickart, eds. *Gender and Reading: Essays on Readers, Texts, and Contexts.* Baltimore: Johns Hopkins University Press, 1986.

Boris Ford, ed. *The New Pelican Guide to English Literature: The Present.* Harmondsworth, 1983.

Frieda Johles Forman with Caoran Sowton, eds. *Taking Our Time: Feminist Perspectives on Temporality.* Oxford: Pergamon Press, 1988.

John Fowles. *The French Lieutenant's Woman.* Boston: Little, Brown, 1969.

Jo Freeman. *The Politics of Women's Liberation.* New York: David McKay, 1975.

Marilyn French. *Her Mother's Daughter.* New York: Summit Books, 1987.

———. *The Women's Room.* New York: Jove Publications, 1977.

Sigmund Freud. *Jokes and Their Relation to the Unconscious. The Standard Edition of the Complete Psychological Works of Sigmund Freud,* ed. James Strachey. 8. London: Hogarth Press, 1960, 169–72.

———. "Medusa's Head," in Strachey, ed., vol. 18, 273.

Betty Friedan. *The Feminine Mystique.* New York: Norton, 1983.

———. "How to Get the Women's Movement Moving Again." *New York Times Magazine,* November 3, 1985, 26ff.

———. *The Second Stage.* New York: Summit Books, 1981.

Alan Friedman. *The Turn of the Novel.* New York: Oxford University Press, 1966.

Susan Stanford Friedman. *Psyche Reborn: The Emergence of H.D..* Bloomington: Indiana University Press, 1981.

Joanne S. Frye. *Living Stories, Telling Lives: Women and the Novel in Contemporary Experience.* Ann Arbor: University of Michigan Press, 1986.

Caryn Fuoroli. "Doris Lessing's 'Game': Referential Language and Fictional Form." *Twentieth-Century Literature* 27, no. 2 (Summer 1981), 146–65.

Nelly Furman. "The Politics of Language: Beyond the Gender Principle?" in Greene and Kahn, 59–79.

Suzanne Gail. "The Housewife." *New Left Review,* 1965–66; in Malos, 105–12.

Jane Gallop. "*Quand nos lèvres se parlent:* Irigaray's Body Politic." *Romanic Review* 74, no. 1 (January 1983).

Irma Garcia. "Femalear Explorations: Temporality in Women's Writing," in Forman, 161–82.

Judith Kegan Gardiner. "On Female Identity and Writing by Women," in Abel, *Writing and Sexual Difference,* 347–61.

———. *Rhys, Stead, Lessing, and the Politics of Empathy.* Bloomington: Indiana University Press, 1989.

———. "A Wake for Mother: The Maternal Deathbed in Women's Fiction." *Feminist Studies* 4, no. 2 (June 1978), 146–65.

Shirley Nelson Garner, Claire Kahane, and Madelon Sprengnether, eds. *The (M)other Tongue: Essays in Feminist Psychoanalytic Interpretation.* Ithaca: Cornell University Press, 1985, 15–29.

Xavière Gauthier. "Is There Such a Thing as Women's Writing?," in Marks and Courtivron, 161–64.

Sally Miller Gearhart. *The Wanderground: Stories of the Hill Women*. Boston: Alyson, 1979.

Blanche H. Gelfant. "Sister to Faust: The City's 'Hungry' Woman as Heroine," in Gelfant, ed., 205–24.

———, ed. *Women Writing in America: Voices in Collage*. Hanover, NH: University Press of New England, 1984.

Graeme Gibson. "Interview with Margaret Atwood," in *Eleven Canadian Novelists*. Toronto: Anansi, 1973, 5–31.

Sandra M. Gilbert. "What Do Feminist Critics Want? A Postcard from the Volcano." *ADE Bulletin* 66 (1980); in Showalter, 1985, 29–45.

Sandra M. Gilbert and Susan Gubar. *The Madwoman in the Attic: The Woman Writer and the Nineteenth-Century Literary Imagination*. New Haven: Yale University Press, 1979.

———. *The Norton Anthology of Literature by Women: The Tradition in English*. New York: Norton, 1985.

———. *No Man's Land: The Place of the Woman Writer in the Twentieth Century*. Volume 1: *The War of the Words*. New Haven: Yale University Press, 1988. Volume 2: *Sexchanges*. New Haven: Yale University Press, 1989.

Carol Gilligan. *In A Different Voice: Psychological Theory and Women's Development*. Cambridge: Harvard University Press, 1982.

James Gindin. *Postwar British Fiction: New Accents and Attitudes*. Berkeley: University of California Press, 1962.

Barbara Godard. "My (m)Other, My Self: Strategies for Subversion in Atwood and Hébert." *Essays in Canadian Writing* 26 (1983), 13–44.

Gail Godwin. "Becoming a Writer," in *The Writer on Her Work*, ed. Janet Sternburg. New York: Norton, 1980, 231–55.

———. *The Finishing School*. New York: Avon, 1984.

———. *A Mother and Two Daughters*. New York: Viking, 1982.

———. *The Odd Woman*. New York: Warner, 1974.

———. Review of Sandra M. Gilbert and Susan Gubar's *Norton Anthology of Literature by Women*. *New York Times Book Review*, April 28, 1985.

———. *A Southern Family*. New York: Avon, 1987.

Herb Goldberg. *The Hazards of Being Male*. New York: New American Library, 1976.

Leona M. Gom. "Margaret Laurence and the Use of Memory." *Canadian Literature* 71 (Winter 1976), 48–58.

Ellen Goodman. "The Doris Lessing Hoax." *Washington Post*, September 27, 1984, 31; in "Doris Lessing as Jane Somers: The Media Response." *Doris Lessing Newsletter* 9, no. 1 (Spring 1985), 3.

Nadine Gordimer. *The Burger's Daughter*. Harmondsworth: Penguin, 1980.

Mary Gordon. *Men and Angels*. New York: Ballantine, 1985.

Lois Gould. *The Final Analysis*. New York: Avon, 1974.

———. *A Sea Change*. New York: Avon, 1976.

———. *Such Good Friends*. New York: Random House, 1970.

Stephen Jay Gould. *Time's Arrow, Time's Cycle: Myth and Metaphor in the Discovery of Geological Time*. Cambridge: Harvard University Press, 1987.

Sherrill Grace. "A Portrait of the Artist as Laurence Hero." *Journal of Canadian Studies* 13, no. 3 (Fall 1978), 64–71.

———. *Violent Duality: A Study of Margaret Atwood*. Montreal: Vehicle Press, 1980.

Gerald Graff. *Literature against Itself: Literary Ideas in Modern Society*. Chicago: University of Chicago Press, 1979.

Antonio Gramsci. *The Modern Prince*. London: International Publishers, 1957.

———. "The Study of Philosophy," in *Selections from the Prison Notebooks*. New York: International Publishers, 1976.

Robert Graves. *The White Goddess*. New York: Creative Age Press, 1948.

Francine Du Plessix Gray. *Lovers and Tyrants*. New York: Simon and Schuster, 1976.

Gayle Greene. "Choice of Evils," review of Atwood's *The Handmaid's Tale*. *Women's Review of Books* (June 1986), 14–15; in 1986 *Contemporary Literary Criticism Yearbook*.

———. "Divided Selves: Women and Men in *The Golden Notebook*," in Garner et al., 280–305.

———. "The End of a Dream," review of Drabble's *The Radiant Way*. *Women's Review of Books* (January 1988), 4–5; in 1989 *Contemporary Literary Criticism Yearbook*.

———. "'Excellent Dumb Discourse': Silence and Grace in *The Tempest*." *Studia Neophilologica* 50 (1978), 173–208.

———. "Feminist Fiction and the Uses of Memory." *Signs* 16, no. 2 (Winter 1990), 1–32.

———. "Margaret Atwood's *The Edible Woman*: 'Rebelling against the System,'" in *Margaret Atwood: Reflection and Reality*, ed. Beatrice Mendez-Egle. Edinburg, TX: Pan American University, 1987, 95–115.

———. "'A New Kind of Knowledge': Doris Lessing's *Landlocked*." *Contemporary Literature* 28, no. 1 (Spring 1987), 82–103.

———. "Shakespeare's *Tempest* and Eliot's *Waste Land*: 'What the Thunder Said.'" *Orbis Litterarum* 34 (1979), 289–300.

Gayle Greene and Coppélia Kahn. "Feminist Scholarship and the Social Construction of Woman," in Greene and Kahn, eds.

———, eds. *Making a Difference: Feminist Literary Criticism*. London: Methuen, 1985.

Germaine Greer. *The Female Eunuch*. New York: McGraw Hill, 1971.

Kirsten Grimstad and Susan Rennie, eds. *The New Woman's Survival Sourcebook*. New York: Knopf, 1975.

Judith Grossman. *Her Own Terms*. New York: Ivy Books, 1988.

Susan Guhar. "The Birth of the Artist as Heroine: (Re)production, the *Kunstlerroman* Tradition, and the Fiction of Katherine Mansfield," in Heilbrun and Higonnet, 19–59.

John Haffenden. "Interview with Anita Brookner," in *Novelists in Interview*, ed. John Haffenden. London: Methuen, 1985, 57–75.

John Hannay. *The Intertextuality of Fate: A Study of Margaret Drabble*. Columbia: University of Missouri Press, 1986.

Gillian Hanscombe and Virginia L. Smyers. *Writing for Their Lives: The Modernist Women, 1910–1940*. Boston: Northeastern University Press, 1987.

Nancy S. Hardin. "An Interview with Margaret Drabble," in Dembo, 89–111.

Elizabeth Hardwick. *Seduction and Betrayal*. New York: Random House, 1974.

Dick Harrison. "Cultural Insanity and Prairie Fiction," in *Figures in a Ground: Canadian Essays on Modern Literature Collected in Honour of Sheila Watson*, Diane Bessai and David Jackel, eds. Saskatoon: 1978.

James B. Harrison. "Review Essay: Men's Roles and Men's Lives." *Signs* (Winter 1978), 324–36.

Frigga Haug and others. *Female Sexualization: A Collective Work of Memory*. London: Verso, 1987.

Marianne Hauser. *The Talking Room*. Brooklyn: Fiction Collective, 1976.

Stephen Heath. "Touch of Evil." *Screen* 16, no. 2 (1975), in Coward and Ellis.

Barbara Hehner. "River of Now and Then: Margaret Laurence's Narratives." *Canadian Literature* 74 (Autumn 1977), 40–57.

Carolyn Heilbrun. *Reinventing Womanhood*. New York: Norton, 1979.

———. *Toward a Recognition of Androgyny*. New York: Knopf, 1973.

———. *Writing a Woman's Life*. New York: Norton, 1988.

Carolyn Heilbrun, Nina Auerbach, Myra Jehlen, Nancy K. Miller, and Catharine R.

Stimpson. Response to Godwin's review. *New York Times Book Review,* April 28, 1985.

Carolyn Heilbrun and Margaret R. Higonnet, eds. *The Representation of Women in Fiction: Selected Papers from the English Institute.* Baltimore: Johns Hopkins University Press, 1981.

Lillian Hellman. *An Unfinished Woman: A Memoir.* Boston: Little, Brown, 1969.

Claudine Herrmann. *Les Voleuses de langue.* Paris: des Femmes, 1976.

Sylvia Hewlett. *A Lesser Life: The Myth of Women's Liberation in America.* New York: William Morrow, 1986.

Marianne Hirsch. *The Mother/Daughter Plot: Narrative, Psychoanalysis, Feminism.* Bloomington: Indiana University Press, 1989.

Molly Hite. *The Other Side of the Story: Structures and Strategies of Contemporary Feminist Narratives.* Ithaca: Cornell University Press, 1989.

———. Review of Claire Sprague's *Rereading Doris Lessing. Doris Lessing Newsletter* 11, no. 2 (Fall 1987), 12–13.

Judith Hole and Ellen Levine. *The Rebirth of Feminism.* New York: Quadrangle, 1971.

Norman H. Holland and Leona F. Sherman. "Gothic Possibilities." *New Literary History* 8 (1976–79), 279–94.

John Holloway. "The Literary Scene," in Ford, 417–49.

Margaret Homans. *Bearing the Word: Language and Female Experience in Nineteenth-Century Women's Writing.* Chicago: University of Chicago Press, 1986.

———. " 'Her Very Own Howl': The Ambiguities of Representation in Recent Women's Fiction." *Signs* 9, no. 2 (1983), 186–205.

Florence Howe, ed. *Tradition and the Talents of Women.* Urbana: University of Illinois Press, forthcoming.

Florence Howe and Carol Ahlum. "Women's Studies and Social Change," in Rossi and Calderwood, 382–407.

Irving Howe. Review of *The Golden Notebook. The New Republic* 147 (December 15, 1962), 17–20; in Sprague and Tiger, 177–81.

Coral Ann Howells. *Private and Fictional Worlds: Canadian Women Novelists of the 1970s and 1980s.* London: Methuen, 1987.

Linda Huf. *A Portrait of the Artist as a Young Woman: The Writer as Heroine in American Literature.* New York: Frederick Ungar, 1983.

Mary Hughes and Mary Kennedy. *New Futures: Changing Women's Education.* London: Routledge, 1985.

Linda Hutcheon. *Narcissistic Narrative: The Metafictional Paradox.* New York: Methuen, 1984.

Earl G. Ingersoll, ed. *Margaret Atwood: Conversations.* Willowdale, Ontario: Ontario Review Press, 1990.

Luce Irigaray. "Plato's *Hystera,*" *Speculum of the Other Woman.* Ithaca: Cornell University Press, 1985.

———. *This Sex Which Is Not One.* Ithaca: Cornell University Press, 1985.

Lorna Irvine. "No Sense of an Ending: Drabble's Continuous Fictions," in Rose, 1985, 73–86.

Wolfgang Iser. *The Implied Reader.* Baltimore: Johns Hopkins University Press, 1974.

Mary Jacobus. "The Difference of View," in Jacobus, 10–20.

———. "The Question of Language: Men of Maxims and *The Mill on the Floss,*" in Abel, *Writing and Sexual Difference,* 207–23.

———, ed. *Women Writing and Writing about Women.* New York: Barnes and Noble, 1979.

Caryn James. "Women's Friendship Thrive in Ambiguity," review of Atwood's *Cat's Eye. New York Times,* January 28, 1989, 15.

Henry James. "The Art of Fiction," in *The Art of Fiction and Other Essays.* New York: Oxford University Press, 1948, 3–23.

Fredric Jameson. *The Political Unconscious: Narrative as a Socially Symbolic Act.* Ithaca: Cornell University Press, 1982.

Alice Jardine. "Gynesis." *Diacritics* (Summer 1982), 54–65.

——. *Gynesis: Configurations of Woman and Modernity.* Ithaca: Cornell University Press, 1985.

Susan Jeffords. *The Remasculinization of America: Gender and the Vietnam War.* Bloomington: Indiana University Press, 1989.

David Jeffrey. "Biblical Hermeneutic and Family History in Contemporary Canadian Fiction: Wiebe and Laurence." *Mosaic* 11, no. 3 (Spring 1978), 87–106.

Nora Johnson. "Housewives and Prom Queens, 25 Years Later." *New York Times Book Review,* March 20, 1988, 1.

Eleanor Johnston. "The Quest of *The Diviners.*" *Mosaic* 11, no. 3 (Spring 1978).

Ann Rosalind Jones. "Writing the Body: Toward an Understanding of *l'Ecriture féminine,*" in Showalter, 1985, 361–77.

Gayl Jones. *Corregidora.* Boston: Beacon Press, 1986.

Erica Jong. "Blood and Guts: The Tricky Problem of Being a Woman Writer in the Late Twentieth Century," in Sternburg, 169–79.

——. *Fear of Flying.* New York: Signet, 1973.

——. *How to Save Your Own Life.* New York: Signet, 1977.

James Joyce. *A Portrait of the Artist as a Young Man.* New York: Viking, 1960.

Suzanne Juhazs. "Towards a Theory of Form in Feminist Autobiography," in *Women's Autobiography,* ed. Estelle C. Jelinek. Bloomington: Indiana University Press, 1980.

Carl Jung. *Mandala Symbolism.* Princeton: Princeton University Press, 1972.

Claire Kahane. "The Gothic Mirror," in Garner et al., 334–51.

Robbie Pfeufer Kahn. "Women and Time in Childbirth and during Lactation," in Forman and Sowton, 20–36.

Wendy Kaminer. *A Fearful Freedom: Women's Flight from Equality.* Reading, MA: Addison-Wesley, 1990.

Louis Kampf. *On Modernism: The Prospects for Literature and Freedom.* Cambridge: M.I.T. Press, 1967.

Carey Kaplan and Ellen Cronan Rose, eds. *Approaches to Teaching Lessing's The Golden Notebook.* New York: The Modern Language Association of America, 1989.

Cora Kaplan. "Speaking/Writing/Feminism," in Wandor, 51–66.

——. "Feminist Criticism Twenty Years On," in Carr, 15–23.

Sydney Janet Kaplan. *Feminine Consciousness in the Modern British Novel.* Chicago: University of Illinois Press, 1975.

Frederick R. Karl. *A Reader's Guide to the Contemporary English Novel.* New York: Farrar, Straus, and Giroux, 1971.

Sue Kaufman. *Diary of a Mad Housewife.* New York: Bantam, 1970.

——. *Falling Bodies.* New York: Bantam, 1975.

Fraya Katz-Stoker. "The Other Criticism: Feminism vs. Formalism," in Cornillon, 315–27.

W. J. Keith. *Canadian Literature in English.* London: Longman, 1985.

Steven G. Kellmann. "The Fiction of Self-Begetting." *Modern Language Notes* 91 (December 1976), 1243–56.

Jean E. Kennard. "Convention Coverage or How to Read Your Own Life." *New Literary History* 13, no. 1 (Autumn 1981), 69–88.

Olga Kenyon. *Women Novelists Today: A Survey of English Writing in the Seventies and Eighties.* New York: St. Martin's Press, 1988.

Christopher Kimball. "What Men Want." *The Peninsula Times Tribune,* August 24–26, 1990, 4, 6.

Gayle Kimball, ed. *Women's Culture: The Women's Renaissance of the Seventies.* Metuchen, NJ: Scarecrow Press, 1981.

Mary King. *Freedom Song: A Personal Story of the 1960s Civil Rights Movement.* New York: William Morrow, 1987.

Mona Knapp. *Doris Lessing.* New York: Frederick Ungar, 1984.

———. "*The Golden Notebook:* A Feminist Context for the Classroom," in Kaplan and Rose, 108–14.

W. F. Jackson Knight. *Virgil: Epic and Anthropology.* London: George Allen and Unwin, 1967.

Annette Kolodny. *The Lay of the Land: Metaphor as Experience and History in American Life and Letters.* Chapel Hill: University of North Carolina Press, 1975.

———. "A Map for Rereading: Or, Gender and the Interpretation of Literary Texts." *New Literary History* 3 (Spring 1980), 451–67.

Richard Kostelanetz, ed. *On Contemporary Literature.* New York: Avon, 1964.

Susan Kress. "Lessing's Responsibility." *Salmagundi* (Winter-Spring 1980), 95–131.

Julia Kristeva. *About Chinese Women.* New York: Urigen Books, 1977.

———. "Breaching the Thetic: Mimesis," in *Revolution in Poetic Language,* ed. Leon S. Roudiez. New York: Columbia University Press, 1984, 57–61.

———. *Desire in Language: A Semiotic Approach to Literature and Art,* ed. Leon S. Roudiez. New York: Columbia University Press, 1980.

———. "Motherhood According to Giovanni Bellini," in *Desire in Language,* 237–70.

———. "The Novel as Polylogue," in *Desire in Language,* 159–209.

———. "Women's Time." *Signs* 7, no. 1 (1981), 13–35.

———. "Word, Dialogue, and Novel," in *Desire in Language,* 64–91.

Annette Kuhn. *Women's Pictures: Feminism and Cinema.* London: Routledge and Kegan Paul, 1982.

Phyllis Gross Kurth. "Wise and Gentle," review of *The Fire-Dwellers. Canadian Literature* 43 (1970), 91–92.

Esther Kleinbord Labovitz. *The Myth of the Heroine: The Female Bildungsroman in the Twentieth Century.* New York: Peter Lang, 1986.

R. D. Laing. *The Politics of Experience and the Bird of Paradise.* Harmondsworth: Penguin, 1970.

Ellen Z. Lambert. "Margaret Drabble and the Sense of Possibility." *University of Toronto Quarterly* 49 (Spring 1980), 228–51.

Elinor Langer. "Whatever Happened to Feminist Fiction?" *New York Times Book Review,* March 4, 1984, 1, 35–36.

Susan Lardner. "Angle on the Ordinary." *New Yorker,* September 19, 1983, 140–54.

Margaret Laurence. "Books that Mattered to Me," in Verduyn, 239–49.

———. *Dance on the Earth.* Toronto: McClelland and Stewart, 1989.

———. *The Diviners.* Toronto: Bantam, 1975.

———. *The Fire-Dwellers.* Toronto: McClelland and Stewart, 1984.

———. "Gadgetry or Growing: Form and Voice in the Novel," in Sorfleet, 54–62.

———. *Heart of a Stranger.* Toronto: McClelland and Stewart, 1976.

———. "Ivory Tower or Grass Roots? The Novelist as Socio-political Being," in New, *Essays and Images,* 15–25.

———. *The Stone Angel.* New York: Bantam, 1981.

D. H. Lawrence. *England, My England.* London: M. Secker, 1924.

John Lawson and Harold Silver. *A Social History of Education in England.* London: Methuen, 1973.

F. R. Leavis. *The Great Tradition.* New York: New York University Press, 1969.

Wolfgang Lederer. *The Fear of Women.* New York: Harcourt Brace Jovanovich, 1968.

Bolivar Le Franc. "An Interest in Guilt." *Books and Bookmen* 14 (September 1969), 20.

Ursula K. LeGuin. *The Left Hand of Darkness.* New York: Ace Books, 1976.

——. *The Dispossessed.* New York: Avon, 1974.

Rosamond Lehmann. *The Weather in the Streets.* New York: Reynal and Hitchcock, 1936.

Lorie Jerrell Leininger. "The Miranda Trap: Sexism and Racism in Shakespeare's *Tempest*," in Lenz et al., 285–94.

Jane Leney. "Prospero and Caliban in Laurence's African Fiction," in Sorfleet, 63–80.

Frank Lentricchia. *Criticism and Social Change.* Chicago: University of Chicago Press, 1983.

Carolyn Ruth Swift Lenz, Gayle Greene, and Carol Thomas Neely, eds. *"The Woman's Part": Feminist Criticism of Shakespeare.* Urbana: University of Illinois Press, 1980.

John Leonard. "In Person." *Newsday*, 3/17/88; part II, 8; in *Doris Lessing Newsletter* 12, no. 2 (Fall 1989), 5.

——. "The Spacing Out of Doris Lessing," in Sprague and Tiger, 204–209.

Doris Lessing. *Briefing for a Descent into Hell.* New York: Bantam, 1972.

——. *The Diaries of Jane Somers.* New York: Vintage, 1984.

——. *The Fifth Child.* New York: Knopf, 1988.

——. *The Four-Gated City.* New York: New American Library, 1976.

——. *The Golden Notebook.* New York: Bantam, 1973.

——. *The Good Terrorist.* New York: Knopf, 1985.

——. *The Grass Is Singing.* New York: New American Library, 1976.

——. Interview by Jonah Raskin, at Stony Brook, in Schleuter, 61–76.

——. Interview with Roy Newquist, in Schleuter, 45–60.

——. *Landlocked.* New York: New American Library, 1966.

——. *The Making of the Representative for Planet 8.* New York: Knopf, 1982.

——. *The Marriages between Zones Three, Four, and Five.* New York: Vintage, 1981.

——. *Martha Quest.* New York: New American Library, 1964.

——. *A Proper Marriage.* New York: New American Library, 1970.

——. *Shikasta.* New York: Vintage, 1981.

——. *The Sirian Experiments: The Report by Ambien II, of the Five.* New York: Knopf, 1980.

——. "The Small Personal Voice," in Schleuter, 3–21.

——. *The Summer Before the Dark.* New York: Bantam, 1974.

——. "To Room Nineteen," in *A Man and Two Women.* New York: Popular Library, 1963, 278–316.

——. *World Press Review*, July 1981, 61.

Bernice Lever. "Literature and Canadian Culture: An Interview with Margaret Laurence," in New, *Margaret Laurence*, 24–32.

George Levine. *The Realistic Imagination: English Fiction from Frankenstein to Lady Chatterley.* Chicago: University of Chicago Press, 1981.

Marion Vlastos Libby. "Fate and Feminism in the Novels of Margaret Drabble." *Contemporary Literature* 16, no. 2 (Spring 1975), 175–92.

Martha Lifson. "Structural Patterns in *The Golden Notebook.*" *Michigan Papers in Women's Studies* 2, no. 4, (1978), 95–108.

Alison Light. "Putting on the Style: Feminist Criticism in the 1990s," in Carr, 24–35.

Amy Ling. *Between Worlds: Women Writers of Chinese Ancestry.* New York: Pergamon, 1990.

Audre Lorde. "The Master's Tools Will Never Dismantle the Master's House," in Moraga and Anzaldúa, 98–101.

George Lukács. "The Ideology of Modernism," in *The Meaning of Contemporary Realism* (1963), trans. John and Necke Mander. London: Merlin Press, 1969, 17–46.

———. "The Problems of a Philosophy of the History of Forms," 1920, in *The Theory of the Novel*. Cambridge: MIT Press, 1971, 40–55.

———. *Studies in European Realism*. New York: The Universal Library, 1964, 1946, Preface, 1–19.

Alison Lurie. "Bad Housekeeping," review of Lessing's *The Good Terrorist*. *New York Review of Books*, December 19, 1985, 8ff.

———. "The Mean Years," review of Atwood's *Cat's Eye*, *Ms.*, March 1989, 38ff.

———. *Real People*. Harmondsworth: Penguin, 1983.

———. *The Truth about Lorin Jones*. Boston: Little, Brown, 1988.

———. *The War between the Tates*. New York: Warner, 1975.

Susan Lydon. "Review of Lessing's *Four-Gated City*." *Ramparts*, January 1970, 48–50.

Samuel L. Macey. *Patriarchs of Time: Dualism in Saturn-Cronus, Father Time, the Watchmaker God, and Father Christmas*. Athens, GA: University of Georgia Press, 1987.

Pierre Macherey. *A Theory of Literary Production*, trans. Geoffrey Wall. London: Routledge and Kegan Paul, 1978.

Catharine MacKinnon. "Feminism, Marxism, Method, and the State: An Agenda for Theory." *Signs* 7, no. 3 (1982), 515–44.

Susan Maclean. "*Lady Oracle*: The Art of Reality and the Reality of Art." *Journal of Canadian Fiction* 28–9 (1980), 179–97.

Angelika Maesar. "Finding the Mother: The Individuation of Laurence's Heroines," in Sorfleet, 151–66.

Sara Maitland. "Futures in Feminist Fiction," in Carr, 193–203.

Christine Makward. "To Be or Not to Be . . . A Feminist Speaker," in Eisenstein and Jardine, 95–105.

Ellen Malos, ed. *The Politics of Housework*. New York: Schocken Books, 1980.

Joan Manheimer. "Margaret Drabble and the Journey to the Self." *Studies in the Literary Imagination* 11, no. 2 (Fall 1978).

Jane Marcus. "Invisible Mending," in Ascher et al., 381–95.

———. "Still Practice, A/Wrested Alphabet: Toward a Feminist Aesthetic." *Tulsa Studies in Women's Literature* 3, no. 1/2 (Spring/Fall 1984), 79–97.

Alice Bradley Markos. "The Pathology of Feminine Failure in the Fiction of Doris Lessing." *Critique: Studies in Modern Fiction* 16 (1974).

Elaine Marks."Women and Literature in France." *Signs* 3, no. 4 (1978).

Elaine Marks and Isabelle de Courtivron, eds. *New French Feminisms: An Anthology*. Amherst: University of Massachusetts Press, 1980.

Paule Marshall. *Brown Girl, Brownstones*. Old Westbury, NY: The Feminist Press, 1981.

Catherine Martens. "Mother-Figures in *Surfacing* and *Lady Oracle*: An Interview with Margaret Atwood." *American Studies in Scandanavia* 16 (1984), 45–54; in Hite, 151.

Wallace Martin. *Recent Theories of Narrative*. Ithaca: Cornell University Press, 1986.

Elaine Tyler May. "Explosive Issues: Sex, Women and the Bomb," in May, 154–70.

Lary May, ed. *Recasting America: Culture and Politics in the Age of Cold War*. Chicago: University of Chicago Press, 1989.

Alice McDermott. "What Little Girls Are Really Made Of," review of Atwood's *Cat's Eye*. *New York Times Book Review*, February 5, 1989, 1ff.

P. W. Frederick McDowell. "The Fiction of Doris Lessing: An Interim View." *Arizona Quarterly* 21 (1965), 315–45.

Brian McHale. *Postmodernist Fiction*. New York: Methuen, 1987.

Susan Jaret McKinstry. "Living Literally by the Pen: The Self-Conceived and Self-Deceiving Heroine-Author in Margaret Atwood's *Lady Oracle*," in Mendez-Egle, 58–70.

Ann McMillan. "The Transforming Eye: *Lady Oracle* and Gothic Tradition," in Van-Spanckeren and Castro, 48–64.

Carol Burr Megibow. "The Use of Story in Women's Novels of the Seventies," in Kimball, 194–214.

W. W. Meissner. *The Paranoid Process*. New York: Jason Aaronson, 1978.

Beatrice Mendez-Egle, ed. *Margaret Atwood: Reflection and Reality*. Edinburg, TX: Pan American University, 1987.

Jack Mezirow. "Perspective Transformation." *Studies in Adult Education* 9, no. 2 (October 1977), 153–64.

Anne Z. Mickelson. *Reaching Out: Sensitivity and Order in Recent American Fiction by Women*. Metuchen, NJ: The Scarecrow Press, 1979.

Rosalind Miles. *The Female Form: Women Writers and the Conquest of the Novel*. London: Routledge and Kegan Paul, 1987.

———. *The Fiction of Sex: Themes and Functions of Sex Difference in the Modern Novel*. New York: Barnes and Noble, 1974.

Nancy Milford. *Zelda*. New York: Avon, 1971.

D. A. Miller. *Narrative and Its Discontents: Problems of Closure in the Traditional Novel*. Princeton: Princeton University Press, 1981.

Douglas T. Miller and Marion Nowak. *The Fifties: The Way We Really Were*. Garden City, NY: Doubleday, 1977.

Jean Baker Miller. *Toward a New Psychology of Women*. Boston: Beacon Press, 1976.

Nancy K. Miller. "Arachnologies: The Woman, the Text, and the Critic," in Miller, 1986, 270–95.

———. "Emphasis Added: Plots and Plausibilities in Women's Fiction." *PMLA* 96, no. 1 (January 1981), 36–48.

———. *The Heroine's Text: Readings in the French and English Novel, 1722–1782*. New York: Columbia University Press, 1980.

———, ed. *The Poetics of Gender*. New York: Columbia University Press, 1986.

———. *Subject to Change: Reading Feminist Writing*. New York: Columbia University Press, 1988.

Sue Miller. *The Good Mother*. New York: Harper and Row, 1986.

Kate Millett. *Flying*. New York: Simon and Schuster, 1990.

Madonne M. Miner. "Guaranteed to Please: Twentieth-Century American Women's Bestsellers," in Flynn and Schweickart, 187–211.

Valerie Miner. *Movement*. New York: Methuen, 1982.

Adrian Mitchell. *Guardian*, October 12, 1967; in Bergonzi, 66.

Juliet Mitchell. "Reflections on Twenty Years of Feminism," in Mitchell and Oakley, 34–48.

Juliet Mitchell and Ann Oakley, eds. *What is Feminism? A Re-Examination*. New York: Pantheon, 1986.

W. J. T. Mitchell, ed. *On Narrative*. Chicago: University of Chicago Press, 1980.

Tania Modleski. *Loving with a Vengeance: Mass-Produced Fantasies for Women*. New York: Methuen, 1982.

Ellen Moers. "Angry Young Women." *Harper's*, December 1963, 89–97.

———. *Literary Women: The Great Writers*. Garden City, NY: Anchor Press, Doubleday, 1977.

Toril Moi. *Sexual/Textual Politics*. New York: Methuen, 1985.

Charles Molesworth, "Culture, Power, and Society," in *Columbia Literary History*, 1023–44.

Cherrie Moraga and Gloria Anzaldúa, eds. *This Bridge Called My Back: Writings of Radical Women of Color*. New York: Women of Color Press, 1981.

Mary Hurley Moran. *Margaret Drabble: Existing within Structures*. Carbondale: Southern Illinois University Press, 1983.

Mark P. O. Morford and Robert J. Lenardon. *Classical Mythology,* 2d ed. New York: David McKay, 1977.

Ellen Morgan. "Alienation of the Woman Writer in *The Golden Notebook,*" in Pratt and Dembo, 54–63.

———. "Humanbecoming: Form and Focus in the Neo-Feminist Novel," in Cornillon, 183–205.

Robin Morgan. "Introduction," in *Sisterhood Is Powerful: An Anthology of Writings from the Women's Liberation Movement.* New York: Vintage, 1970, xv-xlvi.

Patricia Morley. "The Gothic as Social Realism." *Canadian Forum* 56 (December-January 1976-77), 43–51.

———. *Margaret Laurence.*Twayne's World Author Series. Boston: G.K. Hall, 1981.

M. Morris. "Newspapers and the New Feminists: Blackout as Social Control." *Journalism Quarterly* 50, 37–42; in Ferree, 75.

Richard Morris. *Time's Arrows.* New York: Simon and Schuster, 1984.

Toni Morrison. *Beloved.* New York: Knopf, 1988.

———. *The Bluest Eye.* New York: Pocket Books, 1970.

———. Interview with Claudia Tate, in Tate, 117–31.

———. "Rootedness: The Ancestor as Foundation," in Evans, 339–45.

———. *Sula.* New York: New American Library, 1973.

Penelope Mortimer. *Long Distance.* Garden City, NY: Doubleday, 1974.

———. *The Pumpkin Eater.* Plainfield, VT: Daughters, 1975.

Melanie Mortlock. "The Religion of Heritage: *The Diviners* as a Thematic Conclusion to the Manawaka Series," in Sorfleet, 132–42.

Wendy Mulford. "Notes on Writing," in Wandor, 31–41.

Francis Mulhern. *The Moment of "Scrutiny."* London: New Left Books, 1979.

Anne M. Mulkeen. "Twentieth-Century Realism: The 'Grid' Structure of *The Golden Notebook." Studies in the Novel* 4, no. 2 (Summer 1972), 262–74.

Alice Munro. "Baptizing," in *Lives of Girls and Women.* New York: New American Library, 1983, 148–201.

———. *The Beggar Maid.* Toronto: Bantam, 1982.

Iris Murdoch. *An Accidental Man.* London: Triad/Granada, 1973.

———. *The Black Prince.* New York: Warner, 1973.

———. *A Fairly Honourable Defeat.* Harmondsworth: Penguin, 1976.

———. *The Good Apprentice.* Harmondsworth: Penguin, 1987.

———. *Henry and Cato.* New York: Penguin, 1977.

———. *The Nice and the Good.* New York: Penguin, 1978.

———. *Nuns and Soldiers.* Harmondsworth: Penguin, 1982.

———. *The Sacred and Profane Love Machine.* New York: Viking, 1974.

———. *The Sea, the Sea.* New York: Penguin, 1980.

———. *A Word Child.* London: Triad/Panther, 1977.

William New, ed. *Critical Views on Canadian Writers: Margaret Laurence.* Toronto: McGraw-Hill Ryerson, 1977.

———, ed. *A Political Art: Essays and Images in Honor of George Woodcock.* Vancouver: University of British Columbia Press, 1978.

*New Review* on "The State of Fiction: A Symposium." (Summer 1978, 5:1).

Judith Newton and Deborah Rosenfelt, eds. *Feminist Criticism and Social Change: Sex, Class and Race in Literature and Culture.* New York: Methuen, 1985.

Joyce Carol Oates. Review of *The Needle's Eye. New York Times Book Review,* June 14, 1972.

———. "Where Are You Going?" in *The Wheel of Love.* New York: Vanguard Press, 1970.

———. *Wonderland.* Greenwich, CT: Fawcett Crest, 1971.

Edna O'Brien. *Girls in Their Married Bliss, The Country Girls Trilogy.* New York: New American Library, 1968.

Chikwenye Okonjo Ogunyemi. "Womanism: The Dynamics of the Contemporary Black Female Novel in English." *Signs,* 11, no. 1 (1985), 63–80.

Tillie Olsen. *Yonnondio: From The Thirties.* New York: Dell, 1975.

Susie Orbach. *Fat Is a Feminist Issue.* New York: Berkley Books, 1981.

Rebecca O'Rourke. "Doris Lessing: Exile and Exception," in Taylor, 206–26.

Alicia Susan Ostriker. *Stealing the Language: The Emergence of Women's Poetry in America.* Boston: Beacon Press, 1986.

———. "The Thieves of Language: Women Poets and Revisionist Mythmaking," in Showalter, 1985, 314–38.

Erika Ostrovsky. "A Cosmogony of O: Wittig's *Les Guérillères,*" in *Twentieth-Century French Fiction: Essays for Germaine Bree;* in Stambolian, 241–51.

Grace Paley. "A Conversation with My Father," in *Enormous Changes at the Last Minute.* New York: Farrar, Straus, and Giroux, 1974, 161–67.

Gillian Parker and Janet Todd. "Interview with Margaret Drabble," in Todd, 161–95.

Patrick Parrinder. "Descents into Hell: The Later Novels of Doris Lessing." *Critical Quarterly* 22, no. 4 (Winter 1980), 5–25.

Mickey Pearlman, ed. *American Women Writing Fiction: Memory, Identity, Family, Space.* Lexington: University Press of Kentucky, 1989.

Carol Pearson and Katherine Pope. *The Female Hero in American and British Literature.* New York: Bowker, 1981.

Camille Peri. "Witchcraft," interview with Margaret Atwood. *Mother Jones,* April 1989, 26ff.

Marjorie G. Perloff. " 'A Ritual for Being Born Twice': Sylvia Plath's *The Bell Jar.*" *Contemporary Literature* 13, no. 4 (1972), 507–22.

Carla L. Peterson. *The Determined Reader: Gender and Culture in the Novel from Napoleon to Victoria.* New Brunswick: Rutgers University Press, 1985.

Gilbert Phelps. "The Post-War English Novel," in Ford, 65–125.

Marge Piercy. *Braided Lives.* New York: Fawcett Crest, 1982.

———. "Gritty Places and Strong Women," review of *The Diviners. New York Times,* 1974; in *Margaret Laurence,* ed. New, 212–13.

———. *Small Changes.* New York: Fawcett Crest, 1973.

———. *Summer People.* New York: Summit Books, 1989.

———. "Through the Cracks." *Partisan Review* 41 (1974), 202–16.

———. *Woman on the Edge of Time.* New York: Fawcett Crest, 1976.

David Plante. "In the Heart of Literary London." *New York Times Magazine,* September 11, 1988, 42–43, 80–86.

Sylvia Plath. *The Bell Jar.* New York: Bantam, 1981.

George Plimpton, ed. *Women Writers at Work.* The Paris Review Interviews. New York: Viking Penguin, 1989.

Nancy Poland. "Margaret Drabble: There Must Be a Lot of People Like Me." *Midwest Quarterly* 16 (1975), 256–57.

Nancy Porter. "Silenced History—*Children of Violence* and *The Golden Notebook.*" *World Literature Written in English* 12 (November 1973), 161–79.

Marilyn Power. "Falling through the 'Safety Net': Women, Economic Crisis, and Reagonomics." *Feminist Studies* 10, no. 1 (Spring 1984), 31–58.

Annis Pratt. *Archetypal Patterns in Women's Fiction.* Bloomington: Indiana University Press, 1981.

Annis Pratt and L. S. Dembo, eds. *Doris Lessing: Critical Studies.* Madison: University of Wisconsin Press, 1974.

Alison Prentice, Paula Bourne, Gail Cuthbert Brandt, Beth Light, Wendy Mitchinson, and Naomi Black. *Canadian Women: A History.* Toronto: Harcourt, 1988.

Dee Preussner. "Talking with Margaret Drabble." *Modern Fiction Studies* 25, no. 4 (Winter 1979–80), 563–77.

Martin Pugh. "Domesticity and the Decline of Feminism, 1930–1950," in Smith, 144–64.

Ann Quin. *Passages*. London: Calder and Boyars, 1969.

Norman Rabkin. *Shakespeare and the Common Understanding*. New York: The Free Press, 1967.

Janice A. Radway. *Reading the Romance: Women, Patriarchy, and Popular Literature*. Chapel Hill: University of North Carolina Press, 1984.

Catherine Rainwater and William J. Scheick, eds. *Contemporary American Women Writers: Narrative Strategies*. Lexington: The University Press of Kentucky, 1985.

Elayne Antler Rapping. Review of Atwood's *Cat's Eye*. *Guardian*, April 12, 1989, 17.

———. " 'Unfree Women': Feminism in Doris Lessing's Novels." *Women's Studies* 3 (1975).

———. "Youth Ponder Sexual Politics." *New Directions for Women*, March/April 1989, 10.

Barbara Raskin. *Hot Flashes*. New York: St. Martin's Press, 1987.

———. *Loose Ends*. New York: Bantam, 1973.

Walter L. Reed. *An Exemplary History of the Novel: The Quixotic versus the Picaresque*. Chicago: University of Chicago Press, 1981.

Jean Rhys. *After Leaving Mr. Mackenzie*. New York: Vintage, 1974.

Adrienne Rich. "Motherhood: The Contemporary Emergency and the Quantum Leap," in *Lies*, 1979, 259–73.

———. "Disloyal to Civilization: Feminism, Racism, Gynephobia," in *Lies*, 275–310.

———. *Of Woman Born: Motherhood as Experience and Institution*. New York: Norton, 1976.

———. "When We Dead Awaken: Writing as Re-Vision," in *On Lies, Secrets, and Silence: Selected Prose, 1966–1978*. New York: Norton, 1979.

Barbara Hill Rigney. *Madness and Sexual Politics in the Feminist Novel: Studies in Bronte, Woolf, Lessing, and Atwood*. Madison: University of Wisconsin Press, 1978.

Marilynne Robinson. *Housekeeping*. New York: Bantam, 1982.

Anne Richardson Roiphe. *LovingKindness*. New York: Warner, 1987.

———. *Up the Sandbox*. New York: Simon and Schuster, 1970.

Ellen Cronan Rose, ed. *Critical Essays on Margaret Drabble*. Boston: G. K. Hall, 1985.

———. "Feminine Endings—and Beginnings: Margaret Drabble's *The Waterfall*." *Contemporary Literature* 21, no. 1 (1980), 81–99.

———. "A Lessing in Disguise," review of *The Diaries of Jane Somers*. *The Women's Review of Books* 2, no. 5 (February 1985), 7–8.

———. *The Novels of Margaret Drabble: Equivocal Figures*. Totowa, NJ: Barnes and Noble, 1980.

———. "Twenty Questions." *Doris Lessing Newsletter* 4 no. 2 (Winter 1980), 5.

Ellen Cronan Rose and Carey Kaplan, eds. *Approaches to Teaching Lessing's The Golden Notebook*. New York: The Modern Language Association of America, 1989.

———. *The Canon and the Common Reader*. Knoxville: University of Tennessee Press, 1991.

Jerome H. Rosenberg. *Margaret Atwood*. Twayne's World Authors Series, Canadian Literature. Boston: Twayne Publishers, 1984.

Deborah Rosenfelt. "Feminism, Postfeminism, and Contemporary Women's Fiction," in Howe, forthcoming.

———. "From the Thirties: Tillie Olsen and the Radical Tradition," in Newton and Rosenfelt, 214–48.

Deborah Rosenfelt with Judith Stacey. "Second Thoughts on the Second Wave." *Feminist Studies* 13, no. 2 (Summer 1987), 341–61.

Alice S. Rossi. "Equality of the Sexes: An Immodest Proposal." *Dædalus* 93 (Spring

1964), 607–52; in *The Woman in America,* ed. Robert Lifton, Boston: Houghton Mifflin, 1965.

Alice S. Rossi and Ann Calderwood, eds. *Academic Women on the Move.* New York: Russell Sage, 1973.

A. P. Rossiter. "Ambivalence: The Dialectic of the Histories," in *Discussions of Shakespeare's Histories,* ed. R. J. Dorius. Boston: Heath, 1964.

Judith Rossner. *Looking for Mr. Goodbar.* New York: Simon and Schuster, 1975.

Sheila Rowbotham. *Woman's Consciousness, Man's World.* Harmondsworth: Penguin, 1973.

Karen E. Rowe. "Fairy-born and human-bred: Jane Eyre's Education in Romance," in Abel, 1983, 69–89.

Iris Rozencwajg. "Interview with Margaret Drabble." *Women's Studies* 6 (1979), 335–47.

Bernice Rubens. *Go Tell the Lemming.* New York: Pocket Books, 1983.

Roberta Rubenstein. *Boundaries of the Self: Gender, Culture, Fiction.* Urbana: University of Illinois Press, 1987.

———. *The Novelistic Vision of Doris Lessing: Breaking the Forms of Consciousness.* Urbana: University of Illinois Press, 1979.

———. *"The Waterfall:* The Myth of Psyche, Romantic Tradition, and the Female Quest," in Schmidt, 139–54.

Sara Ruddick. "Maternal Thinking." *Feminist Studies* 6, no. 2 (Summer 1980), 342–67.

———. *Maternal Thinking: Toward a Politics of Peace.* Boston: Beacon Press, 1989.

Joanna Russ. "Somebody Is Trying to Kill Me and I Think It's My Husband: The Modern Gothic." *Journal of Popular Culture* 6 (1973), 666–91.

———. *The Two of Them.* New York: Berkley Publishing, 1978.

———. "What Can a Heroine Do? or Why Can't Women Write?" in Weber and Grumman, 158–63.

Mary Russo. "Female Grotesques: Carnival and Theory," in de Lauretis, 1986, 213–29.

Lynn Veach Sadler. *Margaret Drabble.* Boston: Twayne, 1986.

Lorna Sage. *Contemporary Writers: Doris Lessing.* London: Methuen, 1983.

Edward W. Said. *Beginnings: Intention and Method.* New York: Basic Books, 1975.

Linda Sandler. "Interview with Margaret Atwood." *Malahat Review* 41 (January 1977), 7–27.

May Sarton. *As We Are Now.* New York: Norton, 1973.

Curt Schleir. Interview with Erica Jong. *US Air,* April 1989, 86–91.

Paul Schleuter. *A Small Personal Voice: Doris Lessing.* New York: Vintage, 1972.

Dorey Schmidt, ed. *Margaret Drabble: Golden Realms.* Living Author Series No. 4. Edinburg, TX: Pan American University, 1982, 18–31.

Naomi Schor. "For a Restricted Thematics: Writing, Speech, and Difference in *Madame Bovary,*" in Eisenstein and Jardine, 167–92.

Le Anne Schreiber. Interview with Margaret Atwood. *Vogue,* January 23, 1983, 208ff.

Lyn Sharon Schwartz. *Disturbances in the Field.* Toronto: Bantam, 1985.

Lynne Segal. *Is the Future Female? Troubled Thoughts on Contemporary Feminism.* London: Virago, 1987.

Roy Shafer. "Narrative in the Psychoanalytic Dialogue," in W. J. T. Mitchell, 25–49.

Susan Sheridan, ed. *Grafts: Feminist Cultural Criticism.* London: Verso, 1988.

Thelma J. Shinn. *Worlds within Women: Myth and Mythmaking in Fantastic Literature by Women.* Westport, CT: Greenwood Press, 1986.

Elaine Showalter. "Feminist Criticism in the Wilderness." *Critical Inquiry* 8, no. 2 (1981), 179–205.

———. "The Greening of Sister George." *Nineteenth-Century Fiction* 35 (1980), 292–311.

———. "Literary Criticism." *Signs* 1, no. 2 (1975), 435–60.

————. A Literature of Their Own: British Women Novelists from Bronte to Lessing. London: Virago, 1978.

————, ed. The New Feminist Criticism: Essays on Women, Literature, and Theory. New York: Pantheon, 1985.

————. "Women Who Write Are Women." New York Times Book Review, December 16, 1984, 1, 31, 33.

————. "Women Writers between the Wars," in Columbia Literary History, 822–41.

Anita Shreve. Women Together, Women Alone: The Legacy of the Consciousness-Raising Movement. New York: Viking, 1989.

Alix Kates Shulman. Burning Questions. New York: Bantam, 1979.

————. In Every Woman's Life. New York: Knopf, 1987.

————. Memoirs of an Ex-Prom Queen. New York: Bantam, 1972.

Ruth Sidel. On Her Own: Growing up in the Shadow of the American Dream. New York: Viking Penguin, 1990.

Elizabeth Sifton. Interview with Mary McCarthy, in Plimpton, 171–99.

Leslie Marmon Silko. Ceremony. New York: Penguin, 1977.

Alan Sinfield. Literature, Politics, and Culture in Postwar Britain. Berkeley: University of California Press, 1989.

Eleanor Honig Skoller. "The Progress of a Letter: Truth, Feminism, and The Waterfall," in Rose, 1985, 119–33.

Philip Slater. The Pursuit of Loneliness. Boston: Beacon, 1970.

Agnes Smedley. Daughter of Earth. London: Virago, 1977.

Harold L. Smith, ed. British Feminism in the Twentieth Century. Amherst: The University of Massachusetts Press, 1990.

Ann Barr Snitow. "The Front Line: Notes on Sex in Novels by Women, 1969–1979." Signs 5, no. 4, (1980), 702–18.

Barbara Miller Solomon. In the Company of Educated Women: A History of Women and Higher Education in America. New Haven: Yale University Press, 1984.

John R. Sorfleet, ed. "The Work of Margaret Laurence," special issue of Journal of Canadian Fiction 27 (1980).

Patricia Meyer Spacks. The Female Imagination. New York: Knopf, 1975.

Muriel Spark. The Driver's Seat. Harmondsworth: Penguin, 1974.

————. The Hothouse by the East River. Harmondsworth: Penguin, 1975.

————. Not to Disturb. Harmondsworth: Penguin, 1974.

————. The Takeover. Harmondsworth: Penguin, 1978.

————. Territorial Rights. New York: Coward, McGann, and Geoghegan, 1979.

Dale Spender. For the Record: The Making and Meaning of Feminist Knowledge. London: The Women's Press, 1985.

Charlotte Spivack. Merlin's Daughters: Contemporary Women Writers of Fantasy. Westport, CT: Greenwood Press, 1986.

Claire Sprague. "Doubletalk and Doubles Talk in The Golden Notebook." Papers on Language and Literature 18, no. 2 (Spring 1982), 181–97.

————. "Doubles Talk in The Golden Notebook," in Sprague and Tiger, 1986, 44–60.

————. "Dialectic and Counter-Dialectic in the Martha Quest Novels." The Journal of Commonwealth Literature 14, no. 1 (August 1979), 39–52.

————, with Virginia Tiger, eds. Critical Essays on Doris Lessing. Boston: G. K. Hall, 1986.

Madelon Sprengnether. "(M)other Eve: Some Revisions of the Fall in Fiction by Contemporary Women Writers," in Feldstein and Roof, 298–322.

Marlene Springer, ed. What Manner of Woman: Essays in English and American Life and Literature. New York: New York University Press, 1977.

Judith Stacey. "The New Conservative Feminism." Feminist Studies 9, no. 3 (Fall 1983), 559–83.

Susan Stamberg. Interview with Doris Lessing. *Doris Lessing Newsletter*. 8, no. 2 (1984), 3ff.

George Stambolian, ed. *Twentieth-Century French Fiction: Essays for Germaine Bree*. New Brunswick, NJ: Rutgers University Press, 1975.

Bonnie St. Andrews. *Forbidden Fruit: On the Relationship between Women and Knowledge in Doris Lessing, Selma Lagerlof, Kate Chopin, Margaret Atwood*. Troy, NY: Whiston 1986.

Robert Stepto. "Afro-American Literature," in *Columbia Literary History*, 785–99.

Phyllis Sternberg-Perrakis. "*The Golden Notebook:* Separation and Symbiosis." *American Imago* 38, no. 4 (Winter 1981) 407–28.

Janet Sternburg, ed. *The Writer on Her Work*. New York: Norton, 1980.

Randall Stevenson. *The British Novel since the Thirties: An Introduction*. Athens, GA: University of Georgia Press, 1986.

Philip Stevick. "Scheherezade runs out of plots, goes on talking; the King, puzzled, listens: an Essay on New Fiction." *Triquarterly*, 1973; in Bradbury, 186–216.

Grace Stewart. *A New Mythos: The Novel of the Artist as Heroine, 1877–1977*. Montreal: Eden Press, 1981.

Catharine R. Stimpson. "Doris Lessing and the Parables of Growth," in Abel et al., 1983. 186–205.

———. "Nancy Reagan Wears a Hat: Feminism and Its Cultural Consensus." *Critical Inquiry* 14 (Winter 1988), 223–43.

Catharine R. Stimpson with Nina Kressner Cobb. *Women's Studies in the United States. A Report to the Ford Foundation*. New York: Ford Foundation, 1986.

Laurie Stone. *Ms*, July/August 1987, 29.

Nora Stovel. "Margaret Drabble's Golden Vision," in Schmidt, 3–17.

J. R. Struthers. Interview with Margaret Atwood. *Essays in Canadian Writing* 6 (Spring, 1977).

Susan Robin Suleiman. *The Female Body in Western Culture: Contemporary Perspectives*. Cambridge: Harvard University Press, 1986.

———. *Subversive Intent: Gender, Politics, and the Avant-Garde*. Cambridge: Harvard University Press, 1990.

Graham Swift. *Waterland*. London: Picador, 1984.

Patrick Swinden. *The English Novel of History and Society, 1940–1980*. London: Macmillan, 1984.

Tony Tanner. *Adultery in the Novel: Contract and Transgression*. Baltimore: Johns Hopkins University Press, 1979.

Claudia Tate, ed. *Black Women Writers at Work*. New York: Continuum, 1983.

Robert Taubman. "Free Women." *The New Statesman*, April 20, 1962; in Kostelanetz, 402–403.

Jenny Taylor, ed. *Notebooks, Memoirs, Archives: Reading and Rereading Doris Lessing*. Boston: Routledge, 1982.

———. "Introduction: Situating Reading," in Taylor, 1–42.

Emma Tennent. *The Bad Sister*. London: Picador, 1979.

Clara Thomas. "The Chariot of Ossian: Myth and Manitoba in *The Diviners*." *Journal of Canadian Studies* 13, no. 3 (Fall 1978), 55–63.

———. *The Manawaka World of Margaret Laurence*. Toronto: McClelland & Stewart, 1975.

William Flint Thrall and Addison Hibbard. *A Handbook to Literature*. New York: The Odyssey Press, 1960.

Patricia Tobin. *Time and the Novel: The Genealogical Imperative*. Princeton: Princeton University Press, 1978.

Janet Todd. *Feminist Literary History*. New York: Routledge, 1988.

———, ed. *Women Writers Talking*. New York: Holmes and Meier, 1983.

Andrew Tolson. *The Limits of Masculinity*. London: Tavistock, 1977.

Marianna Torgovnick. *Closure in the Novel*. Princeton: Princeton University Press, 1981.

Nissa Torrents. "Testimony to Mysticism: Interview with Lessing." *Doris Lessing Newsletter* 4, no. 2 (Winter 1980), 12.

Diana Trilling. "Review of Doris Lessing." *Times Literary Supplement,* October 1978. 1165.

Lionel Trilling. "Manners, Morals, and the Novel" (1947), in *The Liberal Imagination*. New York: Doubleday, 1953, 199–215.

Victor Turner. "Social Dramas and Stories about Them," in *On Narrative*, ed. W. J. T. Mitchell. Chicago: University of Chicago Press, 1981, 137–64.

James W. Tuttleton. " 'Combat in the Erogenous Zone': Women in the American Novel between the Two World Wars," in Springer, 271–96.

Anne Tyler. *Earthly Possessions*. New York: Knopf, 1977.

Dorothy Van Ghent. "The Dickens World: A View from Todgers's." *Sewanee Review* 58 (1960), 419–30.

———. *The English Novel: Form and Function, Great Expectations*. New York: Harper and Row, 1953.

Kathryn VanSpanckeren and Jan Garden Castro, eds., *Margaret Atwood: Vision and Forms*. Carbondale: Southern Illinois University Press, 1988.

Christl Verduyn, ed. *Margaret Laurence: An Appreciation,* a Journal of Canadian Studies Book. Peterborough, Canada: Broadview Press, 1988.

Brian Vincent. Review of *Lady Oracle*. *Quill and Quire* 42, no. 11 (1976), 6; in Maclean, 196.

James Vinson, ed. *Contemporary Novelists*. London: St. James Press, 1972.

Alice Walker. *Meridian*. New York: Washington Square Press, 1977.

———. *Interviews with Black Women Writers,* ed. John O'Brien. New York: Liveright, 1973.

Michelene Wandor, ed. *Once a Feminist: Stories of a Generation*. London: Virago, 1990.

———, ed. *On Gender and Writing*. London: Pandora Press, 1983.

Patricia Waugh. *Feminine Fictions: Revisiting the Postmodern*. London: Routledge, 1989.

———. *Metafiction: The Theory and Practice of Self-Conscious Fiction*. London: Methuen, 1984.

Jeanette L. Webber and Joan Grumman, eds. *Woman as Writer*. Boston: Houghton Mifflin, 1978.

Fay Weldon. *Down among the Women*. Harmondsworth: Penguin, 1985.

———. *The Fat Woman's Joke*. Chicago: Academy, 1967.

———. *Praxis*. New York: Pocket Books, 1978.

———. *Remember Me*. London: Hodder and Stoughton, 1984.

———. *Words of Advice*. New York: Ballantine, 1977.

Lynn Wenzel. "A Decade Later Burning Questions Remain Unanswered." *New Directions for Women* (May/June, 1990), 23.

Ruth Whittaker. *Modern Novelists: Doris Lessing*. New York: St. Martin's Press, 1988.

Peter Widdowson, ed. *Re-Reading English*. London: Methuen, 1982.

Marianne Wiggins. *Separate Checks*. London: Flamingo, 1985.

Jan Williams, Hazel Twort, and Ann Bachelli. "Women and the Family." *Shrew* (February–March 1970); in Malos, 113–18.

Raymond Williams. *The Long Revolution.;* London: Chatto and Windus, 1961.

———. *Marxism and Literature*. Oxford: Oxford University Press, 1977.

Susan Willis. "Black Women Writers: Taking a Critical Perspective," in Greene and Kahn, 211–37.

———. *Specifying*. Madison: University of Wisconsin Press, 1987.

Elizabeth Wilson. "The British Women's Movement," in Wilson with Weir, 93–133.

———. *Only Halfway to Paradise: Women in Postwar Britain, 1945–1968.* New York: Tavistock, 1980.

———. "Yesterday's Heroines: On Rereading Lessing and de Beauvoir," in Taylor, 57–74.

Elizabeth Wilson with Angela Weir. *Hidden Agendas: Theory, Politics, and Experience in the Women's Movement.* London: Tavistock, 1986.

D. W. Winnicott. "Mirror-Role of Mother and Family in Child Development," in *Playing and Reality.* New York: Tavistock, 1971; rpt. 1985.

Monique Wittig. *Les Guérillères.* Boston: Beacon, 1985.

Nellie Wong. "In Search of the Self as Hero: Confetti of Voices on New Years Night: A Letter to Myself," in Moraga and Anzaldúa, 177–81.

Virginia Woolf. "The Leaning Tower," in *Collected Essays.* London: Hogarth Press, 1966.

———. "Mr. Bennet and Mrs. Brown," in *The Captain's Death Bed and Other Essays.* New York: Harcourt, Brace, Jovanovich, 1950.

———. *A Room of One's Own.* New York: Harcourt, 1957.

Jean Wyatt. "Escaping Literary Designs: The Politics of Reading and Writing in Margaret Drabble's *The Waterfall.*" *Perspectives on Contemporary Literature* 11 (1985), 37–45.

———. *Reconstructing Desire: The Role of the Unconscious in Women's Reading and Writing.* Chapel Hill: University of North Carolina Press, 1990.

Philip Wylie. *A Generation of Vipers.* New York: Rinehart, 1955.

Patricia S. Yaeger. *Honey-Mad Women: Emancipatory Strategies in Women's Writing.* New York: Columbia University Press, 1989.

W. B. Yeats. *The Collected Poems.* New York: Macmillan, 1964.

Anthea Zeman. *Presumptuous Girls: Women and Their World in the Serious Woman's Novel.* London: Wiedenfeld and Nicolson, 1977.

# INDEX

GAYLE GREENE is professor of English at Scripps College in Claremont, California. She is a co-editor of *The Woman's Part: Feminist Criticism of Shakespeare* and *Making a Difference: Feminist Literary Criticism*. She has published articles in journals such as *Novel, Contemporary Literature, Renaissance Literature, Studies in English Literature* and *Signs*.